JOSEPH CONRAD

A Psychoanalytic Biography

JOSEPH CONRAD

A Psychoanalytic Biography

BY BERNARD C. MEYER, M.D.

PRINCETON UNIVERSITY PRESS
PRINCETON · NEW JERSEY

L. C. Card: 66-14312
ISBN 0-691-01296-2

First Princeton Paperback Printing, 1970
Second Princeton Paperback Printing, 1970

Printed in the United States of America
by Princeton University Press, Princeton, New Jersey

To the memory of my father

Acknowledgments

AN UNFORESEEN AND HAPPY CONSEQUENCE of my venturing into the personal world of Joseph Conrad has been my introduction to many individuals who in one way or another have been involved with him. Through Conrad, indeed, I have acquired a number of friends among critics, scholars, librarians, and others, and I am deeply indebted to them for their efforts in my behalf. Through the medium of his perceptive study of Conrad I became acquainted with Thomas Moser at an early stage of my undertaking, and I have since that time enjoyed his steadfast and constructive encouragement. I am equally grateful to Fred Karl, another Conrad scholar, who read the manuscript and made a number of valuable suggestions. Leon Edel and Herbert Weinstock have been generous with advice and support. To Alexander Janta I am indebted for alerting me to Conrad's drawings. He, Ludwik Krzyzanowski, and my colleague Dr. Gustav Bychowski have been most helpful in my understanding of Conrad's Polish background and in their wholehearted endorsement of my efforts. Special thanks are extended to Anne Horan and Peter Spackman of the *Columbia University Forum* and to Herbert Bailey, R. Miriam Brokaw, and Marjorie Putney of the Princeton University Press for their encouragement and constructive criticism. I am most grateful to my colleague, Dr. David Beres, for his valuable criticism of the manuscript, and to Dr. John Frosch, editor of the *Journal of the American Psychoanalytic Association.*

My study has relied heavily on the writing and research of a number of Conrad scholars to whom I acknowledge my indebtedness: notably, Jerry Allen, Jocelyn Baines, Albert Guerard, Eloise Hay, G. Jean-Aubry, Gustav Morf, Thomas Moser, and Zdzislaw Najder.

The facilities of many libraries have been generously extended to me. I offer warm thanks to the distinguished Conrad scholar Dr. John D. Gordan, curator of the Berg Collection of the New York Public Library, to Eugene P. Sheehy (co-author of *Joseph Conrad at Mid-Century*), of the Butler Library of Columbia University, and to Marjorie G. Wynne, who has shown me unfailing generosity and kindness in making available the Conrad Collection at Yale University. I also wish to acknowledge the assistance of Liselotte Bendix, librarian at the New York Psychoanalytic Institute, of the Reference Library of the Australian Consulate-General in New York, as well as of the curators and directors of the libraries at Colgate and Dartmouth Colleges, and at the Universities of Birmingham (England), Indiana, and Texas. I extend thanks to M. Gernet, of the Bibliothèque Municipale de Marseille for supplying me with photocopies of newspaper accounts of Henry M. Stanley's visit to Marseilles in January 1878.

For the use of some of Conrad's unpublished letters, manuscripts, and drawings I am indebted to the Colgate College Library, the Dartmouth College Library, Indiana University Library, Texas University Library, Yale University Library, the Henry W. and Albert A. Berg Collection and the Manuscript Division of the New York Public Library, the Astor, Lenox, and Tilden Foundations, and George Keating. Permission to quote from Conrad's published works (Doubleday, Page and Company were his American publishers), and to quote from manuscripts and unpublished letters has been granted by J. M. Dent & Sons, Ltd., acting for the Trustees of the Joseph Conrad Estate. In addition, Conrad's drawings and a fragment of the manuscript of "The Planter of Malata" are reproduced through the courtesy of the Trustees of the Joseph Conrad Estate. I also wish to thank Sir John Rothenstein, executor of the Rothenstein Estate, for permission to quote from two unpublished letters by Sir William Rothenstein.

Contents

Drawings by Joseph Conrad

Courtesy Estate of Joseph Conrad
Following page 326

JOSEPH CONRAD

A Psychoanalytic Biography

Introduction

"A NOVELIST LIVES IN HIS WORK," wrote Conrad in *A Personal Record*. "He stands there, the only reality in an invented world, among imaginary things, happenings and people. Writing about them he is only writing about himself. But the disclosure is not complete. He remains, to a certain extent, a figure behind the veil, a suspected rather than a seen presence—a movement and a voice behind the draperies of fiction."[1]*

With this statement neither the literary critic nor the psychoanalyst is likely to disagree. "There is always a living face behind the mask," wrote Yeats in his diary,[2] while Freud referred to "His Majesty the Ego" as the "hero alike of every day dream and of every story."[3] Yet it is not every artist whose unseen presence offers so beguiling a temptation for a fuller disclosure of the "figure behind the veil," the "suspected rather than a seen presence," as does Joseph Conrad.

His personal history alone, compounded of strange and unforeseen turns, of seemingly capricious shiftings and irrelevant sequences, can hardly fail to arrest the attention even of the incurious who, accustomed to viewing a man's life as a path threading a more or less discernible course through the thickets and brambles of experience, are understandably confounded and fascinated by the bizarre itinerary of the multifaceted journey of Conrad's life. For in this single life it is possible to trace at least five separate and distinct lives, five lives which might well have belonged to five separate individuals: a Polish gentleman-student; a seafaring adventurer on French ships out of Marseilles; a British sailor who, by dint of his labors, attained the rank of Captain in the Merchant Navy; a Congo River boatman caught in the sordid history of Belgian cupidity; and a lyrical master of English prose, the novelist Joseph Conrad.

Moreover, were his history unknown, and were the reader of his rich prose unaware that its creator was ignorant of the English language until the age of twenty, he could not fail to wonder what complexities in his psychological make-up led to the unevenness

* Numbered references are to Bibliographical Notes, page 364.

in the quality of Conrad's writing, and to the patent deterioration of his artistry during the second half of his literary career. For no perceptive reader can long ignore the enigma posed by the realization that the same sensitive and introspective artist who had written so poignantly of death in *The Nigger of the Narcissus,* so discerningly of moral degradation in "Heart of Darkness," and so poetically of human isolation in *Lord Jim* and *Nostromo,* was the same man who, psychologically transformed, produced such light holiday literature as the melodramatic *Chance,* the banal *Arrow of Gold,* and the partly plagiarized *Suspense.*

Yet despite the varying quality of his writing, to read Conrad at his best or at his worst, to read him a great deal or very little, provides a stimulus to know his history: to discover the roots of those reiterated themes of rescue and betrayal with which he was so manifestly obsessed, and the sources of those recurring images of monolithic women and of their undone, unarmed men who walk across the pages of his novels.

In a much quoted declaration of his literary aims Conrad wrote "My task which I am trying to achieve is, by the power of the written word . . . before all to make you *see.*"[4] Although this statement is usually understood as an expression of his wish to achieve an unusual vividness in his writing, it might also be regarded as an unconscious desire for the self-revelation of the author himself, for perhaps like few other creative artists Conrad asks to be revealed, asks it in his autobiographical as well as his fictional writings, and few critics or biographers have failed to respond to this wish. As a consequence even the most factual-minded chroniclers have paused in the presentation of the raw data of Conrad's life to speculate upon the significance of some curious detail or to offer an explanation for a puzzling inconsistency in the story.

Not all such efforts, however, have reflected either an intuitive or a learned knowledge of the complexities of human behavior or motivation, being based rather, it would seem, upon hunches and uninformed psychologizing.[a] Baines, for example, whose biography

[a] There has been a tendency among some biographers to ignore or gloss over Dr. Morf's thoughtful psychoanalytic study of Conrad published in 1930.[5] In recent years Guerard has come to acknowledge the accuracy of

is undoubtedly the most complete and comprehensive account to date of Conrad's life, ascribes the high incidence of suicide (15 instances) in Conrad's fiction to the "influence" exerted by his own probable suicidal attempt in his youth,[7] rather than recognizing both Conrad's action and the actions of his fictional characters as protean manifestations of the recurring theme of self-destruction that traverses virtually the whole of Conrad's life, be it expressed symbolically, in actual deed, or in the thoughts and behavior of his fictional characters.[b]

It is indeed doubtful whether a truly definitive biography of an individual of such complexity as Conrad can be written today without the skilled use of the tools of contemporary psychoanalytic knowledge. Biographical reconstruction, as Beres has emphasized, is an inherent aim of the psychoanalytic process, and psychoanalysis, aside from its function as a therapeutic instrument, is in essence a science of biography.[9] To ignore its potential contribution to an understanding of the life of the artist is to deprive such a study of a psychological instrument of particular sharpness and precision. At the same time it must be emphasized that analytic training and experience, unmatched by literary or historical scholarship, do not justify an invasion of the field of biography by the psychoanalyst. When this has happened—and it has not been infrequent—the consequences may be unfortunate both for biography and for psychoanalysis. Edel, who is an informed proponent of the application of psychoanalysis to literary biography, has called attention to those analytic practitioners who "venture frequently upon literary ground and sometimes indeed in places

---

Morf's observations, admitting that he treated him "rather severely" in his earlier work. "I had naïvely undervalued Conrad as a psychological novelist," he writes, "because I did not find, for instance, more and better 'Freudian' dreams."[6]

[b] Baines is on no firmer ground when dealing with the subject of Conrad's physical health. Thus in discussing Conrad's gout[8] he advances the suggestion that it may have been caused by bad teeth. But even if this hypothesis were medically valid it would once again emphasize the author's scotoma for psychological matters, for as Baines himself points out Conrad was notoriously neglectful of his teeth, which behavior should again be viewed in the context of self-destruction.

where angels fear to tread, leaving (from the point of view of the student of literature) large muddy footprints in their wake. Possessing neither the discipline of criticism nor the methods of biography, they import the atmosphere of the clinic and the consulting room into the library." At the same time he warned against the inexpert use of psychoanalytic tools on the part of critics and biographers. "We have thus a common problem," he concluded: "that of certain individuals who are perfectly competent in their proper field but who seem prepared to blazon forth their incompetence on ground where they do not belong."[10]

There are other critics, however, who display a more or less overt hostility to any application of psychoanalysis to the study of art or biography. In its most vehement form such an attitude reflects an obscurantist denial of the phenomena of mental conflict, unconscious intention, or the psychological kinship between art, fantasy, and the dream. According to such a point of view a work of art means nothing more or less than its creator affirms, thereby treating the creative process as if it were solely a function of conscious volition. Personal idiosyncrasies of the artist tend to be dismissed as meaningless imitations of current conventions or styles, while the vicissitudes of his life are attributed largely to external forces, often labeled by empty clichés. Thus, Conrad's failure to attain the captaincy of a ship after he had resigned his position on the *Otago* is attributed solely to the real difficulties of securing such a command. Similarly the deterioration of his writing during the second half of his career has been easily ascribed to a variety of ill-considered factors, including financial worry, gout, "exhaustion of creative energy," and Jessie Conrad.

Ideally there should be no conflict between the literary scholar and the analyst, for they each have much to contribute to the other's field, and by complementing each other's efforts may succeed in enriching both.

The application of psychoanalysis to the biography of the artist presents several distinctions from the clinical situation in which a living subject gives continuing expression to his memories, random thoughts, fantasies, and dreams. It is characteristic of the therapeutic process, moreover, that the source of such material is restricted to the verbal utterances of the subject himself, since communication with "outside" persons by the analyst would necessarily jeopardize the confidential nature of the undertaking.[c] Finally the psychoanalytic situation gives rise to a unique relationship between patient and analyst which plays an important role in the therapeutic endeavor. Characteristically the patient endows the therapist with attributes and extends toward him feelings and expectations which have their origin in important, notably parental, relationships of his early years. This phenomenon, known as "transference," may have its counterpart in the feelings and attitudes of the analyst toward his patient, which similarly are not rooted in the current clinical situation, but in the deep-seated and ancient emotional needs of the therapist. Analogous transference phenomena can and often do play a conspicuous role in any biography, psychoanalytic or other, with unfortunate consequences. Freud was well aware of this possibility and warned the biographer against idealizing his subject in order to gratify an infantile fantasy, notably the revival of the childhood concept of his father.[11] There remains, of course, a contrary danger, namely, when the biographer utilizes his subject as a target for unconscious hostile feelings which too have been deflected from their original object.

From the above considerations it is evident that the psychoanalytic biographer can make no claim to "psychoanalyze" a dead artist; what he can aspire to is a painstaking application of psychoanalytic principles and insights to two main sets of data—the available facts of the artist's life and his creative works. As in the clinical situation, in neither instance can the analyst afford to relax his vigilance.

To begin with the stated facts of a man's life are not always reliable, whether they are based upon autobiographical material or upon the testimony of his intimates—the Boswells and the Ford Madox Fords. It is questionable whether even the most secret diary is ever written without one eye on the hoped-for curiosity and titillation of the potential reader. Letters may be equally untrust-

[c] For similar reasons no psychoanalyst can publish a frank and undisguised biography of his patient, however interesting or instructive such a disclosure might be.

worthy, especially when they flow from the pen of a man who more or less consciously anticipates their ultimate destiny as treasured fragments of his literary gifts. No more authentic may be the autobiographical novel with its hints and innuendoes of past experiences which, originating as fantasies, have acquired the stamp of validity with the passing of the years. Some biographers of Conrad, for example, although apparently aware of the implausibility of certain episodes in his own recorded history, have nevertheless tended to accept at face value a few highly questionable "recollections" of the author, thereby helping to perpetuate the notion that some fictional works, notably "A Smile of Fortune" and *The Arrow of Gold*, represent authentic Conrad autobiography. Nor is such an error without consequence, for as long as it persists it obscures from view an important psychological function which Conrad's art apparently did serve—the achievement through his creative fiction of a corrective revision of a painful reality.

Mythmaking, however, need not be viewed solely as a conscious process deliberately designed to distort the true facts of one's life. Every analyst is familiar with the gradual alterations in the patient's past history that emerge as the need for maintaining repression of early painful memories diminishes. Nor is such an unconscious concealment of crucial events behind "screen memories" limited to the analytic process; it is undoubtedly a universal phenomenon which has played no small role in the distortions of both personal and general history. Confronted by such distortions of the past, be it in the analytic situation or in the preparation of a psychoanalytic biography, the analyst does not discard them as false and useless data, but re-examines them as potentially meaningful fantasies whose very content may afford an illumined glimpse into those secret recesses of the mind where lies the rich lode of wishful thought and cherished dream. After his Congo venture, for example, Conrad confided to some of his intimates but failed to mention in print a number of experiences which probably never took place. As authentic biography his claim to have been saved by a native African woman who brought him water every day,[12] and his account of being rescued at the last minute after blowing three times on a whistle as he sank helplessly in a bog,[13] are almost certainly spurious. Yet as expressions of a recurring wish to be rescued, these "recollections" convey an important inner truth. "Men have but very little self-knowledge," wrote Conrad, "and authors especially are victims of many illusions about themselves."[14]

Yet these illusions are fostered not solely by the personal needs of the artist himself, but equally by the emotional demands of the public which seeks to endow its great men with an aura of near legendary glory. It may be to satisfy the world as well as himself, therefore, that a public figure agrees to distortions of his own history and to its embroidery with appealing myths.[d] In some instances these myths present a remarkable stereotype, notably as variants on the theme of the "Family Romance Fantasy" which, as Kris demonstrated, has appeared as a recurring element in the biography of the artist from the time of Giotto well into the twentieth century—the depiction of the future artist as a humble and obscure child, often a shepherd boy, whose latent genius is accidentally discovered by an established master.[15] It will be interesting to discover in the course of the present study that this same fantasy played a prominent role in Conrad's personal life and in his fictional world.

In view of what has been said concerning the potential role of transference factors in relating the life story of a great man, it is not surprising that the temptation to engage in mythmaking is not wanting in the biographer, who may strive consciously or unconsciously, to re-create an idealized image originating in his own past. Such practitioners of the "cherry-tree" school of biography are obliged not only to foster attractive legends about their subject, but to sift out and eliminate those elements in the material that threaten to mar the picture. It was undoubtedly to attain that image of perfection which prompted Anton Schindler, Beethoven's first biographer, to destroy 264 of the 400 priceless Conversation Books by means of which the deaf composer communicated with others.

[d] It is claimed that when Maurice Ravel was once asked why he had never denied the impression held in some quarters that he was Jewish, he replied by saying that since this misconception had evidently brought so much pleasure to the Jewish people he was loath to correct it.

It is not surprising that Schindler referred to his subject as "our hero."[16] A comparable selection of material aimed at creating a simple and idealized portrait is discernible in a number of biographies of Conrad, which more closely resemble pleasing romances than painstaking portrayals of a deeply troubled and highly complicated man; for despite his assertion to his friend Galsworthy that he was "a plain man without tears or sensibility,"[17] he was a creature of sharp contradictions and inconsistencies in whom a search for simple formulas is doomed to fail. Even his expressed opinions on such subjects as Christianity, Bonaparte, and the Russians, for example, must be taken with more than a pinch of salt, for not infrequently they fail utterly to harmonize with other sentiments on those subjects implicit in his fiction. The same may be said of his estimation of himself as an artist, for there came a time in his literary career when it almost seemed as if he failed—or refused—to understand the subtleties of meanings in some of his own earlier writing. Thus he once declared to Lenormand, who had tried to interest him in Freud's writings, "Je ne veux pas aller au fond. Je veux considérer la réalité comme une chose rude et rugueuse sur laquelle je promène mes doigts—rien de plus." ("I have no wish to probe the depths. I like to regard reality as a rough and rugged thing over which I can run my fingers—nothing more.")[18] Yet, like other pronouncements of Conrad, this statement must be read in the temporal context in which it was uttered, namely, toward the close of his life when many of his opinions, especially those about his earlier works, bore the heavy imprint of a vacuous and safe cliché. As an expression of the Conrad who, two decades earlier, had "probed the depths" in such poetic, impressionistic works as *The Nigger of the Narcissus*, "Heart of Darkness," or *Lord Jim*, his comment to Lenormand would seem unthinkable. It is easy enough to quote Conrad, but to do so may be misleading, for the quotation may be but one side of the coin, one facet of those mental conflicts that emerge so distinctly and recurrently in his fictional writings. The latter, therefore, constitute a second important source of data for a psychoanalytic biography.

The interpretation of works of art has been attempted throughout the history of psychoanalysis. Like the interpretation of dreams without the aid of the verbal associations of the dreamer, however, an effort to uncover the latent meaning of a work of creative imagination may be a risky venture. This is particularly true when it is undertaken by individuals who believe they have learned the meaning of symbols and who have "discovered" psychoanalysis, but are untrained in its rigorous discipline. Such efforts, corresponding to what is known clinically as "wild analysis," render a service neither to literary criticism nor to psychoanalysis. Even in the hands of the experienced analyst, the interpretation of a work of art in isolation must be offered in a spirit of tentativeness and conjecture rather than one of unequivocal certainty. There are, to be sure, a few standard themes which may be interpreted with a fair degree of confidence: stories dealing with a competition between an older and a younger man for a woman's love may be safely assumed to carry an allusion to the "Oedipus Complex," and the hostile interference by an older woman in a young girl's romantic life may be viewed as a manifestation of mother-daughter rivalry. Such plot situations occur with particular transparency in fairy tales, like "Jack and the Beanstalk" and "Snow White." Fairy tales too lend themselves readily to thinly disguised depictions of relatively primitive impulses, like death wishes and "cannibalistic" fantasies. It is "permissible," for instance, to "interpret" "Little Red Riding Hood" or "Hansel and Gretel" in terms of "oral" aggression, expressing in particular rather common childhood fantasies linking eating with cruelty and the fear of being devoured. By the same token there are a limited number of symbols which appear to possess universal application to basic biological themes: for example, water for birth and death, fire for passion and anger, snakes and winged creatures for the male genital.

Despite these and kindred aids in deciphering the meanings concealed in a creative work viewed in isolation, the analyst is on much sounder ground when he deals with it as he deals with any manifestation of psychic activity, be it a dream or a fantasy, namely, by correlating it with a host of other remembered details of his subject's life and thought, including other dreams and other works of art. For the psychoanalytic biographer these must serve as partial substitutes for the artist's unspoken associations to his work, for his work is assumed to be in some way related to his life experiences, memories, and fantasies. According to this hypothesis every detail in a story—the names of its characters, the citing of specific dates, the use of language and metaphor, the nature of the plot, and many other elements—must lead to a careful search for their roots in the artist's past, for he cannot take us, as Rickman observed, where he himself has never been.[19] It is the analyst's task to attempt to re-trace those steps and to establish the connections between the art and the artist, connections which indeed may be far more complicated than they at first would seem. Thus, although the artist may fictionalize a real experience or a fragment of recorded history, as Conrad did on more than one occasion, a close look at the fictionalized version may reveal salient details that have no connection with those sources. It has been shown, for example, that the *Patna* episode of *Lord Jim* was based upon the famous case of the *Jeddah*, a steamship which was treacherously abandoned by her crew while transporting nearly 1,000 Moslem pilgrims on their way to Mecca,[20] and that the political events of *Nostromo* were modeled upon an actual chapter in Central American history.[21] Yet in both of these examples there are elements that are plainly extraneous to the simple historical models, elements obviously transplanted from an unrelated corner of the author's past. By the same token, it has been convincingly argued that many of Conrad's invented characters, for example, Jim, Kurtz, and Antonia, were modeled upon real persons. But here again it would be a mistake to conclude that the fictional portrait was drawn exclusively from that simple model—even if the author tells us so—for careful attention to the physiognomy may reveal features that belong to other faces, sometimes, indeed, to the artist's image of himself.

It is undoubtedly the failure to recognize that both Conrad's characters and plots have been derived from multiple sources that has led to some unfortunate controversy about his work. It has been asserted, for example, that critics who discerned in *Lord Jim* allusions to Conrad's guilt over leaving his native Poland had "overlooked the *Jeddah* incident,"[22] the implication being that two such dissimilar "sources" for the *Patna* episode are mutually exclusive. In view of what has been stated, however, it should be clear that there is no incompatibility between them: on the contrary, they complement each other and illustrate how Conrad utilized and modified an actual happening to serve as a vehicle for the expression of an emotionally charged, highly personal statement. It may indeed be justifiably claimed that whether he was writing of events in the Indian Ocean, in the heart of Africa, or in Central America, the insistent shadow of his native Poland inevitably fell across the page.

Psychoanalysis has shown that the dream too is a creation of multiple determinants. The immediate stimulus of a dream is usually an event, an experience, or a thought occurring during the waking hours preceding sleep—the so-called day's residue. But the content of the dream is derived not only from the recent stimulus, but from a host of remote memories and fantasies with which the day's residue is associatively linked. In a sense the real event on which a work of fiction is based may be regarded as analogous to the day's residue of the dream, a stimulus possessing a vague sense of familiarity that is endowed with the power of evoking reverberations from the distant past. Like a dream, a work of fiction—and its characters—is often a composite creation of numerous and disparate elements, a fusion of half-forgotten faces, names, places, and voices imprinted in the mind during the infinite moments of a lifetime.

"Literature, literary creativity," wrote Sainte-Beuve, "is not distinct or separable, for me, from the rest of the man. . . . I might taste a work, but for me it is difficult to assess it apart from my knowledge of the man himself; and I would say quite frankly, *tel arbre, tel fruit*."[23]

The tasting of Conrad's literary fruit offers an abundance of clues concerning the nature of the tree from which it has fallen. Despite the richness of the harvest it contains a relatively limited number of themes and personality types which are displayed in multiple variations, and an equally restricted assortment of symbols and metaphors. The recurring appearance of these few elements in a wide variety of settings and situations furnishes the attentive reader not only with a wealth of cross-references and duplicated meanings within the framework of Conrad's fictional writing, but with an equally rich network of allusions to his personal history. Especially striking, moreover, are the occasional transparent correlations between a given story and the real events occurring in his personal life at the time when it was written. Indeed these events would appear to have played an important role not merely in the content or mood of a particular fictional work, but in its artistic quality as well. "The more perfect the artist," wrote T. S. Eliot, "the more completely separate in him will be the man who suffers and the mind which creates."[24] In Conrad such a separation was occasionally far from complete, with the result that at such times his art declined, contaminated, as it were, by current personal distress. It is noteworthy, for example, that it was during the early troubled months of his marriage that he created two inferior short stories of domestic infelicity: "The Idiots," in which a woman wards off her husband's sexual advances by stabbing him with a pair of scissors, and "The Return," which describes the breakup of a relatively recent marriage. No less significant would seem to be the fact that one of Conrad's gloomiest personal letters, which contains the sentence, "Faith is a myth and beliefs shift like mists on the shore,"[25] was written while his wife was in labor for the first time, or the fact that it was during her second pregnancy that he composed a story in which a man causes a small boy to be blown up by dynamite.

For the psychoanalyst such correlations are remarkable not because they contribute to a larger aesthetic appreciation of a given literary work, but because they may provide hints of forces raging within the mind of the artist that have played a crucial role in facilitating or diminishing the fullest expression of his gift.[e] For while that gift itself, the mysterious thing called genius, lies beyond the confines of psychoanalytic understanding, the possessor of that gift does not. Thus, in his Preface to Marie Bonaparte's study of

[e] By the same token there can be no quarrel with Hewitt's assertion that "concentration on the peculiar circumstances of the creator's upbringing can do little to help us to a fuller appreciation of his work."[26]

Edgar Allan Poe, Freud wrote: "Such studies are not meant to explain the genius of a poet, but to show the motifs which have stirred it up, and the topics imposed upon it by fate."[27]

Far from enhancing the aesthetic value or contributing to a greater appreciation of a work of art, the psychoanalyst, like the critic, is sometimes accused of destroying it. After publishing an article on Conrad in the *Journal of the American Psychoanalytic Association*, the writer received a communication representing an epitaph on a tombstone, which read:

HERE LIES
THE GENIUS
OF
JOSEPH CONRAD
Born
Almayer's Folly, 1895
Died
J.A.P.A. Vol. 12, 1964
Of Symbolic Dissection
R.I.P.

There is, in truth, no cause for such lamentation: genius and great art will endure however closely they may be scrutinized. Psychoanalysis is no more capable of defacing the "Mona Lisa" or of spoiling *Hamlet* than is musical analysis able to diminish by one day the immortality of the "Mass in B Minor." Indeed Bernard Shaw's remarks on the alleged destructive influence of the critic are equally applicable to the reputedly baleful effect of psychoanalytic "symbolic dissection." Replying to the charge that a review by him had "finished" Sardou's play *Tosca*, he wrote: "I am no more able to make or mar artistic enterprises at will than the executioner has the power of life and death. . . . Though the east wind seems to kill the consumptive patient, he dies, not of the wind, but of phthisis. On the strong-lunged man it blows in vain. La Tosca died of disease, and not of criticism, which, indeed, did its best to keep it alive."[28] The fact that today, 75 years after Shaw pronounced it dead, Sardou's play is still enjoying a vigorous existence in the shape of Puccini's opera attests to the correctness of his thesis, if not his diagnostic acumen.[f]

By the same token, there is no reason to doubt that the genius of Conrad will weather the present study. His greatest writings will always grace the high hills of English literature, unshaken by the ravages of time or by the buffetings of the analytic east wind, while the slighter works, weak-rooted in a ground of fallow artistry, will fall of their own accord, unnoticed and unremembered.[g]

Ideally the psychoanalyst seeks to approach the problem of biography unhampered by covert temptations toward either hero-worship or iconoclasm, and equipped with the same capacity for attentive, considered, and detached observation that he strives to bring to his clinical practice. Inevitably in the course of such an inquiry, however, the dispelling of apparent myths concerning the life of a great person arouses a storm of indignation, for man has always tended to resent a confrontation by those realities which threaten treasured belief and happy illusion. In his essay on Leonardo da Vinci, Freud wrote:

> When psychoanalytic investigation, which usually contents itself with frail human material, approaches the great personages of humanity, it is not impelled to it by motives which are often imputed to it by laymen. It does not strive to blacken the radiant and to drag the sublime into the mire; it finds no satisfaction in diminishing the distance between the perfection of the great

[f] After denouncing the play as "an old fashioned, shiftless, clumsily constructed, empty-headed turnip ghost of a cheap shocker," Shaw expressed relief that it was not an opera, for as things stood the producer had only the drama critics to deal with.[29]

[g] It may be claimed that greater attention has been given to some of Conrad's minor works than they deserve. Lest there be any misunderstanding, it should be emphasized that this is not an example of what Hewitt has termed the failure "of practitioners of the [psychoanalytic] method . . . [to] discriminate between the qualities of these novels,"[30] but rather a manifestation of the fact that some works of art, like some people, possessing a greater psychological transparency than others, lend themselves more readily to facile understanding. Just as in fairy tales and in the unsophisticated dreams of little children, it is often among the less subtle and less imaginative stories that this transparency is likely to be found.

> and the inadequacy of the ordinary objects. But it cannot help finding that everything is worthy of understanding that can be perceived through those prototypes, and it also believes that none is so big as to be ashamed of being subject to the laws which control the normal and morbid actions with the same strictness.[31]

It is in such a spirit that the present study of Joseph Conrad has been undertaken, and there is reason to believe that at some unguarded moment his own inquiring mind would have approved, for he once voiced the hope that from the reading of his pages there might "emerge at last the vision of a personality: the man behind the books so fundamentally dissimilar, as for instance, *Almayer's Folly* and *The Secret Agent*—and yet a coherent justifiable personality both in its origin and in its actions."[32]

PART 1

A Skimmer of the Seas

I · Youth

Joseph Conrad was born on December 3, 1857 near Berdichev, in the Russian-ruled Polish province of Podolia. Christened Jozef Teodor Konrad, he was the first and only child of Apollo and Evelina Nalecz Korzeniowski, whose marriage in May 1856 celebrated the ultimate triumph of Apollo over the objections of Evelina's family to his suit. "My parents were by no means anxious to have him as a son-in-law," wrote Evelina's brother, Thaddeus Bobrowski, in his memoirs. "My mother liked his company and his mode of life, but could not perceive in him any qualifications for a good husband; she agreed with my father that having no profession, —for he lived at his father's home, occupying himself with nothing and owning nothing—that he was an undesirable suitor in spite of his pleasant society manners."[1] While Bobrowski was undoubtedly accurate in this report, he was evidently strongly biased against the Korzeniowski family whom he characterized as irresponsible visionaries, impulsive, unstable, and incompetent. Thus he described Apollo's father Theodore, who had lost all of his wife's dowry through the mismanagement of his affairs, as "nothing but a utopian,"[2] deriding him as a man who "considered himself a great politician and a supreme patriot; without listening to common sense he was always ready to saddle a horse and chase the enemy out of the country."[a/3] According to Bobrowski, Theodore's impracticability and quixotic qualities were renewed in his three sons: Robert, "an inveterate card player and drunkard, who having contributed largely to the ruin of his own family was killed in 1863"; Hilary, another "utopian," full of impractical schemes, who died heavily in debt in 1873;[4] and Apollo, described by his brother-in-law as "violent in emotions . . . impractical in his deeds, often helpless and unresourceful."[5]

In contrast Bobrowski sought to depict his own family as conservative, stable, and reliable people, which characterization

[a] Compare Balzac's quip in *Cousine Bette*: "You have only to point out a precipice to a Pole and he will immediately throw himself over. This race has the mentality of a cavalry regiment; they fancy they can ride down all obstacles and come through victorious."

Najder finds based more on wishful thinking than on fact. Thaddeus's own brother Stefan, for example—whose name may have been borrowed by Conrad for more than one fictional character—was the chief of the underground Left in the 1863 Insurrection, and was murdered in a staged duel by his right wing political opponents.[6] Neither politically nor temperamentally does Stefan appear to have differed too remarkably from the "utopian" Korzeniowskis, whose "irresponsibility," observes Najder, "manifested itself mainly in their taking part in the consecutive national insurrections, in which they lost most of their estates."[7]

Another apparent exception to Bobrowski's characterization of his family was his own uncle Nicholas, whose military exploits were one day destined to make a powerful impression on young Conrad. During the Napoleonic era Nicholas had joined the army at sixteen and he served under Bonaparte in the Russian campaign, remaining for the rest of his life an idolizing and awestruck admirer of the Emperor. Many years later in *A Personal Record* Conrad was to devote a number of paragraphs to his illustrious Great-Uncle Nicholas, dwelling particularly upon the disturbing but fascinating fact that to save himself from starvation he had once eaten roast dog.[8] Indeed it is more than likely that the exploits of this soldier of Bonaparte were woven into the fabric of Conrad's own thinly veiled admiration for the Corsican hero.

Thaddeus's sister was sixteen when Apollo first met her and fell in love. Her family's objections to him persisted even after the death of her father in 1850 when she was nineteen. Evelina herself, respecting his wishes, continued to resist Apollo's suit for several years, years during which she apparently manifested conspicuous signs of emotional instability, ascribed many years later by her brother to her conflicting feelings.[9]

Some five years after her father's death Evelina and her mother made a visit to Terekov, in the province of Podolia, not far from where Apollo was working as the manager of an estate. Hearing of their presence in the vicinity, Apollo called on the two ladies and finally succeeded in persuading Madame Bobrowska to permit him to marry her daughter. From the sequence of events, however, it would appear that the mother, believing that marriage might put an end to her daughter's disturbed mental state, had planned the visit with such a result in mind.[10] Thus on May 8, 1856, after eight years, Apollo Korzeniowski was finally able to claim Evelina as his bride. Apollo was then thirty-six and Evelina twenty-three.[b]

From its very inception the marriage of Apollo and Evelina was dogged by trouble, and, in time to come, by disaster. In his role as husband and father Apollo confirmed the estimate of him which his wife's father had once formed. He showed no aptitude for practical matters; he ran through his wife's dowry in a short span of time, and during much of the remainder of his life he was supported by members of her family. Seemingly at the cost of providing for the material—and probably emotional—needs of Evelina and their child, Apollo spent much of his time in writing and in engaging in dangerous political activity. In May 1861 he left his wife and son in the Ukraine and went to Warsaw, ostensibly to take over the direction of a literary periodical, but actually to be in the thick of revolutionary political activity. Toward the end of the summer he was joined by his wife and son in a house in Warsaw which became a clandestine meeting place for the illegal adherents of the cause of Polish nationalism.

On the night of October 21, 1861, when little Conrad was not yet four years old, the house was raided by the Russian police and Apollo was arrested and imprisoned in the Citadel. There he remained for half a year pending the disposition of his case.[12] Many years later Conrad recalled standing beside his mother in a big prison yard from where he caught sight of his father's face peering at them from behind bars.[13] Conrad's recollection of those troubled days may have been somewhat inexact, however, for there is evidence which suggests that Evelina too may have been imprisoned; certain it is that she was accused with her husband in the trial be-

[b] It is noteworthy that when 40 years later their son and Jessie George were married, he was thirty-eight, and she too was twenty-three. Of equal interest is the depiction in Conrad's fictional women of a conflict between an intense attachment to the father and a love for the suitor. It is not surprising that Conrad once confessed that all his life he had been extremely fascinated by the relationship between fathers and daughters.[11]

fore a military tribunal and was sentenced to exile with him.[c] The assumption that she was arrested and separated from her son—at least for a time—gains further support from the fact that, according to Bobrowski, her mother came to Warsaw immediately after Apollo's arrest, which move may have been dictated by the need to look after little Conrad.[14]

On May 8, 1862, escorted by two policemen, Apollo, Evelina, and their child set out upon their long journey into exile to Vologda, in northern Russia. On the way, outside of Moscow, the four-year-old child was taken seriously ill, apparently with pneumonia, but this misfortune was not permitted to interrupt the journey. Apollo later observed that the authorities decided that "as a child is born only ultimately to die, the journey was to proceed at once."[15] Not long thereafter Evelina became ill and so weak she had to be carried from post to post. Finally in early summer the party reached Vologda. "What is Vologda?" wrote Apollo to his cousins:

> A Christian is not bound to know this. Vologda is a great three-verst marsh on which logs and trees are placed parallel to each other in crooked lines; everything rotting and shifting under one's feet; this is the only means of communication available to the natives. . . . The climate consists of two seasons of the year: a white winter and a green winter. The white winter lasts nine-and-a-half months and the green one two-and-a-half. We are now at the onset of the green winter: it has already been raining ceaselessly for twenty-one days and that's how it will be to the end.
>
> During the whole winter the frost remains at 25°-30° [Réaumur; this corresponds to 24° to 30° below zero Fahrenheit] while the wind from the White Sea, held up by nothing, brings constant news from the polar bears. . . . The population is a nightmare: disease-ridden corpses.[16]

In the colony of exiles composed of the three Korzeniowskis and 21 other people, mostly priests from Poland and Lithuania, little

[c] Until recently it was believed—as Conrad evidently believed—that Evelina went into exile of her own volition.

00002.36 ₘ CA
00000.98 ₘ CA
00001.73 ₘ CA
00001.73 ₘ CA
00001.98 ₘ CA
00000.83 ₘ CA
00000.98 ₘ CA
00000.83 ₘ CA
00000.88 ₘ CA
00001.48 ₘ CA
00001.48 ₘ CA
S00015.26 • CA
00001.07 Tx CA
S00016.33 • CA
3 3610 = 10016.33 • CA

his Receipt Must
ompany All Returns

3 3610 = 10016.33 • CA

his Receipt Must
ompany All Returns

Conrad found himself in a completely adult community apparently without a single playmate. During the unsalutary rigors of the "white" winter, moreover, his mother began to show signs of failing health. By the following summer the family was allowed to be transferred to the milder climate of Chernikhov, 125 miles north-east of Kiev. Through the intervention of one of her relatives, Evelina was permitted to take a three months' leave from exile and to bring her small son to her brother's estate in Novofastov. Here little Conrad at last found a playmate, Thaddeus' daughter Josefina, who was but a few months younger than himself. With her and with other children from the neighborhood Conrad now enjoyed for the first time the pleasures of childhood play and the happy and stable atmosphere of home life. It was here too that he met his mother's celebrated uncle, Nicholas Bobrowski, the distinguished former officer in the army of Napoleon.

Although it was apparent that his mother was gravely ill of pulmonary tuberculosis, all attempts to gain permission to extend her stay in Novofastov were rebuffed, and in the autumn of 1863 mother and child were obliged to return to Apollo in Chernikhov, where Evelina's condition steadily deteriorated. In February 1865, Apollo wrote to his friend Kaszewski:

> My poor wife has been dying, for several years, from her sickness and from the repeated blows which have been falling on our family. During the last four months she has been cruelly ill, confined to her bed, with barely enough strength to glance at me, to speak to me with muted voice. . . . May God be with us—for people can do little for us now. I am everything in the house—both master and servant. I do not complain of this as a burden; but how often has it been impossible for me to help the poor, unhappy woman or bring her relief! Our little Conrad is inevitably neglected in the midst of all this.[17]

His state of mind can be judged from another letter to the same friend written two days later:

> I believe, best of friends, that two or three days ago I sent you a letter. . . . I think I did, as I don't know what I am doing—

> what I feel—and I remember nothing. You will understand when I tell you: my wife is very, very ill—there is hope only in God. . . . Homesickness like rust has slowly eaten away my wife's strength . . . sometimes a . . . pressure of her hand in mine, or in little Conrad's, testifies to her courage. . . . We are wretched and unhappy indeed, but thank God that we have been allowed to bear this fate together.[18]

A few weeks later, on April 18, 1865, when her son was but a few months more than seven years old, Evelina died at the age of thirty-two.

Apollo, whose behavior as husband and as father had not hitherto been distinguished by qualities of either resourcefulness or strength, reacted to this latest blow in a characteristic manner. For although he took pains to procure school books in order that he might ensure the education of his son and sought to safeguard his future well-being, he persisted in referring to the boy as "my poor little orphan," and gave the impression of a broken man who, crushed by misfortune and financially dependent upon others, was simply marking time until death would carry him off too. He wrote to his cousins:

> Whatever remains for me to do in life, I cannot either sacrifice or give anything, for I have nothing to sacrifice or offer up. . . . When my bitterness chokes me, I read your . . . letter and the pride of despair changes into divine sadness. My tears flow, but their fount is reason. Then, my composure recovered, I take up my life again, which is entirely centered upon my little Conrad. . . . I shield him from the atmosphere of this place, and he grows up as though in a monastic cell. For the *memento mori* we have the grave of our dear one and every letter which reaches us is the equivalent of a day of fasting, a hair shirt or a discipline. We shiver with cold, we die of hunger.[19]

Apollo divided his time between teaching Conrad and doing translations into Polish of Shakespeare and Victor Hugo. Young Conrad read proofs of his father's translation of *Toilers of the Sea*, a book which undoubtedly made a profound impression on the future mariner and teller of sea stories. These were the years when, shut up with his melancholy and ailing father, the boy devoured whatever books lay at hand, especially those stories of adventure and heroism by Cooper, Captain Marryat, Mungo Park, and others, which were destined to exert so powerful an influence upon the subsequent course of his life. These were the years too when Conrad began to manifest those signs of ill health which were to continue intermittently for the rest of his days. In May 1866, a year after his mother's death, he was sent by his father to spend the summer with his Uncle Thaddeus and his daughter Josefina at Novofastov. When he rejoined his father at Chernikhov in October, however, Conrad became ill, and his grandmother took him to Kiev for a medical consultation, and then to Novofastov. The precise nature of his ailment is unclear. According to his father he suffered from an illness "very rare with children: gravel forms in his bladder and causes gripes."[20] Najder brings forward evidence, moreover, that Conrad was subject to "migraine and nervous fits," possibly epilepsy, which continued at least until the age of fourteen.[21] In view of the paucity of clinical description and data, however, it is quite impossible to evaluate these reports. Suffice it to say that the state of his health often prevented his living a normal child's life, and especially his regular attendance at school.

Apollo, meanwhile, was becoming progressively ill with tuberculosis, and in December 1867, finally received permission to quit his place of exile. With Conrad he visited friends and went to a mountain resort where he sought to improve his health. "Both wandering exiles," he wrote his friend Kaszewski, "we need each other; he needs me as his miserable guardian, and I him as the only power that keeps me alive."[22] In the same letter he once again referred to Conrad's poor health on which account the child had "done virtually no work for the last two years."

At the end of their travels, in October 1868, they settled in Lwow. Here Conrad was again tutored at home, and although he does not appear to have shown much aptitude for studying he continued to be an avid reader and liked to recite poetry, particularly the heroic epics of Mickiewicz, the Polish nationalist.[23] It was at this time too, apparently, that the future novelist began to write, composing patriotic plays which were performed by his young friends.[d] "He writes without my encouragement," wrote Apollo to his friend Stefan Buszczynski, "and writes well."[24]

In February 1869 father and son moved on to Cracow where Apollo's health rapidly declined. "Not only was Apollo himself dying," observes Baines, "but he had become absorbed in a cult of his dead wife." Thus on the anniversary of her death he would sit motionless before her portrait, saying nothing and eating nothing all day.[25] Conrad later wrote of his having "nothing to do but sit and watch the awful stillness of the sick room flow out through the closed door and coldly enfold my sacred heart."[26] On May 23, 1869 Apollo died, and at his funeral, which took the form of a great patriotic tribute, the eleven-year-old Conrad walked at the head of the procession.[27]

Conrad's life now underwent a conspicuous change. In place of his lonely existence under the tutelage of his grief-stricken, dying father, he attended school and experienced the daily companionship of children his own age. In the course of time he began to take an interest in girls, for whom he developed sentiments which were to remain in his memory with undiminished intensity over the years to come. It was during this time too that he first felt the steadfast and sober concern of his Uncle Thaddeus, who until his own death toward the close of the century never ceased to cast a kindly and fatherly eye upon the varying fortunes of his beloved sister's son. In 1871 Thaddeus lost his daughter Josefina, a misfortune which probably intensified the bond between the now childless uncle and his orphaned nephew.

Despite the change in the external appearance of his life, however, Conrad continued to suffer from various manifestations of ill health. For if it had been his good fortune to escape the physical ravages of tuberculosis, it cannot be said that in that survival he emerged uninfected by the atmosphere of sickness that had surrounded him. Not long after his father's death his grandmother took him to Wartenberg in Bohemia to seek a cure for his head-

[d] Despite his later declared aversion for the theater Conrad apparently never lost his interest in writing plays; in time to come he was to adapt several of his stories for stage presentations.

aches, and on several other occasions before leaving Poland for good, he traveled abroad upon the advice of doctors, thus establishing a pattern which he was to follow in the years to come in seeking cures in the spas of western Europe. And, as will be pointed out somewhat later, just as the ailments of his mature years bore a heavy imprint of psychogenicity, so, it may be suspected, his numerous and varied complaints in childhood—beginning so shortly after his mother's untimely death—were related to the mental suffering occasioned by the unhappy events of his young years.

And then, seemingly out of the blue, in 1872, approximately a year after the death of his young cousin, Conrad told her father of his secret wish to go to sea, a confession which evoked a reaction of shocked and bewildered incredulity. "It could not have been greater," he wrote in *A Personal Record*, "if I had announced the intention of entering a Carthusian monastery."[e/28] Nor is this to be wondered at, for why should a young boy, living amid familiar surroundings, cherished by loving kinsmen, and stirred since childhood by the insistent pulse of national consciousness, want to quit his motherland for the life of a sailor, rootless and unmoored, cast adrift upon the high seas in unknown vessels peopled by a motley community of nameless faces? Bobrowski may not have known the answer but he set out to stop him. In May 1873, Conrad was sent on a trip through Germany and Switzerland, accompanied by his tutor, a Mr. Pulman, who was instructed to do his best to persuade his young charge to abandon his foolish idea. Mr. Pulman was apparently making some headway in this endeavor, wrote Conrad in *A Personal Record*, until an unexpected event took place that seemingly shattered the tutor's arguments and made further resistance to the boy's desire futile.

While resting by the roadside on the Furca Pass, Conrad caught sight of an Englishman—"My unforgettable Englishman"—who

[e] Conrad's use of this expression may be an example of his susceptibility to his uncle's influence. In a letter of October 26, 1876, containing the usual scolding for a lack of responsibility in money matters, Bobrowski wrote to Conrad, "Certainly, there is no reason for one to take one's life or go into a Carthusian monastery because of some folly one has committed. . . ."[29] Ironically it would be but a little more than a year later that Conrad apparently did attempt to take his life, as will be recounted in the next chapter.

happened to be passing by. He was wearing a knickerbocker suit, short socks and laced boots and his "calves exposed to the public gaze . . . dazzled the beholder by the splendor of their marble-like condition and their rich tone of young ivory. . . . The light of a headlong, exalted satisfaction with the world of men . . . illumined his face . . . and triumphant eyes. In passing he cast a glance of kindly curiosity and a friendly gleam of big, sound, shiny teeth . . . his white calves twinkled sturdily." Suddenly, the boy who had been feeling "that ghostly unrealized and desired sea of my dreams escaped from the unnerved grip of my will," was fired by a strange and powerful emotion. The Englishman's "glance, his smile . . . his striving-forward appearance helped me to pull myself together. . . ." The argument with Mr. Pulman went on, "But I felt no longer crushed." Realizing the futility of continuing the battle the tutor muttered, "You are an incorrigible, hopeless Don Quixote."[30]

Whether this is a faithful recollection or a romanticized reconstruction by a writer who was notoriously inaccurate in the rendering of his own history cannot be determined, but the question is of small consequence, for either hypothesis carries the same implication of Conrad's pronounced susceptibility, as a child and as a man, to the magnetic influence exerted by images epitomizing strength and masculinity. That Conrad himself felt that this glimpse heralded a crucial moment in his life, is indicated by his query: "Was he in the mystic ordering of common events the ambassador of my future?" For thereafter "there was no more question of my mysterious vocation." Eleven years later, added Conrad, he stood on the steps of St. Katherine's Dock House, a master in the British Merchant Service.[f/31]

Implicit in the account of this little incident is the idea that what the admiring and impressionable Conrad saw he later became, as if in gazing upon the Englishman he took within himself the seeds of his manly qualities, and thus, through a process of incorporation, a hesitant and sickly Polish orphan was transformed into an impressive, vigorous, and substantial figure—Captain Korzeniowski, British Master Mariner.

[f] An inaccuracy: Conrad became a master in November 1886, some 13 years after the Furca Pass incident.

Similar identifications with heroic figures can be repeatedly demonstrated in both the factual and the fictional aspects of Conrad's life. His avid childhood reading of the exploits and derring-do of famous men furnished him with those images of valor and pluck that he sought both to acquire for himself and to re-create in the lives of his invented heroes. A living model for such an image was the Corsican sailor, Dominic Cervoni, whom Conrad came to know on the sailing vessel *St. Antoine* during his career as a French mariner, and later described in *The Mirror of the Sea* and in *The Arrow of Gold.* In the former he likened Cervoni to Ulysses: "a modern and unlawful wanderer with his own legend of loves, dangers and bloodshed,"[32] while in the novel it is Conrad himself (as "M. George") who bears the nickname "The Young Ulysses,"[33] thereby describing a process which begins with hero worship and ends in a fusion of identities between idol and idolator.[g]

What is noteworthy about Conrad's depiction of these and other models of manly strength was his penchant for singling out discrete and isolated parts of the body as the repositories of power. In his account of the episode at the Furca Pass, for example, it is the calves and teeth of the Englishman that are emphasized, as if their marble or ivory-like qualities were magically transferred upon the boy, furnishing him with a sudden adamantine resistance to the arguments of his tutor. In his fiction, too, Conrad bestowed similar attributes of hardness on virtually everyone and everything to such a degree as to suggest an *Idée fixe.*

Thus Tom Lingard, of *The Rescue*, holds his arm "steady as a limb of marble," old Giorgio of *Nostromo* resembles a statue with "an arm of stone."[34] Henry Allègre, of *The Arrow of Gold*, looks "solid as a statue," and the face of Peyrol, in *The Rover*, resembles a "carving of stone." It is among his fictional women, however, where attributes of enduring hardness are most conspicuous. Mrs. Hervey, of "The Return," who is "strong and upright like an obe-

[g] The Marseilles stories were not the only ones in which Conrad revived the reassuring image of Cervoni. The latter in all likelihood was the model for the Capataz in *Nostromo*, for Lingard in *The Rescue*, and for a number of other fictional heroes. His characterization as a latter-day Ulysses is repeated in *The Rescue*, which opens with allusions to the Trojan War.

lisk," displays "marmoreal impassiveness," Captain Hermann's niece in "Falk" is likened to "an allegorical statue of the earth," Antonia of *Nostromo* recalls a "gigantic . . . allegorical statue,"[35] Mrs. Travers of *The Rescue* is "an amazing and solid marvel," and Dona Rita, the heroine of *The Arrow of Gold*, whose "uncovered neck was round like the shaft of a column," reminded one of "the faces of women sculptured on immemorial monuments," or "some impassive statue in a desert."

Allusions to ivory appear not only in his Congo stories but in his descriptions of people, as in the "ivory forehead" of Felicia Moorsom of "The Planter of Malata," and in what amounts to a virtual obsession with teeth. "Conrad's women," observed Visiak,[36] "are dentally superb,"[h] while Ford Madox Hueffer (Ford)[i] wrote that in one of their literary collaborations it was only with difficulty that he was able to persuade Conrad to omit that anatomical detail from the portrait of a fictional character.[37]

Perhaps the most impressive example in Conrad's writings of the attribution of power to isolated body parts concerns hair, which, as will become apparent somewhat later, assumes the quality of a fetish. Conrad's obsessional preoccupation with tokens of solidity, however, was not limited to the marble-like limbs, strong teeth, or helmet-like coiffures of his characters. Even inanimate objects served as epitomes of hardness: thus the sea is compared with a "wall of polished steel," or an "iron plate," and sails are likened to white marble.[j]

This recurring insistence upon hardness, the repeated analogies between persons and statuary, and the seemingly endless pursuit of the quality of solidity in things and people is hardly surprising in a sensitive individual, who in his formative years, had witnessed the merciless march of disaster, disease, and death pass before his frightened eyes. Surely it was to erase the memory of that fearful spectacle that Conrad sought to depict a world in which all persons and all objects possessed the quality of immortality. Thus the ob-

[h] An exception is the downtrodden Mrs. Schomberg of *Victory* whose distinguishing characteristic is a *blue* tooth.

[i] Ford Madox Hueffer changed his name legally to Ford Madox Ford in 1919; Hueffer is used throughout this volume.

[j] The relevance of these observations to the subject of fetishism will be considered in Chapter XV.

servation that Henry Allègre had "silver hairs in his beard but he looked as solid as a statue," suggests that although he displayed signs of ageing he would really never die. By the same token the adamantine qualities which young Conrad saw in his "unforgettable Englishman" presented him with the possibility of his own salvation by linking his fate with that "ambassador of [his] future" and quitting his native land.

It has been suggested that in leaving Poland to go to sea Conrad was expressing a desire to escape the conventional discipline of school life.[38] There is little evidence, however, for such a contention, and Conrad himself wrote, "I didn't suffer much from the various imperfections of my first school. I was rather indifferent to school troubles. I had a private gnawing worm of my own. This was the time of my father's last illness."[39] It would seem more likely that it was that "gnawing worm" which led to the momentous decision of the fifteen-year-old boy to cut himself off from all that was familiar to him. Nor did he underestimate the force of his attachments: "It was within those historical walls [of Cracow] that I began to understand things, form affections, lay up a store of memories and a fund of sensations with which I was to break violently by throwing myself into an unrelated existence."[40] Such a violent break must be viewed, therefore, as an expression of an affirmative pursuit of life, an act of self-preservation, not unlike what he would later fictionalize in Jim's jump from the rusted, leaking steamship *Patna*.[k] It seems likely that in Conrad's eyes to have remained in Poland would have been tantamount to resigning himself to a climate where everyone and everything he had cherished had crumbled, and where he himself might well be the next to perish. Through his reading, however, which he declared had once saved him from going mad in the midst of all the misery about him, he had learned of another life, and of another world—a world of men, of action, of adventure, and of vitality, a world where death was unknown and man is immortal. "After reading so many romances," he wrote in *A Personal Record*, "he desired

[k] Morf has also compared Conrad's leaving Poland with Jim's "jump."[41] Evidence in support of this thesis will be presented in a later chapter.

naïvely to escape with his very body from the intolerable reality of things."[42]

When by the autumn of 1874 there appeared to be no abatement of his yearning to go to sea, his Uncle Thaddeus finally granted his consent, and a few weeks later, supplied with some letters of introduction and the assurance of a small allowance, the sixteen-year-old boy boarded a train at Cracow bound for Marseilles, where he was to begin life anew as a French sailor. "The truth must have been that, all unversed in the arts of the wily Greek, the deceiver of gods, the lover of strange women, the evoker of bloodthirsty shades, I yet longed for the beginning of my own obscure Odyssey, which, as was proper for a modern, should unroll its wonders and terrors beyond the Pillars of Hercules."[43]

If by this act, however, Conrad was signifying his will to live and to link his fortunes and his fate with the immortal adventurers of his childhood reading, it is somewhat startling to learn that a little more than three years after the inception of his new life, he was shot in the chest, apparently by his own hand. It would appear that there were flaws in the elaborate investment of hardness by which he had hoped to attain invulnerability, and that however readily he might array himself in the borrowed armor of powerful men, just as easily could that armor fall away, revealing beneath it no longer a "Young Ulysses" pursuing the vitality of adventure, but a defeated youth courting the finality of death.

The events leading up to this unexpected development will be considered in the following chapter.

II · The Duel

EARLY IN THE WINTER OF 1878 Conrad's uncle received an urgent telegram reading: "Conrad wounded, send money—come."[1] This message which brought Bobrowski to Marseilles heralded the denouement of his nephew's career as a French mariner.

Over the span of the more than three years which had elapsed since his leaving Poland, young Conrad, or Monsieur George as he was called by his fellow sailors, had made a number of trips to the New World. In March 1877 when he was about to embark once again he developed an anal abscess which apparently prevented him from leaving.[2] From this moment on until his departure from Marseilles on a British freighter one year later, Conrad's history is a matter of some doubt and considerable controversy. For some time it had been assumed that his own accounts as written in 1905 in *The Mirror of the Sea*, and again in 1917 in the novel *The Arrow of Gold*, were accurate autobiographic reports of his activities during this year. In recent years, however, new facts obtained from other sources have cast serious doubts upon the validity of this assumption.

It was Conrad's version that he became a member of a syndicate which operated a 60-ton sailing vessel, called the *Tremolino*, which was employed in smuggling arms into Spain for the supporters of Don Carlos de Bourbon, the Pretender to the Spanish throne. The crew was composed of Conrad (or M. George), Dominic Cervoni, and the latter's nephew César. The guiding genius of the syndicate was said to be a certain Spanish woman, Rita de Lastaola, who, in *The Arrow of Gold* is identified as the mistress of the "King," that is, Don Carlos.

In *The Mirror of the Sea* Conrad described the deliberate wrecking of the *Tremolino* in order to avoid her capture by the Spanish coast guard which had been alerted to her illegal activities by the traitorous César. Upon discovering his nephew's perfidy, the indomitable Dominic is supposed to have pitched him overboard with a single mighty blow, causing César, weighted down by a money belt stolen from M. George, to drown.[a]

[a] Conrad used this theme—the drowning of a man weighted down by

A similar cast of characters made its appearance in *The Arrow of Gold* which, like the short account in *The Mirror of the Sea*, is concerned with the Carlist War. In the novel, however, the smuggling of arms into Spain is interwoven with a love story between Rita and M. George. From their retreat in the Maritime Alps, M. George journeys one day into Marseilles where he learns that he is being slandered by a man named Blunt, another member of the syndicate, who is also in love with Rita. Blunt is promptly challenged to a duel in the course of which M. George is shot in the chest. Rita now nurses her lover back to health and then disappears from his life forever, after leaving with him a memento—the gold hair ornament from which the novel obtains its name. Some years later, the author asserts, he lost this precious gift in a storm at sea.

This, in brief, is the version of Conrad's Marseilles history which, until comparatively recent times, had been accepted without much question by his biographers and by the reading public. It goes without saying that it is a story which holds a strong popular appeal. Unfortunately, there are cogent reasons for doubting the accuracy of some parts of his story and for disbelieving others entirely.

In 1937, some thirteen years after Conrad's death, a letter came to light written by Bobrowski on March 24, 1879 to Stefan Buszczynski,[3] an old friend of Conrad's father, which presented a picture quite different from that fictionalized in *The Arrow of Gold*. According to Bobrowski's letter, Conrad had been engaged in smuggling, not for the glorious cause of the Pretender to the Spanish throne, but for his own personal gain. Initially successful in making a profit, young Conrad subsequently lost every penny. Barred by certain legal formalities from serving further as a French seaman, Conrad now found himself in serious straits. He borrowed 800 francs from a friend and then set off for Villefranche, where an American squadron was anchored, in the hope of entering the American naval service. Failing in this he went on to Monte Carlo,

---

heavy metal—in several stories: *Nostromo* (Decoud), and "The End of the Tether" (Captain Whalley). See Chapter XVII, footnote *f*.

gambled away all his money, and returned to Marseilles where he tried to kill himself with a gun. It was at this point that the telegram was sent to his uncle.

It would seem that from the very start Bobrowski was determined to conceal the true circumstances of Conrad's bullet wound, for concerning the suicidal attempt he wrote to Buszczynski, "Let this detail remain between us, for I have told everyone that he was wounded in a duel."[4] Apparently Bobrowski's explanation was widely accepted, for, supported by Conrad's novel, it became an established tenet in the Conrad legend during the ensuing 60 years. The abandonment of the duel story, moreover, has not taken place without encountering an assortment of last-ditch resistances, for, like all public figures who are objects of hero worship, Conrad has long been invested with a romantic aura which many of his admirers are loath to dissipate with the cold touch of unglamorous fact. As noted earlier, the biographer often approaches his subject with that kind of idealization and bias that is characteristic of love, transferring upon the subject sentiments and attitudes not unlike those often directed by a child toward a loved parent. Surely, given a choice, no child would prefer to believe that a father had attempted suicide if it seemed at all possible that he had engaged in a duel, and by the same token some of Conrad's biographers appear to have strained logic to the limit in their efforts to sustain the duel story. There are critics, for example, who have advanced the fanciful suggestion that Conrad told his uncle of the suicide attempt in order to conceal the "true" fact that he had really been wounded in a duel,[5] but insofar as it was Bobrowski himself who disseminated the duel story the logic of this theory is reduced to an absurdity.

A more serious objection to this theory, however, is that it ignores the fact that while duelling at that time enjoyed a status of honor and glamor, suicide, in the Western world, at least, was regarded as a disgrace, a sin, and a crime. (In his unfinished novel, *The Sisters*, Conrad spoke of suicide as "the unpardonable crime."[6]) It seems beyond belief that a young Polish gentleman of that era would have concealed the fact that he had been duelling behind a false confession of attempted suicide. He might at least have claimed that he had shot himself accidentally while cleaning his gun.

It has further been argued that the suicide theory rests upon a faulty translation into English of a letter which Conrad received from his uncle[7] in which the phrase, "you were in a shooting," was erroneously rendered: "You had shot yourself."[8] But the latter expression is precisely how Bobrowski's letter has been translated into English under the careful editorship of the Polish critic Najder,[9] and it is the same phrase rendered in his presentation of the so-called Bobrowski Document, a combined diary and accounting memorandum that Bobrowski prepared for his nephew.[10] In actuality the question of the precise translation of Bobrowski's comments is quite irrelevant, however, for they were written long after the "duel story" had been decided upon, as Bobrowski explained in his letter to Buszczynski.[b]

Granted that the evidence that Conrad made a suicidal attempt seems irrefutable, the attempt itself merits closer scrutiny. The precise setting in which it occurred is arresting: "Having managed his affairs so excellently," Bobrowski wrote sarcastically to his friend, "he returns to Marseilles and one fine evening invites his friend the creditor [whose loan of 800 francs Conrad had apparently lost at Monte Carlo] to tea, and before his arrival attempts to take his life with a revolver."[11] Now this is hardly the behavior of a man unequivocally bent on killing himself; on the contrary it reflects an inner state of indecision, preparing the way for rescue by his tea-time guest in the event that his intended self-injury should not prove immediately fatal.[c] (In current-day psychiatric experience analogous situations are quite common—a would-be suicide takes

[b] It seems reasonable to assume that the "duel story" was invented by Bobrowski, who was motivated by a wish to shield Conrad's name, similar to an earlier wish to conceal from his nephew the fact that his mother had gone into exile not because of faithful devotion to her husband, but because, like him, she had been tried and convicted.

[c] As is the case in many suicidal acts it requires no great perspicacity to discern the hostile element in Conrad's behavior. To invite a friend to tea, and one's creditor at that, and greet him with one's corpse, or at least a bleeding wounded body, might be construed both as questionable hospitality and as a wry means of settling one's accounts.

an overdose of a hypnotic drug and then before losing consciousness puts in a telephone call to a friend, or to the police, to report on what he has done. Many suicides are aborted in this way.) Conrad also took the precaution—so the letter goes—to leave all his family addresses in a conspicuous place[12] so that his rescuer could inform Bobrowski immediately of his nephew's plight, speeding him to Marseilles, and bringing with him, hopefully, urgently needed cash.

None of these observations are intended to minimize the seriousness of Conrad's act, for the report that the bullet went "*durch und durch* near the heart"[13] leaves no doubt of the danger he was risking. At the same time it must be recognized that his act was prompted largely by the desperate and chaotic condition of his immediate situation; once his affairs were set in order and he had once more embarked upon the seas as a sailor, the possibility of a second suicide attempt does not appear to have troubled Bobrowski, who in his subsequent correspondence with his nephew seems to have treated the whole matter more as a temporary lapse in proper conduct[d] than as a cause for future vigilant concern.

Bobrowski's letter to his friend, however, does not constitute the sole basis for disbelieving the authenticity of Conrad's accounts of his experiences in Marseilles. Baines has called attention to several discrepancies in chronology between these accounts and historical fact[15] which would make untenable Conrad's claim to have participated in the Carlist cause at the time when Don Carlos was fighting for the throne, "arms in hand, amongst the hills and gorges of Guipuzcoa."[15a] If indeed Conrad was engaged in gunrunning for his supporters it would have been toward the close of the year 1877, nearly two years after the Pretender had quit Spanish soil. Baines also exposes the fictional nature of an important episode in the *Tremolino* story, namely, Conrad's assertion that he lost all his money during the wreck of the ship, when César, weighted down by M. George's money belt, drowned; in actuality, Baines asserts, César lived for many years after the alleged

[d] "Another absurdity," as he was to characterize Conrad's behavior on a different occasion.[14]

Tremolino affair, and served a long career in the French merchant navy.[e/16]

As for the contention that Conrad was the lover of the mistress of the Pretender, the only evidence for it is *The Arrow of Gold*, and in all fairness to Conrad it should be emphasized that as far as the present writer knows it was not Conrad as much as some of his biographers who have insisted that the novel is authentic autobiography.[f] In seeking to assess the truth of the love affair recounted in the novel, two separate questions must be answered: the identity of Dona Rita, and the nature of Conrad's relationship with that individual.

Beginning at the end of 1876 or early in 1877, and continuing for some years thereafter, the mistress of Don Carlos de Bourbon was a Hungarian actress who ultimately bore the name Paula de Somogyi. It is the opinion of Jerry Allen that Paula was the real Rita of *The Arrow of Gold*.[20] Although Baines dismisses this theory without hesitation,[21] it would appear that his argument concerns

[e] According to Baines this was not the only instance in which Conrad falsely reported losing his possessions on the high seas. On August 10, 1881 he wrote to his uncle for funds, a rather common custom of his in those days, claiming that he had lost all his kit in the wreck of the *Annie Frost*. Baines points out, however, that Conrad was not listed as a member of the crew of that vessel, nor was she wrecked during the particular voyage on which Conrad indicated he had sailed with her.[17] Allen asserts, however, that prior to setting out on a long sea voyage the *Annie Frost* was damaged while being towed out of Le Havre en route to London on June 11, 1881. She believes that Conrad was a member of the crew and was thrown overboard at the time. The same writer attributes his not being listed as a member of the crew to the fact that actual signing on a vessel was often delayed until a new voyage officially began.[18]

[f] Jerry Allen quotes a letter from Professor Marcel Clavel of Aix-en-Provence, of June 9, 1957, assuring her of the authenticity of *The Arrow of Gold*, stating that Jean-Aubry had told him that Conrad claimed "that practically everything was taken from life in his novel." Furthermore, as if offering some added proof of this, Clavel asserted that Conrad and Jean-Aubry "had started from Paris with the purpose of going together to all the places mentioned [in *The Arrow of Gold*], but, unfortunately, Jean-Aubry had to stop at Lyons, and the opportunity was lost forever."[19] (One is reminded of the man who claimed that his horse could encircle a certain race track in 15 seconds and who offered to exhibit the track to anyone who doubted him.)

mainly Miss Allen's assertion that Conrad had an affair with Paula, for he acknowledges certain similarities between her and the fictional Rita and concludes by admitting that there is some evidence to suggest "that Conrad had [Paula] in mind when writing the novel."[22]

Miss Allen seeks to add further proof to her theory that there was a liaison between Conrad and Paula by illustrating her book with a photograph of the latter wearing an arrow-shaped ornament similar to the one worn by Rita in *The Arrow of Gold*, from which the novel takes its name. But the photograph proves nothing about Conrad's relationship with Paula; it merely suggests that he was familiar with her appearance and with the distinctive jeweled ornament which he incorporated in his portrait of the fictional Rita.[g]

In support of this last hypothesis it should be noted that Paula died in November 1917 and that within one month Conrad was at work on *The Arrow of Gold*;[24] this sequence of events is remarkable in view of the fact that shortly after the newspapers carried a false report of her death some 12 years earlier, he had begun to write the *Tremolino* story, which deals again with Dona Rita.[25] Miss Allen claims that it was "out of concern for her" that Conrad refrained from unfolding to the world the story of their love affair during Paula's lifetime. "Conrad wrote that moving love story of his youth," she continues, "when the real people he drew upon for it were truthfully 'all at rest' as he knew. Out of a close feeling of privacy he guarded throughout his life the identity of her whom he called Dona Rita."[26] Despite the strong romantic appeal of this explanation, however, another admittedly less chivalrous one comes to mind, namely, that he was obliged to postpone the writing of this story until the demise of the one individual who might challenge its veracity, for as long as Paula lived both the love affair and the duel could have been exposed by her as figments of a fertile

[g] The fact that the photograph was made in 1880, long after the termination of the alleged affair with Conrad, who by this time had been an English sailor for two years, proves to Miss Allen that Conrad's assertion that Paula had given him the ornament was a romantic fiction, as was his claim that he ultimately lost the precious memento at sea.[23] It does not appear to have dampened Miss Allen's belief in the essential validity of the novel.

imagination. It would appear therefore that Conrad was carefully covering his tracks.

The assumption that Conrad was acquainted with Paula, or at least familiar with her appearance, does not support by any means the thesis that he was her lover, which seems on the face of it highly improbable. From the inception of her relationship with Don Carlos until its dissolution in 1882[27] Paula de Somogyi appears to have retained her position of favor with the Pretender, who finally bestowed on her a generous settlement.[28] If Conrad's story of his duel with another prominent Carlist, Blunt, were true, both its occurrence and the issue over which it was fought would quickly have become common knowledge, sooner or later reaching the ear of the Pretender himself. Why should a woman, suddenly elevated to a position of such eminence, and evidently enjoying the success, excitement, and notoriety of being the favorite of the claimant to the throne of Spain, risk jeopardizing everything by entering into a scandalous liaison with an impecunious sailor? Nor does so bold a venture seem compatible with the character of the inhibited Conrad, who was exceedingly shy and uncomfortable with women who aroused his interest. It would appear highly improbable that the man who later fled in panic and hid for three days after proposing marriage to an unknown English girl named Jessie George would have had the temerity to initiate an affair with so impressive a figure as the mistress of the Pretender to the Spanish throne.

The Marseilles chapter of Conrad's life is not the only instance in which two mutually irreconcilable versions of his personal history exist. At a later point in this work a similar pair of incompatible accounts will be described concerning his brief stay, some ten years after the Marseilles experience, on the island of Mauritius. In this case too it will be seen that the fictional version of what took place held sway throughout Conrad's life, and for some years thereafter, as authentic autobiography, and that it was only many years after his death that new facts came to light which challenged the authenticity of what he had written. Like the Marseilles story, the Mauritius episode concerns a love affair which in the fictional version represents the author as a bold and aggressive suitor, while the factual account reveals him as in truth he was from the time of his first school-boy love affair—an exceedingly reserved person who nourished his unrequited romantic sentiments in the strictest secrecy, and who in the face of discouragement retired in a posture of humiliation and defeat.

In both instances, then, it would appear that Conrad turned to fiction as a means of effecting a corrective revision of a painful reality. If this be true, what was the "painful reality" which he attempted to conceal behind the heroic love affair with the woman he called "Dona Rita"? Was there in Marseilles, as in Mauritius many years later, another girl with whom he was infatuated? If so, some hint of her identity should exist, but aside from Baines' suggestion that Conrad's outspoken antagonism to the theater might have originated in an unhappy experience with an actress in Marseilles,[29] no evidence of such a woman in Conrad's life has so far been discovered.

On the other hand it should be noted that a woman whom he called Rita was of sufficient importance to him to become the subject of three separate literary works, written over widely spaced intervals: the unfinished *The Sisters*, in 1895, "The *Tremolino*," in 1905, and *The Arrow of Gold*, in 1917. Such an insistently recurring reverberation of a name attests to the author's enduring obsession with the memory of someone, who despite the varieties of her fictional representation was evidently modeled, in some details at least, upon the image of Paula de Somogyi.

Whether Conrad was personally acquainted with her is problematical. Baines asserts that there is no evidence that she was ever in Marseilles (the most likely place where Conrad could have met her), adding that Don Carlos would scarcely have used as his emissary there a "young Hungarian chorus-girl, who knew, apart from her own language, only a little German."[30] Miss Allen claims, however, that when he brought Paula to Paris, late in 1876 or early in 1877, Don Carlos set out to "train" and educate her so that within two years she could speak almost any European language.[31] If so she must have possessed a remarkable aptitude, for early in 1877 —a few months after the beginning of this liaison—Paula took a furnished house in Marseilles "to act as the link between Don Carlos and Legitimist circles,"[32] an assignment, one suspects, which would have exacted considerable fluency both in French and Spanish.

While the question must remain unanswered at this time whether Paula was indeed the key figure in the Pretender's cause that Conrad makes her out to be, there can be no denying the fact that Conrad got to know something about this beautiful girl, about her early history,[h] and about her liaison with Don Carlos.[i] However this knowledge was acquired—by hearsay, from the newspapers, or through actual acquaintanceship with her—it is quite possible that Conrad "fell" for her in the manner of a moonstruck adolescent who engages in covert romantic fantasies about movie stars and other celebrities, like the consorts of princes and the mistresses of kings. That Conrad was capable of such a secret infatuation his later behavior in Mauritius would prove;[j] perhaps in Marseilles as in Port Louis he made some half-hearted avowal of his feelings, only to flee in shame and in confusion. Whatever the facts of the matter might be, there would seem to be little doubt that his "memory" of Paula remained alive for virtually the rest of his life, for as late as 1919 he wrote of this adventure in Marseilles: "There are some of these 42-year-old episodes of which I cannot now think without a slight tinge in the chest—un petit serrement de coeur. What a confession!"[36]

In light of the present contention then that Conrad never had a love affair with "Rita," *The Arrow of Gold* may be viewed as a wish-fulfilling fantasy, befitting the daydreams of a man of advancing years, who is unable or unwilling to shake from his thoughts the haunting memory of an unrequited love.

But *The Arrow of Gold* is more than a substitute of a fictional romance for one that probably never was. Viewed together with Conrad's two earlier attempts to deal with a girl named Rita, it supports the suspicion that the latter originated from more than one model in the author's past.

[h] Like the fictional Rita, for example, Paula was apparently a peasant girl, who had been raised by an uncle, a parish priest in a small village.[33]

[i] The "Venetian episode" mentioned in *The Arrow of Gold*[34] was unquestionably inspired by a much publicized stay in that city by Don Carlos and Paula.[35]

[j] See Chapter IV.

The history of Rita of *The Arrow of Gold* has an unmistakable Pygmalion flavor.[k] Of peasant origin, the orphaned Rita tended goats in the hills of northern Spain, where she was molested by the sadistic sexual advances of her depraved cousin, José Ortega. When she reaches the age of thirteen, her priest-uncle sends her to live in Paris with another uncle who is an orange merchant. Sitting upon a stone in a garden, she is one day discovered by a rich artist, Henry Allègre, who, like Shaw's Henry Higgins, proceeds to transform her into a lady. Unlike Eliza Doolittle, however, Rita becomes her benefactor's mistress as well as his model, and following his death inherits his fortune. In the course of time she becomes the mistress of Don Carlos and a key figure in the campaign to place him upon the throne of Spain. This is the general setting when M. George enters the scene and becomes her lover. At the same time she is being sought in marriage by Mr. J. M. K. Blunt, an American who is another member of the syndicate and the adversary of M. George in the alleged duel.

Rita is also the object of the lustful cravings of her cousin, José, who reappears in the latter part of the novel as an agent in the Carlist intrigue. Like M. George, Ortega becomes a casualty because of Rita: in a highly improbable fashion he succeeds in wounding himself with a sword while raging in a fit of wild jealousy outside the bedroom in which Rita and M. George are presumably making love. The physician summoned to treat his "enormous gash in the side"—an incredible consequence of a self-inflicted accidental injury—is the same doctor who, at a later moment in the story, ministers to the chest wound sustained by M. George in the duel. "This is the second case I have had in this house" observes the doctor, "and I am sure that directly or indirectly it was connected with that woman. She will go on leaving a track behind her and then someday there will really be a corpse."[38] The doctor's impression of Dona Rita is supported by the description of her behavior during her liaison with M. George. For despite the writer's efforts to present it as an idyll, "a children's foolhardy adventure,"

[k] Allen makes the same observation about Paula.[37] The significance of the Pygmalion theme will be considered in a later chapter.

The Arrow of Gold is the story of the torments of a weak and hesitant young man who suffers at the hands of an Amazon, a woman older than himself and, like him, afflicted with a conspicuous sexual problem. Although he tries to paint her as "mysteriously feminine," he refers to her head as "delicately masculine," and his characterization of her body as "statuesque, gleaming, cold like a block of marble" hardly conveys an image of yielding femininity. Nor does her response to a kiss: "with a stifled cry of surprise her arms fell off me as if she had been shot . . . the next thing I knew there was a good foot of space between us."[39] She exhibits a violent recoil from any hint of sexual surrender: upon awakening in M. George's arms she "instantly flung herself out of them in one sudden effort."[40] Indeed there is scarcely any indication that sex plays a lively role in this relationship at all. Instead of any intimation of either erotic excitement or the harmonious murmurings of contented lovers, this "affair" which M. George compares with "two infants squabbling in a nursery," conveys rather a mood of melancholy and an atmosphere of neurotic suffering. Indeed the strongest hint of sexual love occurs in M. George's dreams and there a symbolic reversal of the sexual roles takes place:

> Often I dreamed of her with white limbs shimmering in the gloom like a nymph haunting a riot of foliage and raising a perfect round arm. To take an arrow of gold out of her hair to throw it at me by hand, like a dart.[l] It came on, a whizzing trail of light, but I always woke up before it struck. Always. Invariably. It never had a chance. A volley of small arms was much more likely to do the business some day—or night.[41]

Despite his boast, however, the dream has the same meaning whether the dreamer awakens on time or not, for the very conception of being shot at by Rita's arrow conveys the idea of being penetrated by his beloved.

It is apparent therefore, that based upon his seeming adulation of Paula, Conrad utilized *The Arrow of Gold* as a vehicle for a

[l] An identical image is presented in the Mauritius story, "A Smile of Fortune." See Chapter IV, in which additional similarities between that story and *The Arrow of Gold* are noted.

fantasy wherein a weak and passive man is pierced by the shafts of an all-powerful androgynous woman who, untouched and untouchable, elicits from her lover not desire, but awe. But such an image of love and such a conception of a loved woman had their origins in Conrad's life long before he ever heard of Paula de Somogyi.

In his First Note to *The Arrow of Gold* Conrad specifically invoked the memory of a childhood sweetheart, probably a girl named Janina Taube, to whom he proposed to address his tale.[42] In its original form, in fact, the novel was planned as a series of letters to her, now a grown woman, whom the writer had not seen "for something like five and thirty years."[43] "If I once start to tell you" (the story of *The Arrow of Gold*), he wrote, "I would want you to feel that you have been there yourself."[44] This statement certainly suggests that the fictional love story was inspired by his memory of her as an adolescent girl. Indeed in his further comment, "You always could make me do whatever you liked,"[45] the author was apparently recollecting the beginnings of that subservience toward a loved woman which is characteristic of M. George and, for that matter, of virtually all of Conrad's fictional lovers. Yet, while acknowledging this early influence, Conrad explained that *The Arrow of Gold* was purely a work of fiction: "In this form in which it is presented here, it has been pruned of all allusions to their common past, of all asides, disquisitions, and explanations addressed directly to the friend of his childhood."[46]

This was not the first time that Conrad had indicated that a fictional heroine was modeled on a childhood sweetheart. In the Author's Note to *Nostromo* he asserted that the character of Antonia was based on an early love. "How we used to look up to that girl . . . as a standard bearer of the faith to which we were all born but which she alone knew how to hold aloft with an unflinching hope! . . . I was not the only one in love with her [again anticipating Dona Rita]; but it was I who had to hear oftenest her scathing criticism of my levities . . . or stand the brunt of her austere, unanswerable invective."[47]

Thus Conrad's infatuation with Paula and the fictional tapestry made from it were not new-found patterns exhibited for the first time, but rather an only slightly altered design composed of familiar strands well woven into the fabric of his memory. But if in *The Arrow of Gold* Conrad was consciously aware of a psychological kinship between his schoolboy "sweetheart" and the fictional Rita, there is evidence contained within another "Rita" story—the unfinished *The Sisters*—that her haunting image arose from an even earlier period of his life.

The Rita of *The Sisters* is the younger of two orphaned daughters of a handsome Spanish royalist, who was shot and killed while engaged in smuggling. She is raised by an uncle, a fanatical priest, until she is thirteen. She is then sent to live with another uncle, José Ortega, a mild, hen-pecked orange merchant who lives in Passy, outside of Paris. This "wild girl of the Basque mountains" proves to be a joy to her uncle who admires her bravery in standing up to his unpleasant wife. In addition he enjoys Rita's "caressing ways—that were for him only." Rita wonders at her uncle's love for her: "that so much affection must be bound up together with so much weakness. . . . Was it always the most sincere that were the weakest?" Across the street lives Stephen, a young Russian painter, disillusioned and isolated, who has wandered through Europe seeking a "creed." Although this is the end of the fragment of *The Sisters,* Ford Madox Hueffer, who claimed that he knew of Conrad's intentions, contended that Stephen was to marry the older of the two sisters and subsequently to fall in love with the younger with whom he would have what Hueffer called an "incestuous" child.[m] Ultimately both mother and child were to be slain by the fanatical uncle, the priest.[48] Despite his reputation for inaccuracy, Hueffer's assertion that the story was to deal with "incest" is supported by certain details in the text. Stephen's attention to Rita is initially directed by the strong odor of oranges emanating from Ortega's home. In the early pages of the story it is recounted that as a baby Stephen accompanied his parents in a cart, sitting with his loving mother upon the piled-up fruit that his father was en-

[m] This theme of the two sisters would reappear in *Nostromo*, where once again the hero finds himself committed to the older girl although he is really in love with her younger sister. The source of this recurring theme in Conrad's personal life is unknown to this writer.

gaged in selling. The intimacy between mother and child is depicted in imagery that leaves little doubt that it concerns an infant at the breast. "In the daytime, from his mother's arms, he scrutinized with inarticulate comprehension the vast expanse of the limitless and fertile black lands nursing life in their undulating bosom under the warm caress of sunshine."[49] In view of this blissful tableau one suspects that the ultimate goal of Stephen's wandering was to be not merely the finding of an abstract "creed" but the rediscovered establishment of this scene. Evidently this reunion was to be sought with Rita whose presence was announced to him by the same sweet smell of fruit that perfumed the memory of his mother's enfolding arms.[n]

It is not necessary therefore to rely on Hueffer's assertion that the story was to deal with "incest," for in symbolic terms at least, it is implicit in the fragment of *The Sisters* as it exists. "Incest" is hinted at, moreover, in the few written pages, in the relationship between Rita and her weak and adoring uncle, José Ortega. In light of these observations based upon the fragment itself, there is no reason to doubt Hueffer's assertion that it was Conrad's intention that the priest, Rita's other uncle and her surrogate father, was to murder her and her child for her sins.[51] In this denouement it is possible to detect behind the fanatical righteousness of the priest the jealous outrage of a father toward an "unfaithful" daughter—a common theme in Conrad's fiction. In view of its emphasis on both "forbidden" attachments and betrayal it is hardly surprising that a strong hint of guilt and remorse pervades the story.

The autobiographic allusions in this fragment of a story of the "wandering Slav" are self-evident. Aside from the references to

[n] Another allusion to this coupling of fruit and love appears in the short story "The Duel," when D'Hubert, leaving his beloved sister to engage in a duel with his old adversary, plucks a pair of oranges from a tree in her garden and sucks on them as he advances to the place of combat. Despite its intended humor this story carries more than a hint of an incestuous attachment—between brother and sister.

In a later chapter mention will be made of an occasion during Mrs. Conrad's first pregnancy when her husband threatened to shoot some children who were allegedly stealing fruit from the Conrads' orchard.

The house where Conrad was born[50] looked out on a large fruit orchard.

"smuggling," and "suicide," with their suggestive application to Conrad's Marseilles adventures, the author's self-portrait as a young man who has abandoned his motherland is unmistakable. Attention should be paid, incidentally, to the name of the protagonist, Stephen, for throughout his fiction Conrad chose names for his characters which not infrequently contained an important personal significance. Stephen is the anglicized version of Stefan, the name of the murdered brother of Conrad's mother, a heroic figure and a leader in the Polish Insurrection of 1863.[o]

It may be conjectured therefore that in this, the first Rita story, Conrad was confiding his own secret yearnings for his remote homeland, his early origins, and most important, for his dead mother, all subjects which, incidentally, may have contributed to the difficulties he encountered in the writing of it.[p]

It is also apparent that the general outline of this Rita's history is almost identical with that of her namesake in *The Arrow of Gold*, despite certain minor changes, such as the transformation of the weak adoring uncle, José Ortega, of the earlier story into the depraved cousin of the same name in *The Arrow of Gold*. In view of the suggestion that the early Rita represents a symbolic mother it might be anticipated that her later namesakes partake of the same role. Such a suspicion is readily confirmed, for the second Rita, of "The *Tremolino*," is a bountiful woman whose home is a haven for impecunious people. Compassionate and generous, she was "always taking little houses for somebody's good, for the sick or the sorry, for broken down artists, cleaned out gamblers, temporarily unlucky speculators . . . old friends."[q/53] Nor can there be any question that in this portrait, Conrad was drawing upon his imagination, for to Colvin he wrote, "The Rita of the "*Tremolino*" is by no means true, except as to her actual existence."[55]

The maternal qualities residing in the final Rita are com-

[o] Stephen is a name that Conrad would use again, appropriately in a story dealing with revolutionaries and murder—*The Secret Agent*. See Chapter X.

[p] In light of this hypothesis there may be some subtle psychological significance in Allen's report that Conrad abandoned this story on the eve of his wedding.[52]

[q] Cf. Emilia Gould of *Nostromo*: "always sorry for homesick people."[54]

pounded of more Olympian stuff than are ascribed to her more human predecessors. As consort of a near-king she partakes of the symbolic parenthood which uniformly resides in royalty; as a proper subject for a statue crowning a lofty pedestal she is acknowledged worthy of the adoration which befits a queen as the mother of her people.

In light of the contention that all three Ritas represent an idealized and loved mother it is pertinent to dwell on a detail concerning M. George's rival for her love—Mr. J. M. K. Blunt, a man who refers to himself typically as "Américain, Catholique et Gentilhomme."[56] Now, at the age of five Conrad inscribed a photograph of himself as follows: "To my beloved Grandma who helped me send cakes to my poor Daddy in prison—grandson, Pole, Catholic, gentleman—6 July 1863—Konrad."[57] The application of a nearly identical formula to Blunt suggests that while composing this work Conrad was consciously or unconsciously affected by memories of his early childhood, and particularly of a time when an earlier "rival," his father, was away from home and locked up in prison. Thus M. George's rivalry with Blunt assumes an "Oedipal" pattern —the competition between a "father" and a "son" for the same woman, which reaches a climax when the older Blunt shoots the favored younger man in the duel.

One further clue concerning the origin of Rita may be concealed in her name. There is reason to believe that Conrad formed the names of some of his fictional personages by lopping off portions of the names of real persons in his past: e.g., Lena of *Victory* from Eve*lina*, his mother; Nina of *Almayer's Folly* from his supposed childhood sweetheart, Ja*nina*. On this basis it seems plausible to suspect that Rita was derived from Marguerite, or as Conrad's uncle called her, Margue*rita*,[58] the first name of Madame Poradowska, who, until Conrad's marriage, was undoubtedly the most important woman in his adult life, as will become evident in a later chapter. Eleven years his senior, she maintained a warm and loving correspondence with him during some of his loneliest years, and although she was no relative of his, he addressed her invariably as "Aunt," clearly endowing her with parental attributes. Like Rita of *The Sisters*, Madame Poradowska lived in Passy during all but the first 15 months of Conrad's long acquaintance with her.

It is the present writer's contention, therefore, that far from representing a single individual, Conrad's Rita is a composite creation derived from a number of sources, and from various epochs in his life—"Aunt" Marguerite, Paula de Somogyi, a childhood sweetheart, and last and most important, his dead mother.[r] Surely it was the image of her, sick and wasting away, yet steadfastly maintaining a resolute fidelity to her patriot husband, that in his fiction Conrad transformed into the all-powerful Rita de Lastaola, the indestructible supporter of her "king." With this Rita too the author may have realized his secret longings for a "mother's" love, for near the close of the story the stricken hero is nursed back to health by her devoted care. In this tableau of a "son" wounded in the chest and tended by a loving "mother" it is possible to discern the revival of a crucial moment in Conrad's childhood, namely, of the time when during the journey into exile the child nearly died of another chest ailment—pneumonia—and was then nursed by his mother. In the story, upon M. George's recovery, Rita disappears from his life forever; in Conrad's actual past the same pattern unfolded, for not long after his recovery from his own grave illness his mother's health declined, and in all too short a time, she too, like her later fictional recreation, went away never to return. "One's literary life," he wrote in *A Personal Record*, "must turn frequently for sustenance to memories and seek discourse with the shades."[60]

From the foregoing it is apparent that despite young Conrad's brave effort to clothe himself, a "young Ulysses," in the invulnerable armor of an intrepid seafaring adventurer, he was by no means insulated from the dormant longings residing within the memory of his lonely heart. Confronted by the bewitching image of a "Paula," his resolve to hold himself aloof from land-ties melted

[r] Evidence will be produced in Chapter XV which suggests that an additional source of Conrad's portrait of Rita was Wanda in Sacher-Masoch's *Venus in Furs*. According to Retinger the character of Rita was based partly on Jane Anderson, an American newspaper woman whom Conrad seems to have "fallen for" when she was in England in 1916.[59]

away, exposing in his nakedness a grieving boy, orphaned and alone.

Yet, despite his loneliness and the unhappy outcome of his initial venture away from home, Conrad resisted his uncle's suggestion that he return to Poland.[61] Instead, upon recovering from his wound, he found a position on the English freighter *Mavis,* and on April 24, 1878 he embarked upon a voyage which was to prove to be the first step in his career as a British mariner. It also marked the beginning of the next phase of a cycle which had just ended, a cycle which, in one form or another, was destined to become the fixed pattern of his life: a positive thrust of aggressive energy suddenly interrupted by a condition of collapse, inertia, and defeat.

III · The Shadow-Line

THE ARRIVAL OF THE *Mavis* at Lowestoft on June 18, 1878 brought the twenty-year-old Conrad to English soil for the first time; it marked as well the beginning of his familiarity with the English language. During the next 11 years he sailed on many British ships, rising steadily from the rank of ordinary seaman to the position of Master Mariner. Despite the evidence of his determination to achieve advancement in his maritime career, it would be a mistake to conclude that he had committed himself wholeheartedly to a seaman's life or that the realization of his boyhood dreams was embraced by him in a mental atmosphere of relaxed serenity. On the contrary, these were years of skipping from one ship to another, of quarrelling with a series of captains,[1] and they were years in which he engaged in brief and capricious flirtations with careers other than that of a sailor. Constantly in financial difficulties, for which his ever-watchful uncle wrote him words of admonition, Conrad appears to have had no clearly fixed goal in life. As early as the spring of 1880, he wrote to Bobrowski about a plan of becoming the secretary of a Canadian businessman.[2] In 1885, nearly a year after passing his examination as First Mate, he was toying with the idea of whaling,[3] while writing almost simultaneously of the possibility of settling down in London and going into business. In 1886 it is claimed that he tried his hand at writing and submitted a story—"The Black Mate"—to a magazine.[a] During the same year he attained English citizenship and passed his examination for a Master's Certificate. Although the latter entitled him to a command, he failed to secure one, and on February 16, 1887 he accepted the position of first mate on the *Highland Forest*, a sailing vessel bound for Java with cargo from Amsterdam. It was during this stormy voyage that an accident occurred which was destined to alter the course of his life for some months to come. He was struck on the back by a piece of the rigging which

[a] There is some uncertainty about the precise date of the writing of this story. See page 317.

> sent him sliding on his face for quite a considerable distance along the main deck. Thereupon followed various and unpleasant consequences of a physical order—"queer symptoms," as the captain, who treated them, used to say; inexplicable periods of powerlessness, sudden accesses of mysterious pain; and the patient agreed fully with the regretful mutters of his very attentive captain wishing it had been a straight-forward broken leg. Even the Dutch doctor who took up the case in Samarang offered no scientific explanation. All he said was: "Ah, my friend, you are young yet; it may be very serious for your whole life. You must leave your ship; you must quite silent be for three months—quite silent."[4]

On July 1, 1887 Captain Korzeniowski was admitted to a hospital ward in Singapore and then wrote to his uncle describing his condition. Bobrowski's reply on August 20th reflected both his concern and his confusion: "You do not write to me exactly what the actual trouble is; is it ordinary rheumatism? or sciatica?—or perhaps paralysis? . . . I would like to think that it is something slight—but the sad experience I have gone through with persons dear to me continually eggs me on to think the worst."[5]

This was not the first time that his uncle had responded with alarm to Conrad's reports on his own health. Some time before the latter had written about a cough and occasional fever—symptoms which, in light of the history of tuberculosis in the family, could hardly fail to arouse his uncle's anxiety. In general, Conrad appeared to make little effort to spare Bobrowski from such troubles; on the contrary, one gains the impression that the very emphasis on these unhappy details was designed to ensure the steadfastness of his uncle's concern. In this Conrad was presenting a foretaste of the flagrant hypochondriasis of his later years.[b]

[b] It should be pointed out that Bobrowski was hardly the correspondent to discourage reports on the subject of health. His letters to Conrad were replete with details about his own physical condition, focused primarily on his hemorrhoids, his diarrhea, and the condition of his stools. In light of the psychoanalytically established relationship between a preoccupation with anal function and money it is hardly surprising that these two subjects vie with each other for prominence in Bobrowski's letters, while at other times

An additional reason for the vagueness of Conrad's report on his condition arose from the very nature of the disorder. It is manifestly impossible to assess retrospectively the actual severity of the injury he sustained, but the expressions "inexplicable periods of powerlessness" and "sudden accesses of mysterious pain" do not suggest organic symptomatology. On the contrary, if it is permitted to venture any diagnostic opinion, the picture most closely resembles an hysteria—a condition of bizarre motor and sensory phenomena resulting in this instance from the emotional impact of the injury. It is characteristic of such so-called posttraumatic neurotic reactions that there is little correspondence between the severity of the symptomatology and the magnitude of the precipitating injury, which may indeed be of minor intensity. Of special importance in the genesis of such hysterical states is the element of unexpectedness of the trauma, which finds the victim unprepared, and hence unprotected from the shock of the experience. A later consequence of such a "bolt-from-the-blue" injury is a state of exaggerated readiness, manifested by irritability, jumpiness, and a general intolerance for sudden stimuli. In this connection it is pertinent to note the recollections of Paul Langlois (one of the charterers of the *Otago*) of Conrad when the latter was in Mauritius about one year after his hospital stay in Singapore: "Often very quiet and extremely nervous. . . . [He] had a tic of the shoulder and a tic of the eyes and the slightest unexpected happening, such as an object falling on the floor, or the slamming of a door, made him start. He was what one would call today a neurasthenic."[c/7]

The development of a neurotic reaction to a trauma is not solely determined, however, by the state of unpreparedness of its victim.

---

they are introduced almost interchangeably. "I observe that the growing proximity of the payment of your allowance puts you into a feverish state," he writes to his nephew, "which I would call a 'fever of receiving.' I confess frankly that I do not experience a similar 'fever of giving' and I calmly await the time of swallowing this pill, which in the present state of my pocket, may cause a certain diarrhea."[6] In time to come in his correspondence with others Conrad himself would include similar references to his intestinal function.

[c] Today one would speak of an anxiety neurosis.

It is well known that a general trauma befalling several persons simultaneously may lead to more severe emotional consequences in some than in others, indicating that there are specific susceptibilities to this condition, determined by the personality and emotional make-up of the subject and by the psychological significance which the trauma may carry for him at the specific moment of its occurrence.

The application of these considerations to Conrad's injury and its consequence is readily apparent in his autobiographical writings in *The Mirror of the Sea.* Lying on his back in the hospital, he wrote, his thoughts drifted back to Amsterdam where, because until the very eve of her sailing no commander of the ship had yet appeared, he, as first mate, was in charge of the loading of the *Highland Forest.* Apparently his faulty distribution of the cargo contributed to the roughness of the voyage, and hence to the consequent injury he sustained. "It was only poetic justice that the chief mate who had made a mistake—perhaps a half-excusable one—about the distribution of his ship's cargo should pay the penalty." And among his other recollections of Amsterdam was "the elated feeling and the soul-gripping cold of those tramway journeys taken into town" to visit Hudig, one of the charterers of the ship, "with his warm fire, his arm chair, his big cigar, and the never failing suggestion in his good-natured voice: 'I suppose in the end it is you they will appoint captain before the ship sails?' " And although Captain Korzeniowski protested that he had not enough experience for such a post, Hudig "nearly persuaded me that I was fit in every way to be trusted with a command. There came three months of mental worry, hard rolling, remorse, and physical pain to drive home the lesson of insufficient experience."[d/8]

It is clear from these recollections that the matter of assuming command of a ship was very much in the mind of the young captain as he lay incapacitated in his hospital bed. Despite all his protestations of inexperience and his emphasis on his mistake as proof

[d] This account refutes a passage in a letter to Paul Wohlfarth by Jean-Aubry that when Conrad lay in the German hospital in London after the Congo disaster, it was the first moment in his life when he was obliged to be quiet with nothing to do save to reflect.[9]

of it, the fact remains that he was at that time certified as a commander and that he had been subjected to the "never-failing suggestion" that it might ultimately prove to be he who would assume command of the *Highland Forest*. Conrad's comments, therefore, seem to reflect some doubts about his *emotional* readiness to take on the supreme position of captain of a ship: however much it may have satisfied his ambition, it appears to have constituted at the same time a source of anxiety. For a man who held an undisguised admiration for the Dominic Cervonis in this world and who drew a conspicuous feeling of emotional security from serving as their subordinate, the position of commander must have loomed in his mind as a lonely eminence, exposed and unprotected, from which he had no one to turn to for support. Indeed, on a number of occasions in his fiction Conrad referred to this theme. Thus in *Typhoon* the mate Jukes "was uncritically glad to have his captain on hand. It relieved him as though that man had, by simply coming on deck, taken at once most of the gale's weight upon his shoulders. Such is the prestige, the privilege, and the burden of command."[10] Captain MacWhirr, on the other hand, "could expect no comfort of that sort from any one on earth. Such is the loneliness of command."[11] It is no wonder then that while belittling his own fitness for the post of commander, Captain Korzeniowski engaged in nostalgic recollections of the warm security of Hudig's office in the city of Amsterdam.

In light of these considerations it may be questioned whether mere lack of opportunity was responsible for the fact that while Conrad served as mate on four ships during the nearly seven years which elapsed from the time of his certification as master to his ultimate abandonment of a seaman's career, he commanded but one —the *Otago*—and that for only a little more than one year.

Faced by the increasingly likely prospect of his first command, the injury to his back could be viewed as a welcomed respite, and as an escape from the hazards and loneliness of supreme responsibility. Indeed, in this sudden interruption of his steady ascent to the top of the maritime hierarchy by a prolonged siege of inactivity, punctuated by "inexplicable periods of powerlessness," it is possible to discern a repetition of the same oscillating pattern which had characterized his experience in Marseilles and which would soon appear again in his Congo venture, as well as on several other occasions. It is a pattern which would also become discernible in his life as a writer: the final thrust which brought him to the completion of a book would be followed at once by a state of utter collapse, necessitating his taking to his bed for days thereafter. Not surprisingly it is the pattern too of many of his fictional heroes, who, in those moments of crisis calling for a final thrust of affirmative action, suddenly assume the drooping posture of impotence.

Conrad's period of inactivity in Singapore did not last for the prescribed three months. On August 22, 1887, approximately seven weeks after his admission to the hospital, he signed on as mate of the *Vidar*, a steamship based in Singapore, which went on voyages of about three weeks' duration through the Malay Archipelago. All told Conrad made some five or six trips on this ship, gathering those impressions which were later to appear in his Malay novels. The relatively easy-going routine of the steamer no doubt afforded him a gentle transition from his immobilization in the hospital to a rugged life at sea. But Conrad, who disliked steamships, apparently wearied of this protracted convalescence, and on January 4, 1888, he left the ship at Singapore. Through the narrator of the autobiographical *The Shadow-Line*, Conrad described this action:

> One goes on. And the time, too, goes on—till one perceives ahead a shadow-line warning one that the region of early youth, too, must be left behind. . . . This is the period of life in which such moments of which I have spoken are likely to come. What moments? Why the moments of boredom, or weariness or dissatisfaction. Rash moments . . . I mean moments when the still young are inclined to commit rash actions, such as getting married suddenly or else throwing up a job for no reason. . . . This is not a marriage story. . . . My action, rash as it was, had more the character of a divorce—almost of desertion.[12]

There is indeed a familiar ring to these sentiments by which Conrad endeavored to explain his impulsive breaking away from a stereotyped and humdrum existence: they recall his earlier "rash action"—his leaving Poland to go to sea many years before, an action which in some quarters was also labeled as a "desertion." The similarity between these two "desertions" continues as the writer goes on:

> For no reason on which a sensible person could put a finger I threw up my job . . . left the ship of which the worst that could be said was that she was a steamship, and therefore, perhaps entitled to that blind loyalty[13] . . . as to the kind of trade she was engaged in and the character of my shipmates, I could not have been happier if I had had the life and the men made to my order by a benevolent Enchanter. . . . And suddenly I left all this. I left it in that, to us, inconsequential manner in which a bird flies away from a comfortable branch. . . . One day I was perfectly right and the next everything was gone—glamour, flavour, interest, contentment—everything. . . . The green sickness of late youth descended on me and carried me off.[14] . . . The past eighteen months, so full of new and varied experience, appeared a dreary, prosaic waste of days.[15]

Since he had been on the *Vidar* but a little over four months it is evident that he was not speaking of that ship only as a "prosaic waste of days" but of seafaring in general. Indeed, the narrator makes it clear that he intended to find passage back to London in the next mail boat.

Conrad's impulse to quit the sea at this time resembles his quitting Poland not only in language, but apparently in motivation. Throughout his life Conrad displayed an incorrigible restlessness, an inability to tolerate the same ship, the same house, or even the same mode of life for any sustained length of time. Surrender to routine soon became unendurable for him, necessitating the relieving thrust of affirmative action. In his impulsive urge to leave Poland, it has been suggested that he was expressing a wish to survive by identifying himself with vital forces and images far removed from the atmosphere of death and decay of his early years in his native land. Although a sailor's life had once represented to him the epitome of masculine vitality, in time life at sea too could apparently assume the lethal quality of passivity, especially, for

Conrad, life on a dependable, unexacting, and unexciting steamship. Ultimately, in fact, it would seem that any fixed pattern of life came to be viewed by him with an admixture of irritability and alarm, as if in surrendering to it he courted the danger of surrendering to death itself. As a consequence, Conrad behaved like one literally and figuratively unable to sit still.[e] Both in the confining boundaries of day-to-day domestic existence as well as in the broad and comprehensive panorama of life's span, he seemed inwardly driven by the menacing finger of death to keep on the move or, in the words of Lord Jim, to "jump."

From the foregoing, two seemingly contradictory images of Conrad emerge: the man who might welcome a disabling injury as a means of escaping the stress of responsibility and the loneliness inherent in the position of supreme authority, and the man, restless and adventurous, who was unable to tolerate the deadly torpor of a sustained and monotonous routine. In this contradiction lies the essence of one of Conrad's major psychological dilemmas, expressed in the cyclical yielding to and flight from the beguiling seductiveness of helpless inaction. It is this same oscillation which provides a key to an understanding of many of the puzzling inconsistencies and bewildering paradoxes that characterize the vicissitudes of his personal life, and it is this self-same psychological conflict, projected into his novels, which shapes the destiny of those fictional beings born of his creative imagination, who, despite their individual differences, are often but shifting and varying manifestations of their creator. Of these invented projections of his conflict-ridden self, the character of Jim presents special relevancy to the problem under discussion.

Like Conrad, Jim is a sailor with his eye on advancement in the hierarchy of command. Upon attaining the position of chief mate, he, like his creator, is disabled by a falling spar, resulting in a prolonged period of rest in a hospital in an Eastern port.[f] The effect

[e] "I think I never saw Conrad quite in repose," wrote Galsworthy. "His hands, his feet, his lips,—sensitive, expressive and ironical—something was always in motion."[16]

[f] A carefully preserved four-page letter from Jim's father containing advice, "easy morality and family news"[17] is strongly reminiscent of the fatherly letters Conrad received from his Uncle Thaddeus.

of his immobilization is conveyed in terms strikingly reminiscent of Conrad's identical experience:

> [he] spent many days stretched on his back, dazed, battered, hopeless and tormented as if at the bottom of an abyss of unrest. He did not care what the end would be, and in his lucid moments overvalued his indifference. The danger, when not seen, has the imperfect vagueness of human thought. The fear grows shadowy, and Imagination, the enemy of men, the father of all terrors, unstimulated, sinks to rest in the dullness of exhausted emotion. He lay there . . . secretly glad he had not to go on deck. But now and again an uncontrollable rush of anguish would grip him bodily, make him gasp and writhe under the blankets, and then the unintelligent brutality of an existence liable to the agony of such sensations filled him with a despairing desire to escape at any cost.[18]

Following his recovery Jim takes a berth as chief mate, one of the five white officers of the *Patna*, an overaged and rusted steamer engaged to transport some 800 Arabs on a religious pilgrimage. One night during the voyage, unknown to the packed mass of humanity crowded within her and upon her decks, the ship strikes some object which rips a hole in the hull. Four of the officers, believing that the ship is doomed and knowing that there are not enough life boats to save the passengers, lower a boat for themselves and prepare to abandon the ship, calling upon Jim to do likewise.[g] Torn between his sense of seaman's duty and his wish to escape certain drowning with hundreds of anonymous Arabs, Jim hesitates. Suddenly he finds himself in the life boat with the other officers. "I had jumped . . . it seems," he later explains, as if it had been an action beyond his conscious control.

But the *Patna* does not sink. Sighted by a French gunboat the following morning, she is towed safely into port, and thus the scandalous behavior of her crew is exposed. Stripped of his certificate by the Court of Inquiry, Jim wanders over the earth, fleeing in vain from his soiled reputation and pursued by guilt and remorse. At last, aided by the narrator Marlow, he is installed in an isolated

[g] One of the men dies suddenly during these proceedings.

Eastern settlement called Patusan where, sheltered from the accusing world of white men, he becomes the omnipotent overlord and protector, a demigod endowed by the natives with "supernatural powers."[h/19] His rule comes to a sudden end, however, when Patusan is invaded by some piratical whites, led by "Gentleman" Brown, whom Jim finds himself unable or unwilling to destroy. The intruders thereupon massacre Jim's friends, including Dain Waris, the son of Doramin, the native chief. Then inviting retribution in a gesture which is tantamount to suicide, Jim offers himself up to Doramin who shoots him in the chest[i] and kills him.

Whatever other sources may have been drawn upon in the creation of this novel,[j] the autobiographical element is self-evident. From one point of view the *Patna* corresponds to the *Vidar*, and Jim's "jump" to Conrad's act of quitting that steamship, an act which he likened to "a divorce—almost a desertion." Just as this "desertion" of the *Vidar* has been compared to Conrad's "desertion" of Poland, so has Jim's jump from the doomed *Patna*. Morf has even suggested that the very name of that ship was chosen because of its resemblance to *Polska* (Poland), and that her rescue by a French vessel reflects the recurring historical expectation of the Polish people that it is to the French that they must ever look for deliverance.[25] It would seem plausible that Conrad too saw a parallel between his quitting Poland and Jim's "jump," for in *A*

[h] Helene Deutsch equates Patusan to "a state of insanity with delusions of grandeur,"[20] a condition observed clinically in individuals who, like Jim, are seeking to escape from the black depression that accompanies a shattered self-esteem. Once Jim had been established in Patusan—"nobody . . . had been there . . . no one desired to go there"[21]—"it would be for the outside world as though he had never existed."[22] But Marlow, conscious of the futility of Jim's effort to shake off both his unsavory past and the latent depression, shouts at him, "It is not I or the world who remember. It is you—you, who remember."[23] It is indeed Jim's inability to forget that ultimately leads to his self-destruction.

[i] Compare Conrad's self-inflicted chest wound in Marseilles.

[j] Notably the famous case of the S.S. *Jeddah*; see Introduction, page 12. Allen offers evidence proving that the portrait of Jim was drawn partially from Augustine Podmore Williams, the chief officer of the *Jeddah*. (At an earlier time Conrad had used Williams's unusual middle name for the cook in *The Nigger*.) Allen also points out that a steamship bearing the name *Patna* existed at the time of the *Jeddah* scandal.[24]

Personal Record he wrote, "I verily believe mine was the only case of a boy of my nationality and antecedents taking a, so to speak, *standing jump* out of his racial surroundings and associations." (Italics mine)[26]

Over the subject of this "jump" there is no doubt that Conrad suffered keenly throughout his life, despite his later assertion that he had settled the matter "a long time ago with my conscience." "Alas!" he wrote in *A Personal Record,* "I have the conviction that there are men of unstained rectitude, who are ready to murmur scornfully the word 'desertion.' Thus the taste of innocent adventure may be made bitter to the palate."[27] But it is clear both from his sensitivity to criticisms leveled at him from time to time for becoming an expatriate writer and from his preoccupation in his fiction with the theme of desertion that he was as little inclined to regard his leaving Poland as an "innocent adventure," as Jim's jump from the leaking *Patna.*

What then was the origin of his conviction of having himself committed an act of betrayal? In order to answer this question it is necessary to understand one aspect of the mentality of many Polish nationals of the nineteenth century.

Espoused particularly by the poet Mickiewicz, there prevailed throughout that time a doctrine known as Polish National Messianism which asserted that the body of Poland, dismembered and martyred, was akin to Christ crucified, and that the glorious resurgence of the nation, which was to usher in a new epoch in Christianity, corresponded to the Resurrection. According to this conception, the living members of this chosen people were to subordinate personal happiness and private goals to the attainment of the national destiny—Poland resurrected. In addition to his epic poems celebrating the heroism of Polish patriots like Konrad Wallenrod, Mickiewicz composed a "gospel" for Polish refugees living abroad: *Books of the Polish Nation and of the Polish Pilgrimage.*[28] These writings exerted a wide influence in promoting the high-strung and extremist approach to political matters characteristic of many Polish nationals. Needless to say adherents to this doctrine were intolerant of those expatriates who appeared indifferent to this mystique, and Conrad himself was violently attacked—during a time when he was barely eking out a living—for having abandoned his homeland to become a "prosperous" English novelist. A Polish writer, Eliza Orzeszkowa, wrote in 1899:

> And since we talk about books, I must say that the gentleman who in English is writing novels which are widely read and bring good profit almost caused me a nervous attack. . . . Creative ability is the very crown of the plant, the very top of the tower, the very heart of the heart of the nation. And to take away from one's nation this flower, this heart and to give it to the Anglo-Saxons who are not even lacking in bird's milk, for the only reason that they pay better for it—one cannot even think of it without shame."[29]

In the face of such an outcry Conrad was by no means indifferent: it touched him in a vulnerable spot. But there were added reasons of a more personal nature that were bound to intensify his susceptibility to such attacks, for in quitting Poland to become a sailor under foreign flags, and later a novelist writing in a foreign language, he was not merely abandoning his homeland and his mother tongue, but repudiating the very cause and principles for which his parents had dedicated their lives. Indeed, in bestowing the name Konrad upon their only child, they left no doubt of his intended destiny, for he was named for a national Polish hero celebrated in the epic poetry of Mickiewicz.[k] From the very moment of his birth, in fact, the expectations of his father, for whom the doctrine of Polish National Messianism was a ruling passion, were clearly proclaimed. At the time of his christening Apollo composed a poem for his "son born in the 85th year of Muscovite bondage" the significance of which is unambiguous:

> Be a Pole . . . and tell yourself
> That you are without a country, without love,
> Without a homeland, without humanity,
> As long as *Mother Poland* is in the grave . . .

[k] More probably after the hero of *Dziady* ("Forefather's Eve") than Konrad Wallenrod, another subject of Mickiewicz's poetry.[30] A favorite subject of Conrad's "doodling" was a thick and heavy letter "K."[31]

Without her there is no salvation!
With that thought grow in courage!
Give her and yourself immortality.[32]

Pretty strong language and rather plain talk for a christening, one might say. Ushered into this world bearing so heavy a burden of great expectations and severe injunctions, how could Conrad have failed to view his succession of "un-Polish" careers other than as acts of base betrayal?[l] "I have faced the astonished indignation, the mockeries, and the reproaches of a sort hard to bear for a boy of fifteen," he wrote in *A Personal Record*, "I have been charged with want of patriotism, the want of sense and the want of heart too. . . . I went through agonies of a self-conflict and shed secret tears. . . ."[34] It is not to be wondered at that in writing of his ill-starred visit to Poland in 1914 he said: "I felt plainly that what I had started on was a journey in time, into the past: a fearful enough prospect for the most consistent, but to him who had not known how to preserve against his impulses the order and continuity of his life—so that at times it presented itself to his conscience as a series of betrayals—still more dreadful. . . . Nothing . . . could have stayed me on that journey which now that I had started on it, seemed an irrevocable thing, a necessity of my self-respect."[35]

The identity of the 800 pilgrims contained within the friable and corroded belly of the *Patna*, forsaken by Jim in his self-seeking leap into the sea, seems unambiguous: they are the Polish nation, in all likelihood, but they probably represent something else, something dearer and more personal to the troubled heart of an orphaned boy, the sole survivor[m] of the holocaust that had wiped out his little family. It is in Conrad's early unfinished story, *The Sisters*, where once again it is possible to discover a clarification

[l] This view is shared by a contemporary Polish writer, Milosz, who states: "As we go more deeply into the biographical materials we come to the conclusion that a carefully hidden complex of treason is discernible in some of [Conrad's] writings—a feeling that he had betrayed the cause so fanatically embraced by his compatriots, and above all, by his father."[33]

[m] The theme of the sole survivor attains particular emphasis in "Amy Foster."

of the veiled meaning of a later work, for Stephen, the hero of that book, is an obvious precursor of the guilt-ridden wanderer, Jim. Like Jim, Stephen leaves his home to pursue a career, not that of a seafaring man but of an artist. During his prolonged absence his lonely parents pine away for him and die. Learning of this, his world appears to crumble, and the "armor of his art, the armor polished, impenetrable, unstained, and harder than steel, seemed to be stripped off him by a mighty hand, to fall with an ominous clatter at his feet. Defenseless he was pierced by the venomous sharpness of remorse.[n] He had abandoned these two loving hearts for the promise of unattainable things." Urged by his brother to return home, Stephen replies, "I cannot return. You would not understand if I tried to explain . . . to return now they are dead would be worse than suicide which is the unpardonable crime."[36]

Curiously, Jim uses almost identical language when, following the exposure of the *Patna* scandal at the Court of Inquiry, he tells Marlow that now he could never go home again. Speaking of his father—there is not a word throughout the book about his having a mother—Jim says, "I can never face the poor old chap. . . . I could never explain. He wouldn't understand."[37]

The very similarity of the verbal formulation of their remorse suggests an underlying similarity of the misdeeds of these two guilt-ridden wanderers. Jim's dereliction of maritime duty, moreover, originated well before the *Patna* episode: during his period of training he failed to come to the rescue of two sailors who were nearly drowned in a storm at sea. Thus, like Stephen's guilt, Jim's is rooted in an act of infidelity not merely toward a mass of alien people, but toward identifiable individual beings who are of his own kith and kin. In Marlow's eyes even Jim's action on the *Patna* has that connotation, for in explaining to his listeners Jim's refusal to return home, he refers to the "spirit of the land uprising above the white cliffs of Dover, to ask me [he is speaking for Jim] what I—returning with no bones broken, so to speak—had done with my very young brother."[38]

The conclusion seems compelling, therefore, that Conrad's re-

[n] "How sharper than a serpent's tooth it is
To have a thankless child."—King Lear

curring concern with the theme of desertion both in his personal life and in his fiction, arose not merely over his having left his native soil and exporting his literary genius, but over the gnawing conviction that he had perpetrated a perfidious repudiation of the hopes, the ideals, and the expectations of his martyred parents. There is some reason to suspect, moreover, that his guilt toward them was further compounded by the idea that he had been in some way responsible for his mother's death.

A child whose mother dies in the act of giving him birth is almost never set free from the tormenting self-accusation of having been the instrument of her death. It then becomes his unhappy lot to view his own life as continuing at the expense of hers; in the seeming innocence of being born he has become an unwitting murderer. Conrad's mother did not die, to be sure, in giving birth to him (as did the mother of his cousin Josefina in giving birth to her), but from an early moment in his life it was evident that she was dying. Significantly, moreover, it was after tending him in his near fatal illness during the journey of the family into exile that she began to show those ominous signs of physical illness from which she was never to recover. In retrospect it is natural to ask whether, unencumbered by the care of a small and sick child, Evelina might have better endured the arduous hardships which had befallen her. If such thoughts occurred as well to Conrad, it might go far to explain his haunting obsession with the theme of remorse. Viewed in such a light, the *Patna* with its complement of humanity would represent not merely his mother-country, but his mother herself,[o] whom he charged himself with destroying.[p] It is not without significance that for the epigraph of *An Outcast of the Islands*, perhaps his most passionate story, Conrad selected a line from Calderón: "Man's greatest crime is having been born."

For Conrad, then, as for Jim, it may be said that the burden of

[o] Similes between ships and women are common in Conrad's writing. Thus in *The Rescue*, Tom Lingard's brig is described: "Always precious—like old love; always desirable—like a strange woman; always tender—like a mother; always faithful—like a favorite daughter of a man's heart."[39]

[p] Evidence will be brought forward in a later chapter that Conrad also blamed his father for his mother's death.

a guilty past barred all escape from an ultimate retributive destruction. Like Conrad exulting in his new-found freedom in Marseilles, Lord Jim, as the demigod of Patusan, might enjoy his moment of triumph. Yet faced by Gentleman Brown, a criminal who recalls to Jim his own past crime, he offers no resistance, and as a consequence his brief hour of respite from the avenging furies of an inner conscience is brought to a sudden halt—like Conrad's—with a bullet in the chest.

"A man that is born," says Stein, the philosopher-entomologist of *Lord Jim*, "falls into a dream like a man who falls into the sea. If he tries to climb out into the air as inexperienced people endeavor to do, he drowns—*nicht wahr*? No! I tell you! The way is to the destructive element submit yourself, and with the exertions of your hands and feet in the water make the deep, deep sea keep you up."[40] Birth and death and water—these are the familiar joined elements of unconscious mental symbolism which have attained virtually universal expression in the imagery of myth and dream. And just as in art and legend birth is often depicted by an emergence from the water, so may the idea of immersion into it signify a nostalgic wish to return to her in whose liquid envelope an unborn self once floated in idyllic sleep. That these themes exerted a strong appeal upon Conrad's imagination is repeatedly evident, notably in such stories as *Nostromo*, "The End of the Tether," and "The Planter of Malata," wherein the hero seeks his death by drowning. Such a significance is also discernible in *The Sisters* when the orphaned Stephen finally reaches the sea, where "the opening of a wide horizon touched him as an opening of loving arms in a welcoming embrace touches a wayworn and discouraged traveler."[41]

As will be emphasized in a later chapter almost without exception Conrad's heroes are motherless wanderers, postponing through momentary bursts of action their long-awaited return to a mother, whose untimely death has sown the seeds of longing and remorse, and whose voice, whispered from beyond the grave, utters her insistent claim upon her son's return.

Akin to their behavior is the cyclical pattern of Conrad's own life, which may be seen as a recurring oscillation between a repudiation of those objects claiming his "blind loyalty," and a passive yielding up to their engulfing embrace.

In cutting short his prescribed hospital stay in Singapore the pendulum of Conrad's emotional conflict was swinging away from such passive yearnings, and the momentum continued to manifest itself in prompting his sudden and impulsive resignation from the comfortable *Vidar*. While still under the sway of this recoil from inaction, Conrad was unexpectedly offered the command of a sailing vessel, the *Otago*, which ushered in a new and important chapter in his maritime career. Now a captain for the first time, the recent "deserter" from the *Vidar* was psychologically in somewhat the same position as was M. George, a recent "deserter" from Poland, who, freshly arrived in Marseilles, stood upon the threshold of a new career—a French sailor. In view of the parallel between these two phases of his life, it is not surprising that the Captain of the *Otago* was soon involved in an unhappy experience with a woman. Nor should it be wondered at that it was she, like her predecessor in Marseilles, who played a major role in bringing to an abrupt halt the pendulum's swing, thus terminating the one and only experience of Joseph Conrad as commander of a ship at sea.

IV · A Smile of Fortune

THE VALIANT STRUGGLE against bad luck, bad health, and bad weather which plagued the new captain of the *Otago* is recounted in the poetic and moving pages of Conrad's story *The Shadow-Line*. After many vexing delays and a harrowing voyage from Bangkok to Singapore, the *Otago* finally set sail for Sydney, Australia, and from there went to Port Louis, Mauritius, where she remained from September 30 to November 22, 1888.

It was at Port Louis that Paul Langlois, one of the charterers of the *Otago*, first met her new captain and formed those impressions described in the previous chapter. Although he was equally fluent in English and French, Langlois noted, Conrad preferred the latter language, which he "handled with elegance." Their conversations, moreover, were always in French. In appearance Conrad stood out in sharp contrast to other sea captains. Invariably elegant in his dress, Conrad wore a derby and gloves and carried a gold-headed cane. Toward his colleagues, he maintained an attitude of cool politeness, which did not endear him to them and earned him the title "The Russian Count."[1]

For Conrad this brief stay on the island, known as "The Pearl of the Ocean," was to have fateful consequences. Here it was that he committed one of those "rash actions" of which he had spoken as characteristic of the "green sickness of late youth," and one which he was later to regret.

In Port Louis he was introduced into one of the old French families,[a] named Renouf, where he became a frequent visitor. Many years after Conrad's death, it came to light that for him the chief attraction in this household had been the twenty-six-year-old Mademoiselle Eugénie,[3] who was undoubtedly in his mind when in "A Smile of Fortune" he referred to the French girls in Port Louis as "almost always pretty, ignorant of the world, kind and agreeable and generally bilingual; they prattle innocently both in French and English."[4] Eugénie engaged the shy captain in a game

[a] "Descendants of the old colonists; all noble, all impoverished, and living a narrow domestic life in dull dignified decay."[2]

of questions and answers, which has been recorded in a family "Album de Confidences":

1. Quel est le principal trait de votre caractère?
   Laziness.
2. Par quels moyens cherchez-vous à plaire?
   By making myself scarce.
3. Quel nom fait battre votre coeur?
   Ready to beat for any name.
4. Quel serait votre rêve de bonheur?
   Never dream of it; want reality.
5. Où habite la personne qui occupe votre pensée?
   A castle in Spain.
6. Quelle est la qualité que vous préférez chez la femme?
   Beauty.
7. Que désirez-vous être?
   Should like not to be.
8. Quelle est votre fleur de prédilection?
   Violet.
9. Dans quel pays voudriez-vous vivre?
   Do not know. Perhaps Lapland.
10. Quelle est la couleur des yeux que vous préférez?
    Gray.
11. Quel est le don de la nature dont vous voudriez être doué?
    Self-confidence.
12. Que préférez-vous dans un bal?
    Not dancing cannot tell.
13. Quelle est votre promenade favorite?
    Hate all promenades.
14. Que préférez-vous, les brunes ou les blondes?
    Both.
15. Quelle est votre plus grande distraction?
    Chasing wild geese.

16. Dites l'état présent de votre esprit?
    Calm.
17. Que détestez-vous le plus?
    False pretences.
18. Vous-croyez-vous aimé?
    Decline to state.
19. Votre devise?
20. Votre Nom?[5]

Conrad's answers are noteworthy on two counts: first, because they were in English which was not the language of the questions, nor is it likely, in view of Langlois' report, that English would have been used by Conrad in this French colonial household; second, because of their uniformly evasive and cynical tone. Both features suggest an attitude of marked discomfort and guardedness in this shy man, evidently wincing before the flirtatious inquiries of a pretty young girl. Conrad seems to have been secretly infatuated with her—two days before his ship was scheduled to leave Mauritius, he called on her brother Gabriel and asked for her hand in marriage. To his chagrin he was told that Mademoiselle Eugénie was already engaged and planning to marry in two months' time. The effect of this intelligence upon Conrad was evidently crushing: during the few days that elapsed before he was to sail from Port Louis he kept himself in seclusion on the ship and wrote a letter of farewell to Gabriel in which he stated that he could never again return to Mauritius.[6] How determined he was in this resolve can be judged by the fact that when the charterers of the *Otago* later instructed Conrad to sail the ship to Mauritius, Conrad resigned his command and returned to England as a passenger via the Suez Canal.[7]

This episode earns not only the designation "rash" but bizarre, for how else could one characterize a proposal of marriage to a girl of whom he knew so little that he was unaware of her imminent marriage? No less remarkable is his postponing his proposal until the eleventh hour of his stay in Port Louis. It requires little imagination to sense the torments he endured throughout this episode, in which his behavior recalls less that of a grown man proposing marriage than of a terror-stricken schoolboy screwing up his faint courage to ask a girl to dance. And if he knew little about Mademoiselle Eugénie, she in turn must have known next to nothing about the shy captain who concealed his secret yearnings behind a facade of elegant manners and cynical conversation. Only at the last possible moment, when the imminent departure of his ship provided him with an avenue of escape from a scene of failure or disappointment, did he muster the courage to pose the fateful question which, in turn, must have been received in amazement.

It is noteworthy that some seven years later, when Conrad proposed marriage to Jessie George in London he behaved in an almost identical manner. On this latter occasion his proposal was accepted, but this did not prevent his running away in precipitous panic just as he had done in Port Louis.[8] It cannot be concluded, therefore, that his flight from Mauritius was determined solely by a sense of shame or defeat; of equal rank one suspects was the great distress endured in exposing, be it ever so briefly, the raw and tender feelings of a lonely man.

Despite the brevity of his stay in Mauritius, from September 30 to November 22, 1888, Conrad is supposed to have been seriously involved with a second young woman, Alice Jacobus, who was to become the central figure of his Mauritius story, "A Smile of Fortune." Despite Aubry's contention that this story is autobiographical[9]—which Conrad himself denied[10]—it is difficult if not impossible to accept this assertion in view of Conrad's preoccupation with Mademoiselle Eugénie. On the contrary, not only does it appear improbable that he could have been deeply committed to two women at once in the short space of seven weeks, it is even more unlikely that the same man who behaved like the terror-stricken schoolboy toward Eugénie Renouf was capable of the bold seduction of Alice Jacobus in her secluded garden. It is indeed the very contrast and incompatibility between these two "experiences" in Mauritius which makes it appear plausible that in "A Smile of Fortune" as in the Marseilles novel, *The Arrow of Gold*, a fictional romance was created as an antidote for the real one, a suspicion which gains support from a review of the story itself.

Like *The Arrow of Gold,* "A Smile of Fortune" is centered about a young woman, Alice, the illegitimate daughter of a ship's chandler, who keeps her secluded from the world. The narrator, a ship captain, has come to do business with the chandler, but at once becomes fascinated by his seventeen-year-old daughter, who for many years has lived with a governess in her garden, a place of "brilliantly coloured solitude, drowsing in a warm voluptuous silence."[11] Like Rita, Alice has a spectacular head of hair: "a mass of black lustrous locks, twisted anyhow high on her head, with long untidy wisps hanging down on each side of the clear sallow face; a mass so thick and strong and abundant that, nothing but to look at, it gave you a sensation of heavy pressure on the top of your head and an impression of magnificently cynical untidiness."[b/12] Alice is a strange withdrawn girl whose abrupt and fragmentary speech—"Don't care!" "Shan't!"—resembles the hostile utterances of an emotionally troubled child. At the same time, like Rita, "her attitude, certain tones of her voice, had in it something masculine."[14]

The captain is plainly bewitched and sets himself the task of making her smile. When she refuses to come to the dinner table he carries a plate of food to her on the verandah—"it was like offering food to a seated statue. . . . 'I haven't been able to swallow a single morsel thinking of you out here, starving yourself in the dark,' " he tells her. " 'It's positively cruel to be so obstinate. Think of my suffering.' "[15] The captain is puzzled by the intensity of his fascination:

> I cared for the girl in a particular way, seduced by the moody expression of her face, by her obstinate silences, her rare scornful words; by the perpetual pout of her closed lips, the black depths of her fixed gaze turned slowly upon me as in contemptuous provocation, only to be averted next moment with an exasperating indifference. . . . She was like a spellbound creature

[b] The governess' hair is also abundant—a "mop" into which from time to time she plunged a knitting needle and "stirred it vigorously."[13]

> with the forehead of a goddess . . . even her indifference was seductive. I felt myself growing attached to her by the bond of an unrealisable desire . . . what folly was this? It was like being the slave of some depraved habit. And I returned to her with my head clear, my heart certainly free, not even moved by pity for that castaway (she was as much of a castaway as any one ever wrecked on a desert island) but as if beguiled by some extraordinary promise.[16]

Impulsively in that garden, in that "mass of gloom, like a cemetery of flowers buried in darkness," he seizes her and covers her with kisses; she offers no resistance, but suddenly she breaks away from his embrace, for she has seen her father watching. In her flight she drops a slipper, which her father picks up, and holding it as a symbol of his momentary authority, he concludes a commercial agreement with the defenseless captain. On his next meeting with Alice the spell is strangely broken: no more would he find again "near her the strange, half-evil, half-tender sensation which had given its acrid flavor to so many days, which had made her appear tragic and promising, pitiful and provoking. That was all over. . . . I realized clearly with a sort of terror my complete detachment from that unfortunate creature."[17] And so he leaves her, feeling "like a thief retreating with his ill-gotten booty. . . . During that stealthy act I experienced the last touch of emotion in that house, at the thought of a girl I had left sitting there in the obscurity . . . staring into the walled garden, silent, warm, odorous with the perfume of imprisoned flowers which, like herself, were lost to sight in a world buried in darkness."[18] The captain returns to his ship and sails away, soon to resign his command because the owners insist upon another voyage to Mauritius. But this he cannot do, ". . . the Indian Ocean and everything that is in it has lost its charm for me. I am going home as passenger by the Suez Canal."[19] Here the story becomes identical with Conrad's actual experience after the unfortunate episode with Eugénie Renouf: fact and fiction merge into one as both Captain Korzeniowski and the captain of "A Smile of Fortune" leave the island of Mauritius unalterably determined never to return.

It goes without saying that if that decision was dictated by Conrad's refusal to re-visit the scene of a humiliation by one woman, it cannot be ascribed at the same moment to his discomfiture resulting from his seduction of another. It is indeed the incompatibility between these two romances, both allegedly occurring concomitantly during a seven-week interval, which supports the impression that, far from possessing autobiographic validity, "A Smile of Fortune," like *The Arrow of Gold*, was a fantasy designed to convert humiliation and defeat into bittersweet success, from which the author might retire with honor.

If "A Smile of Fortune" was conceived as an antidote to the memory of Conrad's unhappy experience with Mademoiselle Eugénie, apparently it did not altogether fulfill its purpose. Three years later he composed another long short story, "The Planter of Malata," which, despite its presentation as pure fiction, seems to sound louder the echoes of his Mauritius experience in particular, and of his larger personal history in general. "The Planter" concerns a dazzlingly beautiful redheaded English girl, Felicia Moorsom, who arrives with her father and aunt at a "great colonial city" in the East in search of a man to whom she was once engaged. The man had left home under suspicion of having been involved in financial irregularities, but somewhat later his innocence was proved and Felicia, seized with remorse for having believed in his guilt, has resolved to find him and make amends by marrying him. In the Eastern city she makes the acquaintance of Geoffrey Renouard, a shy and solitary young man who is engaged in experimental silk culture on the island of Malata, which is located some several days sailing distance from the mainland. Renouard is struck by Felicia's beauty and soon finds himself madly in love with her. Whether she feels comparable sentiments for him is questionable, but also irrelevant, for she is a rather self-righteous girl (on no fewer than three occasions she asserts, "I stand for truth here!") who is clearly too dedicated to her zealous mission of reparation to be deflected by the promptings of a tenderer passion. Renouard, his infatuation mounting, discovers to his horror that the man she is seeking was his assistant on the island until his recent death. Unable to terminate the search and cause Felicia to depart from his life, Renouard conceals the information and offers to take the Moorsoms to Malata, where Felicia expects to reclaim the man she wronged. On the island, however, Renouard confesses the truth and then passionately declares his own love; Felicia, however, with characteristic loftiness, spurns his advances and returns to the mainland with her companions, leaving behind a broken Renouard, who commits suicide by swimming out to sea.

In its final version the actual locale of "The Planter" was left obscure. No island by the name of Malata is listed in the gazetteer, but the text clearly places it in the Pacific Ocean.[c] In the published version the "great colonial city" is unnamed, but in the original manuscript it was identified as Sydney, Australia.[20] Although there is no evidence that Conrad engaged in a romantic misadventure in Sydney, it was from that city that he sailed in August 1888 for Mauritius, where he experienced his unhappy infatuation with Mlle Eugénie Renouf. In view of the momentous consequences of this voyage—it was destined to put to an end Conrad's career as a ship's captain—it would seem reasonable to suspect that the point of departure was closely associated in Conrad's mind with the events taking place at its ultimate destination. Such a view gains support from the similarity between the names *Renouard* and *Renouf*. Indeed the original manuscript reveals that Conrad experienced some difficulty in committing the former name to paper, for on a number of occasions, as is shown in the accompanying extracts, he wrote the first two syllables without hesitation, only to stumble on the last.

"The Planter of Malata" has other overtones of Conrad's experience with Mlle Renouf. In spurning Renouard's passionate declaration of love, Felicia suddenly—and unaccountably—speaks out in French: "Assez! J'ai horreur de tout cela!"[21] Now this is precisely the reverse of what Captain Korzeniowski did in his re-

[c] The origin of Malata is a matter of speculation. There is a lake by that name in southern Australia near the coast, northeast of Coffin Bay in Eyre's Peninsula. In a personal communication to the author, however, Miss Jerry Allen states that it is derived from TANJONG (POINT) MALATAJOER, on the south coast of Borneo, which was a landmark on one of the voyages between Singapore and Pulau Laut of the *Vidar*, the steamship on which Conrad sailed in 1887-88.

The younger's man's name was
Renouard. That ~~he~~ he was ~~[illegible]~~

...! But Renouard restrained himself. His friend was not a person

---

As he spoke ~~Renouard~~ Renouard saw
her rise, ~~the~~ sway of her figure in a

plies to Mlle Eugénie's French questionnaire. Felicia's linguistic switch is bizarre unless it is viewed in the context of his own involvement with Mlle Renouf: "*in her trouble, perhaps prompted by the suggestion of his name* . . . she spoke to him in French."[22] (Italics mine)[d] It was evidently not only to Felicia, but to Conrad, that the name brought associations; for him it evoked memories of the girl in Port Louis, who, like Felicia, was betrothed to another man. If these considerations are valid, it would make of "The Planter" a more accurate psychological reflection of Conrad's unhappy Mauritius experience than what he set down in "A Smile of Fortune."[e]

[d] Further implications of this linguistic shift in terms of the use of an alien language as the vehicle of his writing will be discussed in Chapter XVII.

[e] There is reason to suspect that aside from his Mauritius experience, in composing "The Planter" Conrad drew upon other sources, which in time he took pains to conceal. As already noted he finally disguised the locale of the story after spelling it out in the manuscript. The latter also reveals several changes in the proper names of fictional characters as the writing progressed. He failed to give the heroine any name whatever until page 128 when he called her *Ida*; by page 142 he had changed it to *Felicia*. Her surname also underwent a change: before becoming *Moorsom* her father is known as *Professor Wright*. The "eminent Colonial statesman," *Old Dunster*, moreover, was originally *Old Deacon*.[23] Efforts to trace the sources of the names *Ida* and *Wright* have so far been unsuccessful, but it seems quite

It should be emphasized that, like the report of his attempted suicide in Marseilles, Conrad's experience with Mlle Renouf was not generally known during his lifetime. The former came to light in 1937, and Conrad's first major biographer, Jean-Aubry, made no mention of the Eugénie story until he published a second biography in 1947.[25] Whether this dampened the French writer's belief in the authenticity of "A Smile of Fortune" is questionable; in his earlier biography, written in 1927, he left little doubt that he accepted it as historically true, and even recounted an episode which for him apparently clinched it. Talking with Conrad about the story one day, Conrad asked, " 'Do you think that Jacobus [Alice's father] had seen something?'," referring to the amorous scene between the captain and Alice. "When I confessed," replied Jean-Aubry, "that for my part I could not decide and in my turn, asked him the same question, he answered, 'I never knew.' "[26] But this anecdote proves nothing beyond the observation that Conrad took considerable pains to lend an aspect of verisimilitude to a work of fiction by posing an artless inquiry to his future biographer. The same may be said of Jessie Conrad's statement that her husband used to accuse her of being jealous of Alice Jacobus.[27]

This does not mean that Alice Jacobus was but a fiction of Conrad's imagination. It is quite possible that during his stay in Mauritius he met or heard of such a woman living in seclusion in her father's garden. Yet the granting of her existence, like that of the

---

possible that *Deacon* was derived from Alfred Deakin (1856-1919), a prominent political figure who ultimately became the second Prime Minister of Australia. By the time Conrad had arrived at Sydney as captain of the *Otago*, Deakin, like his later fictional "namesake," had gone to England on a political assignment and had returned in triumph to that city. Whether Conrad ever knew him personally is not known to this writer, but he could hardly have avoided knowing about him, and may even have felt some kinship with this versatile man, who was also a writer of sea romances, and who, like Conrad, had been nourished in childhood on a literary diet of Marryat, Cooper, and Scott.

As will be noted in a later chapter, Herndon has advanced the suggestion (with considerable plausibility) that the portrait of Renouard's friend, the Editor, was based on Conrad's then estranged friend, Ford Madox Hueffer.[24] See Chapter XII.

mistress of Don Carlos de Bourbon, proves nothing about Conrad's relationship with either of them; it merely suggests that the rumor or knowledge of them was stored in his memory as strands that he might one day unwind to weave into the colorful fabric of fictional romance. In this process, moreover, it is evident that the original imprint underwent a distinct change, for in the final tapestry the portraits of these personages came to resemble each other like repeated figures on a patterned cloth. There is a similarity not only between Rita and Alice, but between them and Felicia Moorsom too. All three are motherless girls living under the protective guardianship of an older man: Dona Rita is the successive protégée of an uncle, of the rich artist, Henry Allègre, and finally of the Pretender to the Spanish throne; Alice and Felicia live under the watchful eye of a father. In all three stories an older woman is a member of the ménage and looks upon the girls' lovers with distrust.[f] All three women are severely inhibited emotionally and evoke recurring comparisons with cold statuary. Physically, all are distinguished by a spectacular head of hair.

The similarity of the women in these stories is matched by a similarity of thematic material, of which the motif of rescue or rehabilitation occupies a central position. The prominence of the Pygmalion theme in *The Arrow of Gold* has been mentioned in an earlier chapter. Like the ragged waif Rita, Alice Jacobus too is discovered in a garden, and like Henry Allègre, the captain-narrator of "A Smile of Fortune" is seized by a desire to rescue the hapless girl from her pitiable state and transform her into a vibrant animated woman. *The Arrow of Gold* presents a second treatment of the rescue theme with an opposite polarity, for here it is the wounded hero who is saved and nursed back to health by the powerful heroine, Rita. It is this version of the theme that appears in "The Planter," for in that story it is again the heroine who seeks

[f] Just as in *The Arrow of Gold* M. George dreams that Rita hurls her gold hair ornament at him "like a dart," so does the captain in "A Smile of Fortune" believe that Alice's governess intends to attack him. Suspicious of his attentions to the girl, the old woman "turned upon me. She was, I perceived, armed with a knitting needle; and as she raised her hand her intention seemed to be to throw it at me *like a dart*."[28] (Italics mine)

to rehabilitate the man she once had wronged.[g] Just as the statement of the rescue theme of "A Smile of Fortune" is reversed in "The Planter," so is there a reversal of the personalities of the protagonists of both stories. The dynamic Felicia, who has traveled halfway across the globe on her mission of reparation is reminiscent of the typical Conrad wanderer-hero, while Alice, the lonely recluse, bears more temperamental kinship to the isolated Renouard. The latter resembles Alice in still another respect, for it is his fate to be ultimately forsaken by his beloved Felicia, who, like the captain-narrator of "A Smile of Fortune," sails home to England *via the Suez Canal*, resolved never to return, and leaving behind a lover's broken heart.

Of these several variations of the Pygmalion theme, "A Smile of Fortune" is the most literal, for the mute girl whom the captain seeks to arouse is virtually a lifeless creature, sitting silently "like a statue" in her garden—that "mass of gloom, like a cemetery of flowers buried in the darkness."[29] Alice Jacobus is indeed the symbol of a dead soul whom the captain would recall to life.

Death, in fact, is the note upon which the story unfolds: on the very day that the captain brings his ship into Port Louis he learns of the death of the baby of another sea captain, the skipper of the *Stella*. "Poor Captain H. and his wife were terribly cut up. If they had only been able to bring it into port alive it could have been probably saved."[30] What follows is a mournful procession to the cemetery where the little body of the child is buried in the earth.[h]

Nor is this the only misfortune of which the captain hears. The captain of still another ship, the *Hilda*, is grieving over the loss at sea of the figurehead of his ship: "A woman in a blue tunic edged with gold, the face perhaps not so very, very pretty, but her bare white arms beautifully shaped . . . who would have expected such a thing. . . . After twenty years too!" When it is suggested that he could replace the lost figurehead with a new one, the captain of the

[g] Like the two other heroines Felicia makes her initial appearance in a garden.

[h] This is one of the rare appearances in Conrad's fiction of an infant; it is noteworthy that the child is dead.

Hilda, a widower, grows indignant, exclaiming "I would just as soon think of getting a new wife."[31]

With these somber beginnings—a dead little boy and a figurehead of a woman lost forever at sea—the atmosphere of melancholy and death is soon established, setting the stage for its reappearance in the deathlike garden of Alice Jacobus. Clearly then "A Smile of Fortune" is more than a simple love story that may have served its creator as an antidote for his humiliation in Mauritius at the hands of Eugénie Renouf. It is a tale of death, of recall to life; it is, above all, a tale of rescue.

Psychoanalytic investigation of fantasies of rescue—of which the Pygmalion theme is a variant—have revealed that they contain consistent allusions to the Oedipus Complex, namely, derivatives of the daydreams of a small boy of gaining the undisputed possession of his mother.[32] In their later elaborations such rescue fantasies may include the notion of saving a woman from danger, degradation, poverty, and even death.[i] Characteristically the rescuer has to contend with another man—usually a representative of the father, hence often older, and sometimes evil—who has some prior claim on the girl. In the "Rita stories" such men are easily identified in the persons of her relative Ortega, Mr. J. M. K. Blunt ("Américain, Catholique et Gentilhomme"), and even Don Carlos himself; in "The Planter" he is Felicia's father as well as her dead fiancé; in "A Smile of Fortune" he is Alice's father, Alfred Jacobus.[j] It may be suspected therefore, that, like Rita, Alice Jacobus is a representative of a mother,[k] a figurative symbol of someone beyond the grave whom the author would summon back to life.[l]

[i] To Felicia, Renouard declares: "If I saw you steeped to the lips in vice, in crime, in mud, I would go after you, take you to my arms—wear you for an incomparable jewel on my breast."[33]

[j] Curiously he has the same first name as the father of Eliza Doolittle in Shaw's *Pygmalion*. The latter was written after "A Smile of Fortune," but well before Conrad wrote *The Arrow of Gold*, wherein Rita's rescuer, Allègre, has the same first name as Shaw's Professor Higgins—Henry.

[k] There is reason to believe that Felicia is also a maternal symbol. When Renouard succeeds in fighting off an impulse to throw himself at her feet, he suddenly begins to speak to her about his mother.

[l] A restatement of this theme may be discerned in the episode of the lost

There is another facet to Alice, however, far removed from her representation as an object of adult desire, namely, her manifest childlike behavior. To this the captain responds in a manner that is unmistakably maternal, coaxing her to eat and pleading with her to talk and smile as a devoted mother might encourage an ailing or a withdrawn child. In this reversal of roles one suspects that Alice represents a self-portrait of the author. Alice's "moody expression" and "obstinate silences" readily recall the moodiness and taciturnity which so many observers remarked in Conrad himself. To the captain's parting words to Alice, "You must love this garden!" Alice had retorted bitterly, "I love nothing!" To Eugénie Renouf's question: "Que désirez-vous être?" the embittered captain of the *Otago* had written, in words reminiscent of the "rare scornful words" of Alice, "Should like not to be." In short, it is he who is shut-in, cold, and aloof; it is he who, alone in a "cemetery of flowers," longed to be rescued from a living death; it is he, sunk in a chronic melancholy, who hungered for the nourishing love which might entice him to enter the animate world of the living.[m]

No reader of Conrad can remain long unaware of his intense preoccupation with the subject of rescue. In his childhood he had read of the African adventures of Mungo Park, and in "Geography and Some Explorers" he recounted an episode of that man's rescue from death by a native woman: "A young emaciated fair-haired man, clad simply in a tattered shirt and worn-out breeches, gasping painfully for breath and lying on the ground in the shade of an enormous African tree, while from a neighboring village of grass huts a charitable black-skinned woman is approaching him with a calabash full of cold water, a simple draught, which according to himself, seems to have effected a marvelous cure."[34] Not only did this story make a deep impression on Conrad as a boy, but in his later years he seems to have believed that it had happened to him, for he described it to Garnett as a personal experience of his own

figurehead of the ship *Hilda*, whose grieving captain equates his loss with his widowed state.

[m] Quite possibly it is as an allusion to this self-image that the story opens with an account of the death and funeral of a small boy.

in the Congo,[35] although he omitted to mention it in any of his published writings, e.g., "A Congo Diary" or "Heart of Darkness." As an insistent theme in his fiction, however, the offering of food and water as an act of rescue appears not only in "A Smile of Fortune," but in "Amy Foster" where it occurs with dramatic force.[n] As in "A Smile of Fortune," the story of the rescue of the Central European castaway, Yanko Gooral, presents a picture of false promises. Like Alice Jacobus, before whose hungry eyes the bright prospect of succoring love has been dangled, Yanko too is ultimately forsaken. To his unheeding wife and one-time savior Yanko screams in vain for water, while when Alice Jacobus suddenly realizes that the faithless captain is about to sail away, she pours a glass of water which she drinks "with the avidity of a raging thirst."[o]

That both of these "castaways" suffer a similar fate attests to the underlying similarity of their identity: in both can be seen a self-portrait of their creator, Joseph Conrad, who too can be regarded as a castaway from Central Europe washed up on the shores of England.

Out of these and other complex strands of shifting and multiple self-identifications, Conrad spun out the numerous and varied patterns of those themes of rescue and betrayal which appear so insistently in his writings. But if the idea of rescue was associated in his mind with the concept of reunion between mother and child, wherein arose the equally forceful theme of betrayal? What was the origin of his seeming distrust of women? Who raised his early hopes and later played him false?

In the previous chapter it has been suggested that Conrad may have felt in some way responsible for his mother's early death. Whether this conjecture is true or not it cannot be doubted that his misfortune engendered within him a sense of having been abandoned. For however well a small child may seem to accept a ra-

[n] See Chapter XI.

[o] An allusion to the same theme occurs in *Lord Jim*—just before his desertion of the *Patna*, Jim is accosted by one of the Arab passengers begging for water. It reappears in *Nostromo* when a sudden feeling of compassion prompts Decoud to offer water to the despised Hirsch.

tional explanation of illness and death, such explanations usually fail to obliterate the feeling of having been rejected. For such a child the reasons for a mother's untimely and total disappearance are irrelevant—all he knows and feels is: "She left me." (In this sense, any mother, however unsatisfactory or inadequate, is better than a dead one.) It was, one surmises, this experience of little Conrad, enjoying but a few short years with a mother who then went away forever, which the artist Conrad felt impelled to reiterate in story. In imitation of his own unhappy fate an invented Alice Jacobus is subjected to the same misfortune: like the five-year-old Conrad rescued from the brink of death by a patient and a loving mother, so is Alice recalled from her living death by the succoring maternal captain. But having brought her back to life, the rescuing captain, like Rita after tending M. George's wound, and like Conrad's own mother, abandons his charge and vanishes forever.

Although the writing of "A Smile of Fortune" may have succeeded at least in erasing the frown of melancholy from the countenance of Joseph Conrad, it cannot obscure the painful reality of Conrad's actual experience many years before on the island of Mauritius. In describing the captain's teasingly seductive advances to Alice, Conrad may well have been recollecting Eugénie's flirtatious games which encouraged him to seek in his wildest dreams, perhaps, some hope of rescue by her love. That such a hope came to naught is not surprising. It may be asked, rather, whether Conrad truly expected to be successful in his quest, for far from acting the part of an ardent suitor, his awkward manner, his cynical talk, his bitter aloofness, and the strange timing of his proposal suggest far more a man who is courting disappointment and seeking out hurt at the hands of a woman.

So came to a close Conrad's one and only command, the command "that was like a foot in the stirrup for a young man."[36] On this occasion, as once before in Marseilles, it was a woman who seemed to prove his undoing. And if this time unlike Renouard he did not try to kill himself,[p] what followed can be viewed as a

[p] In view of her kinship with Renouard it is not surprising that Alice Jacobus hints at her own suicide.

figurative self-destruction: he surrendered his command and, reduced to the status of a mere passenger, sailed home for England. Not long thereafter he turned his back upon all he had achieved in the slow and laborious ascent of his maritime career, and undertook a voyage into the heart of Africa, where disease and death menaced him in that far-off tropical cemetery of flowers.

PART 2

The Flow and Ebb of Artistry

V · 'Twixt Land and Sea

UPON HIS RETURN to England early in the summer of 1889 Conrad appeared devoid of any distinct plan of action or purpose: The "oscillating pendulum" seems to have come to a temporary halt. Legal formalities delayed a long-awaited visit to his uncle in Poland. How diligently he then sought a position on a ship is questionable; suffice it to say he obtained none. "My whole being was steeped in the indolence of a sailor away from the sea," he wrote, "the scene of never-ending labour and of unceasing duty. For utter surrender to indolence you cannot beat a sailor ashore when that mood is on him, the mood of absolute irresponsibility tasted to the full."[1]

It was in such a mood of dead calm during the autumn of 1889 when, without any perceptible warning, his torpor suddenly abated and the wind of active impulse began to stir. From three unexpected directions it blew upon him, and, filled with the breath of renewed vigor, Conrad soon found himself again upon the high seas of adventure, embarked on three new voyages. The first of these he undertook while sitting in his furnished rooms, where, pen in hand, he sailed forth upon the waters of a literary career; the second, following soon thereafter, consisted in a strange journey to the heart of Africa; while a third found him involved, for the first time in his adult life, in a warm and affectionate relationship with a woman—Marguerite Poradowska. Even though these three ventures were seemingly separate, it will in time become apparent that this was not quite so, for they were interwoven in a manner both remarkable and significant.

It was one morning after breakfast that ostensibly "out of the blue" Conrad started to write the story that was ultimately to be *Almayer's Folly*, the first of several novels born of his Malay experience, but a book which was not destined to be finished for nearly five years.

His recollections many years later of that memorable day when he started writing included a memory of his landlady's daughter who cleared away his breakfast dishes. "Of late it was the landlady's daughter who answered my bell. I mention this little fact with pride, because it proves that during the thirty or forty days of my tenancy I had produced a favorable impression."[2] Despite the seeming triviality of this detail, it may contain a more important significance, for the creation of a favorable impression on a girl had been, some months ago on the island of Mauritius, a matter of no small concern to him. For despite his awkward shyness, his suit for the hand of Mlle Renouf revealed the direction of his longings, longings which presumably constituted an important symptom of the "green sickness of late youth" which had prompted him to quit the *Vidar* with the avowed intention of going home. That he did not do so at once was the consequence of the unexpected opportunity to assume command of the *Otago*, and even if the voyage on that ship to Port Louis resulted in a humiliation and a disappointment over a girl, there is no reason to suppose that, at thirty-one years of age, his desire for a romantic attachment was permanently dampened. Indeed he craved some surcease from his loneliness and his despair. "Life rolls on in waves of bitterness," he wrote sometime later, "like the dark and cruel sea under a sky flecked with clouds of sadness, and there are days when it seems to those poor souls embarked on that voyage of despair, that never has the sun's rays penetrated that doleful veil; that never will it shine again, that it never did in fact exist."[3]

It would appear then that in taking up his pen he was seeking to combat his loneliness by creating a world of fiction teeming with people and bursting with action. If his own existence seemed empty, devoid of purpose and direction, lacking in human companionship and fulfilled passion, through invented characters loving and raging in an invented world, the shy and lonely Conrad could enjoy vicariously a vibrant participation, achieving there a release of feeling and an unmasking of himself rarely permitted in his real life. Just as in the unhappy solitude of childhood he had avoided going mad, he declared, by discovering a life of adventure and excitement in the world of books, so in this later moment of renewed loneliness it would seem that he made a similar effort to save himself—not through reading, but through writing. The familiar theme of rescue is once more in evidence, but it was a rescue of the self through a creative act which in time to come afforded him the companionship not only of invented characters but of fellow artists and an ever-increasing reading public.

In initiating his literary career with an exotic tale of action and romance, moreover, he was following in the footsteps of those very writers whose exploits had fired his childhood imagination with the excitement of adventure. But in the wish to be a writer he possessed an even more compelling model in the image of his father, a poet and playwright, who had dangled before his son's excited eyes his own translations of such romantic tales as Hugo's *Toilers of the Sea.* Indeed, as pointed out earlier, a wish to emulate his father was manifest soon after the latter's death, when the eleven-year-old Conrad began to write plays, and announced without hesitation that one day he would become a great writer.[a/4] Thus, in setting out to tell the story of Kaspar Almayer and his faithless daughter, Conrad was fulfilling an ambition of his youth, even as his venturing upon a sailor's life had signified the realization of his early daydreams, and even as his journeying into central Africa would mark the vindication of a childhood boast. As for the third "voyage" initiated during this fateful autumn of 1889—his drifting into the warm climate of a woman's tender affection—this too, it will appear, was rooted in the reveries of a distant past.

Although the origins of these new "travels" can be traced to dreams of early years, it cannot be denied, in light of Conrad's maritime occupation during the preceding 15 years, that they loom as striking irrelevancies. That a man certified as a ship's captain should with seeming suddenness forsake the sea to compose a love story is surprising indeed, though no more so, it must be acknowl-

[a] To what an extent the desire to make good this early prophecy occupied his later conscious thoughts during his seafaring days is uncertain. On one occasion he claimed to have written the short story "The Black Mate" in 1886, although in *A Personal Record* he asserted that until he had begun to write *Almayer's Folly* in 1889, he had "never made a note of a fact, of an impression, or of an anecdote" in his life, that he had written nothing, in fact, but letters.[5] Captain Craig of the *Vidar*, however, reported that he had often found Conrad writing in his cabin, and writing far more, it would seem, than could be ascribed to his correspondence with his uncle.[6] Scrupulous reliability about his past was not one of Conrad's outstanding traits. He was notoriously inaccurate about dates, and according to his wife he invariably fixed the time of events two years later than when they actually occurred.[7]

edged, than was the abrupt impulse of this same man, schooled in the craft of guiding huge sailing ships upon the ocean's vast expanse, to seek the post of steamboat skipper on the Congo River.

What prompted this strange voyage into Africa is problematical. For a while during that summer of 1889 Conrad worked for a firm of shipping agents; somewhat later he apparently made some effort to get a ship's command without success. In *A Personal Record* he wrote that in 1868 when he was "about nine years old,"[b] "while looking at a map of Africa of the time and putting my finger on the blank space then representing the unsolved mystery of that continent, I said to myself with absolute assurance and an amazing audacity . . . 'When I grow up I shall go there.' "[8] His narrator Marlow repeats the same episode in "Heart of Darkness," adding, however, "that it had ceased to be a blank space of delightful mystery . . . it had become a patch of darkness. But there was in it one river especially, a mighty big river, that you could see on the map, resembling an immense snake uncoiled, with its head in the sea, its body at rest curving afar over a vast country, and its tail lost in the depths of the land. And as I looked at the map . . . it fascinated me as a snake would a bird—a silly little bird."[c/9]

But while these romantic evocations of the daydreams of his youth point to the origin of his interest in the Congo, they do not account for his impulse to go there in the autumn of 1889. Like his sitting down one morning after breakfast to write a novel, the idea of his entering the heart of Africa at that very moment in his life must have been initiated by particular circumstances which mobilized a long dormant fantasy and prodded it into action. The "particular circumstances" are not especially difficult to identify, for in the year 1889 the newspapers of the world were filled with dramatic reports from the Congo and East Africa of the latest exploits of the celebrated Henry Morton Stanley. The man who had

[b] If the date is correct he was closer to eleven. See footnote *a*.

[c] It will be recalled that Conrad had previously compared himself to a bird: "I left [the *Vidar*] in that inconsequential manner in which a bird flies away from a comfortable branch." The bird imagery reappears again in the story "Amy Foster" and elsewhere. Its significance will be discussed in Chapter XVI.

found Dr. Livingstone in 1871, and had discovered the course of the Congo River some years later, had journeyed into Africa again in 1887 on another errand of mercy—to rescue Emin Pasha, the German-born governor of an Egyptian province in the Sudan. News of the success of this enterprise began to arrive in January 1889 when the London *Times* printed a letter from Stanley, dated August 17, 1888, announcing, "I found the white man whom I was looking for." In Paris at about the same moment *Le Temps* advised its readers that "the return of the great traveller, when everybody supposed him certainly lost, will make a great stir in Europe." On April 3, 1889 the *Times* printed a letter asserting that "the relief of Emin Pasha will stand out as one of the highest achievements in the history of Central African exploration," and on the 14th it provided detailed descriptions of Stanley's latest geographical discoveries in the Congo area which were reported to the Royal Geographic Society. Dispatches from Africa continued to arrive as the year rolled on, relating the hardships endured by Stanley's expedition and adding further luster to his already near-legendary image.

It was during this period of mounting excitement over Stanley that Conrad returned to England in the early summer of 1889, and it cannot be doubted that he was affected by these reports of heroism and rescue much as during his childhood he had been stirred by his reading about Mungo Park and other intrepid explorers. Indeed it is difficult to avoid the conclusion that the news from Africa played an important role in causing him in September of that year to begin to make inquiries concerning the possibility of obtaining employment in the Congo, and it is safe to assume that subsequent reports of Stanley's doings did little to dampen his enthusiasm.

On the 27th of September the *Times* published a report of a lecture in London by Mr. Herbert Ward, a former member of the Emin Pasha Expedition, whose personal impressions of Stanley might well have referred to a demigod: "Astride a magnificent mule, whose silver-plated trappings shone and sparkled in the bright morning sun, came the great explorer, attired in his famous African costume." The lecturer also related how Stanley had invited him to smoke "the cigar of peace," which the explorer produced from a silver case presented to him by the Prince of Wales. This linking of Stanley with royalty, however, was but a mild foretaste of things to come. Upon his arrival in early December at Bagamoyo in Tanganyika all the vessels in the harbor were dressed in bunting to welcome the hero, who, at a banquet in his honor was proclaimed "Master in African Exploration." On the 9th of the month Wilhelm II of Germany sent a congratulatory telegram to Stanley, which was followed in short order by messages from Queen Victoria and President Harrison. When he reached Cannes in France on the 14th of April, 1890, Stanley was welcomed by the Prince of Wales and a week later he was received "with almost royal honors" in Belgium where he dined with the King and Queen.

So gorgeous a spectacle of glory could hardly have failed to re-kindle the ever-smouldering embers of Conrad's passion for fame. When, in "Heart of Darkness," the narrator, Marlow, says of Kurtz, "Sometimes he was contemptibly childish. He desired to have kings meet him at railway stations on his return from some ghastly nowhere, where he intended to accomplish great things,"[10] surely it was of himself that Conrad was writing, confessing and at the same moment deriding his own grandiose ambition to become a savior and a hero of world renown.[d] In seeking to follow in the

[d] "The monuments left by all sorts of empire builders," Conrad wrote, cannot "suppress for me the memory of David Livingstone."[11] Conrad's youthful susceptibility to the Stanley mystique was undoubtedly rekindled during his Marseilles era when the famed explorer, returning from his second major African expedition, arrived in triumph in that city on January 13, 1878, a few short weeks, incidentally, prior to Conrad's suicidal gesture. Whether Conrad was among the capacity audience that attended a reception in Stanley's honor on January 14, or was part of the crowd that accompanied the celebrated traveler to the railroad station on the following day is unknown, but he could hardly have missed the colorful and detailed coverage of the stirring occasion in the local press. The *Gazette du Midi* of January 18 devoted several columns to Stanley's visit, describing his appearance, reviewing his heroic career (including his encounter with Livingstone), and recording in detail Stanley's speech before the Société de Géographie de Marseille. On January 19 *Le Sémaphore de Marseille* reported that the president of the Société had shown Stanley a number of articles which had belonged to Livingstone, including a pistol given to him by Stanley at the time of their meeting. The same paper noted that Stanley had received three medals of honor during his stay in Marseilles.

footsteps of the famed Stanley, it would seem that Conrad was once again repeating his experience at the Furca Pass, when, dazzled by the tokens of manly power and the attributes of individual distinction which he found in the Englishman, he was moved to acquire them for himself, thus buttressing his own uncertain sense of masculinity and individuality. Indeed there is little difficulty in discerning the sexual implications of the "Congo fantasy" of Conrad's childhood. The boast of a young boy that on attaining manhood he will enter into some dark mysterious place in which a river, shaped like "an immense snake uncoiled," penetrates the body of the land, offers self-evident symbolic meaning. Moreover, the contention that the need to prove his manliness was an inherent, albeit unconscious, element in the realization of this fantasy is supported from a passage in "Heart of Darkness" in which Marlow apologizes to his audience for having stooped to enlisting the aid of a woman in securing him his Congo job: "Then—would you believe it?—I tried the women. I, Charlie Marlow, set the women to work—to get a job."[12] A man secure in the image of his virility would hardly consider that he had compromised it by accepting a woman's help. Marlow protests too much.

Yet even more fundamental than his apparent need to shore up his dubious virility and potency was Conrad's constant search for a distinct image of his very identity, for, as pointed out in an earlier chapter, he behaved as one who, when stripped of the borrowed trappings of impressive men, evidently viewed himself as nothing, as no one—like Kurtz, "hollow at the core."[13] Such a concept of himself is succinctly conveyed in Conrad's explanation for his becoming a sailor: "I had elected to be one of them very deliberately, very completely, without looking back or looking elsewhere. The circumstances were such as to give me the *feeling of complete identification*, a very vivid comprehension that *if I wasn't one of them I was nothing at all. . . .*"[14] (Italics mine) It is hardly surprising then to learn from his friend Hueffer that Conrad was often discovering presumed resemblances between himself and distinguished figures of history, like Napoleon, Louis XVIII, and others, and that when he learned of Doctor Johnson's habit of collecting dried orange peel Conrad passed through a phase of engaging in that strange practice himself.[e/15] Of related significance is Curle's report that Conrad used to scribble his initials over and over again on the flyleaves of books as if he were continually driven to remind himself of his own identity.[16]

Unfortunately such methods of attaining either an abiding conviction of one's masculinity or of one's personal identity are like bailing out a badly leaking boat: there can be no resting and no stopping. There is, moreover, an inevitable will-o'-the-wisp quality to such emblems of strength which enjoy but an ephemeral effect: last year's triumph is soon devalued and this year new and better "proofs" are wanted.

In the year 1889 it may be surmised that Conrad was in urgent need of such "proof," and a return to the sea would no longer supply it. Some ten years earlier he might have regarded the position of Captain in the British Merchant Navy as the awesome epitome of manliness and as an undeniable and impressive imprint of a "self"; however, having reached that position of eminence himself it presumably had lost value in his eyes. Something new and spectacular was needed to still the gnawing inner doubts. What he desired to re-establish was that "absolute assurance and . . . amazing audacity" which he believed he had possessed as a child of nine, but which, he asserted "are no longer in my character now."[17]

And so, it would appear, with his gaze fixed upon the glorious example of Henry Morton Stanley, Conrad set out once more to prove himself. On February 5, 1890 he arrived in Brussels and sought the help of the wife of a distant cousin, Marguerite Poradowska, a well-known literary figure, who had influence and important connections with the administrators of the Société Anonyme Belge pour le Commerce du Haut-Congo. Two days after Conrad's arrival her husband, Alexander Poradowski, died, an

[e] This chameleon-like quality was also reflected in his letters in which he colored his language in order to harmonize with the image of his correspondent. Thus he addressed the Hispanophilic Cunninghame Graham with the salutation, "Ah! Amigo," while in writing about his son to the American Stephen Crane he used such phrases as "yelled like an Apache," and "on the warpath again"—expressions which never appeared in his letters to Englishmen.

event which may have contributed to the increasingly warm attachment that subsequently sprang up between Marguerite and her late husband's distant cousin. Madame Poradowska succeeded, moreover, in securing for Conrad a position in the Congo, and in May he sailed from Bordeaux, France, to begin the strange new chapter in his life that would one day prove to be the cradle of one of his literary masterpieces. Among his belongings was the manuscript of the few chapters he had already written of *Almayer's Folly.*

Unfortunately if the Congo venture was conceived as the epitome of a masculine adventure, designed to cover Conrad with a mantle of glory and infuse him with a conviction of omnipotence, it was a signal failure. His hopes for the command of a river steamboat were frustrated; he found himself repelled by the behavior of the so-called civilized Europeans with whom he had to deal; and, finally, like so many others, he fell ill. The brave boast of his childhood—"When I grow up I shall go *there*"—now echoed in a hollow note of melancholy. Alone at night in a silence broken only by the "subdued thundering mutter of the Stanley Falls"—the name itself accentuates the irony—he reminded himself, "Yes, this was the very spot. But there was no shadowy friend to stand by my side in the might of the enormous wilderness, no great haunting memory, but only the unholy recollection of a prosaic newspaper 'stunt,'[f] and the distasteful knowledge of the vilest scramble for loot that ever disfigured the history of human conscience and geographical exploration. What an end to the idealized realities of a boy's daydream! I wondered what I was doing there, for indeed it was only an unforeseen episode, hard to believe in now, in my seaman's life. Still the fact remains that I have smoked a pipe of peace[g] at midnight in the very heart of the African continent, and felt very lonely there."[18]

Once again a bold manly gesture had ended in failure, in dis-

[f] This presumably refers to the fact that Stanley was originally sent to find Livingstone by the editor of the *New York Herald*, James Gordon Bennett. It certainly has no bearing on Conrad's Congo venture.

[g] Perhaps an allusion to Mr. Herbert Ward's report of having smoked "the cigar of peace" with Stanley.

appointment, in melancholy, and in a bodily affliction, but on this occasion the physical consequences were less transitory than before, for Conrad came out of the Congo with an ailment of the joints which was to harass him intermittently to the end of his days. The period of the pendulum came to a halt; a new and opposite phase began and in its downward motion the man who presumably had dreamed of a hero's welcome by kings and queens and cheering crowds soon found himself a lonely patient in a London hospital.

Alone he was, yet not so alone as before the Congo, for it was in the course of this "unforeseen episode" that he made the acquaintance of Madame Poradowska, a woman some 11 years his senior whom he soon chose to call "Aunt," though she was no relation of his whatever.[h] In her he had found at last a woman to whom he could open his heart—by correspondence, at any rate—and from whom he could receive expressions of maternal concern. "You have given my life a new interest and a new affection," he wrote to her from Africa in June 1890. "I am grateful . . . for all the sweetness . . . of this priceless gift. . . . For a long time I have been uninterested in the end to which my road leads. I have gone along it with head lowered, cursing the stones. Now I am interested in another traveler; this makes me forget the petty troubles of my own road."[19] And when, sick and disillusioned, he recognized the utter failure of his once high hopes, he confided to her: "I feel rather weak and equally demoralized; and then I believe I am lonesome for the sea, desiring to see once more that vast expanse of salt water which has so often rocked me gently, which has smiled upon me so many times in the dancing sunlight of a beautiful day. . . ."[20] Indeed in his relationship with her—strange as it proved to be—Conrad seemed to find some compensation for all the heartbreak he had encountered in the Congo.

Upon his return from there it was to his "Aunt" in Brussels that he went almost at once before entering the hospital in England, and for the next five years he was to maintain with her an active correspondence, writing often every week and keeping her in-

[h] It is curious how many of Conrad's biographers have ignored this fact, referring to Madame Poradowska as his aunt.

formed of virtually every detail of his physical and mental suffering. "I have never before spoken to anyone like this," he wrote. "My nervous malady torments me, depresses me, and paralyzes all action and all thought. I ask myself, why do I exist?"[21]

Clearly he was addressing her with the accents of love, but the love not of a grown man for a woman but of a hurt and weeping child for a compassionate mother. Thus in one letter he compared himself to a doll of his childhood whom he begged her to place upon her lap, a doll whose back was "broken in two, the nose dragging in the ground between his feet; the legs and arms flung aside, in an attitude of profound despair, so pathetically funny, toys thrown into a corner. He had no phosphorus; I know, for I had licked all the paint off his rosy cheeks, kissed and even bitten his nose many times without my being any the worse for it. He was a faithful friend. He received my confidences with a sympathetic air while regarding me with an affectionate eye. I say 'an' eye because during one of the first days of our friendship I broke the other one in a sudden outburst of mad tenderness. Despite which he never appeared to pay any attention to it lest he cause me any distress. He was a 'gentleman.' Other puppets which I have known since scream if you step on their feet . . . after all nothing replaces the friendships of our childhood. This evening it seems to me that it is I who am in a corner, my back broken, my nose in the dust. Would you have the goodness to pick up the poor devil, place it tenderly on your apron, introduce it to your dolls, and permit it to eat with the others. I can see myself from here at that feast, my nose smeared with jam, while the others stare at me with that cold look of wonder which is so natural to well made dolls. I have been looked at like that many times by innumerable 'manikins.' "[22]

Nor was the ever-watchful Uncle Thaddeus unaware of this growing attachment, for in his letters he warned Conrad that this "worn-out female" (Madame Poradowska was then in her middle forties) ". . . would be a stone around [his] neck."[i/23] Nonetheless the letters continued.

[i] "You were a stone round my neck," Willems tells his wife Joanna, in *An Outcast of the Islands*, when he is about to leave her.[24]

Meanwhile, after failing to improve in the London hospital, Conrad was advised to undertake a course of hydrotherapy in a sanitarium at Champel, near Geneva, Switzerland, which provided among other therapeutic techniques a rigorous measure which Conrad later referred to as "active fire hose."[25] He was later to return there on a number of occasions, thereby reviving the practice of seeking a cure in spas which had been established in earlier years with his grandmother and his father. At Champel, in a condition of enforced idleness, where the luxurious submission to the play of supposedly magical waters and to soothing massage seems to effect beneficial results by re-invoking the passive pleasures of loving childhood care, Conrad's health improved. Not only were his symptoms relieved, but while at the sanitarium he was able to resume writing *Almayer's Folly*.

Back in England, however, his spirits seemed no better and he continued to write letters of lamentation both to his "Aunt" and to his Uncle Thaddeus, who responded with his usual words of advice and friendly exhortation. Suddenly in November 1891, Conrad was offered a position as first mate on the celebrated clipper ship *Torrens*, on which he made two voyages. Despite his complaints to Madame Poradowska about his low spirits and poor health, it does not appear that physical suffering interfered significantly in the discharge of his duties.[j] The second trip was noteworthy on two counts: it was during this voyage that he made the acquaintance of John Galsworthy and Edward Sanderson, who were later to become his friends, and it was during the same voyage that apparently for the first time Conrad was bold enough to show the unfinished manuscript of *Almayer's Folly* to another person, a man

[j] Cf. Moby Dick: "Whenever I find myself growing grim about the mouth; whenever it is a damp, drizzly November in my soul; whenever I find myself involuntarily pausing before coffin warehouses, and bringing up the rear of every funeral I meet; and especially whenever my hypos [hypochondriasis] get such an upper hand of me, that it requires a strong moral principle to prevent me from deliberately stepping into the street, and methodically knocking people's hats off—then, I account it high time to get to sea as soon as I can. This is my substitute for pistol and ball. With a philosophical flourish Cato throws himself upon his sword; I quietly take to the ship."

from Cambridge named Jacques, whose reaction to the story was evidently decidedly encouraging.[26]

Upon his return to London on July 26, 1893, Conrad found a letter from his uncle urging him to visit him in the Ukraine. This visit which took place shortly afterward was to afford Conrad the last glimpse of his uncle, for in the following February he received word of Thaddeus' death. It affected him profoundly. "It seems to me that everything within me is dead," he wrote to Madame Poradowska. "He seems to have taken my soul away with him."[27] Yet, despite these melancholic sentiments Conrad promptly attacked the closing chapters of his novel, displaying far greater energy than at any time since the beginning of the work four and one-half years before. Indeed, the work seemed to capture his entire attention, causing him to write, "I regret every moment which I spend away from my writing."[28] To Marguerite he wrote at last on April 24, 1894, "I have the painful duty of announcing to you the death of Mr. Kaspar Almayer, which took place at 3 o'clock this morning."[k/29] Both the sudden speed of bringing the work to a close and the manner of his announcing it to his "Aunt" suggest that the death of his beloved Uncle Thaddeus had acted as a stimulus upon him. It seems quite likely, moreover, that his announcement of the death of Almayer was a paraphrase of the message he had received not long before announcing the unhappy news from the Ukraine. This would suggest that Conrad was attempting to master a painful real loss by "advertising" a fictional one, thus becoming the active-author, rather than the passive recipient of a piece of bad news. As a defense against painful experiences, the device of "active repetition" is a familiar psychological phenomenon,[l] and in the present instance it can probably be held accountable for the rapid completion of a book, which, prior to Bobrowski's death, had been limping along for nearly five years. Here an affirmative action apparently served Conrad as a protection against the threat

[k] A year and one-half later he was to announce the completion of his second novel, *An Outcast of the Islands*, in an identical manner.

[l] This psychological mechanism is a common determinant in causing individuals who have been conspicuously ailing as children to choose a medical career.

of emotional annihilation occasioned by the loss of virtually the last close link with his family.[m]

Conrad was aware of the "therapeutic" efficacy of activity and action. "There were moments when I felt, not only that I would go mad, but that I had gone mad already . . ." he wrote in *The Shadow-Line*. "Luckily I had . . . my orders to give, and an order has a steadying influence upon him who has to give it."[31] Even more relevant to the matter of grief are his comments in *Nostromo* concerning the death of Charles Gould's father. "It hurt [Charles] to feel that never more, by no effort of will, would he be able to think of his father in the same way he used to think of him when the poor man was alive. His breathing image was no longer in his power. This consideration, *closely affecting his own identity*, filled his heart with a mournful and angry desire for action . . . *action is consolatory. It is the enemy of thought and the friend of flattering illusions.*"[32] (Italics mine)

Like Charles Gould, too, Conrad reacted to the death of his cherished relative as if his very identity were affected—"He seems to have taken my soul away with him." For just as tokens of individuality and strength borrowed from others served to sustain Conrad's sense of identity and manliness, so did the loss of the man who had served him so long as a devoted and responsible foster father apparently threaten to re-awaken that sense of inner dissolution which after the untimely loss of his parents menaced him throughout the rest of his life. It was indeed such a picture of disintegration which Conrad later provided in *Nostromo* in the events leading up to the ultimate suicide of Martin Decoud, of whom Conrad would say: ". . . *in our activity alone do we find the sustaining illusion of an independent existence* as against the whole scheme of things of which we form a helpless part." But cut off from all human contact, all distractions, and all means of action on the island of the Great Isabel,

[m] Guerard, too, connects Bobrowski's death with the rapid completion of *Almayer's Folly*, but he offers a different explanation from the one given here, suggesting that Conrad's uncle was an "inhibiting substitute father," preventing Conrad from doing creative work until his "critical presence was out of the way."[30]

> the brilliant "Son Decoud," the spoiled darling of the family, the lover of Antonia, and journalist of Sulaco, was not fit to grapple with himself single-handed. Solitude from mere outward condition of existence becomes swiftly a state of soul in which the affectations of irony and skepticism have no place. It takes possession of the mind, and drives forth the thought into the exile of utter unbelief. After three days of waiting for the sight of some human face, Decoud *caught himself entertaining a doubt of his own individuality*. It had merged into the world of cloud and water. . . . Decoud lost all belief in the reality of his action past and to come. On the fifth day an immense melancholy descended upon him palpably.[33] (Italics mine)

Finally after ten days of solitude and after ten nights of unrelenting sleeplessness, Decoud pushes off from the shore in a small boat, his pockets weighted down with ingots of silver; and when he shoots himself in the chest[n] his body falls to the bottom of the sea. "The truth was that he died from solitude, the enemy known but to few on this earth, and whom only the simplest of us are fit to understand."[34]

Fortunately, unlike Decoud but like Gould, Conrad possessed the means of engaging in that action which is "the enemy of thought," and on July 12, 1894, after making many revisions, he sent the manuscript to the publisher Fisher Unwin.

But as the weeks rolled by and Conrad received no word of the fate of his novel, his old complaints of depression and nervousness reappeared in his letters to Madame Poradowska, and as he had once before turned to her for help he now did so again. Ostensibly because of her influence and reputation as a writer, he made the curious proposal to her that his book be produced in French under her name, with his participation as a junior collaborator signified by the addition of his name, in the form of a pseudonym, in small letters under hers.[35] Even assuming that such a plan might further the chances of getting his book published, it is difficult to see how such a proposal would really have helped launch Conrad on a literary career, for it would have meant surrendering his identity

[n] Cf. Conrad in Marseilles.

as an author and remaining merely as a disguised minor appendage to an already established writer.

It would have meant more than that, one suspects, for in a man so seemingly obsessed by the issue of manliness, the sacrifice of the authorship of his first work to a woman must have loomed as a disturbing thought. Surely if in pursuing a literary career Conrad was unconsciously seeking to emulate—or even outstrip—his father, it would have done little to promote that masculine aim to hide his authorship behind a woman's skirts.

Yet it must be recognized that the proposal for "collaboration" came from Conrad,[o] and it came too soon after he had submitted his manuscript to ascribe it solely to a fear of its rejection. The suspicion arises, therefore, that he may have used this latter possibility as a pretext to yield to an unconscious impulse to play a subordinate role toward a strong and beloved woman. Seen in this light his suggestion to Marguerite Poradowska may be viewed as a means of achieving a closer bond with her through an act of loving submission, a gesture that anticipates the behavior of virtually every love-struck hero in Conrad's fiction.

From Bobrowski's letters and from Conrad's own correspondence with Madame Poradowska there is reason to suspect that from time to time he might have toyed with the idea of marrying her.[36] Such an idea would have appealed to him not only because he saw in her a loving maternal being, but because of the realistic support she might lend him, for Marguerite was a personage of some reputation as a writer and wielded considerable influence with important and prominent people. Finally she was, according to the later testimony of Jessie Conrad, a woman of great beauty.[37]

And yet her relationship with Conrad, sustained over a number of years by occasional meetings and frequent letters and bathed in an atmosphere of warmth and closeness, appears to have come to a sudden halt, for beginning in June 1895 there occurred a gap in their correspondence which continued over the next five years.[p]

[o] As would similar proposals for collaboration with other writers in the years to come. See Chapter VII, footnote *c*.

[p] Baines brings forward evidence that some exchange of letters continued

Two events seemingly ushered in the rupture of this "romance": in October 1894 Conrad received word that his book had been accepted for publication, and a month later he met Miss Jessie George. During the following year, 1895, which marked the apparent interruption of his correspondence with his "Aunt," Conrad's relationship with Miss George became closer, and on March 24, 1896, following a precipitous and bizarre courtship of six weeks, they were married.

It has been suggested that Conrad may have turned to Jessie George on the "rebound" after Marguerite Poradowska had turned him down on a proposal of marriage.[40] There is no evidence for such an hypothesis, however, and a closer view of Conrad's actual relationship with Madame Poradowska should suffice to dismiss the idea altogether, for it will soon be apparent that their "romance" existed more on paper than in the flesh. Despite the fervent and often imploring tone of his letters, despite his declaration of a sense of mystical union with her, and the embraces and kisses with which he concluded so many of his letters, Conrad was remarkably rarely in her physical presence. During the five and one-half years which elapsed between their initial meeting in 1890 and June 1895 when their correspondence apparently came to a temporary halt, Conrad wrote her close to 100 letters. Yet during the same interval, aside from the two visits in 1890 when he was enlisting her aid in his Congo venture, Conrad seems to have seen her but four times: immediately upon his return from the Congo in January 1891, and again in June of that year; once in March 1894; and finally in June 1895. Moreover, save for his two-day visit of January 1891, none of his other visits with her exceeded a single day. Furthermore, one gains a distinct impression that the infrequency and the brevity of his glimpses of her arose more out

---

during this interval.[38] His suggestion that Conrad's letters to her during this period were either destroyed or withheld because they "contained matter which she thought was better not revealed,"[39] seems unlikely, however, for as his relationship with Jessie George grew in intimacy it seems improbable that his feelings for his "Aunt" maintained their erstwhile importance. If indeed Marguerite did destroy his letters after June 1895, one might conjecture that she was motivated by pique, the pique of a woman scorned.

of choice than out of practical necessity. There were several journeys from London to the continent and back, for example, when a stop in Paris, where she was then living,[q] would have been a simple matter if he had wished to make one. In September 1893, for instance, he could have seen her on his return trip to England from the Ukraine; he had in fact advised her that this was his intention. Yet, although he had not seen her in over two years, he went home via Amsterdam, offering the dubious explanation that he was anxious to return home and find work.[41] Two months later he was in Rouen awaiting the departure of the steamship *Adowa* on which he had obtained a position as second officer. Ultimately the voyage was abandoned, but Conrad was in Rouen for a period of six weeks, during which time he found it impractical to travel to Paris, a mere 75 miles away. This did not prevent his writing to her, however, and furnishing her with what appears to be a series of rationalizations for his failure to visit her. "It seems unnatural to be in France without seeing you," he wrote. "I have a mind to escape and run off to Paris—even to leave the ship for good—but I have had to give up all these dreams. The fact is that I can't afford this little luxury of affection. And anyhow they wouldn't let me go. So there you are! What can I do!"[42] He appears to protest too much about the alleged impossibility of his undertaking the little trip, much as he did a few months later when he wrote to her of another possible visit to her—"It is not that I don't want to. I am trying to find employment and I dare not leave London just now for fear of missing an opportunity."[43] Moreover, when he did decide to see her he apparently found it necessary to explain the reasons for his visit. Upon his return from the sanitarium in Champel he warned her, "I am stopping a day just for the novel [one of hers]—not for any other thing."[44]

This discrepancy between the intensity of their correspondence and the paucity of their meetings leads to the conclusion that however much Conrad cherished his acquaintance with his "Aunt" he earnestly desired to maintain his relationship with her from afar, confining his expressions of tenderness and love to the me-

[q] More precisely in Passy, like Rita. (From Marguer*ita*?)

dium of the postal service. It is probably significant therefore that his most ardent letters to her were written from the safe distance of central Africa. The picture indeed is reminiscent of the celebrated "love affair" between Tchaikovsky and his "beloved friend" and patroness, Madame Nadejda Von Meck, who exchanged passionate love letters over many years without ever setting eyes upon each other. In this instance too, in which the element of distance constituted a *sine qua non* of love, the woman was approximately ten years older than the man.

Conrad himself undoubtedly realized that he had fashioned Marguerite into an idol, an object to be worshipped from a distance, and a being whom he shrank from touching. "Do not come down from the pedestal where I have set you," he wrote, "even though that would mean to come nearer to me."[45] What he undoubtedly meant was that only if she remained upon her pedestal could he continue to love her. Viewed in this light Marguerite Poradowska was a precursor of his statuesque fictional heroines who inspire not so much sensuous longing as awe-filled adoration. Just as Razumov in *Under Western Eyes* confides his love of Nathalie Haldin not to her directly but to his diary, so did Conrad confine his love for his "beloved Aunt" to the written page. His own evident discomfort in her presence, moreover, is mirrored in his fiction in the undisguised awkwardness which pervades those love scenes in which his "goddesses"—the women "of all time"—are involved.

Under the circumstances, the notion that Conrad seriously contemplated marriage with a woman whose company he took such pains to avoid seems highly unlikely. On the contrary, to judge again from the pattern of love discovered in his fictional characters, Conrad could have attained a physical relationship only with a woman who failed to inspire such worshipful sentiments. For the sensuous women in Conrad's fiction are not the monolithic Rita and her like, but those creatures who spring from a much lower station in the hierarchy of social organization, women like Aïssa, Winnie Verloc, and the simple hired girl, Amy Foster. The girl with whom the Russian student Razumov finds final peace is not the revered Nathalie Haldin but the bedraggled Tekla. In like manner, Conrad could have given little if any consideration to the idea of experiencing erotic excitement with Madame Poradowska, but by the same token he might encounter a much less formidable psychological barrier in seeking the hand of the relatively obscure and undistinguished English girl, Jessie George.

Yet the fact of his having met Miss George does not alone account for his courting her nor for his "dropping" Marguerite Poradowska. Earlier in this chapter it was pointed out that there was a subtle interrelationship between the three new ventures embarked upon by Conrad toward the close of the year 1889. It was through the efforts of Marguerite that he secured his position in the Congo, to which remote quarter he carried the manuscript of the early chapters of his novel. Upon his return to Europe it was to Marguerite that he turned for comfort and it was to her that he proposed to "sacrifice" his finished book. She was indeed a good fairy who presided over the fortunes of both his African and his literary adventures, touching him with the wand of kindness in his hours of misery and defeat.

But suddenly his fortunes turned. His novel[r] was accepted for publication and Edward Garnett, his publisher's reader, encouraged him to write another.[46] Before him rose the prospect of a new career and of a new and distinguishable "self"—a man of letters. Now, much as if he had returned from the Congo a hero instead of a sick and broken man, he could afford to relinquish his child-like grasp on his "Aunt," and heartened by new tokens of identity and power, he was ready to undertake another bold adventure, another proof of manliness.

That he did not regard this new venture without trepidation, however, is apparent from the whistling-in-the-dark tone of the announcement of his impending marriage to his cousin Karol Zagorski: "I cannot say I am terrified," he wrote, "being, as you know accustomed to leading a life full of adventure, and to wrestle with terrible dangers. Besides, I must add that my fiancée does not appear at all dangerous."[47]

Despite this bantering disclaimer subsequent events would show that upon the threshold of this new phase of his life Conrad was

[r] Dedicated appropriately to "T. B.," his Uncle Thaddeus.

indeed terrified and even panic-stricken. It will also soon become apparent that like all of Conrad's positive actions his entry into matrimony was but another phase of that movement of the pendulum, which, as in the past, would reach its apex and then begin its downward motion, accompanied by characteristic signs of dissolution and collapse.

VI · An Outcast of the Islands

THE CONTRAST between Marguerite Poradowska and Jessie George serves to emphasize another aspect of Conrad's attitude toward love, sexuality, and marriage. In 1896 the forty-nine-year-old Marguerite enjoyed a reputation as an established writer. Like Conrad she was a cultivated European intellectual. Jessie George, then twenty-three, was an obscure English girl of humble birth and modest education, who, when Conrad met her, was employed as a typist.[1] While Marguerite was called "Aunt," placing her in the psychological position of a parent, Jessie was so young that she was occasionally taken for Conrad's daughter—to his great annoyance.[2] In turning from Madame Poradowska to Jessie George, therefore, Conrad was not merely replacing a celebrated woman, much older than himself, by an unknown girl less than half her age; he was replacing a person with whom he shared a common background and common interests by one with whom he shared almost nothing. In these substitutions of the alien for the familiar, and the young girl for the mature woman, Conrad was introducing into his own life an allusion to two matters which he frankly admitted held a marked interest for him: the theme of exogamy and the relationship of father and daughter. Of the former he once wrote: "A dash of orientalism on white is very fascinating, at least for me, though I must say that the genuine Eastern had never the power to lead me away from the path of rectitude; to any serious extent, that is."[3] Indeed the element of dissimilarity between the lovers appears to have been a necessary condition for the emergence of passionate love in his stories, for it is mainly in those novels in which a conspicuous element of exogamy is implied that Conrad's lovers convey a credible impression of erotic feeling: "Amy Foster," *An Outcast of the Islands*, *Lord Jim*, "A Smile of Fortune," "Heart of Darkness," and possibly *Almayer's Folly*. But in those stories like "The Return," "The Planter of Malata," *Chance*, *Victory*, *The Arrow of Gold*, and *The Rescue*, in which the protagonists are both white and of comparatively similar backgrounds, the lovers appear to expend most of their sexual energies by backing and filling in a morass of inhibition, all the while engaging in a ruminative chatter that at times approaches sheer double-talk.[a]

An implied insistence upon exogamy as a necessary condition for erotic arousal can be uniformly interpreted as an effort to dissociate such feelings from those individuals who constitute the familiars of childhood, thereby creating an illusion of "distance" designed to eliminate any hint of an incestuous component in the sexual objects of adult life. Such a sense of distance may be achieved literally by removing one's love life geographically from the locale of the scenes of childhood, or psychologically, by choosing as sexual objects individuals whose social and racial origins and history are so foreign to one's own as to convey the illusion that they belong virtually to another species.[b]

Whereas occasionally devices aimed at creating "distance" lead to felicitous relationships, often enough unions composed of conspicuously exogamous elements end in sexual maladjustment and highly unstable marriages. Nor should it be difficult to understand such failures, for the very urgency of including an exogamous ingredient only emphasizes the compelling attraction of its opposite—the incestuous object. Flight into exogamy may therefore be but a chimera, and that which is so strenuously avoided is at the same moment the secret object of an unconscious pursuit. The white man who hopes to achieve an uninhibited erotic experience in the embrace of an exotic half-caste may find in her the same mother or sister from whom he is ostensibly fleeing: in *An Outcast of the Islands* when the motherless Willems sleeps upon the tan breast of the young Polynesian girl Aïssa, she murmurs, "I shall watch your sleep, child."[6]

Expressed figuratively, then, Conrad's fascination with "a dash of orientalism on white" may be regarded as one side of a coin on

[a] Moser, who characterizes love as Conrad's "Uncongenial Subject," suggests that it may have been his inability to deal with the theme of love between white people that caused Conrad to abandon *The Sisters*, and to labor with such difficulty over *The Rescue*.[4]

[b] "How I loved her! How wildly, how irrationally—this woman of another race, of another world . . ." exclaims the hero of *Romance*.[5]

whose reverse is stamped his unmistakably equally intense preoccupation with the subject of incest. In his stories this theme is portrayed most commonly by the possessive and jealous love which a father displays towards his daughter. Indeed it is this relationship which often overshadows the more conventional love affairs in such romances as *Almayer's Folly*, "Freya of the Seven Isles," and especially *Chance*, in which De Barral angrily accuses his daughter of being in love with her own husband.[c] Other variations on the incest theme appear in *The Arrow of Gold* (Ortega's passion for his cousin Rita), and in the unfinished novel *Suspense* (the foreshadowed love affair between Cosmo and his half-sister Adèle).[d]

It is noteworthy, however, that despite the several patterns in which Conrad presented the theme of incest, one is conspicuously absent—mother and son. Indeed, Conrad saw to it that such a relationship could virtually never exist in his stories, for there is scarcely a major male character in all his fiction who has a living mother, and there is but one important female character who has a living male child, namely, Amy Foster.[e] Thus despite his obvious interest in the subject of incest Conrad not only pointedly avoided depicting it in terms of mother and son, but selected his characters in such a manner as to make such a relationship impossible.[f] It goes without saying that this omission is in itself important, and that, like the emphasis upon exogamy, the admitted fascination with the theme of father and daughter may be viewed as signifying an equal albeit undeclared interest in its opposite: the relationship between mother and son.

These considerations have a distinct bearing upon Conrad's substitution of Jessie George for Marguerite Poradowska. For just

[c] The setting in which De Barral plots to murder his son-in-law contains obvious allusions to *Othello*.[7]

[d] Evidence for the presence of the "incest" theme in the unfinished *The Sisters* has been given in Chapter II.

[e] In *The Secret Agent* Stevie Verloc occupies the position of Winnie's son, although in reality he is her very young brother. It is noteworthy that her husband is responsible for Stevie's death. See Chapter X.

[f] Conrad showed no reluctance, on the other hand, in portraying a son's attachment to a father, as in the case of Charles Gould, Heyst, etc.

as his choice of the former conforms to his interest in exogamy and the "approved," "father-daughter" relationship, his relinquishment of the woman he called his "Aunt" constitutes a rejection both of a woman of his own "kind" and of a representative of a mother. In turning from her, the European intellectual who had once been married to a member of his family, to an unknown English girl, Conrad evidently strove to establish an exogamous "distance" between childhood attachments and adult sexual objects. In turning from her, a considerably older woman into whose lap he had once begged to be placed, to a girl in her twenties, Conrad may also have been seeking to eliminate from his adult sexual life any hint of an attachment between a "mother" and "son."

Unfortunately, as already stated, such devices often fail to gain in adult life the hoped for freedom from the emotional conflicts of childhood. Sooner or later the mate chosen because of a seeming lack of similarity to the parent may become endowed with all the attributes of the latter: age, race, and nationality tend to be obliterated in the dark.[g] If the choice of Jessie George represented an effort to achieve a dimension of "distance," detaching her from Conrad's image of a European mother, it cannot be said to have met with signal success. For despite her youth and the exogamous character of her origin, his courtship, honeymoon, and subsequent life as husband and father fail to reflect the image of a grown man who, unencumbered by the residua of the emotional conflicts of childhood, was psychologically equipped to enjoy the satisfaction of love, marriage, and family life.

Curiously his courtship of Jessie George coincided precisely with the creation of his second novel, a love story which epitomized Conrad's fascination with a "dash of orientalism on white." He began writing *An Outcast of the Islands* during the same month when he was introduced to Jessie; their marriage took place during the very month of its publication. The book stands, therefore, as a creative accompaniment, or a literary obligato, to events in Conrad's personal history: the love affair between Willems and Aïssa evolved and collapsed as an artistic parallel to Conrad's courtship

[g] For somewhat analogous reasons some men begin to experience disturbances in potency after their wives become mothers.

of Jessie George. Nor is this merely a parallel in time: it is equally a parallel in feeling, in sense, and in structure. Despite the remoteness of its exotic Malay setting and the seeming dissimilarities of the characters, the fictional love story illumines the real one.

Like Conrad, the Dutchman Willems, a motherless child reared by a father, leaves his native land in his middle 'teens to go to sea. Disillusioned in time by a sailor's life—for what "had looked so charming from afar but proved so hard and exacting on closer acquaintance"[8]—he finds a protector in the prosperous white trader, Captain Lingard, who offers to send him home. "But the boy begged hard to be permitted to remain."[h/9] Becoming "soon perfect in English" he obtains a position with Hudig,[i] a Dutch merchant, and later he marries the latter's illegitimate daughter, Joanna. But when Willems is caught stealing from his father-in-law he abandons his wife and child—"those encumbrances of his life"[11]—and is once more taken under the protection of Lingard, who enjoys a flourishing monopoly in an up-river Malay settlement, called Sambir. Here Willems is installed to work for Lingard and to rehabilitate himself, but instead he falls desperately in love with Aïssa, a bewitching native girl, the devoted daughter of a blind Arab chieftain, Omar. Maddened by passion, "possessed of a devil," Willems betrays his benefactor by revealing to Aïssa's Arab people Lingard's secret entrance to the river from the sea. Later, overcome with remorse, Willems pleads with Lingard for forgiveness, begging him to save him from Aïssa, whose possessiveness has now become oppressive and loathsome to him. But Lingard refuses, abandoning his traitorous protégé to the girl who shoots him fatally when he tries to escape.[j]

[h] To his friend Buszczynski Conrad's uncle wrote after the Marseilles debacle, "I suggested that he return to his country—he flatly refused."[10]

[i] This was the name of the man in Amsterdam, one of the charterers of the *Highland Forest*, who predicted that Conrad would be called upon to be her captain, as recounted in Chapter III.

[j] Viewed symbolically, Willems's betrayal of his benefactor has the unmistakable stamp of an "Oedipal" crime, which is compounded by his piloting the Arab chieftain's ship through the opening which heretofore had been known only to Lingard. (That a man piloting a vessel through the narrows carried an erotic significance to Conrad is again suggested by his

Summed up by Conrad as the story of the "physical enslavement of a man by a totally savage woman,"[13] *An Outcast of the Islands* epitomizes Conrad's reiterated insistence upon the destructive and devouring nature of a woman's love. Aïssa is likened to "an animal as full of harm as a wild cat,"[14] whose words "rang out shrill and venomous with her secret scorn, with her overpowering desire to wound, regardless of consequences; in her woman's reckless desire to cause suffering at any cost, to cause it by the sound of her own voice."[15] Unable to escape from her he foresees himself eaten by "endless and minute throngs of insects, little shining monsters . . . in eager struggle for his body . . . till there would remain nothing but the white gleam of bleaching bones in the long grass."[16] In short, Aïssa's love is likened to being eaten alive.

In the course of his proposal of marriage to Jessie George, which was as dismaying as it was abrupt, she later reported Conrad conveyed a similar forecast of his early destruction by informing her that he had not long to live—an assertion for which there was not the least evidence. Following her acceptance, she noted on his face an expression of "acute suffering." Suddenly he left her, hailed a passing cab, and, urging the driver on to greater speed, fled from her presence. During the next three days she did not hear from him, and when he finally saw her again he insisted that the marriage take place in less than six weeks' time and that they go abroad to live. Just before the wedding he demanded that she burn all his letters in his presence.[17] He was a half hour late in arriving for the ceremony which he postponed even longer by entering into an argument with the cab driver.[18] On their wedding night he kept her up to pack and to address the wedding announcements until two in the morning, and he then insisted upon going into the street to

---

later characterization of the tugboat Captain Falk as a "centaur"—"not a man-horse, but a man-boat." See Chapter IX, footnote *b.*) "It's the madness that drove me to it," Willems tells Lingard, seeking to account for his faithless action. Abandoned by his protector, Willems is ultimately stricken by figurative blindness: "All was night within him. All was gone from his sight. He walked about blindly in the deserted courtyards," etc.[12] Apropos of this emphasis on the "Oedipal" flavor of this story, it is noteworthy that Almayer, another protégé of Lingard, calls the latter "Father."

mail them. Early the next morning, on bidding farewell to her mother at the station, Mrs. Conrad was under "the strictest orders that there should be no tears or display of emotion."[19] On the channel crossing to Brittany the former Captain Korzeniowski was seasick.[20]

Hardly had they reached their Brittany destination—a small house on Ile Grande, a rocky barren island near Lannion—when Conrad, not pausing to unpack, plunged into the business of writing. Nor do his letters to England convey so much the image of a romantic idyll as that of a man suffering over his difficulties in writing *The Rescuer* and pining for his friends at home. To Garnett he wrote one month after his arrival at Ile Grande, "I am thirsty and hungry for news from you . . . just be for once immorally charitable and drop me a line quick."[21] A few weeks later he was promising to write again "whenever . . . the loneliness becomes insupportable."[22]

Then suddenly he became ill with fever and delirium, frightening his wife by raving incomprehensibly in Polish, and later upsetting her by letting loose a "stream of disjointed accusations," in English, "concerning [her] moral and spiritual character."[k/23]

Rather than a picture of amorous bliss, the account of these nuptials reflects a sense of nervousness, of sickness, and of discomfort hardly compatible with an atmosphere of felicitous physical intimacy. The suspicion that Conrad was disturbed by the sexual aspects of marriage gains support from a short story written by him during the early months of his stay at Ile Grande. Unable to get ahead with the troublesome *The Rescuer*, he wrote "The Idiots," a story which was inspired by a meeting with a family of mentally retarded children. It is the story of Susan, who, having given birth to several idiot children, stabs her husband in the throat with a pair of scissors when he tries to make love to her. Haunted by the dead man's voice and believing him still lusting after her, she hurls herself into the sea. Perhaps of equal significance, this time as a measure of his sense of isolation and vulnerability, is

[k] The picture recalls a scene in "Amy Foster" in which the delirious Yanko Gooral screams for a glass of water at his uncomprehending English wife.

another tale written in July of the same year—"An Outpost of Progress." Placed in a Congo setting, the story concerns the steady deterioration of two white men whose quarrelling culminates in murder over a bit of sugar for a cup of coffee. Like Susan in "The Idiots," the murderer then commits suicide.

It is difficult indeed to envisage a grimmer accompaniment to a song of love than these two tales, the first complete stories written by Joseph Conrad as a married man. (The theme of the murdering woman, moreover, recalls the close of the *Outcast.*) Like Willems, Conrad's behavior both during his courtship and during his honeymoon invokes the image of a trapped man constantly plotting his escape. When touched by Aïssa's hand Willems sits up suddenly, as if shot, and flings her hand away, "brutally, like something burning."[l/24] Accepted in his suit for Jessie George's *hand,* Conrad dashed off in a seeming panic and disappeared for three days. Like Willems who begs Aïssa to go away with him from her people, Conrad demanded that Jessie abandon all her English attachments and settle down with him in a small Breton village where neither of them knew a soul. Willems berates Aïssa for mourning her dead father; Conrad insisted that upon leaving her mother Jessie should show "no tears or display of emotion." Both men, restless in their snares, become sick and delirious, and both vilify their women: "Take that woman away!—she is sin,"[26] cries Willems, while Conrad uttered a "stream of disjointed accusations" concerning his wife's "moral and spiritual character." Isolated, both men grow restive and long for the company of their protectors—"Take me away, I am white!"[27] pleads Lingard, while Conrad wrote to Garnett, "just be for once . . . charitable and drop me a line quick!"

Although at the time of his marriage proposal Conrad had stated that he intended to take his wife abroad indefinitely, by September 1896, they were back in England, having been persuaded without too much difficulty of the unsalutary effects of the Breton climate upon his health, thus bringing to a close the first chapter in their married life. For six months they had lived an isolated life far

[l] In *The Rescue,* Lingard drops Mrs. Travers's hand "suddenly as if it had burnt him."[25]

away from all that was familiar to them, a pair of outcasts from the islands across the English Channel. From this moment on such isolation was not to recur, for never again were they alone with each other for any appreciable amount of time.

Conrad's apparent neurotic suffering throughout these early months of marriage, however, did not prevent his creating a work which is considered a masterpiece by many critics—*The Nigger of the Narcissus.* Begun while he was still at Ile Grande, probably in June 1896, and finished early in the following year,[28] *The Nigger* was the first of those sea stories which caused Conrad to be classified as a writer of sea tales, a designation which persists in some quarters to this day,[m] and one which continued to elicit a protest from him throughout his life.[29] Of course the novel is a sea story, a vividly impressionistic evocation of a ship and its men, of wind and water, of storms and near disaster. But *The Nigger* is more than the story of a sea voyage, more too than what its author called "an effort to present a group of men held together by a common loyalty and a common perplexity in a struggle, not with human enemies, but with the hostile conditions testing their faithfulness to the conditions of their own calling."[30] More too than a gallery of sharply etched portraits of men of the sea, the novel is a literary tone poem whose theme is death—the grim spectacle of gradual death unfolded before the uncertain and anxious eyes of the ship's crew. Viewed in such terms it is clear why Conrad insisted that the problem confronting these men was not a problem of the sea,[31] for it was indeed one which he himself had faced as a child in witnessing the slow dying of his mother and later his father. Noteworthy is the fact that the very illness which caused their death —tuberculosis of the lungs—is the same sickness which slowly kills James Wait, the "nigger" of *The Narcissus.*[n] Recognizing Conrad's apparent tendency to come to terms with painful personal experiences by actively re-ordering them, so-to-speak, in creative fiction, there is justification for believing that the same psychological "mechanisn" was at work in his telling the story of Jimmy's

[m] The title of the English translation, published in 1957, of Jean-Aubry's *Vie de Conrad* is *The Sea Dreamer*.

[n] And presumably also Yanko Gooral of "Amy Foster."

dying and its effect upon the others.[o] Indeed, one wonders whether the very description of Jimmy's coughing when he went to bed, his "wheezing regularly in his sleep"[33] might have been based upon real models, particularly upon his father whose final illness and death could hardly have failed to leave a vivid and lasting imprint in the memory of his son, then in his twelfth year. There are subtleties and nuances surrounding Jimmy's dying which too may have originated in Conrad's own early experience. Suggestive of a child's disbelief and inner turmoil when faced with the bewildering image of death is the uncertainty of the crew: was Jimmy really sick, or was he faking and exploiting them? They despise him, yet they cannot refrain from mothering him tenderly and from rescuing him when he becomes entombed in his cabin during the storm.[p] "We hated James Wait. We could not get rid of the monstrous suspicion that this astounding black man was shamming sick, had been malingering heartlessly in the face of our toil, of our scorn, of our patience—and now he was malingering in the face of our devotion—in the face of death."[34]

Jimmy is not the only demoralizing force on board the *Narcissus*. The solidarity of the crew and its devotion to duty is also threatened by the troublemaker Donkin, who seeks to incite the others to mutiny. Indeed it is Karl's view that these two men are the first of a long line of Conradian anarchists; "not men who throw bombs, but those who refuse their duties and know nothing of courage and endurance and loyalty; men who know only of their rights."[35] But if the Negro James Wait is to be viewed as an "anarchist" he may also be regarded as a particularly sharply delineated example of the "outsider," the disruptive alien, who elicits hatred and distrust, and occasionally compassion from the crowd, as well as from the reader. He would appear again in Conrad's

[o] Suggestive of this attempt to master an early trauma through active repetition is the message sent to Garnett by Conrad as he was finishing the novel: "Nigger died on the 7th at 6 P.M." To which he added, "I can't eat—I dream—nightmares—and scare my wife." In the context of the present hypothesis it is regrettable that Conrad failed to mention the content of those dreams.[32]

[p] The claustrophobia implicit in this scene will be discussed in a later chapter.

fiction, notably as the Central European castaway, Yanko Gooral, washed up on the English coast, and as the Jew, Señor Hirsch of *Nostromo*. In a larger sense, however, the designation "outsider" is applicable to virtually every major character in Conrad's fiction, and in the course of the present study evidence will be offered which suggests that aside from whatever real models he may have used in fashioning these individuals alienated from their surroundings, ultimately they represent multiple self-portraits of the author himself. Viewed in this light the picture of James Wait as a childlike helpless creature, whose physical sickness appears to be admixed with malingering, and who still succeeds in holding those about him in a kind of "weird servitude,"[36] may be regarded as an incisive and scornful confession. Support for this hypothesis is not wanting, for there is abundant evidence that these same attributes were always present in Conrad's personality, and conspicuously so after his marriage.

That during the early troubled months of married life he was able to compose a generally acknowledged masterpiece is noteworthy, for his other literary efforts of that time were somewhat less than that. The ill-fated *The Sisters*, begun shortly after he had finished *An Outcast of the Islands* and permanently abandoned around the time of his marriage in March 1896, prompted Conrad to complain to Garnett in February of his "horrible inability (for the last fortnight) to write a line."[37] Nor did he fare much better with *The Rescuer*, which, under the title of *The Rescue*, was not to be completed for 23 years. In June, the same month which apparently witnessed the beginnings of *The Nigger*, Conrad wrote from Brittany, "And every day *The Rescuer* crawls a page forward —sometimes with cold despair—at times with hot hope." Some notion of his state of mind is conveyed by the sentences that follow: "I have long fits of depression, that in a lunatic asylum would be called madness. I do not know what it is. It springs from nothing. It is ghastly. It lasts an hour or a day; and when it departs it leaves a fear."[38] By mid-August he was writing: "I wish I could tackle *The Rescuer* again. I simply can't."[39]

Conrad wrote three short stories during his honeymoon on Ile Grande, two of which, "The Idiots" and "An Outpost of Progress" have already been mentioned. A third, "The Lagoon," which Conrad characterized as "a tricky thing with the usual forests—river—stars—wind—sunrise, and so on—and lots of second-hand Conradese in it,"[40] anticipates a fourth short story, "Karain," which he composed after finishing *The Nigger* early in 1897. It is doubtful whether any of these stories would have made the author a reputation as a great literary figure, although "An Outpost of Progress," which Conrad called "the lightest part of the loot [he] carried off from Central Africa,"[41] provides a hint of the power and atmosphere that would later appear in his great Congo story, "Heart of Darkness." If "An Outpost" stands above the rest of the short stories written during this period it should be noted that it is the only story of this era—except *The Nigger*—which is virtually devoid of women and love interest. Indeed, it would seem likely that it was this same remoteness from any overt allusion to the emotional conflicts which Conrad's courtship and marriage had apparently intensified, that made *The Nigger* "possible." In this story with "its conditions of complete isolation from all land entanglements,"[42] Conrad could escape from the stifling atmosphere of a close relationship, and, of probably even greater importance, from the oppressive embrace of physical intimacy. It is true he wrote of death (did he long for it?), but he wrote easily and produced a work that may be said to fulfill his definition of artistic aim: " . . . to aspire to the plasticity of sculpture, to the colour of painting, and to the magic suggestiveness of music—which is the art of arts."[43] Unhindered by the burdens of love and sexuality that had caused his other literary craft to drag or founder in their course, the *Narcissus* moved swiftly, a thing of grace and beauty, carrying her creator, in his fancy, once again into the familiar serenity of the open seas.

If in actuality he did not escape from Jessie in the sense that Willems sought deliverance from Aïssa, there is reason to believe that from time to time the idea of flight occurred to him. In April, just one year after his marriage, and a few weeks after finishing *The Nigger*, Conrad began to compose "The Return," a story concerning the disintegration of the five-year-old marriage of the Alvan Herveys, a middle-class English couple. By this time events were taking place which could hardly fail to augment the author's restlessness. Not surprisingly, in view of the subject of the story and of the circumstances surrounding its origin, Conrad experienced great difficulties in the writing of this work.

"The Return" represents Conrad's first attempt to compose a story set, so-to-speak, at his own back door. Not only are Alvan Hervey and his wife white, they are Londoners. Their relationship is presented as the epitome of superficiality and remoteness. "They understood each other warily, tacitly, like a pair of cautious conspirators in a profitable plot. . . . They skimmed over the surface[q] of life hand in hand, in a pure and frosty atmosphere . . . like two skillful skaters cutting figures on thick ice for the admiration of the beholders, and disdainfully ignoring the hidden stream, the stream restless and dark, the stream of life, profound and unfrozen."[49] Like many of Conrad's male protagonists Alvan Hervey is weak, inarticulate, and seemingly impotent. He is moreover submissive before his wife, who "strode like a grenadier,"[50] and whose veil is likened to a vizor.[51] Returning home from work one day he discovers that she has left him for another man. Hardly has he recovered from the shock which has momentarily shaken him into experiencing some "real feelings," when his wife returns; she was unable to carry out her plan. What follows is a rambling, redundant, and very "talky" conversation, the pointlessness of which suggests a confusion in the author over both his conception of his created characters and the plot. While Alvan pleads with his wife, before whom he feels "insignificant and powerless" as she towers above him, she suddenly snaps her ivory fan and the fragments fall to the floor. Automatically he stoops and picks them up, giving

[q] Conrad used this expression to designate an attitude of detachment on other occasions. Thus Captain MacWhirr of *Typhoon* "had sailed over the surface of the oceans as some men go skimming over the years of existence to sink gently into a placid grave,"[44] and Peyrol of *The Rover* is told, "You have been the best part of your life skimming the seas if the truth were told."[45] Although not specifically called a "skimmer," Heyst of *Victory* fits into this category: "In this scheme he had perceived the means of passing through life without suffering and almost without a single care in the world —invulnerable because elusive."[46] The first ship in which Conrad sailed out of England was named *Skimmer of the Sea*[47] which name Conrad gave to Captain Hagberd's ship in "Tomorrow."[48]

expression to a self-debasing gesture which, as Moser has noted, is typical of a number of Conrad's male characters.[r/52] When he essays an amorous advance she recoils in "undisguised panic. She panted, showing her teeth, and the hate of strength, the disdain of weakness, the eternal preoccupation of sex came out like a toy demon out of a box. 'This is odious!' she screamed."[s/53]

Threading his uncertain path through the confusion of this relationship, Conrad suffered over the writing of this story from the start. "I feel helpless," he wrote in July, "the thing has bewitched me."[55] By October he was complaining, "It has made me ill; I hated while I wrote."[56] One difficulty in particular tormented him—how to end it. In its final form Alvan Hervey impulsively runs off, a gesture which to this writer, at least, appears quite out of character.

That Conrad suffered so keenly over the writing may be explained in part by the fact that he was trying to write about the intimate life of a white man and a white woman, a subject which, as previously noted, may have caused him trouble in the past and was surely destined to do so again. However, there is good reason to suspect that the subject of the story—the breakup of a marriage—was too close to his own discomfort as a married man to permit him to compose with ease and detachment. If Conrad had already displayed restiveness under the yoke of marriage, the sense of being trapped was undoubtedly enhanced when Jessie Conrad became pregnant presumably in mid-April 1897, the very month in which he began to write "The Return." In proposing marriage Conrad announced that there were to be no children (a stipulation which he enforced on most of his fictional characters) and there is no reason to suppose that he had changed his views. His attitude toward this pregnancy was far from joyous. To his friend Sanderson he wrote on July 19, 1897: "There is no other news—unless the information that there is a prospect of some new kind of

[r] Thus in *An Outcast* Willems picks up a kriss thrown down by Aïssa; in "A Smile of Fortune" the Captain retrieves the dropped slipper of Alice Jacobus; in *The Arrow of Gold* M. George gathers up the cigarettes which Rita throws on the floor; and in *The Rescue* D'Alcacer picks up a fan dropped by Edith Travers.

[s] Cf. Felicia's outburst at Renouard's passionate advances in "The Planter of Malata": "Assez! J'ai horreur de tout cela!"[54]

descendant may be looked upon in the light of something new. I am not unduly elated. Johnson [the Doctor] says it may mend Jess' health permanently—if it does not end her. The last he does not say in so many words, but I can see an implication through a wall of words." In the same letter he referred to "The Return" as "too contemptible for words."[57]

Mrs. Conrad's account of her husband's behavior during this time confirms the impression that Conrad was disturbed by the new state of affairs. "I had a very clear notion that my husband was not exactly pleased . . . it seemed to me that I had played him false, as it were. . . . I wondered what would happen afterwards. Could I continue to fill this post of general guardian of my husband's peace and do my duty to my child? I saw quite plainly that my allegiance must be somewhat divided."[58] She strongly suspected, moreover, that in order to safeguard his share of that allegiance, he would frequently "indulge in a fit of gout." During this pregnancy, she added, "I had perforce to be mostly nurse."[59] His thinly veiled displeasure over the prospect of a baby who would usurp his position burst out into frank rage on one occasion when he threatened to shoot some school children who were stealing fruit from the Conrad orchard.[60] It is more than likely that this murderous anger was displaced upon the anonymous school children from the real thief of his "fruit"—the expected baby.[t]

Such hostility toward a pregnancy is typical of those husbands who, having experienced an unsatisfactory early relationship with their own mothers, for one reason or another, are constantly seeking to be the only child of a loving, nourishing woman. Characteristically the subject of food and eating occupies a central position in the feelings and behavior of such men, who may react to a wife's pregnancy—seemingly threatening their position of "only child"—with a show of demanding helplessness, with an intensification of previous idiosyncrasies concerning eating, or with the

[t] The apparent symbolic importance of fruit for Conrad, and its psychological association with the blissful unchallenged union of mother and child, has been discussed in Chapter II.

This theme of the newborn baby who robs his father of a woman's love is depicted with stark clarity in the story "Amy Foster."

appearance of a variety of gastrointestinal disturbances, ranging from loss of appetite or gluttony to ulcer of the stomach. Moreover, insofar as the emotional problems ignited by the new life circumstance are usually repetitions of childhood experiences, it is often possible to discover a history of "stomach" disturbances in the remote past, e.g., feeding or digestive problems.

Husbands fearing that the advent of a child will unseat their position in their wife-mother's affection may display a variety of reactions: first, an overtly hostile attitude toward the mother or her unborn child which may attain the intensity of a matricidal or infanticidal impulse or fantasy. Since the latter are rarely acceptable as conscious thoughts they may be displaced upon other, indifferent objects, or experienced as their opposite, namely, as a fear lest something untoward befall the pregnant wife or her unborn child. Such husbands often display evidence of an identification with the expected baby, manifested by an intensification of habitual child-like behavior, by a conspicuous hypochondriasis, or by a tendency to become accident prone. Under the same circumstances other men seek to resolve their dilemma by identifying themselves with the pregnant wife. (It should be noted, however, that such identifications, and indeed the total negative attitude toward a woman's pregnancy, may originate in pregnancy wishes residing in the man himself.) Finally there are men who seek to run away, hoping to find in some unencumbered soul a suitable substitute for the "unfaithful" spouse.

It is not difficult to discover the application of these observations to Conrad who, anticipating Jessie's confinement, wrote that he envisaged "toutes sortes de désastres."[60a] His wife, who described herself as the "mother to an overgrown baby,"[61] gave a number of examples of his arbitrariness concerning food, including one occasion when he sent her out late at night to fetch a cauliflower to appease his pica-like craving,[62] and another when he commented on her efforts with, "A damn rotten tea, let me tell you, my dear, a damn rotten tea."[63] Through his recurring bouts of gout embellished by hypochondriasis, moreover, he succeeded in being nursed like a baby.[u] The suspicion that he also unconsciously identified himself

[u] He once claimed that moving his fingers caused an acceleration of his

with his pregnant wife gains support from his letters describing the difficulty he was having in writing "The Return," which contain frequent references to the number of *months* occupied in completing it. After telling Sanderson of Jessie's pregnancy in a letter of July 19, 1897, he added, "This attitude does not contribute to my peace of mind—and now, when I think of it, there is nothing very shocking in my not being able to finish a short story in three months."[66] To Garnett he wrote later, "It has embittered five months of my life. I hate it,"[67] and on another occasion he referred to it as "A heavy trial."[68] Still later he wrote to Garnett, "And the question presents itself: is it to be put away in an unhonored grave or sent into the world?"[v/69]

In view of the probable meaning which this story contained for him, it is hardly surprising that its production was neither smooth nor a labor of love. It would also seem that his comment, "I hated while I wrote," referred no less to Jessie's creation than his own. Like Willems he undoubtedly foresaw his wife with a child as one of "those encumbrances of life."

As the time approached for the baby's arrival Conrad's thoughts carried a note of mournful gloom. " 'Put the tongue out,' why not?" he wrote to Cunninghame Graham on January 14, 1898.

> One ought to really. And the machine will run on all the same. The question is whether the fatigue of the muscular exertion is worth the transient pleasure of indulged scorn. On the other hand one may ask whether scorn, love, or hate are justified in the face of such shadowy illusions. . . . Life knows us not and we do not know life,—we don't know even our own thoughts. . . . Faith is a myth and beliefs shift like mists on the shore;

---

pulse, itself a remarkable phenomenon, and an observation that could only be made by someone given to obsessional self-examination.[64] Mrs. Conrad insisted that "in nine out of ten cases . . . irritation produced the gout."[65]

[v] If during his wife's first pregnancy his infanticidal impulses were expressed by means of displacement upon the fruit-stealing children, during the second pregnancy he appears to have dealt with them through the medium of artistic sublimation, for it was during those months that he composed *The Secret Agent*, a story in which a "father" causes a small child to be blown to bits. See Chapter X.

thoughts vanish: words, once pronounced, die: and the memory of yesterday is as shadowy as the hope of tomorrow . . .

In an appended postscript, he added, "This letter misses this morning's post because an infant of male persuasion arrived and made such a row that I could not hear the postman's whistle. It's a fine commentary upon this letter. But salvation lies in being illogical."[70]

In light of his mood on the threshold of Jessie's confinement, it should not be wondered at that when she went into labor and he was sent to fetch the obstetrician, Conrad, assuring the doctor that there was no hurry whatever, leisurely sat down to accept the offer of a second breakfast. When Jessie later remonstrated with him for his disregard for her comfort and welfare he became annoyed, she wrote, declaring himself "very displeased with me, and adding that my behavior was 'most unseemly and disturbing.' "[71] Some notion of Conrad's seeming last ditch efforts to deny the reality of the situation is conveyed by an account of his reaction to the baby's first cry. "Send that child away at once; it will disturb Mrs. Conrad," he is supposed to have told the housemaid, who replied, "It's your own child, sir."[72]

Needless to say the birth of Borys on January 15, 1898, was not followed by any perceptible diminution in Conrad's manifestly ambivalent feelings toward the child. On the contrary, his behavior reflected an intensification of his desire to escape from the domestic trap in which he found himself encased. More gout followed and by the end of January he was writing to Cunninghame Graham: "Last night a heavy gale was blowing and I lay awake thinking that I would give ever so much for being at sea, the soul of some patient faithful[w] ship standing up to it . . . and no land anywhere within a thousand miles. Wouldn't I jump at a command if some literary shipowner suddenly offered it to me!"[73] Failing to find such a means of escape from his wife and baby he behaved at times as if they didn't exist. In anticipation of a visit to Stephen and Cora Crane, Conrad suggested to the latter that as a means of transporting the two-week-old Borys—"the ominous baby," he called him—"perhaps a strong iron cage would be the most effec-

[w] Not like the "faithless" Jessie.

tive expedient."[74] To Jessie he gave strict orders that during the trip there was to be no indication that there was any connection between himself and the mother and baby. In the train compartment he buried himself behind his newspaper. When the baby cried and refused to be comforted, "I caught a glance of warning directed at me from over the top of the paper," wrote Jessie Conrad. "All my efforts to soothe the infant proved unavailing, and the whole carriage re-echoed with his lusty howls. The paper was flung aside and from all sides came murmurs of consternation and sympathy for him—the only man; the stranger in the carriage," Joseph Conrad, the infant's father.[75] No less conspicuous than his irritability is the evidence of mental depression. "An extreme weariness oppresses me," he wrote a few weeks after Borys' birth. "It seems as though I had seen and felt everything since the beginning of the world. I suspect my brain to be yeast and my backbone to be cotton."[76]

Not long thereafter he put his desire to escape into action and left his home to stay with his friend Garnett for a while. When Jessie, alone with the child, wired him that she was afraid of being alone and unprotected, he arranged for them to stay nearer to Garnett's home. Upon their arrival he hastily installed them in their new quarters and promptly dashed off, complaining that he was already late to dinner at his friend's home, where he continued to remain for an additional week before rejoining his wife and child.[77]

Difficulties in writing the vexing *The Rescuer* continued to harass him. In March he wrote to Garnett of being in bed—"this beastly nervous trouble"—adding, "I ask myself sometimes whether I am bewitched, whether I am the victim of an evil eye?" His pent-up emotions appeared near the bursting point as he continued: "Sometimes it takes all my resolution and power of self-control to refrain from hitting my head against the wall. I want to howl and foam at the mouth, but I daren't do it for fear of waking that baby," he added, avoiding the possessive pronoun which would acknowledge whose baby he was complaining about.[x/78]

[x] In some respects it would seem that Conrad never succeeded entirely in

Thwarted in his desire to escape by taking to the high seas, Conrad now once again achieved a token release from his oppressive surroundings through the creation of a stirring retrospective tale of the sea, "Youth." In a spirit of obvious relief from the agonies of the unfinished love story, *The Rescuer*, Conrad evoked an exultant and poetic memory of an exciting and adventurous past, when, in a diminutive universe—the gallant and ill-fated ship *Judea*—a band of heroic men, unencumbered by the importunities of women's passion or the howls of babies, struggle valiantly against the raw and savage forces of nature to emerge triumphant and free.[y]

Meanwhile, during this first year of Borys' life, Conrad resumed his efforts to obtain a ship's command. To his friend Cunninghame Graham he wrote in July of being "almost frantic with the longing to get away."[79] However, despite the efforts of friends and his own inquiries among shipowners, nothing came of it. By autumn the urgency of this desire appears to have abated considerably. "I feel less hopeless about things and particularly about the damned thing called *The Rescue*,"[z] he wrote to Garnett at the end of September,[80] and a few weeks later he wrote to Cunninghame Graham, "The fact is from novel writing to skippering *il y a trop de tirage.* This confounded literature has ruined me completely. There is a time in the affairs of men when the tide of folly taken at the flood sweeps them to destruction. *La mer monte, cher ami; la mer monte,* and the phenomenon is not worth a thought."[81]

This seemingly abrupt about-face deserves attention, for there is no indication that the forces impelling him to flee his wife and child had lessened perceptibly, nor were his difficulties in making headway with the exasperating *The Rescue* significantly diminished.

---

reconciling himself to Borys' existence, as will become evident in a later chapter.

[y] One element in the tale, however, which links the recollected past to the present time is the device of a narrator, Marlow, introduced for the first time in Conrad's fiction. For the narrator tells his story in London and his occasional interruptions serve to recall both writer and reader to the hard reality of the present moment. From now on Marlow was to become a familiar figure in Conrad's writings.

[z] The revised title of *The Rescuer*.

The suspicion arises that a new element had entered into Conrad's life on land which made it more tolerable and which reconciled him in fact to abandoning the sea for good. Such a suspicion requires little confirmation: at the beginning of September 1898, while staying with the Garnetts, the Conrads were introduced to Ford Madox Hueffer and his wife Elsie.[82] The meeting was an eventful one, destined to exert an effect upon them all. For Conrad it marked the beginning of a relationship which not only influenced his literary career, but brought to him emotional satisfactions which clearly played a role in diminishing the urgency of his craving to return to the sea. Nor were these satisfactions unreciprocated, for Hueffer, too, was a chronically troubled man, then chafing under the yoke of marital burdens. Like Conrad, he too had recently become a father (his daughter Christina was born in July 1897), and like Conrad he seems to have responded to this new role by manifestations of restlessness and an itching to get away from his wife and child.[83] In July 1898 the Hueffers had left their home, Pent Farm, and had moved to Surrey in order to live near the Garnetts, and it was here, two months later, that the two fugitive fathers met.

Like Lingard who makes a protégé and partner of the Dutchman Willems when that disenchanted husband finds himself cast adrift from "those encumbrances of his life" (his wife Joanna and their baby), Ford Madox Hueffer came to the rescue of the disgruntled Conrad, offering him the hand of friendship, and in time establishing with him a literary partnership in a country where, if he did not possess the sole monopoly of his craft, he at least wielded a considerable influence among the literate "natives." Like the fictional partnership in *An Outcast,* Conrad's friendship with Hueffer ended in an atmosphere of bitterness and enmity, but not before it had bestowed on Conrad a steadying hand and had nourished his art with its enriching fruit.

A consideration of some of the psychological undercurrents which permeated this interesting liaison will be presented in the following chapter.

VII · The Rescue

In 1868, at the age of twenty-three, Dr. Franz Hüffer, a German music scholar and an authority on the troubadours of French Provence, left his native Münster to settle in England where, as Dr. Francis Hueffer, he became an esteemed music critic. Not long after his arrival he married Catherine, second daughter of Ford Madox Brown, the well-known Pre-Raphaelite painter and intimate of the celebrated Rossettis.[a] Their oldest child, Ford Hermann Hueffer, born on December 17, 1873, was reared in an atmosphere rich in artistic and intellectual achievement and graced by a seemingly endless array of Victorian celebrities. Encircled by such a dazzling environment, and advised by his father that if he could not reach comparable heights he might "just as well not cumber the earth,"[1] little Ford could hardly have felt cherished and loved merely for being himself. At the age of eight this "patient but extremely stupid young donkey,"[2] as his father called him, was sent away to boarding school, and since Dr. Hueffer, an ardent champion of Richard Wagner, was usually in Bayreuth during the summer holidays, Ford grew up experiencing little contact with him, recalling him mainly as a man of enormous stature (which he was not) with a great red beard.[3] Nor did Ford seem to fare much better with his mother, a painter like her own father, who supposedly had sacrificed her career for her family, and who is said to have manifested an undisguised partiality for her younger son, Oliver.[b]

Thus, despite his illustrious origins—or perhaps because of them—Ford apparently grew up harboring a highly fragile sense of personal worth and personal identity, a condition no doubt responsible for a lifelong penchant for elaborate and conflicting confabulations concerning his past history.

[a] Brown's oldest daughter Lucy married William Rossetti, a brother of Dante Gabriel and Christina.

[b] Following her husband's death at the age of forty-three, when Ford was about fifteen, she became ill and was "away" for quite some time, during which period her sons lived with her father, Ford Madox Brown, and her daughter Juliet was sent to live with the William Rossettis.[4]

This *folie de grandeur* manifested itself in an assortment of claims concerning his educational and other distinctions; he asserted that he was a graduate of both Eton and Westminster,[5] and he once pointed out a table in a Paris café where he said he had written his thesis for the Sorbonne,[6] although his precise connection with that institution is a matter of considerable uncertainty.[7] He also claimed to have been an officer in the Bonn Hussars,[8] and in *Return to Yesterday* he mentioned a number of improbable duels he had fought—or almost fought—and claimed one of them took place at Bonn after another student trod on his dog's tail.[9] Hueffer could "lie most pleasantly," wrote Norman Douglas.[10] Similar motivations presumably led to a recurring tendency to change the name he chose to go by. Born Ford Hermann Hueffer,[11] he was provided with two new names, Joseph and Leopold, when at the age of eighteen he was baptized in the Roman Catholic Church. To his other names he added Madox.[12] Thereafter he was known by various combinations—he once claimed he was the German *Baron Hüffer von Aschendrof*[13]—until after the First World War, when he dropped his surname and became Ford Madox Ford for the rest of his life. Parallel with these shifting identities or *personae*, were the instabilities of his mode of life, of his relations with women, and of his mental health. "What he is really or if he is really," wrote H. G. Wells, "nobody knows now and he least of all; he has become a great system of assumed personas and dramatized selves. His brain is an exceptionally good one and when first he came along, he had cast himself for the role of a very gifted scion of the Pre-Raphaelite stem, given over to artistic purposes and a little undecided between music, poetry, criticism, the Novel, Thoreau-istic horticulture and the simple appreciation of life."[14] At the time of the initial meeting with Conrad, the twenty-four-year-old Hueffer, who had already published a number of works, was occupied in the horticultural phase of his shifting interests—he was growing potatoes and lettuce.

His emotional instability was marked by a number of depressions during his adult life, and on one occasion he announced his intention of taking his own life.[15] He suffered, moreover, from a variety of nervous complaints including phobias and writer's cramp,[16] and during the First World War advanced the fanciful notion that he had been subjected to gas poisoning, not in France, but back home in England, where some noxious fumes which he had inadvertently enclosed within his portmanteau on the battlefield escaped when he unpacked his belongings.[17] It is not surprising that Florence, a central figure in his novel *The Good Soldier,* is a malingerer who feigns heart disease throughout her marriage.

Hueffer's inability to achieve lasting and gratifying relationships and his restless quest in search of new ones were particularly evident in his love life. The collapse of his marriage was followed by a liaison with the writer Violet Hunt, 11 years his senior, which was followed in turn by other attachments, including an Australian painter, Stella Bowen, who had a child by him, and Janice Biala, an artist more than 20 years his junior. Miss Bowen declared that personal relationships were not really important to him at all, but that "in order to keep his machinery running he requires to exercise his sentimental talents from time to time upon a new object. It helps to keep him young. It refreshes his ego. It restores his belief in his powers."[18] Goldring notes that "the real 'wife of the bosom' was the art he practiced,"[19] to which should be added, however, that the discovery and promotion of fellow artists was one of Hueffer's conspicuous achievements, and at the same time, an important source of gratification. Both as an editor of periodicals in which he launched the literary careers of more than one of his "finds," and in his personal life, Hueffer displayed a penchant toward playing Pygmalion to inarticulate or unknown castaways. Like other romantics, wrote Violet Hunt, "Ford was . . . tainted with the lust of rescue-work."[20] Although Conrad, to be sure, was no unknown castaway at the time of his initial meeting with Hueffer, he did complain of difficulties in expressing himself fluently in English—"the particular devil that spoils my work for me as quick as I turn it out"—[21] and undoubtedly saw in the native-born Hueffer a means of his achieving a more articulate ease in his adopted literary language. There is little doubt, moreover, that as Baines suggests, he may have looked upon a collaboration with Hueffer as an escape from the relative stagnation which had characterized his literary efforts during the greater part of 1898.[22] The author of *The Rescuer* wanted rescuing.

It is doubtful, however, that these considerations alone would have sufficed to lead to the literary partnership.[c] Indeed, the intimacy which grew up between Conrad and Hueffer and the vehemence of the feelings which it generated in their wives leaves little doubt that the literary aspect of their collaboration was but one facet of a broader emotional attachment. In 1898 Conrad was forty-one, almost old enough to be the father of the twenty-four-year-old Hueffer. Like Hueffer's father, Conrad was a non-practicing Catholic, a European, who wore a prominent beard and who spoke his adopted English tongue with a heavy accent. Although one was a Pole and the other a German, both were well versed in French literature and French was in both cases their second tongue. Both were expatriates who had arrived in England in their early twenties and acquired British citizenship.

If Hueffer found in Conrad physical and other resemblances to the father from whom he had received so little, Conrad in turn wove Hueffer into the fabric of his own past by evoking "memories" of Hueffer which extended far back across the years. Like lovers who enjoy inventing a remote common past he "remembered" seeing the four-year-old blond "Fordie" playing with a shovel and bucket on the beach when the ship *Mavis* first brought Conrad to Lowestoft 20 years before.[23] He also claimed that the sight of one of Hueffer's books at the railroad station in Geneva first caused him to entertain the possibility of writing in English,[24] a "circumstance" which permitted Conrad to regard Hueffer as his literary godfather. Granted that these "recollections" were presented perhaps in but a half-serious vein, they nevertheless convey an impulse to enrich the quality of the relationship by endowing it with a "pre-history." In general when such fantasies arise, they express the wish that the persons involved have always known each other, have partaken in each other's childhood experiences,

[c] During the course of his literary career, both before and after the Hueffer era, Conrad proposed collaboration with at least four other writers: Madame Poradowska, Stephen Crane, Edward Noble, and Richard Curle.

and thus, possessing a virtually common origin, share in a common identity, or one-ness.[d]

The nature of the personalities of Conrad and Hueffer undoubtedly facilitated such a conception of a common identity, for aside from whatever qualities Conrad might have held in common with Hueffer's father, there were other aspects of his nature which more closely resembled Hueffer himself. Perhaps the most compelling reason for their mutual attraction lay in the sense of isolation shared by both men. In his memoir on Conrad, Hueffer recounted an anecdote which illustrates both this common feeling of alienation from the environment and the nearly telepathic quality with which they liked to endow their relationship: "Once we were sitting in the front row of the stalls at the Empire. . . . On that night . . . there was at least one clergyman with a number of women: ladies is meant—. And during the applause by the audience of some *too* middle class joke one of us leaned over towards the other and said: 'Doesn't one feel lonely in this beastly country!'—Which of us it was that spoke neither remembered after: the other had been at that moment thinking so exactly the same thing."[25]

Both men were evidently seeking for a firm human relationship of a parent-child configuration to compensate for weak, frustrating, and unstable childhood attachments. As a consequence both were attracted to women who were either strikingly older or much younger than themselves, toward whom both men engaged in active and passive fantasies of rescue, which theme, incidentally, occupies a conspicuous position both in their separate fictional creations and in the books they wrote together. Other points of similarity between them included emotional instability, nervousness, hypochondriasis, gastrointestinal disturbances, a tendency toward chronic depression, and a preoccupation with the subject of suicide. According to Goldring they even shared queer sensations of being no longer in this world. Suffering from a kindred sense of inner instability and weakness, each pursued in his own fashion a pattern of life designed to establish an impressive imprint of personal identity.

[d] The relevance of these observations to the fantasy of the "Family Romance" will be discussed in a later chapter.

At the time of their first meeting, in the early autumn of 1898, they possessed an additional common bond: an undisguised desire to escape from a wife and her new-born child. It is not surprising, therefore, that the picture of their relationship, as described by Hueffer in his memoir on Conrad, is that of two bachelors, who when not discussing Gustave Flaubert, the *mot juste*, the *progression d'effet*, and other aspects of literary technique, played dominoes and engaged in the possibly significant pastime of shooting rats with a rifle.[26] Hueffer's book is noteworthy, moreover, for its complete omission of any reference to his friend's wife. Needless to say the banding together of these two men was accompanied by various crosscurrents of antagonism, of which the most conspicuous manifestations concerned Hueffer and Jessie Conrad. In their frequent conflicts, however, the latter asserted that her husband almost invariably sided with his new friend, while treating her as a servant whom he would sometimes order to leave the room.[27] To her chagrin he would also neglect to consult her before inviting the Hueffers to join them on holidays.[28] On one of these joint vacations, however, when Borys became seriously ill, Hueffer's behavior elicited Jessie's admiration and praise: "He was always at hand to shift my small invalid, fetch the doctor and help with the nursing."[29] Evidently this was a moment when Hueffer, presented with an opportunity to play the rescuer, was at his best and could display those qualities of resourcefulness and strength which were conspicuously wanting in Conrad, who, under such circumstances, far from lightening the load, could generally be counted on to augment it by joining the ranks of the helpless and the disabled. However, when Hueffer's "lust for rescue work" was frustrated for lack of helpless or needy subjects, the tensions between him and Jessie broke out anew. During her second pregnancy, as will be pointed out later, Hueffer, the erstwhile "mother's helper," behaved toward her in a manner that she found baiting and hostile.[30]

With Hueffer, Conrad also shared confidences about the state of his health which he described with an exposure of intimate detail that recalls his correspondence with his Uncle Thaddeus and with Marguerite Poradowska. Thus in one letter he wrote of being "beastly seedy with cold, cough and piles and a derangement of the bowels.[31] No doubt paralysis isn't far off," he added, conveying the same note of hypochondria and gloom that had once pervaded his letters to his "Aunt." Also reminiscent of his correspondence with her was another line written to Hueffer: "I want you and have wanted you for some time."[32]

It would appear then that during this phase of their relationship Conrad transferred upon Hueffer attitudes, feelings, and desires which at an earlier time had been directed toward persons who had occupied the position of substitute parents. One such desire, which not so long before he had imparted to Madame Poradowska and which was now to gain renewed expression with her seeming successor, was the wish to enter into a literary partnership. It has already been suggested that the earlier proposal for collaboration was motivated not only by a wish to ensure the publication of *Almayer's Folly*, but also by a desire to achieve a closer emotional bond with her, even at the cost of surrendering his identity as the sole author of the book and of accepting the obscure position of the junior partner of a strong and influential woman. It is possible that similar considerations prompted Conrad's proposal to join literary forces with the quasi-maternal Hueffer, for whatever benefits emerged from the partnership certainly did not lie in the quality of their joint literary efforts, none of which enhanced the reputation of either author. In all they produced three works together, none of which has enjoyed high critical acclaim. On the contrary, far from profiting by it, these works seem to have suffered from their dual origin which, placing these books in the category of curiosities, constitutes their main reason for survival.[e]

The first of these ventures, *The Inheritors*, written largely by

[e] "Collaboration, where a work of intelligence is concerned," wrote Théophile Gautier, "is something quite incomprehensible. . . . Just imagine Prometheus with a collaborator seated in front of him, watching his struggles as the sharp-beaked vulture skillfully probes his heart and liver, and not only watching, but making notes in pencil on a small sheet of paper!"[33] Similar sentiments were expressed by Edward Noble, another writer to whom Conrad proposed collaboration: "Collaboration was a goddess I did not understand, nor could I worship her. It seemed that worship must entail sacrifice, for one of us, of some part of his individuality."[34]

Hueffer, is a kind of allegorical romance. Interspersed with elements of political satire, it is the story of the author's infatuation with a beautiful girl who is a member of a sect, "The Fourth Dimensionists." The latter, devoid of all ideals, conscience, ethics, tradition, sympathy for suffering, capacity for love, reverence for life, and feeling for art, are committed by means of intrigue and callous trickery to inherit the earth. It goes without saying that these are not qualities likely to be compatible with requited love and the author is ultimately destroyed by his passion for the bewitching girl.[f] She is "like Fate; like the abominable Fate that desolates the whole length of our lives; that leaves of our hopes, of our plans, nothing but a hideous jumble of fragments like those of statues smashed by hammers; the senseless, inscrutable, joyless Fate that we hate, and that debases us forever and ever."[35] "All your misery," says the girl, "your heartache comes from love. If you had not loved you would not be wretched now."[36]

In short, the book presents a picture of the ruthless destructiveness of a woman, who is evidently regarded by the authors as an epitome of her sex. Despite the paucity of Conrad's contribution to the work, its pages evoke familiar reflections of the recurrent misogyny in his own works, in which he was evidently seconded by his fellow-sufferer Hueffer.[g] The fact that Elsie Hueffer was pregnant once more during the writing of *The Inheritors* may have supplied additional fuel to its denunciation of the woman, who, like Fate, "leaves of our hopes . . . nothing but a hideous jumble of fragments." Nor can it be without significance that it was to Borys and Christina, the seeming source of the grievances of both authors, that the book was dedicated.

The second collaboration, *Romance*, begun in 1900, was dedicated to the women who presumably had caused all the "misery and heartache," Elsie and Jessie. Developed out of an unfinished

[f] An incestuous relationship between the "author" and the girl is hinted at since she poses as his sister.

[g] Thus, reminiscent of some of Marlow's intemperate comments on women in *Chance*, Hueffer (then known as Ford) wrote in *Women and Men* (1923) of the "monstrous regiment of women," banded together "in a sort of freemasonry to extort always more and more money from the unfortunate camel who bears them all upon his back."[37]

story of Hueffer's, originally entitled "Seraphina," *Romance* is an undistinguished adventure yarn filled with piracy, intrigue, and photo-finish escapes. The familiar theme of rescue of a beloved woman, Seraphina, constitutes the central theme of the story. Her own portrayal is entirely unconvincing, and she remains throughout the narrative a pure, devoted, and utterly lifeless cliché.[h] Indeed, as Moser has pointed out in comparing the lovers of *Romance* with those in "Falk," although they have three long scenes together, circumstances invariably arise which virtually prevent their talking to one another, an observation which would suggest that the discomfort Conrad experienced in dealing with love in his own stories crept into his collaborative ventures as well.[39] The publication of the book in 1903 met with a disappointing reception by the critics.

Meanwhile tensions were high and tempers short in the households of the two authors. Apparently much of the misery experienced by these four people found expression in physical illness, in accidents, and in hypochondriacal complaints. While Conrad suffered from gout and was prophesying his imminent paralysis, Hueffer became a victim of a so-called nervous dyspepsia (a condition said to be baffling to the specialists) which was characterized by an inability to tolerate any food. In November 1903, Elsie Hueffer, already a partial invalid, fell down a flight of stone steps and broke her arm.[40] Three months later Jessie Conrad suffered a fall in the street causing injuries to her knees from which she never again recovered and which left her, like Mrs. Hueffer, a semi-invalid for the rest of her life.[41] Not long after Elsie's fall, Hueffer suffered a so-called nervous breakdown, which led to his leaving his home in order to seek help in German spas in the company of his mother.[42] The ensuing years were marked by a steady deterioration of Hueffer's marriage and its ultimate replacement in 1908 or 1909, by his liaison with Violet Hunt. Noteworthy is the fact that the develop-

[h] In light of Conrad's preoccupation with "armed" women it is not surprising that she is labeled "The Girl with the Dagger." In contrast to the suggestion of an incest element in *The Inheritors*, in *Romance* the love relationship, as noted earlier, is explicitly exogamous: "How I loved her! . . . this woman of another race, of another world. . . ."[38]

ment of the latter coincided closely in time with a quarrel between Hueffer and Conrad which soon led to their estrangement.

It would not be long before Conrad was writing about Hueffer: "His conduct is *impossible*. . . . He's a megalomaniac who imagines that he is managing the Universe and that everybody treats him with the blackest ingratitude. A fierce and exasperated vanity is hidden under his calm manner which misleads people . . . he is behaving like a spoilt kid—and not a nice kid either."[43]

Ostensibly the quarrel grew out of Conrad's failure to contribute further installments of his reminiscences[i] which were being published under Hueffer's editorship in *The English Review*,[j/44] but it is difficult to accept at face value this explanation as either the sole or the major reason for Conrad's seeming sudden disenchantment with Hueffer, whose "fierce and exasperated vanity" could hardly have become revealed to him for the first time in the year 1909. Hueffer's idiosyncrasies must have been as well known to him as they had been to Stephen Crane, who many years before had written to a friend: "You must not be offended by Hueffer's manner. He patronizes Mr. James. He patronizes Mr. Conrad. Of course he patronizes me and he will patronize Almighty God when they meet, but God will get used to it, for Hueffer is all right."[47] Indeed in a letter to H. G. Wells in 1905, Conrad referred to Hueffer as "a sort of lifelong habit—of which I am not ashamed, because he is a much better fellow than the world gives him credit for."[48] Under the circumstances it would seem most unlikely that it was because of his friend's "manner" that Conrad conceived a sudden hostility to him. On the contrary, like the rupture of most intimate relationships, this one must be examined in the light of its under-

[i] Later published as *A Personal Record*.

[j] In a letter to Galsworthy,[45] Conrad explained that the reason for his action was that "A Russian has got hold of the E.R. and I cannot contribute any more." The "Russian" was Dr. David Soskice, a brother-in-law of Hueffer, who hardly deserved to be regarded as the epitome of Russian imperial oppression, for like Conrad's father he had been imprisoned by the Czarist regime, and would on those grounds at least seem entitled to Conrad's sympathy. A more likely cause of Conrad's antipathy to this man may have been the fact that he was engaged in assisting Mrs. Garnett in her translations of the writings of Conrad's *bête noir*, Feodor Dostoevski.[46]

lying emotional basis and in terms of those happenings which made its continuance untenable.

In seeking to contribute to a further understanding of these questions it may prove instructive to refer at this point to the third collaborative venture of Conrad and Hueffer, *The Nature of a Crime*. Although it was not published in book form until 1924, the actual writing occurred some time prior to their estrangement.[k] This little book is not a novel but a series of letters written to a married woman with whom the "writer" has been in love for over seven years. The author confesses to her that he is in imminent danger of being discovered to have committed a fraud as trustee of young Edward Burden, a man who is soon to be married. Two choices now lie before him; either to commit suicide by biting the glass covering of his poison-bearing ring or to set Burden's affairs in order. He will do the latter only if his lady love consents to be his. Thus his fate is in her hands and he awaits her "verdict." What her decision is the reader never learns, but one thing is quite clear: this is indeed a strange image of adult love, for what the letter writer seeks is not physical possession but her "consent to be mine to the extent of sharing our thoughts alone." Boasting that they "could have broken the rules of the game" by deceiving her husband and going off together, he reminds her that they rejected such an action "because we sought the difficulty which sanctifies. . . . For is it not a thing to be very proud of—to be able to say that, for a whole lifetime, one has abstained from that which one most desired?" This "sanctification" of self-denial has apparently gone even further, for far from destroying her husband the author indicates that he has been secretly weaning her husband from drug addiction.

Since sexual intimacy is evidently not an element in this love, it is some other goal which prompts the writer to declare, "I cannot live without you any longer," and "unless I can have you I must die." Yet "in dying I surrender to you," he adds, "and thus, for the inner self of myself, death is no ending, but the commencement of who knows what tortures . . . what I seek is only forgetfulness of

[k] The precise date of the writing is unknown. Herndon believes it was written in 1908,[49] although Baines suggests it may have been even earlier.[50]

you, or some sort of eventual and incomprehensible union with you . . . hardly at all, I think, a union of the body, but a sort of consciousness of our thoughts proceeding onwards together. That we may find in the unending Afterwards."[51]

Despite the seeming inconsistencies and contradictions, the essential theme is that of eternal union, and thus, by implication, dying together. In view of this *Liebestod* motif, it is not surprising that the narrative contains pointed references to Wagner's *Tristan und Isolde*. Having just returned from a performance of that opera the author writes, "We are held—simply by the idea of a love philtre—it's that alone that interests us, that performs the miracle . . . we see a vision of a state of mind in which morality no longer exists: we are given a respite, a rest: an interval in which no standard of conduct oppresses us." This "state of mind in which morality no longer exists," in stark variance with the sentiment that one may be proud for having "abstained from that which one most desired," points up the sharp moral conflict which permeates these letters. Conscience indeed is a conspicuous *leit-motif* of this little book, this confession of theft and fraud.

The true identity of the beloved woman is not hard to discover. As the "loved woman of the first cry that broke the silence"[52] she is a symbolic mother with whom the "writer" aspires to attain an "eventual and incomprehensible union." Anticipating Conrad's later characterization of Rita de Lastaola, the "author" exclaims, "you are of all time."[53]

The Nature of a Crime appeared originally under the pseudonym of "Baron Ignatz von Aschendrof" in 1909 in the April and May numbers of *The English Review*. It is generally acknowledged that Conrad's contribution to the work was slight, and there is little difficulty in recognizing in it the hand of Hueffer, for the pseudonym is almost identical with the name he was later to use in attempting to legalize his liaison with Violet Hunt: "Baron Hüffer von Aschendrof."[54] Another apparent allusion in the story to this phase of Hueffer's personal life concerns the matter of rescue from suicide. In the former the heroine is given the power of saving her lover from taking his own life; according to Miss Hunt, when she called on Hueffer one summer day in 1909, she arrived just in time to prevent his swallowing a fatal dose of poison.[55] What is arresting about this parallel between fact—if indeed it is fact—and fiction is that the writing of the story *preceded* the "real" event, suggesting that in the real or fancied rescue by Miss Hunt, Hueffer was living out a pre-existing fantasy of being saved from death by a woman.

As was the case with Conrad, the idea of being rescued from death was not a new one for Hueffer. During the years 1903-1906, when he was seeking "nerve cures" in various European spas, he apparently entertained the notion that his death was imminent, and informed his physicians to that effect. Like Florence in *The Good Soldier*, he believed he had some "weakness of the heart" although he lived on for nearly another 35 years. What is of particular significance about the quest for health of this thirty-three-year-old man is that he left his wife and children and traveled about in the company of his mother, as if her presence, creating the illusion of childhood regained, might succeed in warding off the specter of death. Under the circumstances it is hardly surprising that when he met the woman who allegedly saved him from suicide some years later, he immediately identified her with his mother. "I've just met a Miss Violet Hunt," he is supposed to have told Goldring. "She says she was at school with my mother and used to see me in my perambulator."[56] But Goldring points out that while it was true that Mrs. Francis Hueffer and Violet were educated at the same school their difference in age made it impossible for them to have been there at the same time. Hueffer's misleading remark, therefore, must have been based on a wish to view Violet Hunt, 11 years his senior, as a *contemporary* and alter ego of his mother. Another effort to create the same illusion accounts for his additional remark that Violet used to see him in his pram, i.e., when he was a baby. Whether true or not, it is possible to discern here the same efforts to reconstruct a common past that Conrad made in his "recollection" of "Fordie" at the age of four. But the common past which Hueffer was creating aimed at establishing a mother-infant tableau of Violet Hunt and himself, a tableau already anticipated in the writing of *The Nature of a Crime*. That the latter contains recurring allusions to *Tristan und Isolde* is not surprising, moreover, when it is recalled that Hueffer's father was an enthusiastic champion of Richard Wagner.[l]

There is yet another aspect of *The Nature of a Crime* which seems to bear upon Hueffer's personal life, namely the matter of obligation toward a younger man—Burden. Knowing the propensity of the real authors for logomachy, it may be that they chose the name to identify him as "a young burden," that is, someone for whom an older person is obliged to assume reluctant responsibility.[m] In light of Hueffer's childhood history it is conceivable that Burden refers to his younger brother, Oliver, who, according to Hueffer, was "the sparkling jewel of the family whilst I was its ugly duckling."[58] Oliver, says Goldring, "seems to have had all those qualities of humour and gaiety which enable a man to steal a horse and get away with it. Ford, on the other hand, could never so much as look over a hedge without provoking an outburst of denunciation."[59] As an example of their mother's favoritism Goldring cites an occasion when Oliver stepped on his own pet rabbit and killed it, whereupon Mrs. Hueffer commanded that Ford surrender his own animal to his brother. When Dr. Hueffer was asked by the older boy if this was deemed just, the father replied that in his opinion it was not, but that since his mother had demanded it she was to be obeyed at once, "et plus vite que ça!"[n/60] Although

[l] Aside from the *Liebestod* motif, Wagner's *Tristan* deals with the theme of the rescue of a stricken man by a woman: at some time prior to the action of the opera the wounded Tristan is nursed back to health by Isolde.

[m] Although Herndon connects *The Nature of a Crime* with Hueffer's liaison with Violet Hunt, he also suggests that it may have been inspired by the love affair of Dante Gabriel Rossetti with Mrs. William Morris, née *Burden.* He also points out that the element of drug addiction in the story may be a reflection of the fact that Dante Gabriel, the brother of Hueffer's uncle-by-marriage, William, was addicted to chloral.[57] Whatever the origin of *A Nature of a Crime,* the interpretation of its significance to Hueffer or to Conrad would not be affected.

[n] Whether this story is true or not is less important than the fact that Hueffer presented it as typical of his impression of the state of affairs that prevailed during his childhood. A suggestion of revenge against the obligation to defer to Oliver may be discerned in an episode in 1906, when, persuaded that Edmund Gosse would not print anything of his "at any price," Hueffer submitted one of his poems under the pseudonym "Jane Wardle," and was accepted. "Jane Wardle" was Oliver Hueffer's *nom de guerre.*[61] It

Goldring asserts that "no trace of jealousy, at least on Ford's part, seems ever to have affected their relations," it is difficult to believe that such manifest partiality toward a younger brother could possibly have failed to evoke intense resentment, however deeply it may have been buried.

Characteristically feelings of jealousy toward a favored younger brother or sister and old resentments toward the "faithless" mother who bore them, tend to be revived in adult married life with the advent of a child. It would seem probable that similar considerations prompted Hueffer's disenchantment with his marriage shortly after the birth of Christina, and his spending long hours away from home playing golf[62] and later escaping into the company of Conrad, who, for reasons arising out of his own past, in turn seemed to feel similarly threatened by the arrival of a "young burden."

In his study on Hueffer, Cassell has drawn attention to the recurring theme of the relationship between brothers in his novels, suggesting its origin in the circumstances of Hueffer's childhood.[63] It is no less plausible to suspect that a variation on the same theme, and of a similar genesis, found its way into *The Nature of a Crime*, which book, admittedly written chiefly by Hueffer, concerns the seizure of the undisputed possession of a woman's love.[o]

Such an undisputed possession of a "mother," however, involves not only stealing from younger brothers and kindred rivals, but the removal of her husband—a figurative father—as well. But from this crime of "patricide," the narrator obviously recoils; not only does he refrain from poisoning the lady's husband, he secretly rescues him from the poison to which he is already addicted. It seems, then, that in this story (as in many of Conrad's tales) the hero desires possession of the woman not as an adult sexual being replacing her husband (as Tristan replaces King Mark in the opera) but as one whose aim—"some sort of eventual and incom-

---

should be observed parenthetically that this Achilles-like use of a female pseudonym by a man is most unusual.

[o] It is not without significance that in the narrative the danger of being discovered in his fraud is precipitated by the fact that Burden is about to get married. Hence, a realistic consequence of the writer's stealing would be to ruin the young man's relationship with another woman.

prehensible union"—is to achieve a revival of those blissful days when as an only child he basked within the warmth of a mother's innocent embrace.

Seen in relation to Hueffer, *The Nature of a Crime* presents a patently autobiographical picture, including both a retrospective and an anticipatory commentary on his history. In view of the major theme of the book, it should be recalled, moreover, that unlike Elsie Hueffer, Violet Hunt was not only much older than Hueffer but unencumbered by children. By the same token, the story offers familiar echoes of Conrad's fictional themes, however little of it he may have written. Like Hueffer, Conrad also reacted to the advent of a "young burden," Borys, as if he were a usurper threatening Conrad's position of "only child," and like Hueffer he responded to the new circumstances of his life by seeking to escape. What arrested both men in their moment of flight was their discovery of each other, their recognition of their kindred plight, and their realization of salvation through the establishment of a sympathetic union. So long as they shared a common grievance they enjoyed a harmonious friendship, joined together in common cause.

But suddenly things changed: Hueffer found Violet Hunt and realized—for a time, at least—the fulfillment of this long unanswered yearning for a union with a symbolic mother, unencumbered by other claimants for her love. In the attainment of this goal his need for the supporting friendship of a fellow-suffering ally must have all but vanished: Conrad became expendable. To the latter, Hueffer's new found attachment must have been tantamount to a betrayal, as indeed from a psychological point of view it was.[p] It left him alone once again, without his "life-long habit." Torn, one suspects, between envy, resentment, and disapproval of his late friend's action it would seem likely that he welcomed the opportunity to quarrel with him over something, and the matter of *The English Review* was a convenient screen to conceal his far greater grievance. It is not surprising that in his bitterness he denounced Hueffer as an indulged child reveling in popularity. He wrote to a

[p] Many years later Conrad would again react with fury to his "desertion" by a younger man—the secret marriage of his son Borys. See Chapter XIII.

friend of the reports he had received of Hueffer's "furies, his agonies, his visits to various people of distinguished quality and his general carryings on like a spoilt kid—together with a report of the male and female devotions attending upon his mental and moral convulsions."[q/64] Clearly he was terribly hurt, and although in time he succeeded in replacing Hueffer with another younger man—Richard Curle—it is doubtful whether he ever truly recovered from the loss of Hueffer. Indeed, as will be pointed out later, there is good reason to believe that their estrangement played an important role in the grave mental illness which befell Conrad in the beginning of the year 1910.

And so, the partnership—"our welded collaboration," Conrad had called it[67]—was dissolved, never to be reformed.[r] As far as

[q] This was not the first time Conrad reacted with seeming jealousy and sarcasm to a show of success on Hueffer's part. When the latter went to America in 1906, Conrad wrote to the Galsworthys: "Ford, I guess, is now being entertained in America. I manage to write something nearly every day but it is like a caged squirrel running in his wheel—tired out in the evening and no progress made. It's very mysterious that thing. I feel as if I should like to sit down for a couple of years and meditate [in the skyscraping wigwams of the unpainted savages of the great continent. I hope he'll find the war dances agreeable and soothing to his nerves.] No doubt they'll feast him on intellectual roast dog, too. Perhaps his next book will be written with an eagle's feather."[65] It should be noted that the bracketed portion of this rather bitter letter is omitted from Jean-Aubry's published version.[66]

[r] It must not be supposed that the break with Hueffer was ever complete or final. Even during the latter's liaison with Miss Hunt, Conrad maintained sporadic contact with them, although his attitude seems to have been extremely ambivalent. Miss Hunt recorded receiving several cordial notes from Conrad, and described automobile outings with the Conrads in 1911-12.[68] However, in 1912 Conrad wrote sarcastically to Galsworthy that "The great F. M. H. . . . was here shortly after New Years with the somewhat less great V. H."[69] Yet in the following year he sent a friendly letter to Hueffer concerning a long standing debt of £100 plus interest which Conrad owed him. The letter opens "Mon très Cher" and refers to Violet Hunt as Hueffer's "wife" which she never was. It also contains sentimental allusions to bygone days and closes with "Au revoir. Yours ever."[70] In 1914 Conrad wrote a warm letter of thanks to Miss Hunt—"Chère Madame et Confrère"—who had dedicated her book, *The House of Many Mirrors*, to him.[71] During the following year he sent her a copy of *Victory*.[72] While serving with the B. E. F., Hueffer wrote to Conrad from France on several occasions. One of his letters closes with "God bless you, my dear. Love to Jessie. I hope

their joint literary creations were concerned, this was surely no great loss, but viewed in the broader context of a mutual sympathy and rapport its dissolution appears to have brought about far-reaching consequences, notably upon Conrad's creative artistry. For while it is true that prior to his meeting with Hueffer he had already written a number of works, including an acknowledged masterpiece—*The Nigger of the Narcissus*—there can be no question that the advent of Hueffer marked the beginning of a period of rich productivity during which he created the greater part of that wealth of fiction which has earned for him his position of eminence in English literature. It was during the "Hueffer decade" that he wrote "Heart of Darkness," *Lord Jim*, *Typhoon*, *Nostromo, The Secret Agent, A Personal Record*, "The Secret Sharer," and *Under Western Eyes*, as well as many shorter works, including "Falk," "Amy Foster," and "The End of the Tether." And if after the breakup of his relationship with Hueffer, Conrad continued to create novels which some critics have acclaimed as possessing equal greatness, there are others who have detected a noteworthy deterioration in the quality of the later Conrad. Galsworthy, for one, felt that beginning with the publication of *Chance* in 1913, none of his work, except perhaps "The Secret Sharer" and some parts of *Victory*, "in that late period was up to his exalted mark."[76] This opinion has been more or less endorsed in a later day by Guerard,[77] Hewitt,[78] Moser,[79] and others. Moser too names "The Secret Sharer" as marking the end of that high quality of writing that he terms "major Conrad." Although "The Secret Sharer" was published in 1912,

you have good news of Borys."[73] By 1921, Conrad's debt to Hueffer was still unpaid, which is noteworthy inasmuch as by that time his financial condition was greatly improved. "Thinking hard about it," he wrote Hueffer, "I fancy I may owe you still something," and he enclosed £20, adding, "I have to keep indoors just now but later, perhaps, we could arrange a meeting in town."[74] (One suspects that Conrad may have persisted in his indebtedness as a means of maintaining a subtle tie with Hueffer.) In 1923, again Conrad wrote a very warm letter to Hueffer wishing him well in his new venture, *The Transatlantic Review*, but within a year he was once again denouncing his estranged friend as "a swell-headed creature who seems to imagine that he will sweep all Europe and devastate Great Britain with an eventual collected edition of his own works."[75]

it was completed in the autumn of 1909, the very year which saw the collapse of the Conrad-Hueffer friendship. If one accepts these judgments it would follow that most of Conrad's greatest literary achievements were created during those years when the emotional atmosphere surrounding him was warmed by the inspired breath of Ford Madox Hueffer.

It is not necessary, moreover, to rely on conjecture in proposing that Hueffer exerted a quasi-catalytic effect upon Conrad's creative energy, for Conrad himself told Hueffer, "It is a fact I work better in your home, in touch with your sympathy,"[80] and for all her undisguised hostility toward Hueffer, Jessie Conrad's sense of justice prompted her to state, "*The Mirror of the Sea* owes a great deal to [Hueffer's] ready and patient assistance—not perhaps to the actual writing, but that book would never have come into being if Joseph Conrad had had no intelligent person with whom to talk over these intimate reminiscences."[81]

In light of the partisanship which often invades biography and criticism it is not remarkable that the Hueffer-Conrad controversy has given rise to violent and passionate feelings. Hueffer's biographer Goldring, for example, regards Conrad, "except for two or three of his early novels and short stories" as a "total loss," whose prose is "largely pastiche Flaubert translated into English by someone with no great ease in the use of the language."[82] On the other hand when Hueffer published an account of his contribution to Conrad's literary career, he was denounced as "a pathological liar,"[83] "a fat patronizing slug upon the Conradian lettuce,"[84] and as "a megalomaniac with systematized delusions of grandeur."[85] Yet despite these outraged howls a careful inquiry into the facts of the matter has led Morey to the conclusion that although Hueffer's "impressions may be exaggerated . . . they are essentially true." Morey produces evidence not only of Hueffer's moral and financial support—the latter remaining un-repaid as late as 1921—but also of the probable validity of his claim to have written some 20 pages of the manuscript of *Nostromo*. Morey also calls attention to the interesting fact that on the reverse side of the half-title page of the first edition of *A Set of Six* which listed the works of Conrad, *The Secret Agent* was mentioned as a work of collaboration with Hueffer, which Morey claims is suggestive proof that the latter had a considerable hand in that story.[86] In the Author's Note to *The Secret Agent*, Conrad clearly acknowledges the correctness of Hueffer's claim that he had supplied his friend with the story of the real attempt to blow up the Greenwich Observatory which was fictionalized in the novel.[87] Whether, as Morey suspects, Hueffer's contribution to the writing of the book went beyond this is uncertain, but there is a suggestive allusion to Hueffer's past in the opening pages of the novel. Along with the pornography[88] which Mr. Verloc sells are some "obscure newspapers," one of which, *The Torch*, bears the same name as the anarchist leaflet printed by the Hueffers and their Rossetti cousins when they were children.[s]

Morey cites a number of other services rendered to Conrad by Hueffer: copying the dialogue for Conrad's play "One Day More" (based on his short story "Tomorrow"), assisting in the re-writing of the burned portions of "The End of the Tether," and taking down from dictation portions of *The Mirror of the Sea* and *A Personal Record*. That these latter services transcended the role of an amanuensis is attested to by Conrad himself, who wrote to Hueffer in 1923, "The mere fact that it was the occasion of your putting on me that gentle but persistent pressure which extracted from the depths of my then despondency the stuff of the *Personal Record* would be enough to make its memory dear."[89] In the face of this evidence, there is no reason to doubt Hueffer's word that during one of their collaborations Conrad exclaimed: "By Jove, it's a third person who is writing!"[90]

To the psychoanalyst such manifestations of both literary and spiritual collaboration are arresting, for they carry a hint of a sublimated representation of biological creativity, a hint which is hardly diminished by Hueffer's account of his method of coaxing Conrad to write: "I would manoeuvre him towards writing as the drake manoeuvres the sitting duck back to the nest when she has abandoned her eggs."[t/91] Whether Conrad on his part would have

[s] Other allusions in Conrad's stories to this chapter in Hueffer's life will be noted in Chapter XVII.

[t] Hueffer's simile is particularly striking when compared with Mencken's statement that Mrs. Conrad had denounced Hueffer as "a cuckoo, shame-

accepted this imagery or subscribed to its thinly veiled sexual implications is doubtful; suffice it to say that it is true enough in spirit to discount the importance of assessing the precise literal contribution that Hueffer brought to Conrad's writing. For whether Hueffer did or did not suggest this plot or revise that paragraph is a relatively unimportant question compared with the influence he brought to bear, an influence, which, viewed within the context of the next chapter, might earn for him the title of Conrad's "Secret Sharer."

---

lessly laying eggs in her late husband's nest."[92] Writing of the Hueffer-Conrad collaboration she referred to *Romance* as "the child of their joint fabrication."[93]

VIII · The Secret Sharers

SOON AFTER he had made Conrad's acquaintance, Hueffer suggested to his new friend that he rent Pent Farm, near Aldington in Kent, lately vacated by the Hueffers who had moved to Surrey in order to be near the Garnetts. The Conrads accepted the proposal and a few weeks later moved into the house which was to be their home for the next nine years. Not long thereafter the Hueffers moved again and took a cottage at Aldington, which not only facilitated the literary collaboration of the two men, but established a proximity between them which was to endure for some time.

This change in his physical and human environment was accompanied by an unmistakable lift in Conrad's spirits. His letters, which so recently had been filled with melancholy complaints, now began to manifest a distinct note of hopefulness. Thus on the eve of moving to Pent Farm he wrote to H. G. Wells, "I am writing in a state of jubilation at the thought we are going to be nearer neighbors than I dared to hope a fortnight ago,"[1] and it was not long after this that from his new home he wrote the letter to Cunninghame Graham which heralded his seemingly sudden reconciliation to the life of a literary landlubber. Parallel with this change in mood there was a vigorous thrust of creative energy, for at Pent Farm Conrad seemingly struck a vein rich with the gold of inspiration. Wearying of the literary dystocia occasioned by the vexing *The Rescue*, Conrad once again laid that troublesome story aside, and in December 1898 began to write "Heart of Darkness," which he finished with unaccustomed speed by the beginning of February 1899. It proved to be an achievement of singular importance.

On the surface the book is an account of Conrad's experience in the Congo. Indeed, in his Author's Note, written in 1917, he himself gave it credit for being little more than that: " 'Heart of Darkness' is experience pushed a little (and only very little) beyond the actual facts of the case for the perfectly legitimate, I believe, purpose of bringing it home to the minds and bosoms of the readers."[2] But to even the least perceptive reader this statement must seem unsatisfactory, for like many of his Author's Notes, often written long after the initial publication of the stories, it is clearly an evasion of the subtlety and depth of the work.

There had been a time, however, not long after the publication of the story, when Conrad himself agreed that it had a deeper meaning, for he charged himself with "the fault" of making the character Kurtz "too symbolic or rather symbolic at all."[3] Indeed, for Hewitt "Heart of Darkness" is a typical example of Conrad's ability to "make an appeal at two different levels: the natural and the symbolical."[4] Thus, when telling his audience of the effect upon him of the country and of Kurtz, Marlow says: "It was the farthest point of navigation and the culminating point of my experience,"[5] Conrad is alluding to a voyage "both into the impenetrable darkness of Africa and into the darkness of Marlow's thoughts . . . . We know that what Marlow finds in the heart of the African continent is a darkness which every man may be forced to meet within himself."[6] Clearly, "Heart of Darkness" is far more than "experience pushed a little beyond the actual facts." Unlike anything Conrad had written up to this point, the story is an introspective journey into the self, a daring attempt, in the narrator's words, "to find yourself . . . your own reality . . . what no other man can ever know . . ."[7] Going up that river, says Marlow, the captain of the Congo River steamboat, "was like travelling back to the earliest beginnings of the world."[8]

At the farthermost point in his penetration of the river, Marlow discovers Kurtz, a European who had entered this wilderness "equipped with moral ideas of some sort," which he had memorialized in a scholarly 17-page report written for the "International Society for the Suppression of Savage Customs." In it he noted, among other lofty sentiments, that because of the almost godlike view that the savages took of the white man, "by the simple exercise of our will we can exert a power for good practically unbounded," etc.[a/9] But in the course of his stay in the wilderness,

[a] In his address before the Société de Géographique de Marseille on January 15, 1878, Henry M. Stanley spoke glowingly of the potential benefits that the white man might confer on the African natives, including their spiritual uplift: "When these people behold the white man stricken by ill-

a strange and ominous transformation had taken place in Mr. Kurtz's personality; like a snake shedding its skin, he had cast off all his fine European habits and ideals, revealing a creature whose condition of moral degradation and animal primitivism made him indistinguishable from the savages for whom he had once expressed such touching concern. Having reached this state he amended the sober 17-page report by scrawling across the bottom, "Exterminate all the brutes!"[b]

Mr. Kurtz, observes Marlow, "lacked restraint in the gratification of his various lusts . . . the wilderness had found him out early, and had taken on him a terrible vengeance for the fantastic invasion. I think it whispered to him things about himself which he did not know, things of which he had no conception till he took counsel with this great solitude—and the whisper proved irresistibly fascinating. It echoed loudly within him because he was hollow at the core."[12] Mr. Kurtz was under the spell, "the heavy mute spell of the wilderness—that seemed to draw him to its pitiless breast by the awakening of forgotten and brutal instincts, by the memory of gratified and monstrous passions. . . . This alone had driven him out to the edge of the forest, to the bush, towards the gleam of fires, the throb of drums, the drone of weird incantations; this alone had beguiled his unlawful soul beyond the bounds of permitted aspirations."[13]

These are hardly the thoughts of a man recording his recollections of "experience"; they are the thoughts of a reflective and troubled man, for the narrator of this tale (and of *Lord Jim*), is quite a different person from the Marlow of *Youth*, who interrupts

---

ness, mortally wounded, and dying with the calm and peaceful resignation of a Christian, they wonder what is this Faith that sustains him, whence comes this confidence in a better future."[10] These remarks, widely quoted in the local press, were made on the occasion of Stanley's triumphal arrival in Marseilles, which took place while Conrad was living in that city. See Chapter V, footnote *d*.

[b] Aside from the suggestive allusions to Stanley, the character of Kurtz was apparently based on two other models: Georges Antoine Klein, a French agent of the Société Anonyme Belge pour le Commerce du Haut-Congo, and Major Edmund M. Bartellot, an Englishman noted for his "merciless ferocity" in the Congo.[11]

his fond and wistful reminiscences with asides to his listeners such as, "Pass the bottle"; he is even further removed from his garrulous and misogynous namesake who tells the story of *Chance*, which Conrad finished in 1912. For the narrator of 1899 and 1900 is a thoughtful soul, skeptical, inquiring, and self-doubting—a perceptive and sensitive observer of the human condition.

Fascinated by what he sees in the wilderness, he is at the same time struck by the realization that the potential for a regression to primitive savagery to which Mr. Kurtz had succumbed resides within himself as well. What was shocking about the savages, he declares, was "the suspicion of their not being inhuman—the thought of your own remote kinship with this wild and passionate uproar. Ugly: yes, it was ugly enough; but if you were man enough you would admit to yourself that there was in you just the faintest trace of a response to the terrible frankness of that noise, a dim suspicion of there being a meaning in it which you—you so remote from the night of first ages—could comprehend. And why not? The mind of man is capable of anything," observes the astute narrator, "because everything is in it, all the past as well as all the future."[c/14]

What, then, are the forces that spell the difference between the fate of Marlow and Kurtz? Why, despite his admitted "fascination of the abomination" did the former resist the temptations to which Kurtz had surrendered? "You wonder I didn't go ashore for a howl and a dance?" Marlow asks his listeners. "Well, no—I didn't. Fine sentiments, you say? Fine sentiments be hanged! I had no time. I had to mess about with white lead and strips of woolen blanket helping to put bandages on these leaky steam pipes."[16] Yet even this explanation does not appear to satisfy Marlow entirely, for he is aware that there are pressures exerted by elemental impulses that are kept in check not by the demands of practical necessity alone, but by the rules and conventions of organized society. "Here you all are," he tells his listeners in London, "each moored with two good addresses, like a hulk with two good anchors, a butcher

[c] "Man is an evil animal," wrote Conrad to Cunninghame Graham at the moment he was completing this work. "Crime is a necessary condition of organized living. Society is basically criminal."[15]

round one corner, a policeman round another, excellent appetites, and temperature normal."[17] What happens, however, when civilized means of gratification are absent and external restraints are lacking? By way of example Marlow cites extreme and insatiable hunger: "No fear can stand up to hunger, no patience can wear it out, disgust simply does not exist where hunger is." Under such circumstances regression to savagery can become a powerful temptation: "Don't you know the devilry of lingering starvation, its exasperating torment, its black thoughts, its sombre and brooding ferocity? Well, I do. It takes a man all his inborn strength to fight hunger properly. It's really easier to face bereavement, dishonor, and the perdition of one's soul—than this kind of prolonged hunger."[18] In short, there are circumstances under which a man, even a good man, may be hard put to resist reverting to the beast which lies dormant within everyone. That which distinguishes Kurtz from Marlow, therefore, is not a difference in their basic primitive impulses, but in their ability or willingness to resist them. Stripped of these defenses against temptation, Kurtz and Marlow are one and the same—"secret sharers" of the same primitive core.

Indeed, in "Heart of Darkness," the first work completed after establishing himself in the former home of his new friend Hueffer, Conrad was embarking upon the first of what may be called "secret sharer" tales. A radical departure from most of what had gone before, in these stories Conrad employed the device of the "double" in his attempt to explore and discover those half-secrets hidden in the remote reaches of the mind. By recognizing his occult kinship with the monstrous Kurtz, Marlow too discovers "things about himself which he did not know . . . what no other man can ever know," and because he is dealing with perceptions hidden below the level of naked conscious awareness, this recognition contains an unreal and eerie quality, imbued with the strange elusiveness of dreaming. "It seems to me," he observes, "I am trying to tell you a dream—making a vain attempt, because no relation of a dream can convey the dream sensation, that commingling of absurdity, surprise, and bewilderment in a tremor of struggling revolt, that notion of being captured by the incredible which is of the very essence of dreams."[19]

Clearly then, despite his later apologetic disclaimer, in "Heart of Darkness" Conrad had permitted himself to be "captured by the incredible," as he sought to open the doors guarding the slumbering chambers of the human mind. During the decade which was ushered in with the writing of this story he continued this inquiry, writing with poetic and imaginative daring, and often with an almost uncanny awareness, about that perhaps most fascinating of all subjects, man. In these years Conrad depicted him with all his inconsistencies, complexities, and unpredictabilities, caught in a hopeless web of twisted thought and tangled dream.

His earnest concern with psychic conflict revealed itself anew in *Lord Jim*, the novel to which he turned upon finishing "Heart of Darkness."[d] Like the latter, *Lord Jim* is a tale of "secret sharing," but it presents a far more painful and more searching depiction of mental conflict than is found in the earlier story. In "Heart of Darkness" the device of the secret sharer permits the "good" protagonist to maintain his integrity after he has succeeded in recognizing his potential identity with his evil double. Thus, while it is true that Marlow discovers that but for the grace of circumstance he might turn into a Kurtz, he is nonetheless able to emerge from the Congo with his ideals and his civilized character intact, albeit somewhat less sure of himself. In the case of Jim no such safe detachment is available, for when he encounters his "secret sharer" he is reminded not of any potential capacity for evil but of a real past in which he has exhibited a fatal flaw in his character.

The son of an English parson, Jim is a "good" boy, who, confronted by the supreme test of his moral fiber, fails. In the certain expectation that the leaky *Patna* will sink, he scuttles his seaman's code of conduct, and gripped by the instinct for self-preservation, he jumps overboard. Here Conrad's explanation for Jim's action discloses an astute awareness of the strength of obscure mental forces. Jim does not *decide* to jump as the other officers did. On

[d] Actually Conrad had begun, "Jim, A Sketch," toward the middle of 1898, but after writing a few thousand words he put it aside.[20]

the contrary when much later he tries to explain his action to the sympathetic Marlow, he speaks of it as if it had been perpetrated in a state of reduced consciousness, as in a hypnotic trance: "I had jumped . . . it seems."

" 'Looks like it,' I muttered," replies Marlow.

" 'I knew nothing about it till I looked up,' he explained hastily. And that's possible, too . . . He didn't know. It had happened somehow."[21]

Psychologically these pages reveal Conrad in what may well be his most perceptive hour, for here he acknowledges not only that man may be torn by mental strife but that the outcome of such a struggle may stem from hidden sources of far greater magnitude than the forces of conscious resolve. Such a conflict is much more subtle and infinitely more frightening than is the picture of Razumov in *Under Western Eyes*, torn between conflicting conscious impulses: to safeguard Haldin's escape or to betray him to the police and thus save his own skin. When, on deliberately choosing the latter course, Razumov informs on Haldin, he does not say, "I turned him over to the police . . . it seems." Nor does Marlow ascribe the moral disintegration of Kurtz to forces lying beyond the rim of conscious control: since he was "hollow at the core," Kurtz consciously chose to answer the "mute spell of the wilderness" with a full-throated appetite for "forgotten and brutal instincts." There is no suggestion that Jim is hollow at the core. On the contrary, since he is a young man of high ideals and good character, his action is not a manifestation of a defect in his standards of conduct but a testimonial to the vast and undreamed of power of elemental instinct in times of crisis, instinct which resembles a reflex action in that, despite all contrary conscious intent, it asserts itself as the supreme dictator of behavior: "The mind of man is capable of anything."

Nor was the Conrad of *Lord Jim* any less perceptive in following Jim's slippery efforts to dissociate himself from his own action by ascribing it not to an impulse within himself but to forces without —a rationalization of behavior and action, incidentally, which Conrad was to espouse in his later novels. During his trial, for example, Jim tries to excuse his jump by blaming it on the officers calling to him from the lifeboat. "It was their doing as plainly as if they had reached up with a boat hook and pulled me over," he explains to Marlow, who observes, "It is my belief no man ever understands quite his own artful dodges to escape from the grim shadow of self-knowledge."[22] Nor does Jim himself, deep within his heart, really succeed in persuading himself of his innocence or accept his wishful efforts to project the origins of his shame-ridden conduct upon external agencies. For throughout the remainder of his life he embodies the image of a man seeking to undo his guilty deed. In this he never succeeds, and even when he has achieved the position of the beneficent overlord of the Malay settlement of Patusan, a new crisis arises which fans the ever-smoldering fires of his unextinguishable guilt: Patusan is suddenly invaded by Gentleman Brown and his piratical crew. Abandoning his habitual role of strong leader, Jim, instead of seizing Brown and his men and thus safeguarding the community, offers no resistance to the invaders and presents them with an opportunity to do their worst.

Thus, despite the fact that the seemingly redeemed Jim had achieved the status of a demigod over his people, the arrival of the evil Brown becomes the signal for him to betray them as he had once betrayed the Arabs on board the leaky *Patna*. But clearly, the motivations for these two betrayals are not the same: Jim's jump from the *Patna* was prompted by a wish to survive, but his failure to defend his people from Brown's treachery serves no such purpose. Indeed, it causes him to destroy all that he held dear, all that he had so laboriously created; it causes him to topple from his lordly eminence and to lose his own life. It would seem therefore that it is precisely to attain this end—his own destruction—that he commits the second betrayal, for in so doing he acknowledges and advertises his earlier crime.[e] What stimulates Jim's action, or better his inaction, is his discernment in the brigand Brown of a "secret sharer." Placing a finger unwittingly on a sensitive spot in Jim's defenses, Brown asks him, "Whether he himself—straight now—didn't understand that when it came to saving one's life in the dark, one didn't care who else went—three, thirty, three hun-

[e] His behavior recalls those misdeeds that are committed in order to "relieve" an already existing sense of guilt.[23]

dred people."[24] He asks Jim, about whose past he knows nothing, "Whether he had nothing fishy in his life to remember . . . there ran through the rough talk a vein of subtle reference to their common blood, an assumption of common experience; a sickening suggestion of common guilt, of secret knowledge that was like a bond of their minds, and of their hearts. . . . 'I made him wince,' boasted Brown. . . . 'He very soon left off coming the righteous over me. He just stood there with nothing to say, and looking as black as thunder—not at me—on the ground.' "[25] Brown's words thus rekindled Jim's sense of guilt and gave the lie to his assertion to Marlow at the Court of Inquiry about the *Patna* scandal that "there was not the thickness of a sheet of paper between the right and wrong of this affair."[26] Faced by the villainous Brown, Jim recognizes their underlying common identity just as Marlow had seen his "secret sharer" in Kurtz.

Lord Jim was completed in July 1900, and upon his return from a joint holiday in Belgium with the Hueffers, Conrad began a new story, *Typhoon*, a sea tale again, but one which presents a sharp contrast to the recently completed *Lord Jim*. For *Typhoon* is the story of a ship's captain whose conduct under conditions of incalculable stress, unlike Jim's, epitomizes the best tradition of seamanship.

Like the *Patna*, the *Nan-Shan*, under Captain MacWhirr, is engaged in transporting a vast cargo of humanity—not 800 Arab pilgrims this time, but 200 Chinese coolies. Toward them Captain MacWhirr behaves precisely as Jim failed to do as first mate of the *Patna*. For MacWhirr not only guides his ship through terrible storms but concerns himself as well with the welfare of the anonymous coolies whom he brings safely to port.

The fact that Conrad was moved to write a straightforward tale of simple valor and steadfast adherence to purpose and principle only a few short weeks after finishing the story of the tormented Jim and his flagrant violation of the maritime code suggests that he was composing an antidote to the novel. It is as if in telling a story of quiet heroism and undeviating devotion to duty he was seeking to cleanse his mouth of the bad taste left there by Jim's neurotic suffering and erratic behavior. Moreover, in creating the character of Captain MacWhirr, an essentially simple man who is unencumbered by corrosive inner doubts or remorseless ruminations over what might have been, Conrad was providing himself with a respite, a breather, as it were, from the unlit and airless depths of the human soul into which he had recently descended.

Not surprisingly, Captain MacWhirr, for all his simple nobility, is hardly more than a caricature, a cliché. Although he has a wife —"a pretentious person with a scraggy neck and a disdainful manner,"[27]—she too is obviously a cliché; they have no personal relationship whatever. "The only secret of her life was her abject terror of the time when her husband would come home to stay for good." Their two children—also clichés—are "slightly acquainted with their father." Twelve times a year the captain writes home, begging to be "remembered to the children," and signing his letters unvaryingly, "your loving husband." And if the Captain's family is completely indifferent to him, the feeling is plainly mutual; Captain MacWhirr is first and last a simple sea captain, who "had sailed over the surface of the oceans as some men go skimming[f] over the years of existence to sink gently into a placid grave, ignorant of life to the last, without ever having been made to see all it may contain of perfidy, of violence, and of terror. There are on sea and land such men thus fortunate—or thus disdained by destiny or by the sea."[28] "*Typhoon*," wrote Maugham, "is a tale of the sea, which he [Conrad] knew better than the land, and it is concerned with men, whom he knew better than women. These sailor chaps are a little simpler than most of us now think human beings really are."[29]

But if Conrad chose to tell the story of one of these "simpler chaps" as a way of coming up for air from the neurotic broodings of Jim, it was but a temporary relief. Hardly had he finished the heroic saga of Captain MacWhirr when he immersed himself in the passion and the mental torment of the one-time cannibal, Falk, and, shortly thereafter in the perplexing admixture of tenderness and cruelty of Amy Foster. Although lightened by the jointly written cloak and dagger yarn, *Romance* (1902), and interspersed with personal reminiscences in *The Mirror of the Sea* (1905) and

[f] A favorite expression of Conrad's which he uses to denote an attitude of emotional detachment. See Chapter VI, footnote *q*.

A Personal Record (1909), Conrad's writing during this decade continued to reflect his imaginative and perceptive commitment to the complexities of the human mind. Upon the large canvas of *Nostromo* (1904), painted against a background of South American politics, commerce, and intrigue, Conrad drew the sensitive portraits of the neurotic and depressed Decoud, of Charles Gould, a man "haunted by a fixed idea," and of Emilia, his frustrated and neglected wife. His evident fascination with man's capacity for regression to jungle morality was revealed again in *The Secret Agent*, while the themes of betrayal, desertion, guilt, and atonement, so conspicuously presented in *Lord Jim*, appeared again in *Under Western Eyes* (1908-1910). Then as the "Hueffer decade" drew to a close, in late November and early December 1909, Conrad wrote "The Secret Sharer," a work which for some critics marks his last important literary creation.

"The Secret Sharer" presents the most explicit expression of the theme which Conrad had already developed in "Heart of Darkness" and in *Lord Jim*: the underlying kinship between all men—saint and sinner, Marlow and Kurtz, Jim and Gentleman Brown. The actual name of the story as well as some alternates suggested by Conrad—"The Second Self," "The Secret Self," and "The Other Self,"[30]—leave no room for doubting that this too is the story of a "double."

It concerns a young and inexperienced sea captain, who, taking the anchor watch one night, sees a man in the water clinging to a rope ladder lowered over the side of the ship. When the Captain brings the man on board he learns that the stranger, named Leggatt, has just escaped from a nearby ship, the *Sephora*, where shortly before in a storm at sea, he, the First Mate, had killed a disobedient member of the crew. Almost at once the Captain notices a "mysterious communication . . . already established between us two," while Leggatt observes that the Captain acts " 'as if you had expected me.' " The Captain says, " 'It was, in the night, as though I had been faced by my own reflection in the depths of a sombre and immense mirror.' "[31] During the following days the Captain hides the fugitive Leggatt (legate?) in his cabin. The Captain experiences a curious disturbance in his sense of identity—an alienation from himself. When he is temporarily separated from Leggatt it seems as if "part of me is absent."[32] His mind is affected, he believes, for he has become unsure of himself, neglecting to give orders which had always been second nature to him. Finally, after several days at sea, he selects a spot where Leggatt can safely disembark; the Captain brings his ship perilously close to the shore and his "double" secretly lowers himself into the water and quietly swims to the land, to become, like Jim, "a fugitive and a vagabond on the earth."[33]

There are other aspects of this story which evoke echoes of *Lord Jim*. Like Jim, Leggatt is an English parson's son, a subtle detail which imparts an accent of irony to their crimes. In another respect it is the Captain who resembles Jim—Jim in *Patusan*, seemingly secure in his isolation from the troubled world outside. On board his ship just prior to Leggatt's mysterious appearance, the Captain experiences a sense of satisfaction in his new task: "Suddenly I rejoiced in the great security of the sea as compared with the unrest of the land, in my choice of that untempted life presenting no disquieting problems, invested with an elementary moral beauty by the absolute straightforwardness of its appeal and by the singleness of its purpose."[34] For a moment one might have the impression that Captain MacWhirr is speaking, but suddenly this sweet tranquility is shattered by the irruption of Leggatt, just as Jim's idyll is broken by the sudden arrival of Gentleman Brown and his evil crew. And both the Captain and Jim, recognizing their kinship with these invading criminals, perceive that their dreamless sleep has become a nightmare, as they confront their evil other selves, their "own reflection in the depths of a sombre and immense mirror."

There is indeed a dreamlike quality to the nocturnal happenings in "The Secret Sharer," recalling Marlow's comments to his audience in "Heart of Darkness," for the language of "The Secret Sharer," the strangeness of its story, and the eerie atmosphere that pervades it conspire to recreate what Marlow calls "the dream sensation, that commingling of absurdity, surprise, and bewilderment in a tremor of revolt, that notion of being captured by the incredible."

What, above all, imparts to both of these stories their dreamlike texture is their amazingly intuitive intimacy with unconscious mental processes. The "notion of being captured by the incredible" expresses a flooding of the conscious mind by thoughts and feelings submerged or long forgotten which, seemingly without warning, pour forth and threaten to engulf rational thought and purposeful action. Faced by such sensations, man experiences uncertainty over his actual identity, anxiety over the nature and the power of his unknown impulses, and a deep concern over the cohesive strength of his mental organization. These are, in fact, the disturbing dream-like questions which obtrude themselves upon the Captain, jarring him rudely even while he is rejoicing securely in the quiet serenity of life at sea. "Who am I?" he seems to ask, when he confesses that "if all the truth must be told, I was somewhat of a stranger to myself."[35] "What am I?" he also demands to know, in remarking, "I wondered how far I should turn out faithful to that ideal of one's own personality every man sets up for himself secretly."[36] Was he the epitome of "immaculate command," like the Captain of the *Sephora*, or was he his "double," the killer Leggatt? And finally he is assailed by doubts concerning his sanity: "All unconscious alertness had abandoned me. I had to make an effort of will to recall myself back . . . to the conditions of the moment. . . . I had come creeping quietly as near insanity as any man who has not actually gone over the border."[g/37]

That these terrifying doubts and questions were projections of the author's own fears about himself seems certain. What is striking about them is that their expression in Conrad's writing was confined largely to a delimited phase of his literary career beginning with "Heart of Darkness," completed shortly after his first meeting with Hueffer in the fall of 1898, and ending with "The Secret Sharer," written just after overt signs of hostility to Hueffer began to appear in the summer of 1909. It cannot be without significance that these introspective journeys within the dark and shadowy passages of his secret self coincided so closely with the period of his intimate friendship with Hueffer, whose moral influence was in

[g] There is a prophetic irony in this line for it would not be many months after its writing that its author would actually go over that "border."

itself apparently akin to that of a secret sharer, and who provided Conrad with a view of his own reflection "in the depths of a sombre and immense mirror." Just as two boys banded together exhibit far greater daring than each one alone—for the presence of an accomplice serves to dilute and divide the sense of guilt—so apparently did the spiritual union of these two inhibited men lend to Conrad, at least, a certain boldness in his willingness to search his inner self. He had rarely displayed this quality before he knew Hueffer and he was destined to show it with decreasing frequency following the dissolution of their relationship. And just as it is difficult to visualize Conrad shooting rats as a solitary pastime, although with Hueffer it became a source of joint amusement, so it is equally questionable whether Conrad alone, deprived of his friend's moral support, would have possessed the daring to explore man's "forgotten and brutal instincts" with the audacity manifested by him during the "Hueffer decade." What Marlow says at one point about Jim could have been said equally well by Hueffer about Conrad: "He was not speaking to me, he was only speaking before me, in a dispute with an invisible personality, an antagonistic and inseparable partner of his existence—another possessor of his soul. The issues were beyond the competency of a court inquiry: It was a subtle and momentous quarrel as to the true essence of life, and did not want a judge. He wanted an ally, a helper, an accomplice."[38]

"The artist descends within himself," wrote Conrad, "and in that lonely region of stress and strife, if he be deserving and fortunate, he finds the terms of his appeal."[39] Secure in the company of the "inseparable partner of his existence," Conrad could make that descent, emerging from time to time for breath and to reassure himself of the presence of his "ally" and "accomplice," and then descend once more.

And then, one day, his friend was gone and the alliance of the secret sharers was broken. Now Conrad resembled the Captain of "The Secret Sharer" when separated from Leggatt: part of him was absent, and no reflection of himself appeared in the depths of a sombre and immense mirror. A closer view of what Conrad had seen there will be related in the succeeding chapters.

IX · Heart of Darkness

ALTHOUGH in "Heart of Darkness" Marlow fails to spell out the precise nature of all the "forgotten and brutal instincts" and the "monstrous passions" to which Mr. Kurtz had succumbed, the row of human skulls adorning the fence posts around his jungle house removes any doubt that above all else this is a tale of cannibalism. To his audience on the river Thames, "each moored with two good addresses . . . a butcher round one corner, a policeman round another," Marlow describes a far-off land where neither of these safeguards exists, a land where every man, possessed of the "devilry of lingering starvation," may become a butcher and where human flesh may be man's meat.

Conrad's evident fascination with the subject of cannibalism was not limited to the writing of "Heart of Darkness." Two years after the completion of that story he introduced the subject again in "Falk." Falk is the mate of a stricken ship; most of the crew is sick or dying, and all of the food is gone or spoiled. Faced by inevitable starvation, the mate and the carpenter, the sole remaining healthy members of the crew, hunt each other down, each with the undisguised intention of killing and eating the other. It is Falk who prevails; he eats the carpenter and ultimately he is rescued. Upon his return to civilization he becomes an inflexible vegetarian.[a]

Conrad's interest in the subject of eating that which is usually forbidden appears to have originated in his childhood. As noted earlier, in *A Personal Record* he recalled the profound impression made upon him when his grandmother told him that his Great-Uncle Nicholas Bobrowski, an officer in Napoleon's army, had once killed and eaten a dog. When the child assured her that he could never have done such a thing, she replied, "Perhaps you don't know what it is to be hungry."[1] This account is presented in a manner which pretends to lightness and jocularity, but which somehow it never achieves. "The childish horror of the deed clings absurdly to the grizzled man. I am perfectly helpless against it."

[a] Conrad had dealt with a variation on this theme of hunger and murder in the one short story which came out of his Congo experience—"An Outpost of Progress," written in 1896. See Chapter VI.

Seemingly unable to drop the subject, he explains that it was not only hunger that drove Great-Uncle Nicholas to eat dog, "but also for the sake of an unappeasable and patriotic desire . . . Pro Patria!" The author then names all the varied and bizarre substances which he too had eaten—"ancient salt junk . . . shark . . . trepang . . . snake," but, he insists, "of the Lithuanian village dog, never! I wish it to be distinctly understood that it is not I, but my grand-uncle Nicholas, of the Polish landed gentry—*Chevalier de la Legion d'Honneur*, etc., etc., who, in his young days had eaten Lithuanian dog."[2]

Despite this pointed and humorous disclaimer, the very belaboring of the subject of eating a household pet suggests that it was closely related in Conrad's mind to the disturbing but fascinating topic of cannibalism. In view of the insistent recurrence of the subject in his writings the conclusion that cannibalism (and kindred practices) contained some personal significance for Conrad might seem justified. In an effort to gain an understanding of this puzzling preoccupation, a more detailed examination of his story of the cannibal Falk is necessary.

At the outset of the tale the narrator and his friends are eating dinner in a small inn. The chops "brought forcibly to one's mind the night of ages when the primeval man, evolving the first rudiments of cookery from his dim consciousness, scorched lumps of flesh at a fire of sticks in the company of other good fellows; then, gorged and happy, sat him back among the gnawed bones to tell his artless tales of experience—the tales of hunger and hunt—and of women, perhaps!"[3] It is in fact toward women, or a woman, rather, that the story eventually turns.

Some years after he had eaten the carpenter, Falk, now a captain, falls desperately but secretly in love with a young woman, who is the niece of Hermann, the captain of a ship lying in an Eastern port. The niece, who looks after Hermann's children, remains nameless and fails to utter a single word throughout the narrative. Despite the fact that he is now a confirmed vegetarian, Falk is haunted by his past. "I have eaten man," he declares, implying that the evil deed renders him unworthy of the girl. Nor is it difficult to see why, for his feelings for her partake of a quality strongly reminiscent of his cannibalism. "He was a child. He was frank as a child too. He was hungry for the girl, terribly hungry, as he had been terribly hungry for food."[4] But at last he confesses to her his terrible secret; she forgives him and they marry.

In this story Conrad poses the physical love of man for woman as if it were almost equivalent to cannibalism: "Don't be shocked," says the narrator of "Falk," "if I declare that in my belief it was the same need, the same pain, the same torture."[5] The fact of his having devoured human flesh, therefore, would seem to disqualify Falk from satisfying his kindred hunger for the girl, as if, having once succumbed to such "forgotten and brutal instincts," he might do so again, despite his renunciation of meat.[b] In light of this equation between devouring love and devouring brutality, it is not surprising that in Conrad's fiction carnal love is usually tainted with attributes of cruelty and evil, characterized conspicuously by biting sadism. Such lovers are found characteristically among his villains who are usually snarling, teeth-grinding fiends: Ortega, Dona Rita's perverse cousin who bites his own fists when he is enraged; Scevola, the "blood drinker" of *The Rover* who lusts after Arlette; and Count Helion of *Suspense* whose wife Adèle is reluctant to let him kiss her hand "lest he should lose his self-control and bite it."[7] Captain Falk is indeed the only Conrad character who, despite his carnivorous propensity, is treated sympathetically, and this indulgence he achieves only by virtue of a process of redemption; he renounces all meat and achieves forgiveness from the woman for whom he hungers.

Conrad's other male protagonists reveal no hint of latent cannibalistic temptation. On the contrary, despite his vigorous efforts to shore up their masculinity, the Alvan Herveys, the Heysts, the Captain Anthonys, the Tom Lingards, the M. Georges, and others are sexually speaking a rather vegetarian lot, like Bunthorne in *Patience*:

[b] The bestial component in Falk's make-up is underscored by his resemblance to a centaur. "He was a composite creature," says the narrator. "Not a man-horse, it is true, but a man-boat. . . . Separated from the boat, to me at least, he seemed incomplete. The tug herself without his head and torso on the bridge looked mutilated as it were."[6]

If he's content with a vegetable love
Which would certainly not suit me;
Why what a most particularly pure young man
This pure young man must be.

Conrad's "pure young men," in truth, are not only devoid of any suggestion of biting sadism; they are virtually edentulous from the viewpoint of masculine aggression. Not so his women, however, who, as previously noted, are "dentally superb." The teeth of his heroines are a conspicuous feature of their attractiveness, while among the villainous women they comprise an especially terrifying element in their total feral aspect: they are the fangs of predatory creatures, like the female piano player from whom Heyst rescues Lena in *Victory*—"more disagreeable than any cannibal I have ever had to do with"[8]—and the governess of Flora in *Chance* who "pushed her face so near mine and her teeth looked as though she wanted to bite me."[9] The girl in "The Inn of Two Witches" resembles a "hungry cat watching a bird in a cage or a mouse inside a trap";[10] and Clelia in *Suspense* "has the appearance of a cat ready to fly off at one."[11] However, images of biting and clawing aggression are not restricted to Conrad's evil women. Under certain circumstances such attitudes are displayed even by his heroines: Winnie Verloc of *The Secret Agent* who is described as "ready to fly at her father's eyes—like a cat";[12] Aïssa who is called "a she-dog with white teeth";[13] and Mrs. Hervey of "The Return" who, in response to an amorous advance by her husband, "panted, showing her teeth."[14]

Another fictional female who appears to be endowed with a latent capacity for "oral" sadism is Amy Foster, and in light of Conrad's evident preoccupation with that subject in the early years of the "Hueffer decade," it is not surprising that a few weeks after he had finished the tale of the cannibal Falk in May 1901, he wrote the story that bears her name. The hero of "Amy Foster," Yanko Gooral,[c] is a refugee from central Europe who is the sole

[c] Yanko means "little John." Gooral is derived from the Gooralians, a Polish mountain folk living in the Carpathians where Conrad spent several holidays with his tutor, Mr. Pulman.[15]

survivor of a ship wrecked off the English coast. When he wanders into a nearby town his wild appearance and incomprehensible speech so frighten the natives that he is locked up like an animal in a woodshed. There he is discovered by Amy Foster, a good-hearted village girl, whose sympathy gives her an understanding that transcends the barrier of language. Recognizing his hunger and thirst she cares for him and brings him food and water.[d] In time they fall in love and, despite the objections of the neighbors, they marry. For a short time their relationship gives the appearance of an idyl, but when a child is born Amy turns against her husband to bestow all her love upon her son. Excluded from this mother-child union, Yanko falls ill with lung trouble, and after nearly drowning in a puddle of water, he dies, abandoned by the same woman who had once nursed him so tenderly.

It is evident, therefore, that Amy is not quite as consistently tender-hearted as she at first appears. Apparently she can be a devoted nurse to a helpless castaway, but she can as easily spurn him when she has a child of her own. Like the captain in "A Smile of Fortune," she holds out promises and then reneges.

There are hints, moreover, that even in her seeming tenderheartedness there lurks a streak of biting cruelty which is akin to cannibalism. For although she is described as a girl who was "never heard to express a dislike for a single being . . . and [was] tender to every living creature,"[16] she displays some strikingly opposite behavior when her employer's parrot is attacked by a cat. (The familiar cat.) The parrot's peculiarities, the reader learns, "exercised upon her a positive fascination. Nevertheless when that outlandish bird was attacked by a cat and shrieked for help in human accents, she ran out into the yard stopping her ears, and did not prevent the crime."[17]

Now this is precisely how Amy behaves when her husband is calling for help in his final delirium: "Suddenly coming to himself, parched, he demanded a drink of water. She did not move. She had not understood, though he may have thought he was speaking in English. [Amy had understood his need for water very well when he

[d] One of Conrad's favorite themes. See Chapter IV, page 85.

was locked in the woodshed and knew no English whatever.] He waited, looking at her, burning with fever, amazed at her silence and immobility, and then he shouted impatiently, 'Water! Give me water!' . . . She jumped to her feet, snatched up the child . . . opened the door and ran out."[18] As he lies dying Yanko reminds the narrator of "a wild creature under the net; of a bird caught in a snare."[19] Thus is Yanko equated with the unfortunate parrot, and Amy with the cat that killed it. Nor does Yanko appear to be the final victim of Amy's feline destructiveness, for although she exhibits "a very passion of maternal tenderness to her son," the narrator darkly hints that his fate will in time resemble his father's: "The little fellow was lying on his back, a little frightened at me, but very still, with his big black eyes, with his fluttered air of a bird in a snare. And looking at him I seemed to see again the other one —the father, cast out mysteriously by the sea to perish in the supreme disaster of loneliness and despair."[20] Thus it is hinted that Amy will one day destroy her son Johnny, as she did his father Yanko. Like the parrot, these two "birds" will be devoured by a "cat"—Amy Foster, the tender-hearted "cannibal."

Nor are these the only references to the devouring of birds in this bird-filled story. In the wreckage of the ship from which Yanko escaped there was a hen coop containing 11 drowned ducks which was washed ashore. One of the local families cooked and ate the ducks and used the hen coop for firewood. It was suspected by some that Yanko's survival was accomplished by his floating into shore clinging to the hen coop. Viewing Yanko, then, in terms of his ultimate depiction as "a bird caught in a snare,"[e] the hen coop carried not 11 but 12 birds, all of whom suffer the same fate— they are eaten up. Before the ducks are eaten, moreover, they are cooked, and although literally Yanko is spared from that grim experience, figuratively this befalls him too, when, forsaken by his faithless wife, he dies "burning" with fever.

This linking of devouring and incendiary destructiveness with a woman was by no means a new idea for Conrad; it recurs in his fiction before the writing of "Amy Foster" and would reappear in

[e] A discussion of the significance of Conrad's frequent comparisons between people and birds is reserved for a later chapter.

his later stories. In *An Outcast of the Islands*, for example, Willems flings aside Aïssa's hand "like something burning,"[f/21] while in "The Return," Alvan Hervey's annihilation by his wife takes place in a setting of glaring incandescence: "The coals glowed without a flame; and upon the red glow the vertical bars of the grate stood out at her feet, black and curved, like the charred ribs of a consumed sacrifice. Far off a lamp . . . burned under a wide shade of crimson silk; the center, within the shadows of the large room, of a fiery twilight that had in the warm quality of its tint something delicate, refined and infernal."[23] Mrs. Hervey, too, partakes of these same qualities: her husband finds himself "unable to touch her as though she had been on fire."[24] A similar incinerating effect is wrought upon Renouard by Felicia Moorsom in "The Planter of Malata." Felicia is described as the personification of fire: "the flame of her glorious head scorched his face"; Renouard envisages "his wits burned to cinders in that radiance."[25] The destruction of a man by fire attains its most literal expression, however, in *Victory* in which because of his love for Lena, Heyst is burned to death.

It is evident from these examples that a number of Conrad's female characters possess attributes generally ascribed to fire-breathing dragons or devouring witches. In the story "The Return," there is a seemingly unimportant detail, in the form of an object of art, which combines the several elements of this "cannibalistic" theme—the jaws, the fire, and the winged victim—into a composite whole: a figure of a bronze dragon, "nailed by the tail to a bracket writhed away from the wall in calm convolutions, and held, between the conventional fury of its jaws, a crude gas flame that resembled a butterfly."[26] It is, to be sure, a most appropriate symbol for the Herveys' marital relationship, but it could serve equally well as an armorial emblem of Amy Foster.

Amy possesses another characteristic, moreover, that emphasizes the nuclear importance of the mouth in the psychologic make-up of this unpredictable woman: she stutters. Clinically, stuttering is a common manifestation of an underlying conflict concerning

[f] As previously noted Willems foresees the consequences of his involvement with her in terms of being devoured "till there would remain nothing but the white gleam of bleaching bones in the long grass."[22]

the act of speaking, which, for the stutterer, usually has an unconscious aggressive significance. Consequently the symptom may make its appearance at moments when a powerful destructive impulse is being opposed by an equally strong recoil or inhibition. The resultant stutter bears a crude resemblance to the jerky movement of an automobile driven by a hesitant novice whose foot oscillates impulsively between accelerator and brake pedal.[g] Similar to this is the pattern of Amy's speech in which the smooth flow of words is broken up by sudden staccato spasms; this is in keeping with the pattern of her behavior which oscillates erratically between flowing tenderness and sudden unexpected outbursts of biting destructiveness.[h]

In this connection, it is pertinent to observe that Hermann's niece in "Falk" remains mute throughout the narrative. In this story of man-eating she is represented as the epitome of kindness, her muteness testifying to her lack of any "oral" cruelty. Psychologically speaking she is an ideal mate for the vegetarian Falk.

Despite certain similarities between "Falk" and "Amy Foster" in their presentation of the inter-related themes of love and man-eating, it is possible to discern a fundamental difference between the "cannibalistic" behavior of the two characters after whom these stories are named. Falk's cannibalism, it may be noted, occurred as a desperate measure when his very survival was at stake. Like Conrad's Great-Uncle Nicholas, who ate roast dog, Falk is regarded as a good man at heart whose indulgence in his horrible act was dictated by dire necessity. Moreover, he displays later on a full expression of his remorse by forswearing meat of any kind. This does not appear to apply to Amy Foster whose destructiveness is attributed to the same feral instincts that govern the behavior of a cat silently advancing upon an unsuspecting bird. In this implied distinction between the two characters, Conrad gives

[g] This relationship between stuttering and aggression is dramatically portrayed in Melville's *Billy Budd*. Prevented by his speech impediment from proclaiming his innocence to the charge of conspiring to mutiny, the enraged Billy delivers a blow to the head of his accuser and kills him.

[h] Little Stevie in *The Secret Agent* is like Amy a stutterer, and like her he enjoys a questionably deserved reputation for tenderness. See Chapter X.

a hint of the misogyny which permeates much of his writing and which attains overt explicitness in the asides of the narrator of *Chance.*

Expressive of this distrust of women is a short story entitled "Tomorrow" which Conrad wrote in January 1902, about six months after he wrote "Amy Foster." "Tomorrow" concerns Hagberd (a pun?), a retired sea captain, who is daily awaiting the return of his seafaring son Harry, who had left home 16 years before. Despairing of his return, his mother has died of "impatience."[i] Next door to Hagberd lives Bessie, a single girl who takes care of her old blind father. Captain Hagberd tries to persuade Bessie that when his son returns "tomorrow" he will marry her, but when Harry does finally appear it is only to get some money from his father to pay some shady debts. Like the captain in "A Smile of Fortune," he engages in a brief and passionate erotic scene with the girl, but he has no intention of settling down and complying with his father's plans to have him marry her and become "a blamed tame rabbit in a cage." Extolling the freedom of life at sea, Harry says, "a ship's a ship. You love her and leave her, and a voyage isn't a marriage."[27] And with that he goes off again, leaving the girl who is overwhelmed with despair.

Unlike Yanko Gooral and his little son Johnny, Harry Hagberd has no intention of allowing himself to be caged by a woman or of subjecting himself to the precarious whim of those creatures who take care of a man today and abandon him tomorrow. In contrast with the earlier story, in "Tomorrow" it is the man (Harry), not the woman, who offers a false promise of love. So complete indeed are the reversals of the theme of "Amy Foster" in the story "Tomorrow," that the latter might appropriately deserve the subtitle, "Yanko Gooral's Revenge."

This was to be the last story, for a while at least, in which Conrad focused his attention upon the intense and passionate emotions raging within the confines of domestic life, and in which he displayed once more his evident preoccupation with the themes of ensnarement and man-eating, as well as their derivatives. These

[i] Cf. the death of Stephen's parents in *The Sisters.*

same themes, it should be noted, occupy a prominent position in myths and fairy tales, and no less frequently in the fantasies of children. There are two tales of Grimm, "The Twelve Brothers" and "The Six Swans," which in some respects show a remarkable correspondence with the Conrad stories under discussion.

In both of these fairy tales boys are turned into birds by the action of a woman. In the first story a royal couple has 12 sons who are destined to die if a sister should be born. When the queen is about to have her 13th child she warns her sons to watch for a signal; if another son is born a white flag will appear and it will then be safe for the boys to come home; if a girl is born the queen will unfurl a red flag and the boys must leave home and remain in hiding. A daughter is born and in time, learning of the existence of her brothers, she sets out to find them in order that she may look after them. One day, after she has established herself in their retreat, she prepares a great feast. Before sitting down to eat she goes into the garden and picks 12 lilies, intending to give one to each brother. Instantly all the boys are changed into ravens and fly away. The princess is distressed until she learns that by remaining mute for the next seven years she can cause them to revert to human form. In "The Six Swans" it is a wicked stepmother who turns her husband's sons into six birds. Here again it is a sister who by remaining mute has the power of transforming the birds back into boys again.

In both stories the mute princess marries a king whose jealous mother speaks ill of her silent daughter-in-law: "even if she is really dumb and cannot speak she might at least laugh. Not to laugh is the sign of a bad conscience." In "The Six Swans" the old woman steals each baby born to the young queen and marks the latter's mouth with blood, declaring to her son, the king, that his wife is an evil thing, an eater of human flesh. At first the king resists these slanderous accusations against his wife, declaring "she is too tender and good to do any such thing, and if she were only not dumb, and could defend herself, then her innocence would be as clear as day."

Finally, the king's evil mother prevails and the mute queen is condemned to be burned at the stake. Happily at the last minute, however, her period of mutism is at an end, and her brothers, ravens in one story and swans in the other, fly to her rescue and then revert to their human form. The young queen is saved and her wicked mother-in-law dies a horrible death—in the second story, appropriately enough, by burning at the stake.

According to Morf,[28] Grimm's fairy tales were among Conrad's earliest reading. To what extent he was influenced by a conscious recollection of these tales in writing "Amy Foster" and other "cannibalistic" stories is conjectural. Suffice it to say, however, that the similarities between the two are sometimes quite striking. The number of brothers turned into birds—12—for example, is precisely duplicated in "Amy Foster" by the depiction of the 11 ducks and the bird-like Yanko floating in to shore on a hen coop. The transformation of boys into birds, moreover, through the action of a girl in the fairy tale corresponds to the fate of Amy's husband and son who come to resemble "birds in a snare." Moreover, the penalty of mutism assumed by the princess in order to restore her brothers to human form finds its counterpart both in the speech disturbance of Amy Foster and in the mutism of Hermann's niece. As a complement to Falk's renunciation of meat, the niece's silence symbolizes her sharing in the penance demanded by his cannibalistic crime. An additional element shared by the fairy tales and the Conrad stories concerns fire and burning. The condemning of the young princess to burning at the stake signifies an application of the *lex talionis*; for allegedly consuming her children she herself is condemned to be consumed by fire—a not unusual fate for witches who plot to eat children.

A pivotal role in both the fairy tales and in "Amy Foster" is assigned to the advent of a child. Psychologically "The Twelve Brothers" is concerned primarily with envy within the family circle. During the early part of the story the birth of a daughter is held to imperil her brothers; her arrival in fact is announced by a classical signal of danger: a red flag. Some time later, presumably upon her attaining sexual maturity, the girl inadvertently turns her brothers into ravens—symbols of death—as a result of picking 12 lilies. Thus, despite her presumed sweet nature, the princess fulfills her father's prophecy that she will bring ruin upon her brothers. In this insistence upon her inevitable destructiveness, the princess resembles Conrad's Amy Foster, whose propensity for inflicting injury on males (and birds) is presented as if it were an inherent female attribute. The red cloth[j] which advertises the birth of the princess, may be viewed as a symbolic allusion to blood, and particularly to menstruation, that condition which among many diverse people is regarded with fear and revulsion, for the association of blood and genitals often serves to rekindle childhood fears of genital mutilation or "castration."[k] Implicit in such fears is the idea that since a woman is in actuality a castrated individual she may be consumed with envy for the male's superior genital equipment and secretly aims to rob him of it.[l] Viewed symbolically it is this act of mutilation that is wrought by the princess upon her brothers at the very moment when they are about to partake of a feast, and, from the nature of her subsequent punishment—mutism —the biting nature of her deed is implied.[m]

Like the princess in the fairy tales, Amy Foster is also depicted as an emasculator of males, or a castrator;[n] this characterization,

[j] Aside from Yanko, only one other person is identified among the victims of the shipwreck in "Amy Foster": a dead fair-haired girl clad in a red dress.[29]

[k] Although technically inexact, the word *castration* in psychoanalytic parlance has acquired the meaning of injury to the external male genitals.

[l] Such a view of some women is far from delusional, particularly around the time of menstruation which may give rise to states of extreme irritability and aggressive rage. The menstrual period, or the "curse," may engender such attitudes not only because it serves as a reminder of a state of barrenness, but because it may symbolize a general sense of deprivation.

[m] Clinical experience reveals that some women become temporary vegetarians during the menstrual period as a defense against any hint of "cannibalistic" aggression. The writer has encountered cases in which women refused to eat any red-colored foods during this time. It is also striking to observe that a number of women unconsciously restrict the wearing of red attire to the catamenia, as if they were advertising their condition and issuing a warning of their noxious potential.

[n] In keeping with her propensity for destroying birds it should be pointed out that the latter are common symbols for the phallus, e.g., "cock," "pecker," and that in several languages the figurative castration of a man is expressed in terms associated with birds: *cuckold* in English; *cocu* in French; *Hahnrei* in German.

The transformation of a man into a bird as a symbolic depiction of his castration is dramatically illumined in the motion picture "The Blue Angel," incidentally, is equally applicable to the majority of Conrad's fictional women, heroine and villainess alike.

But the Grimm tales are concerned with other themes than the "castration complex." When later on the princess in "The Six Swans" becomes a queen and a mother she is accused by her jealous mother-in-law of devouring her own children. The latter part of the story, therefore, deals with a somewhat different envy and rivalry—competition between the king's wife and his mother (a situation not entirely limited to the world of fairy tales). When the young wife begets a child, the envy of her mother-in-law knows no bounds—she kidnaps the baby while insinuating to her son that his wife is an evil person (an opinion not unknown in the real world). At this point the king is torn between conflicting loyalties which he finally resolves by dutifully succumbing to the authoritative voice of his slandering mother. Fortunately, his wife has relatives, even if they are all birds, and in the nick of time they arrive to save her from burning and to straighten matters out generally.

Rivalry is also the basic theme of "Amy Foster," but so long as there are but two individuals on the scene—Amy and Yanko—their relationship is as peaceful and harmonious as was life for the king and queen and their 12 boys prior to the birth of the princess. "People saw her going out to meet him in the evening, she standing with unblinking, fascinated eyes up the road where he was expected to appear, walking freely, with a swing from the hip, and humming one of the love tunes of his country."[30] But then Johnny is born,[o]

---

in which, as a result of his infatuation with a voluptuous music-hall tart, a pompous Prussian schoolteacher forfeits his respectable position and is reduced to the ignominy of appearing on the stage as a ridiculous crowing rooster. His degradation becomes complete when he is forced to perform before an audience composed of hooting and jeering former students. A preview of what lies in store for him takes place in an early scene in which the professor discovers that his beloved pet bird is dead. Anticipating the subsequent behavior of his inamorata, his housekeeper removes the dead bird from its cage and without a vestige of either pity or regret callously throws the corpse into the fire.

[o] Little children are a distinct rarity in Conrad's writing. The only other important stories in which they appear are "Falk" and *The Secret Agent*, and in neither of these is the child the offspring of the principal characters.

and, as in the fairy tales, trouble comes with him; like the children of the young queen, Johnny becomes an object of rivalry. One day when Yanko is singing to the child, as the *mothers* (italics mine) in his country used to sing to babies, Amy snatches the child from his arms.[32] She also objects vigorously when her husband proposes to teach his son to speak his own European tongue.[p] These episodes are soon followed by Yanko's illness, his unheeded cries for water uttered in his burning delirium, and finally his unlamented death.

At first glance, then, the rivalry in "Amy Foster" seems to concern the struggle between two adults over the "ownership" of the child. Seen in this light the rivalry resembles that between mother and mother-in-law in the fairy tales, particularly when it is recalled that Yanko's approach to his son is modeled upon the behavior of the mothers in his native land.

There is a second facet to the theme of rivalry in this story which is implied rather than stated: that between father and son for Amy. The tale presents an unmistakable picture of the usurpation of a husband's position by his son, yet aside from complaining to the narrator of the story that "women are funny," Yanko's reaction to the alienation of his wife's affection, like the behavior of all of Conrad's fictional "good" men, is completely passive: like a neglected older child he silently witnesses the total withdrawal of Amy's love from him and its lavish bestowal upon her baby. Indeed, his only protest is expressed by the unspoken utterance of bodily sickness and ultimately by death itself.

But if the basic pattern of love in "Amy Foster" concerns the relationship between mother and child it is no less so in the cannibalistic story "Falk," where the silent niece is compared to a classic symbol of motherhood—"an allegoric statue of earth,"[34]—

The four children appearing in "Falk" belong to Captain Hermann, not to the mute niece who looks after them. Stevie in *The Secret Agent* is the little brother of the maternal Winnie Verloc. Nina appears briefly as a small child in *Almayer's Folly*, but it is as a mature woman that the story is concerned with her. A baby was included in an early plan of *Under Western Eyes* but discarded subsequently.[31]

[p] Conrad felt apologetic toward his compatriots because his sons could not speak Polish.[33]

and where Captain Falk himself is referred to as a child, in so many words. How then is this seemingly innocent image of a united mother and child related to the frightful specter of cannibalism?

As noted in previous chapters the re-establishment of a blissful intimacy between mother and child seems to represent the deepest significance of the conception of love in many of Conrad's stories, in which, like superimposed pictures, the pale outlines of adult sexuality are barely visible against the brighter background of the child at his mother's breast. Indeed, in his fiction the love of a man for a woman is so fused with fantasies of nursing as to confer upon all masculine aggression the significance of unrestrained biting. It is for this reason that while Yanko can accept the succoring love of Amy when it is freely offered, he cannot fight for it when she abandons him to nurse her real child, for necessarily his behavior would assume the character of infanticide or a carnivorous assault on her; as already noted, and as will become even more evident in the following chapter, in Conrad's fiction the men who perpetrate such acts are never the heroes: they are the evil rivals of the hero.

It may be suspected therefore that the image of a woman as a devouring, incinerating, and ensnaring creature is derived in part, at least, from a psychological projection upon her of the evil impulses which the good hero must disavow within himself. There is reason to believe, however, that this image arises also from a totally different origin: paradoxically, as a distorted representation of a wish.

Psychoanalytic observations have shown that ulterior to many fears of castration, as well as fears of being devoured, swallowed, pinned down, or trapped, are deep-seated wishes for helpless passivity. Hence phobias characterized by fear of falling, drowning, entrapment, and even dying, may be derivatives of an unconscious desire to re-experience a child's blissful pleasure in sinking sleepily within the warm encircling arms of an all-powerful loving mother.[q] The fear of dying, moreover, may carry a particular significance

[q] By the same token, ideas of being devoured are remotely related to the affectionate terms employed in conversing with little children, who are compared with delicious comestibles: "You're so sweet I'm going to eat you up."

when the beloved mother is in fact dead, for it may then point to a hidden fantasy of joining her in death.

Some evidence that Conrad himself nourished such a fantasy has already been cited; further evidence is provided by the quasi-autobiographical story of the lonely European "castaway."[r] Yanko is not only abandoned by his wife-mother, but, like Jimmy in *The Nigger*, is stricken with a disease of the lungs, presumably "consumption," the very illness which robbed Conrad of his own mother.[s]

Seen in the light of autobiography, moreover, the advent of little Johnny corresponds in the author's personal life to the birth of his son, an event which Jessie Conrad recognized as posing a threat in her husband's eyes to his position in her affection. When she wrote, "I saw quite plainly that my allegiance must be somewhat divided," she was acknowledging her realization that Conrad would regard her not so much as a wife bestowing upon a husband the priceless gift of a child, but as an "Amy Foster," a faithless "mother," who "played him false." Unlike his fictional counterpart, Conrad did not subsequently die of neglect, but there is good reason to believe that he suffered keenly because of the unwelcome intrusion of his son until the timely arrival of the similarly de-throned Hueffer provided him with solace and companionship.

Curiously, that companionship, flourishing in a domestic atmosphere of jealousy and rancor, was accompanied by a series of mishaps which in some instances seem almost inspired by the Brothers Grimm. It is true that no one was transformed into a bird, although toward the end of 1901 Hueffer claimed that he was unable to continue working with Conrad on *Romance* because of the ill effects which resulted from his getting a chicken bone stuck in his throat;[37] and although no one was burned to death, six months after Huef-

[r] Before choosing the present title for the story Conrad had considered naming it "A Husband" or "A Castaway."[35] According to Jessie Conrad, a girl named Amy Foster was employed by the Conrads for many years.[36]

[s] In a later chapter the hypothesis will be advanced that, aside from its origins in fairy tales and elsewhere, "Amy Foster" has roots in Conrad's Catholicism, and that Yanko, and presumably Conrad himself, were identified with the martyred Christ.

fer's unfortunate encounter with the chicken, a good part of Conrad's manuscript of "The End of the Tether" was destroyed by fire when a lamp exploded in Conrad's home.[38] More serious accidents were to follow, for, as previously noted, in November 1903 Elsie Hueffer fell down a flight of steps and broke her arm,[39] and three months later Jessie Conrad suffered a fall in the street, causing injuries to her knees which left her a partial cripple for the rest of her life.[40] In October 1904, a few weeks after Conrad had completed *Nostromo*, Jessie was obliged to undergo surgery, and when at the beginning of the new year the Conrads embarked at Dover for a winter holiday in Capri, she had to be carried on board in a chair.[41] They returned to England in May 1905, and later in that year, presumably in November, Jessie became pregnant again, an occurrence which, not surprisingly, served to reignite all the tensions and turmoil which had accompanied the arrival of their first child, Borys. The literary obligato which accompanied the new pregnancy was *The Secret Agent*, a tale of violence which unfolds a grim drama concerning a man, a woman, and a child.

X · The Character of the Foe

Although Jessie Conrad wrote about her second pregnancy, "I believe my husband was more pleased this time than he had been when the first one was coming,"[1] the sentiment does not altogether harmonize with other observations made by this usually perceptive person. Her account of her husband's behavior during these months hardly conveys the image of a man eagerly awaiting the emergence of the new life germinating within her. Indeed, at times his thoughts would seem to have traveled in an altogether different direction. When one day a farm hand failed to appear, Conrad insisted that the man had committed suicide. Although Jessie affirmed that there was not a shred of evidence for this notion, which was merely a product of Conrad's "fertile imagination," he ridiculed her, saying, "You don't know these young men; his whistling and being, or appearing, happy is nothing to go by." Following this anecdote she wrote, "I suppose the expected event had a good deal to do with my husband's excess of restlessness. He could settle to nothing for long enough to achieve any measure of work."[2] Nor did the hovering presence of Hueffer make matters any easier for Jessie, however much spiritual balm he may have brought to her restless husband. Returning to England after spending the winter of 1906 in Montpellier, the Conrads were invited to occupy Hueffer's house in Winchelsea. This move further inflamed the mutual antipathy between Jessie and Hueffer, for the latter came down to stay with the Conrads on weekends and according to Jessie rarely overlooked an opportunity to vent his hostility upon her. On one very hot day during that summer, when Jessie, who was extremely uncomfortable as well as self-conscious over her ample size (she had become markedly obese even before the pregnancy), was about to enter a train, she found her way blocked by the teasingly playful Hueffer, who refused to let her pass.[3] On another stifling day, ostensibly to spare some guests a view of the proceedings, he shut her up in the hot kitchen where she was preparing a meal.[4] On still another occasion he angrily accused her of mutilating one of the Hueffer tablecloths, exclaiming, "Look at that! Elsie will be furious." But Jessie, who claimed she had anticipated just such a situation, had brought all her own linens with her when she came down to Winchelsea; the "mutilated" tablecloth was her own.[5]

Nor did Hueffer's repeated efforts to demean Jessie seem to elicit from her husband manifestations of that fidelity which he held in such high esteem. One day when she was cooking lunch, Hueffer opened the oven and placed his freshly washed hat just above the roast. "It was a real Panama, but [as] his washing had been strictly confined to the outside only, there was much grease inside the lining for my liking—even had I not had our meat underneath, and I would have liked above everything to have put it on the fire." But Jessie apparently refused to play the role of the incinerating witch. She removed the hat to a chair and "resolutely closed the oven." On the following morning, however, her humiliation was compounded when Conrad told her to put a new ribbon on the hat.[6]

It is noteworthy that much of the friction with Hueffer which Jessie recorded concerned food and its preparation. In view of the discussion in the previous chapter this is hardly surprising, for the kitchen would appear to have been a most appropriate arena in which these two combatants might hope to settle their basic quarrel: which was the better "mother" to Conrad—the wife or Hueffer, her quasi mother-in-law, who allegedly noised it abroad that Jessie was "the daughter of a Folkstone boatman."[a/7]

Conrad's demanding irascibility grew as the day approached for the confinement. They had been invited to stay at the Galsworthys for the baby's birth and arrived there on a Thursday to await the event. By Sunday Conrad was in the throes of an attack of gout, irritable and unreasonable. Suddenly he discovered that a favorite book had been left behind at Pent Farm. "Like a spoilt child no other would do; he must have that book at once," and Jessie, awaiting the imminent arrival of her child—which occurred four days later—took the long train ride back to Pent Farm to fetch the book. When her physician learned of it he became angry and ordered

[a] "The king's mother, who was a wicked woman, began to slander the young queen, and said to the king, 'She is only a low beggar maid that you have taken to yourself.' "—"The Six Swans"

her to bed.[8] On Thursday, August 2, 1906, a baby son was born. He was named John, for Galsworthy.

In the middle of December the Conrads went to France for the winter. During the railroad journey the father performed a strange act: suddenly, and for no apparent reason, he opened a window and threw out a package containing the infant's clothes—"months of hard work," wrote Jessie, who added wryly, "Well, I am sure the man who finds that bundle will be looking for the baby's corpse."[9] Indeed, as a manifestation of Conrad's inhospitality toward the new baby the action speaks for itself.[b] What is equally

[b] Jessie Conrad's observations seem to be compounded out of varying mixtures of intuition and naïveté. Her naïveté, however, often seems somewhat forced, as it does when she claimed to be puzzled by her husband's demeanor during her second pregnancy: "As I did not know what the book [*The Secret Agent*] was about, I could not account to myself for the grimly ironic expression I used often to catch on his face, whenever he came to give me a look-in. Could it have reference to the expected baby? No! it was only a reflection of the tone of the book's."[10] It is possible that she assumed this tone of simple innocence to dampen her criticism of her husband, but despite this effort her revelations about him contain a sufficient wealth of uncomplimentary innuendoes and reports to raise the suspicion that she used her books on Conrad as a means of discharging a generous supply of resentment and anger.

The nature of Jessie Conrad's basic personality configuration is a matter of speculation. Whatever she may have been prior to her relationship with Conrad, there can be no doubt that being married to him must have been a trying experience. Not only do her books reflect her feeling of having been exploited, but they convey the impression that she harbored a sense of inferiority toward him and toward his intellectual friends, who in turn probably felt little in common with her. As already noted, Hueffer apparently took little pains to hide his disrespect for her, and Virginia Woolf referred to her as Conrad's "lump of a wife."[11] Just how Jessie dealt with these attitudes is not altogether clear, but one suspects that her progressive obesity was at least partly the result of her utilizing overeating as a means of warding off depression and anger, as is so often the case in markedly obese individuals. Whether the fall in the street which ushered in her chronic invalidism was unconsciously motivated is conjectural, but it is worth noting that shortly before the accident she visited a doctor because her heart seemed to be troubling her.[12] In all likelihood she was experiencing palpitations—that tell-tale sign of anxiety—for on another occasion when she consulted a doctor for that complaint Conrad was told that she was "suffering from a nervous breakdown of some sort."[13]

striking, however, is its oblique allusion to the behavior of Adolf Verloc, one of the principal characters of the story that Conrad had just completed, *The Secret Agent.*

Conrad began writing *The Secret Agent* early in 1906 during the second or third month of Jessie's pregnancy, and he finished it in the beginning of November, about three months after the birth of the baby.[14] It may be considered therefore a literary accompaniment to the pregnancy and to the immediate postpartum period.

The pivotal event of this tale of violence—an abortive attempt to blow up the Greenwich Observatory—was based upon an actual undertaking which was similarly unsuccessful: the bomb exploded prematurely and Bourdin, the man who was carrying it, was killed.[15] In Conrad's story, Adolf Verloc, an agent of a European power, assigns the task of planting the bomb not to a man, but to a boy—Stevie, his wife Winnie's little brother. While carrying the bomb, Stevie trips, the bomb goes off too soon, and, like Bourdin, Stevie is blown to bits. When Winnie learns what has happened she murders her husband with a butcher knife and then commits suicide by leaping off a boat in the English Channel.[c]

Despite the stated relationships of the three members of the Verloc household, Conrad leaves no doubt that psychologically Stevie, a "weak-minded" boy, is Winnie's child. Winnie had been Stevie's protector since the time when he was a little boy, shielding him from their cruel father, a drunkard and a man "bad enough for murder."[16] After his death Winnie continues to mother Stevie, and in marrying Mr. Verloc she was seeking, among other advantages, to supply the child with a happy home. Indeed, in this she seems for a while at least to have succeeded: noting her husband's growing affection for little Stevie, she thinks with pride that they "might be father and son." Thus in spite of the thin disguises employed, the family group concerns a father, a mother, and their child. Moreover, in being responsible for killing the boy, Verloc becomes an appropriate substitute for the child's murderous real father.

[c] This violent outcome is identical with the end of "The Idiots": the wife stabs the husband and then leaps into the sea.

This theme of *The Secret Agent*—a father kills his son—is essentially the mirror image of the theme of "Amy Foster," wherein the birth of a son leads indirectly to the death of his father. In view of the reciprocal relationship between the two stories, it is not surprising to discover that *The Secret Agent* abounds with references to eating, biting, and even cannibalism. Mr. Verloc, for example, who is described as a fat, slothful, and disgusting slug, gnaws on his fingers when he is "upset." Confronted by his wife's "unreasonable" refusal to understand that he had not meant to kill her little brother, that it was "a pure accident; as much an accident as if he had been run over by a bus," Mr. Verloc finds himself seized by "unappeasable hunger," and, with a sharp carving knife, cuts thick slices of meat which he promptly devours.[d/17] It happens to be the same knife which Winnie employs a few minutes later, when, seeming to respond to the note of wooing of her recumbent ample mate, she plunges it into his heart. "Into that plunging blow, delivered over the side of the couch, Mrs. Verloc had put all the inheritance of the immemorial and obscure descent, the simple ferocity of the age of caverns, and the unbalanced nervous fury of the age of bar rooms."[18]

Mrs. Verloc's capacity to revive her connections with her primitive impulses, her "simple ferocity of the age of caverns," is in harmony with the jungle atmosphere of London as Conrad depicts it in *The Secret Agent*. "Then the vision of an enormous town presented itself," he wrote in 1920, in an introduction to the story, "of a monstrous town, more populous than some continents and in its man-made might as if indifferent to heaven's frowns and smiles; a cruel *devourer* of the world's light. There was room enough there to place any story, depth enough there for any passion, variety enough for any setting, *darkness* enough to bury five millions of lives."[19] (Italics mine) The element of cannibalism in this tale need not be inferred, however, through metaphor: it attains explicit expression. Thus, the anarchist Yundt declares: "Do you know how I would call the present social conditions? I would call them cannibalistic. The minority, a mere handful, are nourish-

[d] Some years prior to her marriage to Mr. Verloc, Winnie had been in love with a young impecunious *butcher*.

ing their greed on the quivering flesh and warm blood of luckless human beings. You can almost hear the scrunching of the bones."[e]

Overhearing these bloodcurdling sentiments, little Stevie screams, "Eating human flesh! That can't be allowed, can't, can't!"[21] For Stevie is a tenderhearted child, suffering acutely at the merest suggestion of cruelty. He implores a cab driver not to whip his horse, and, in his compassion for the overworked animal, leaps to the pavement in order to lighten the beast's burden. In his compassion Stevie is reminiscent of the tenderhearted Amy Foster; with her, moreover, he shares another trait—he stutters, a fact which in itself prompts the question whether, like Amy, his seeming tenderness may be tainted with a streak of savage ferocity.[f] The truth of this suspicion is readily confirmed, because long before his "father," Verloc, devises his plan for blowing up the Greenwich Observatory, Stevie sets off some explosions of his own in the building where he is employed; they are a protest against the alleged maltreatment of two office boys. His fireworks create a general panic, and he is forthwith dismissed from his job. On another occasion, after hearing of some maltreatment accorded a recruit by an army officer, Stevie becomes outraged. "I had to take the carving knife from the boy," Winnie confides to her husband. "He was shouting and stamping and sobbing. He can't stand the notion of cruelty. . . . He would have stuck that officer like a pig if he had seen him then."[23] Apparently reports of cruelty are capable of arousing Stevie to a pitch of sadistic fury.

These several resemblances between Stevie and Amy Foster suggest that in a sense they are cut from the same cloth and espouse a common cause. Amy, however, is not the only "mother" with whom Stevie apparently shares an identity. At the moment when, knife in hand, Winnie Verloc approaches the fat form of her unsuspecting husband, her face undergoes a strange and fleeting

[e] From the dramatized version, in which Yundt's speech is slightly more extended than in the book.[20]

[f] The "oral" nature of the sadism in Conrad's fiction is also indicated in the torture meted out to Dr. Monygham by Father Beron in *Nostromo*. After the torture, Beron would display "that dull, surfeited look which can be seen in the eyes of gluttonous persons after a heavy meal."[22]

transformation: "As if the homeless soul of Stevie had flown for shelter straight to the breast of his sister, guardian and protector, the resemblance of her face with that of her brother grew at every step, even to the droop of the lower lip, even to the slight divergence of the eyes." But as soon as Mr. Verloc expires, Winnie's "extraordinary resemblance to her late brother had faded."[24]

By means of this mysterious fusion of their appearance the murdered Stevie becomes united with his murdering sister-mother. "Mother" and "son" become one, sharing an ancient and elemental enmity toward the "father" who has come between them, an enmity no less powerful than that which could induce a man to invite a child to carry a deadly bomb.

The identities shared between Stevie and Amy Foster and between him and Winnie Verloc emphasize the basic similarity of the themes of the two stories. In both "Amy Foster" and *The Secret Agent*, a family of three—man, woman, and boy—constitutes an inherently intolerable situation demanding the elimination of one of the males in order to permit the remaining two to enjoy an unmolested mutual possession. In the former story it is the "good" passive father who is eliminated; in the latter, it is the "son." The "triumph" of the "father" in *The Secret Agent*, however, is short-lived, for he is promptly despatched by his unforgiving wife, who at the moment of his extinction, is joined in a mystical corporeal union with the "homeless soul" of her beloved "son."

This depiction of a symbolic reunion of mother and child is by this time a familiar Conrad theme. What is especially arresting about its re-statement in *The Secret Agent* is that it concerns a child bearing the name Stevie, which is a standard diminutive of Stephen, the name of the central male figure in *The Sisters*. Like Stevie, whose soul had flown "straight to the breast of his sister," his namesake Stephen is described as an infant basking in his mother's arms. It has already been suggested, even on the basis of the slight extant fragment of the work, that it was to achieve a reunion in death with a representative of his mother that the story of Stephen's relationship with Rita was conceived. Moreover, if Hueffer's account of the projected plot of the book is accurate, *The Sisters* was to have anticipated the denouement of *The Secret*

Agent in other aspects as well, for, like the latter story, a violent end was envisaged for Rita and her child; they were to have been murdered by the fanatical priest, her uncle and surrogate father.[25]

The fact that in these two analogous stories, written in two widely separated phases of his literary career, Conrad duplicated the name of a central character merits attention, for, except for the at least fivefold appearance of the name "Charles" (or its equivalents),[g] repetition of names in Conrad's fiction is rare. In *Victory* he supplied a clue to his method of selecting names: the narrator explains that the girl was given the name "Lena" by Heyst "after several experimental essays in combining detached letters and loose syllables."[26] Although it is stated that Lena was in some way fashioned out of Magdalen, it would appear just as likely that ultimately the name was created out of some "loose syllables" of Eve*lina*, the name of Conrad's mother.[h] If this hypothesis is correct it would lend significance to the fact that Conrad had used the name Lena once before, for in "Falk" one of the four children of Captain Hermann bears that name.[i] In naming another of the Hermann children Nicholas, Conrad was again drawing on his mother's family for names in that "cannibalistic" story, for Nicholas, it will be recalled, was the name of his mother's uncle, the notorious eater of roast Lithuanian dog. The same source was tapped in *The Secret Agent*: Adolf, Verloc's first name, was the name of another uncle of Conrad's mother—Adolf Pilchowski, at whose home, incidentally, arrangements were finally concluded for the marriage of Conrad's parents.[28] By the same token, as mentioned earlier, the name Stephen in *The Sisters* and Stevie, in *The Secret Agent* can be traced to Evelina's youngest brother, Stefan. The fact that Conrad's Uncle Stefan was murdered in the

[g] Charlie Marlow; Charley of *The Nigger*; Karl (one of the children in "Falk"); Charles Gould (*Nostromo*); and Sir Charles Latham (*Suspense*). The origin of Conrad's apparent attraction to this name is conjectural: perhaps the name "Don Carlos" was the source.

[h] See Chapter II, page 51.

[i] Baines erroneously applies the name Lena to Falk's beloved, the silent niece of Captain Hermann.[27] The error is understandable in light of the above hypothesis since it reflects an unconscious realization that the niece represents an epitome of motherhood.

course of the Polish Insurrection of 1863 confers an element of logic upon Conrad's borrowing his name for Winnie Verloc's brother Stevie, who, like his namesake, meets a violent death in an atmosphere of revolutionary activity.[j]

The fact that in these tales culminating in a symbolic reunion between mother and child Conrad was moved to choose names from the family of his lamented mother is noteworthy and lends further support to the thesis that his preoccupation with that theme arose from his own unanswered kindred yearnings originating in the distant past. Like so many of his invented characters, Conrad evidently hoped to be an "only child" of his wife; like them, too, he may have hoped to find in an early death the fulfillment of a wish for eternal peace.

But the actual circumstances of his married life turned out quite differently. Conrad lived for nearly 30 years after his ominous prediction of a short life, and he became the father of the two children whose advent gave rise to the stormy feelings and strange behavior which have been described. It goes without saying that in several respects Conrad was emotionally ill-suited to the role of father, and especially a father of boys. When his son Borys was about a year old he wrote to a friend who had just had a daughter, "I don't mind owning I wished for a daughter. I can't help thinking she would have resembled me more and would have been perhaps easier to understand."[30] In light of his admitted fascination with the relationship between fathers and daughters, this frank declaration is in itself not surprising, but his explanation for his preference is, to say the least, extraordinary, for it carries the implication that he viewed himself as having more in common with girls than with boys.

In the same letter he made it clear that he was repelled by the manifestations of uninhibited instinctual behavior in the baby, declaring, "If my affection for him depended on his angel-like quali-

[j] A possible allusion to this uncle may be contained in a comment of Victor Haldin in *Under Western Eyes*: "They say I resemble my mother's brother. . . . They shot him in '28."[29] The theme of the uncle who is murdered during a political uprising also occurs in *Nostromo* where it concerns Henry Gould, one-time President of the State of Sulaco and the brother of Charles Gould's father.

ties, it would be very evanescent. At the age of thirteen months he is an accomplished and fascinating barbarian full of charming wiles and of pitiless selfishness. It is not his innocence but his unconsciousness that makes him pathetic,—besides making him just bearable." Undoubtedly he regarded little girls as more "angel-like," and hence more like what he himself strove to be. A daughter, too, would have been less of a rival for Jessie's love.

Yet even if he might have preferred a daughter, his attitude toward children of either sex was something less than joyous, and he apparently doubted the sincerity of those who were enthusiastic. "I can't confess to any reverential feeling for childhood," he wrote to the same friend. "I've heard people, more or less sentimental, talk about it, but I question whether it is not a rather artificial attitude."[31] Then, apparently somewhat troubled by these frank "confessions," he added, "You must forgive—if you can detect—the tinge of cynicism upon my opinions. It is a false light after all. At the bottom of all these cheap reflections there is love for the young souls committed to our blind guardianship, which must fit them for the hazard of life." Despite this appended retraction, however, there is little difficulty in discerning both in this letter and elsewhere his irritation with the little "barbarian," which he would reveal again later on with John, Borys' younger brother.[k]

Thanks to his artistry, however, Conrad was able to direct some of these troubled feelings into the channels of fiction, thus sparing himself an even greater degree of suffering than that which he actually endured. One suspects that through his "cannibalistic" tales in particular, he was able to discharge not only intense feelings of hostile aggression but equally intense feelings of guilt. Thus, while there is little difficulty in perceiving a parallel between Mr. Verloc's destruction of his "son" Stevie and Conrad's act of throwing the new baby's clothes out of the train window, there is also no problem in discerning in his description of Verloc and his associates an expression of mordant self-hatred. Nor is it possible

[k] A clue to the origin of Stevie's stutter may be contained in a letter to Galsworthy in which Conrad wrote: "Poor B. stutters painfully on some days and on others not at all. Something will have to be done with his nose and throat."[32] "B" was undoubtedly Borys.

to escape the self-portrait of the gout-ridden Conrad in his depiction of the anarchist Karl Yundt: "When he rose painfully the thrusting forward of a skinny groping hand deformed by *gouty* swellings suggested the effort of a moribund murderer summoning all his remaining strength for a last stab . . . his worn out passion, resembling in its impotent fierceness the excitement of a senile sensualist," etc.[33] (Italics mine)

Yet even if Verloc and his ilk are a despicable lot, Conrad hints that in some respects they do not differ significantly from the agents of law and order who hunt them down. "You revolutionists," says the Professor, " . . . are the slaves of social convention, which is afraid of you; slaves of it as much as the very police that stands up in the defence of that convention. . . . The terrorist and the policeman both come from the same basket."[34] A similar opinion is voiced from the side of the law by Inspector Heat, who recognizes that the common type of criminal is "of the same kind as the mind and the instincts of a police officer."[35] This familiar reference to the theme of the "secret sharer" gains added emphasis in the dramatized version of *The Secret Agent.* In his stage directions for Act III, Scene 3, for example, Conrad says this of Verloc and Inspector Heat: "There is a certain similarity in their personal appearance—both big men, clothes same sort of cut, dark blue overcoats and round hats on."[36] Like the Captain and Leggatt in "The Secret Sharer," a physical resemblance between the upholder of the law and the criminal underscores their basic moral kinship.

Like "Heart of Darkness," and those other tales of secret sharing, *The Secret Agent* represents an introspective journey into the self, another attempt to find "what no other man can ever know." Like "Heart of Darkness," it is an avowal of the elemental savagery which lurks within the human breast, a renewed affirmation and a renewed confession that "man is an evil animal." Unlike the earlier novel, however, in which the evil slumbering in the heart of Mr. Kurtz was awakened by the seductive whisperings of the wilderness enfolding him, *The Secret Agent* asserts that even within the confines of regulated and organized civilization man may succumb easily to the primitive impulses which seethe within his savage soul: cannibalism resides not only in the heart of Africa but in the heart of London as well. Geography sets no limits upon the dark thoughts of a pregnant woman's jealous husband, who, gazing upon her body swollen with an unborn and unwanted rival, nourishes a secret hope that it will suddenly explode.

In keeping with a pattern which has been noted before, it was not long after the completion of *The Secret Agent* that Conrad composed its "antidote," the short story "Il Conde."[l] The former was finished early in November 1906, and by the 4th of December Conrad had completed the short story.[38] It concerns an elderly Count, a man of culture and elegance, who lives in Naples because of his frail health. One evening while listening to an open air band concert he is accosted by a young man who, holding a knife against the Count's breastbone, demands his money. But the Count has left his money at his hotel and his watch is being repaired. The young man disappears leaving the Count badly shaken. Suddenly, he recalls that he has a 20 franc French gold piece hidden away in his clothing and he goes to a nearby restaurant, paying for his restorative with the gold piece. But the young man is not far off. Approaching the elderly gentlemen he snarls, "Ah! So you had some gold on you—you old liar! . . . But you are not done with me yet." This proves to be the final crushing blow for the Count. Degraded and humiliated he determines that he must leave Southern Italy at once, never to return, and since he believes that his health cannot prosper in any other climate, the decision is tantamount to suicide.

Clearly "Il Conde" is in several respects a reversed image of *The Secret Agent*. For not only is the setting of the tale in a lovely music-filled Neapolitan evening in marked contrast with the sordid grime of sprawling London, and the character of the aristocratic Count the antithesis of the crude and porcine Verloc, but the essential action of the story constitutes a complete reversal of the theme of the novel. For "Il Conde" is not a tale of a gross and venal older man who causes a boy's death, but of a vicious, snarling

[l] It is a matter of speculation why Conrad mixed an Italian article and a Spanish noun in naming this story—an error which Conrad acknowledged and never corrected. Morf has noted a second similar error: "Riviera di Chiaja" for Riviera di Chiaia, a famous avenue in Naples.[37]

youth whose ruthless action leads to the ultimate destruction of an elderly gentleman.

The swift execution of this tale, reversing the thematic action of its predecessor, recalls Conrad's writing of the antidotal "Tomorrow" after "Amy Foster." In keeping with the suggestion offered regarding the latter pair of stories, "Il Conde" might bear the suitable subtitle: "Stevie's Revenge."

Yet, despite Conrad's apparent need to reverse the guilt-laden child-killing of *The Secret Agent* in "Il Conde," upon closer scrutiny the differences between these two tales of violence fade. It is noteworthy, for example, that the knife which the young Neapolitan uses on the Count is described as "perhaps a kitchen knife,"[39] as if it is Winnie Verloc's old knife which is held against the body of the Count at almost the precise point where Winnie stabbed her husband. It should also be recalled that at the moment of the stabbing Winnie's face was fused with the face of Stevie. Psychologically in both stories it is the "son" who ultimately annihilates the "father."[m]

In mid-December 1906, shortly after the completion of "Il Conde," the Conrads left London to spend the winter in Montpellier, stopping in Paris to visit Marguerite Poradowska. (It was on this trip that Conrad threw the baby's clothes out of the window.) The winter turned out badly for the family: both children became ill and for a while it was suspected that Borys might have tuber-

[m] "Il Conde" is said to have been based upon an experience befalling a Count Szembek—an elderly Polish nobleman whom Conrad had known during his stay in Capri in 1905.[40] As in other stories which Conrad drew from actual happenings, however, the psychological significance of "Il Conde" resides in its total presentation as a creative work. Conrad himself denied that it had any such significance: referring to all the stories in the volume entitled *A Set of Six*, which includes "Il Conde" and "The Duel," he wrote, "they are not studies—they touch no problem. They are just stories in which I've tried my best to be *simply entertaining*."[41] But Conrad's critical comments about his own work were often singularly lacking in perception, as if he had a scotoma—real or contrived—toward the remarkable insights residing in his fiction. He was to sum up the theme of *Lord Jim* as "acute consciousness over lost honor,"[42] and one suspects that had he written *Macbeth* he would have insisted that it was nothing but a ghost story. "Il Conde" may not be his most important short story, but it does an injustice to this psychologically subtle tale to dismiss it as "simply entertaining."

culosis. Despite the strain imposed by these added troubles, Conrad managed to make extensive revisions of *The Secret Agent* and to compose "The Duel." This short story which concerns a protracted feud, interspersed with a succession of duels between two officers in Napoleon's army, may be viewed as a third variation of the vexing theme of rivalry between males. If *The Secret Agent* may be summed up as "father murders son," and "Il Conde" as "son kills father," "The Duel" represents a humorous attempt to portray an even draw, a stalemate.

Ostensibly because Lieutenant D'Hubert disturbs Lieutenant Feraud while the latter is visiting a lady, D'Hubert is challenged to a duel in which Feraud is wounded. By the time both men reach the rank of General they have fought several more duels: in the second D'Hubert is wounded and the third ends in a standoff. Thus, the very pattern of the outcome of this succession of duels imitates the outcome of the rivalries in the three stories under consideration.

For all the fighting, it is difficult to give serious credence to the mutual antipathy of the two officers of "The Duel." Moreover, despite the alleged cause of their first duel—a woman—there is little to account for the perpetuation of their feud; certainly women do not furnish motivation since they play a negligible role in their protracted quarrel. There is a servant girl, a stock Conrad "wildcat," who nurses the wounded Feraud after the first duel, but she soon drops out of the picture and no successor appears to grace Feraud's life thereafter. D'Hubert too remains a bachelor during most of the story, and, until his marriage at forty, the only important woman in his life is his sister. Although he has seen his sister rarely over the years he is chagrined to hear of her impending marriage, fearing that it will result in his being "ousted from the first place in her thoughts, which had been his ever since the girl could speak."[43] He seeks to reconcile himself to the event, however, by observing that the day is not long off when he too must think of getting married. He is in the process of writing a letter of congratulations to her when a fourth duel interrupts him. Finally, when D'Hubert is on the point of marrying, his old adversary shows up again and a fifth duel ensues, with pistols. Feraud is disarmed in the fight but D'Hubert, refraining from pressing his advantage, spares the other man's life. D'Hubert then proceeds with his marriage. When, sometime later, he learns that his old foe has lost his government pension, D'Hubert and his wife contrive to support the unsuspecting Feraud for the rest of his life.

Despite D'Hubert's decision to get married, it would appear that his main reason for doing so is that his sister, once the only woman in his life, has turned her affections upon another man. Indeed the very fact that he interrupts writing a letter to her in order to go out and fight another duel with Feraud suggests that in this encounter psychologically his real adversary is the man who is about to rob him of her. Such an impression gains added support from a detail connected with the final duel: while preparing to meet his old enemy D'Hubert stops and plucks a pair of oranges from a tree in his sister's garden and sucks on them as he advances to the duelling ground.[n]

A further if indirect allusion to an incestuous attachment is furnished by a pair of names: D'Hubert's first name is Armand; his wife's, Adèle. Many years later Conrad combined these two names for Adèle D'Armand,[o] the half-sister of Cosmo in *Suspense*, an unfinished novel in which an incestuous love affair between these two individuals was clearly foreshadowed.

Thus, despite the suggestion that "The Duel" was conceived, albeit unconsciously, as a mild antidote for the grim brother-sister drama of *The Secret Agent*, an unaccentuated and watered-down version of the same relationship finds its way into the short story. "The Duel" achieves its light and essentially comic effect because the "real" issues over which the fighting takes place are so obscure as to be virtually invisible. The real adversary of D'Hubert, the suitor for his sister's hand, fails to make a single appearance throughout the story.

As for the protracted feud between the two officers, plainly it is not all it is reputed to be, for it appears less an expression of im-

[n] Attention has already been directed to this detail in connection with the symbolic significance of fruit in *The Sisters*. See Chapter II.

[o] Her name was derived from Adèle D'Osmond, the Countess de Boigne, whose *Memoirs* served as the base of the plot of *Suspense*, passages of which were lifted almost verbatim from the *Memoirs*. See Chapter XVII, page 36.

placable hatred than of a long standing attachment between two lonely bachelors, whose fighting provides an excuse for their coming together when they are not engaged in fighting a common enemy. During the retreat from Moscow, for example, they had fought shoulder to shoulder like inseparable comrades, and D'Hubert had carried both muskets when Feraud was tired. After the Restoration, D'Hubert intervenes with Fouché, the notorious minister of police, to spare the life of the overzealous Bonapartist, Feraud. Indeed, considering how often and how energetically D'Hubert comes to Feraud's rescue, it is difficult to believe in the alleged lethal antagonism between these two men, for it would appear to be affection rather than hate that binds these old combatants together, a sentiment echoed at the close of the story by D'Hubert himself, who says, "It's extraordinary how in one way or another this man has managed to fasten himself on my deeper feelings."[44]

In its spirit then, "The Duel" occupies the opposite end of the spectrum of rivalry between males to that depicted in "Falk," "Amy Foster," and *The Secret Agent*. Whereas in these three tales, suffused with an atmosphere of cannibalistic violence, either a man or a boy is destroyed, leaving his rival in undisputed possession of the wife-mother,[p] in "The Duel" there is no real killing although the men play at killing each other over women, and the women are but mere shadows. At the end of the story all three characters are still alive—the woman, her husband, and his so-called implacable foe, who, far from being eliminated, is generously supported by the married couple as if he were their beloved son.

Thus, the fierce and murderous rivalry of the earlier tales is replaced in "The Duel" by a loving attachment, an attachment achieved by minimizing the importance and even the desirability of women. Indeed, the ultimate union between mother and son which appears to occupy so central a position in the earlier stories gives way in "The Duel" to a seemingly eternal bond between the alleged enemies.

[p] In the cannibalistic episode in "Falk," the fight to the death is not over sole possession of a mother's love but over a symbolic manifestation of motherliness—food.

Seeking to account for the ancient enmity between the two soldiers, one observer, "who affected to believe in the transmigration of souls, suggested that the two had met perhaps in some previous existence,"[45] a sentiment which is reminiscent of Conrad's penchant for inventing a common "pre-history" of his relationship with Hueffer. Indeed the strong underlying attachment between the two combatants of "The Duel" bears more than a passing resemblance to the Hueffer-Conrad friendship, which, for a while at least, prospered in a climate where masculine rivalry was apparently supplanted by a fraternal embrace. It was such a truce that resulted in Conrad's apparent failure to defend his wife against Hueffer's impertinences, and which made their literary and spiritual collaboration a far more rewarding emotional experience than were certain aspects of their respective marriages.

Despite the gratification provided by this relationship it does not seem to have dampened Conrad's apparent unappeasable yearning to be a mother's only child. With the birth of a second son in the summer of 1906 this wish was dealt another blow, and despite his efforts during Jessie's pregnancy and after her delivery to cope with his rekindled feelings of resentment and rivalry toward the little usurper, the gnawing pain of isolation continued to harass him, demanding some new vehicle of discharge. It is not without significance, therefore, that in the autumn of 1907, roughly a year after John's birth, Conrad wrote once more of a lonely and unloved outcast in a story entitled *Under Western Eyes*, in which he immersed himself again in the grim themes of betrayal, guilt, and retribution, occurring in a setting of political anarchy and violence.

XI · Under Polish Eyes

ALTHOUGH Conrad began writing *Under Western Eyes* in the autumn of 1907 and finished the major part of it in 1908,[1] he laid it aside from time to time for his "Reminiscences"[a] and late in 1909 for "The Secret Sharer," so that the novel was not completed until the beginning of 1910.[b] Its completion, therefore, followed not long after the dramatic change in his relationship with Hueffer, a circumstance which, it is suspected, played a part in the emotional and physical upheaval that came as the aftermath of its final pages. Although a collapse of his health was a common consequence of the completion of one of his novels, what happened to Conrad after he finished writing *Under Western Eyes* exceeded anything that had gone before.

Under Western Eyes is Conrad's only major work in which the entire cast of characters, excepting the narrator, is Slavic. The story concerns Razumov, a student at St. Petersburg University, who is the illegitimate child of a Russian prince and the daughter of an arch-priest. Like nearly all the mothers of Conrad's main characters, Razumov's mother is dead, and until the action of the story begins he has seen his father but once in his life. Having neither roots nor family he has decided that the only way to success open to him is to distinguish himself in his studies. Consequently he has little to do with his fellow students and with their social and political activity, but this detachment has fateful consequences. One day a prominent minister of the state is assassinated by a bomb thrown by Victor Haldin, another student. Haldin, mistaking Razumov's aloofness for unspoken sympathy in political matters, takes refuge in the latter's lodgings. The fugitive tells Razumov what he has done and prevails upon him to make arrangements for his escape by sleigh during the night, but Razumov finds the driver dead-drunk when he tries to complete the arrangements. Enraged by this unforeseen predicament, Razumov gives the driver a violent thrashing and he then seeks out his father, the

[a] Later published as *A Personal Record*, the "Reminiscences" were written initially for *The English Review*.

[b] The date "January 22, 1910" is written on the manuscript at Yale.[2]

prince, and informs on Haldin. Returning to his rooms, Razumov tells Haldin that the arrangements for his escape have been completed; when Haldin leaves at midnight he is apprehended by the police and hanged a few days later.

The scene then shifts to Geneva, where a colony of Russian revolutionaries are living and where Victor Haldin had sent his mother and sister Nathalie for safety's sake; it is there that they learn of his death. Razumov, now in the employ of the Russian secret service, enters this circle of compatriots, and, taken for a loyal friend and comrade of Victor, is greeted with open arms. When he is faced with the grief-stricken mother and the trusting Nathalie, however, Razumov's arrogant callousness melts. He falls in love with Nathalie to whom he exposes himself as the betrayer of her brother, and subsequently he makes a second confession before the entire circle of revolutionaries. One of their strong men shatters Razumov's hearing and then throws him into the street, where the deafened Razumov is hit by a tram car, causing injuries which are ultimately fatal.

It is evident that here as in *Lord Jim* and in other stories Conrad was once again dealing with the theme of betrayal and atonement. But while Jim betrays 800 anonymous Arab pilgrims, the Russian betrays a fellow student, a "brother," a young man like himself. Yet in Razumov's eyes he has little in common with Haldin, for the latter has a loving mother and an adoring sister, while Razumov has no one, not even his father. "The most miserable outcast hugs some memory or some illusion,"[3] observes the narrator, and for Razumov that memory was of his single meeting with his father and of the latter's handclasp. "The most amazing thing of all was to feel suddenly a distinct pressure of the white shapely hand just before it was withdrawn: a light pressure like a secret sign. The emotion of it was terrible. Razumov's heart seemed to leap into his throat."[4] Bereft of any steady and trustworthy human contact, Razumov cannot permit himself to be diverted from pursuing his own ends by the importunities of a Victor Haldin, for having nothing himself he can feel only hatred for the fellow student who appears to have everything. Hatred, and perhaps jealousy, for while gazing on Haldin's grief-stricken mother he asks himself "was it something like enviousness which gripped his heart, as of a privilege denied to him alone of all men that had ever passed through this world?"[5] In depicting Haldin's loving relationship with Nathalie, moreover, Conrad was returning again to the intimacy between brother and sister which evidently held so strong an appeal for him, and which he depicted in *Nostromo*, *The Secret Agent*, "The Duel," and Suspense.[c] Indeed, in falling in love with Nathalie, Razumov sought to replace the brother he had betrayed. "Victor Haldin had stolen the truth of my life from me, who had nothing else in the world, and he boasted of living on through you [Nathalie] on this earth where I had no place to lay my head. . . . And do you know what I said to myself? I shall steal his sister's soul from her . . . he has delivered her into my hands."[7]

It is noteworthy that in an early plan of this story, which then bore the title *Razumov*, Nathalie Haldin was to marry her brother's betrayer and have a child by him. However, the remarkable resemblance of the child to Victor Haldin was to evoke Razumov's confession and lead "to the death of all these people."[8] Implicit in this preliminary sketch is the familiar theme of a father undone by his own child, whose resemblance to Haldin, incidentally, would have symbolized the real indestructibility of the betrayed man. Even in the final version of the book, in which no child appears, the dead Haldin appears to be joined in an eternal union with his mother: Miss Haldin "pointed mournfully at the tragic immobility of her mother, who seemed to watch a beloved head lying in her lap."[9] Thus even in death Haldin "continued to exist in the affection of that mourning old woman, in the thoughts of all these people."[10] Because he had been loved, Razumov realizes, "it was impossible to get rid of him. It's myself whom I have given up to destruction. . . . I can't shake him off."[d/11]

[c] According to Martin Decoud in *Nostromo* friendship between a man and a woman is impossible save between brother and sister, "meaning by friendship the frank unreserve, as before another human being, of thoughts and sensations; all the objectless and necessary sincerity of one's innermost life, trying to re-act upon the profound sympathies of another existence."[6] Conrad's meaning here would appear to be that sexuality precludes the possibility of friendship.

[d] Baines cites this sentence as one example of the "verbal echoes" of

Yet, despite his terrible deed and despite his abject loneliness, Razumov in the end attains the love which has been so long denied him. Crippled and dying, he is cared for by Tekla, one of the exiles, who, coming upon him after the tram-car accident, pushes her way through the crowd, exclaiming, "The young man is a Russian and I am his relation."[13] From her, thereafter, Razumov receives those loving maternal caresses which had once caused him such envy. "She sat down calmly, and took his head in her lap; her scared faded eyes avoided looking at his death-like face."[14] During the remainder of his days it was Tekla, "the Samaritan," who "tended him unweariedly with the pure joy of unselfish devotion."[15] Thus in his dying hours Razumov achieves that blissful sweet repose in the arms of a loving maternal woman that appears to be the ultimate goal and the final salvation of so many of Conrad's heroes.

No such repose awaited the author, however, upon his completion of the work, for it was swiftly succeeded by a state of progressive irritability and dangerous excitement. A few days before he was to journey to London to deliver the manuscript to his agent Pinker, an unpleasant scene took place in the Conrad home in the presence of Hueffer's estranged and aggrieved wife, Elsie. When the latter unleashed a long tirade against the literary world in general and against Conrad's friend Galsworthy in particular, Conrad flew into a rage and stamped out of the room. Jessie Conrad later insisted that "there was some connection between that incident and the cause of my husband's agitation when he had to go down [to London] a few days afterwards."[16] On his way to the railroad station Conrad drove recklessly and broke a spring in the cart; at his publisher's he smashed the back of a chair and he got into a violent and bitter row with Pinker, a man Jessie called "a very old and tried friend."[17] During his sleep that night he kicked out the foot of the bed. Upon his return home Conrad was acutely ill, suffering from a large swelling in the neck, a fever of 104°, and a delirium in which he rambled in Polish, save for interpolations of

Crime and Punishment heard in Conrad's novel. In the former, Raskolnikov declares, "I murdered myself, not her."[12]

the English burial service.[18] Although the physical symptoms soon subsided, he continued to manifest a bizarre mental state, causing his wife to write:

> Months of nervous strain have ended in a complete nervous breakdown. Poor Conrad is very ill and Dr. Hackney says it will be a long time before he is fit for anything requiring mental exertion. . . . There is the M.S. complete but uncorrected and his fierce refusal to let even I touch it. It lays on a table at the foot of the bed and he lives mixed up in the scenes and holds converse with the characters.
>
> I have been up with him night and day since Sunday week, and he, who is usually so depressed by illness, maintains he is not ill, and accuses the doctor and I of trying to put him into an asylum.[19]

In the weeks that followed, Conrad's behavior was characterized by childishness and deceit. According to his wife he consumed huge quantities of aspirin, consulted three physicians simultaneously without alerting any one of them to the services of the other two, and he poured their medicines down the drain. "I know what is wrong with me," he told her, "but I'm not going to tell them. I'm not going to do half the damn doctor's work for them."[20]

Altogether he was laid up for three months. In mid-May he wrote to Galsworthy, "I am coming back to the world. Yet that isn't exactly it. It's very much like coming out of one little hell into another."[21] Two days later he wrote to Sir Hugh Clifford: "I am somewhat shaky all over. It seems I have been very ill. At the time I did not believe it, but now I begin to think that I must have been. And what's more, I begin to see that the horrible nervous tension of the last two years (of which my wife knows nothing) had to end in something of this sort. . . . Perhaps it was the only way of relief?"[22]

Despite his evident improvement he continued to feel the effects of his illness for some time to come. "I am all of a shake yet," he wrote to Norman Douglas toward the end of June. "I feel like a man returned from hell and look upon the very world of the living with dread,"[23] and as late as September he was still referring to the "horrible nightmare of my long illness," and lamenting the "seven months . . . of my declining life wiped off in one fell swoop."[24]

Although it is admittedly impossible, unaided by medical data, to make a definitive diagnosis of an illness occurring more than 50 years ago, it seems probable, on the basis of his own subjective reports and the observations of his wife, that Conrad had developed a psychosis as a complication of an acute infectious-toxic process. Its initial phase, ushered in during an acute febrile state, bears a strong resemblance to the delirium he had experienced some 14 years before on his honeymoon.[25] But while the earlier illness soon ran its course, the delirium of 1910 was followed by a phase of physical and psychological invalidism, in which paranoid and possibly hallucinatory phenomena occurred. Finally there was a protracted phase of convalescence marked by depression, inertia, and childish behavior. Viewed as a whole the picture bears a strong resemblance to what is known clinically as the "Infection-Exhaustion Psychoses," which have been observed accompanying or following a variety of acute physical conditions: infectious illness, hemorrhage, poisoning, etc.[26] And just as these latter conditions may precipitate a latent psychic disorder, so, one suspects, did Conrad's acute febrile illness hasten to uncover a gathering emotional storm which, there is reason to believe, had been brewing for some time. Indeed when he himself spoke of his illness as a "way of relief" he was probably not far from the truth, and although he failed to specify precisely what he had in mind when he spoke of "the horrible nervous tension of the last two years," there is good reason to believe that it concerned above all the growing strain in his relationship with Hueffer resulting from the latter's liaison with Violet Hunt. There can be no question that from the moment of her entrance into Hueffer's life the Hueffer-Conrad friendship was never the same.

It was at a dinner party at John Galsworthy's in 1907 where Hueffer met Miss Hunt,[27] and where presumably he learned those gratifying vignettes of their shared past history that prompted his assigning to her, a woman 11 years his senior, the role of mother. Although that night they walked home together they apparently saw nothing of each other again until some time in 1908, when prodded by H. G. Wells, she called on Hueffer to submit some short stories to *The English Review*, which was at that time in the planning stage. After glancing rapidly through them Hueffer selected one, "The Coach," which was subsequently printed in the March 1909 issue.[28] Three days later they lunched together, and from that moment on she apparently worked closely with the magazine.[29]

Meanwhile Hueffer's marriage was foundering: his wife broke up their home at Winchelsea and moved into a cottage with her children; there was some intimation that she might seek a divorce.[30] It was at about this time, according to Herndon that *The Nature of a Crime* was written—mainly by Hueffer, who, like the protagonist of that work, was "suffering from a desire for a woman whom his chivalrous scruples and sense of obligation to his wife and others prevented him from possessing."[e/31] In time these scruples proved surmountable, although just when he and Miss Hunt began their affair is uncertain. In her memoir, *The Flurried Years*, there is a hint that it may have been in the late summer or early autumn of 1908, after she had written him a letter "containing vague messages of sympathy, as of an angel stooping from heaven to a mortal in durance."[32] In any event, there soon came a time when they were living together openly.

Conrad's reaction to these developments can only be surmised. That some ripples in his hitherto smooth relationship with Hueffer were developing in the latter part of 1908 is evident from a plaintive and distinctly apologetic letter written by Conrad in mid-December:

Dearest Ford:

I have almost lost the hope of seeing you here. My foot is very swollen yet and I have still less hope of being able to come and see you in town.

I can't get somehow rid of the idea that I have been in some

[e] Mention has been made in an earlier chapter of evidence suggesting that *The Nature of a Crime* may have been based partially upon the personal tribulations of Dante Gabriel Rossetti. See Chapter VII, page 146.

way indiscreet—I can hardly say offensive—vis à vis de vous. I have said something to that effect in a letter to you which was not worth answering, the supposition being too silly. If so—good. And indeed it is incredible that you should suspect me of an offensive intention on the ground of some remarks which are not and could not have been of any consequence. And considering our friendship and the confidence you gave me in that particular matter even the charge of mere impertinence would not stand. It was an expression which was *not* critical in its intention. But enough of that. I daresay you think I am mad—and truly sometimes I think so myself.[33]

In what way Conrad had been "indiscreet" or "offensive" and what the particular "confidence" was that he had received is conjectural, but in light of the events occurring at the time it would seem not unlikely that it concerned Miss Hunt, about whom Conrad may have made a tactless remark.

By mid-1909, however, when he began denouncing Hueffer as a "megalomaniac" with "a fierce and exasperated vanity," Conrad had clearly changed his course and had swung to the offensive. Instead of "Dearest Ford" he was addressing his errant friend as "Dear Hueffer" in a letter stating his refusal to contribute further to *The English Review*: "The E.R., I hear, is no longer your property and there is, I believe, another circumstance which for a purely personal reason (exceptionally personal, I mean) makes me unwilling to contribute anything more to the E.R."[34]

For Conrad this decision must have been painful for he had been identified with *The English Review* from its inception and was indeed one of its most enthusiastic sponsors.[f] As for the "exceptionally personal reason" for his withdrawal, Morey's suggestion that it referred to Hueffer's illicit affair seems quite plausible,[36] for by this time the latter had reached the proportions of a scandal. After Miss Hunt had allegedly saved him from suicide, Hueffer took steps to obtain a divorce in order to marry her. In the fall of 1909, Henry James retracted an invitation he had just extended to

[f] The very name of the magazine is said to have been suggested by Conrad.[35]

her with the observation that her position had become "lamentable."[37] All this must have been most distressing to Conrad, imposing upon him the burden of conflicting loyalties as well as the unhappy prospect of losing his friend, for, despite his aggressive attack upon Hueffer in July, he was far from reconciling himself to his loss. "After eleven years of intimacy," he wrote to a friend a few short weeks before the outbreak of his illness, "one feels the breach."[38]

Such was the highly charged atmosphere when on the eve of his breakdown Elsie Hueffer unleashed her attack on Conrad's friend Galsworthy, a man who, like her own husband, had sought a divorce in order to marry the woman he loved. But if Galsworthy had succeeded in this aim, Mrs. Hueffer was at that very moment determined that her husband would not. Far from being granted a divorce, Hueffer was ordered on January 11, 1910 by the court for the Restitution of Conjugal Rights to return to his wife in 14 days. This he did not do, nor did he comply with the order to pay his wife a weekly allowance, declaring that he would prefer to go to prison.[39] It is indeed ironical that within the space of a few days one of the "secret sharers" was in Brixton Gaol[g] while the other was suffering a psychotic delirium.

Although the break with Hueffer appears as an important factor in precipitating Conrad's psychosis it is pertinent to inquire into possible contributory causes, especially in light of his previous history of a decidedly shaky psychic equilibrium.

As already noted, Conrad characteristically succeeded in warding off physical and mental suffering through action—that action which for Charles Gould was "consolatory—the enemy of thought and the friend of flattering illusions."[41] During his earlier days Conrad sought action on the high seas and in adventure; later on he found it in the act of literary creation, which he himself defined as "just simply the conversion of nervous force into phrases."[h/42]

[g] After spending ten days in jail Hueffer paid the allowance.[40]

[h] It may be suspected that it was of himself he was thinking when referring to Razumov's diary he wrote: "He had regained a certain measure of composure by writing in his secret diary. . . . It calmed him—it reconciled him to his existence."[43]

Clearly, however, there are limits to the "therapeutic" efficacy of action, for sooner or later an adventure, a voyage, or a work of art must come to an end, and in the ensuing period of inaction all the hitherto contained suffering may break out anew. This indeed is what happened repeatedly to Conrad and was undoubtedly largely responsible for the condition of physical collapse and mental depression that followed the termination of so many of his actions.[i] It may be surmised, therefore, that the conclusion of the writing of *Under Western Eyes* had exposed him once again to that characteristic condition of physical and mental vulnerability.

There are reasons to believe, moreover, that his state of vulnerability was particularly heightened on this occasion by the nature of the book he had just completed, for *Under Western Eyes* proved to be an exceptionally personal work—so personal, indeed, that in his delirium the characters slipped almost unnoticed into the very content of his psychotic thought. From this observation and from others soon to be presented, it may be suspected that emotionally the story itself imposed a great strain upon him and threatened to engulf him in the currents of his own introspection. Conrad was evidently all too aware of that risk, for in this story as in others he employed a narrator in an effort to keep himself at a safe psychological distance from his work. Unlike the Marlow of "Heart of Darkness" or of *Lord Jim*, moreover, the narrator of *Under Western Eyes*, the "English teacher of languages," is portrayed as a person who is utterly uncommitted to the story he is telling; he is, in his own words, "unidentified with anyone in this narrative."[j/44] An attitude of detachment is also implied in the title of this work, as if its entire drama were being viewed through the wrong end of a pair of binoculars by a foreign correspondent for a British newspaper. Yet the very pointedness of this detachment is suspect, for

[i] An analogy to the condition of postpartum depression comes to mind.

[j] In actuality the detachment of the narrator is quite uneven. The term is hardly appropriate to the man who asks: "Who knows what true loneliness is—not the conventional word, but the naked terror?" On the other hand, there are sections of the book, particularly after Razumov leaves Russia, where the detachment assumes at times the quality of near indifference—a characteristic which Howe believes to be responsible for the weaknesses of the work.[45]

despite the forced nature of the title, and despite Conrad's effort to masquerade as a tourist among an alien people—detached "from all passions, prejudices and even from personal memories"[46]—it is all too apparent that the eyes through which the story of Razumov is seen are the eyes of an Eastern European, a native writer, whose narrative bears a clear imprint of Russian literary masters and reflects an unmistakable identification of the author with the Slavic temperament and people of the story.

The influence of Dostoevski, notably of *Crime and Punishment,* upon Conrad's Russian novel has been remarked upon by several critics. Baines has called attention to a number of striking parallels between the two stories, providing a number of examples of what he calls "verbal echoes" of the earlier work in Conrad's story.[k/47] Hay, too, comments on the similarities between the two works and cites other Russian sources of Conrad's material.[48] Conrad himself was evidently aware of this not inconsiderable indebtedness for he confided to his wife his fear that his work would be considered derivative by the critics: "They will be trying to drag in comparisons with Russian writers of a certain kind."[49] In this, of course, he was quite right, and had these same critics had access to earlier versions of the work they would have discovered even further evidence of his preoccupation with Russian writers while composing it. For if he engaged in thinly disguised borrowing from Dostoevski in the published novel, in the earlier versions, as Baines[50] and Hay[51] have pointed out, Conrad utilized the story as a vehicle for pouring ridicule on Leo Tolstoi, notably through the character of Peter Ivanovitch, who is credited with the authorship of a number of literary works whose names are obvious parodies of Tolstoi's titles.[l]

Seen in this light *Under Western Eyes* may be regarded as Conrad's Polish entry into the competitive field of Slavic literature.

[k] See footnote *d*, page 204.

[l] Hay has also called attention to a slip of the pen in Conrad's manuscript where he erroneously applied Tolstoi's patronymic, Nikolaievitch, to Peter.[52] An ambivalence toward Tolstoi is suggested by a letter in which Conrad praised Constance Garnett's translations of Russian novels, adding that "Turgeniev (and perhaps Tolstoi) are the only two really worthy of her."[53]

Moreover, if imitation be a high form of flattery, and parody the tribute paid to genius, it would seem that implied in the writing of his novel was the acknowledgment of at least a covert admiration for his Russian confreres, and particularly for Dostoevski. This hypothesis has importance, moreover, for not long after recovering from his psychosis Conrad was to unleash a stream of violent abuse at the author of *Crime and Punishment.*

This seeming ambivalence toward Russian literary masters is no more impressive, however, than is the patent contradiction between Conrad's professed Russophobia and the unmistakable sympathy extended to the lonely Razumov and to almost all of the other Russians in *Under Western Eyes.* It is startling to realize that the man who would one day declare that "Russians are born rotten"[54] was the same person who in 1908 had written to Galsworthy, "I think that I am trying to capture the very soul of things Russian."[55] There is little doubt that in this aim he succeeded; indeed, as Guerard has noted, Conrad appears to have been captured by that very soul himself.[56]

This remarkable capacity to steep himself so deeply in the atmosphere and feelings of a supposedly hated nation is indeed arresting, and causes one to wonder whether in the more obscure reaches of his mind there may not have lurked a hidden sense of identification with that nation as an expression of a fundamental Slavic affiliation. Hay brings forward evidence in support of such a view, pointing out that while throughout his later writing life Conrad repeatedly insisted that Poland was a Western nation, during his seafaring days he had apparently advanced the idea that Poland might one day become the leading *Slavic* nation in the Panslavonic movement. "What interests us here," she adds, "is that Conrad obviously had embraced for a time certain aspects of the Russian mystique."[57] That many years later he was to declare that "between Polonism and Slavonism there is not so much hatred as a complete and ineradicable incompatibility"[58] only serves to emphasize once again the wavering uncertainty of his own position between East and West, an uncertainty which he fictionalized in a Russian novel told by an English narrator.

Viewed dispassionately there is logic to the proposition that

Conrad felt a deep-seated affinity for Slavism, even Russian Slavism. It must be recalled that throughout his formative years he had been a Russian subject, and although he belonged to a family and to a nation that strove desperately to free itself from Czarist oppression, Russian history, Russian culture, Russian people, and the Russian language[m] were immanent elements in the environment of those impressionable years and could hardly have escaped inclusion within the cherished memories of his past and in the unfolding image of his own identity.[n]

It is indeed tempting to picture a subjugated people as imbued with an unequivocal and undying hatred for every facet and every member of the oppressing nation, but the lessons of history teach that things are seldom that simple. It would appear closer to the truth to assert that ever since the days when the children of Israel wandered in the wilderness of Sinai, refugees from tyranny have often sighed for the fleshpots of their native land:

> Why brought ye us from bondage,
> Our loved Egyptian night?

Moreover, although a regime, a policy, or a class may be despised, the various institutions of the "motherland" are often held dear and may be preserved relatively unchanged following the successful establishment of political independence. Thus refugees from British religious oppression named their American settlement Plymouth after their point of embarkation in England, and despite the efforts of Irish nationalists to foster the use of Gaelic, English continues to be the dominant language in Ireland.[o] It is a commonly observed clinical phenomenon, moreover, that even bad parents and unhappy childhood surroundings may become, despite

[m] Despite Conrad's assertion that he never knew Russian,[59] Najder brings forward evidence suggesting that he might have possessed at least a smattering knowledge of that language.[60] His father, who, like Razumov, had been a student at the University in St. Petersburg, knew it well.

[n] It is also somewhat difficult to reconcile Conrad's professed Russophobia with his naming his son Borys, a name which, as Najder points out, is typically Russian.[61]

[o] Even in contemporary America it is possible to discern vestiges of a sentimental affection for the British crown.

considerations of logic and reason, the fixed and haunting objects of nostalgic longings in later life.

That such nostalgic longings permeated the creation of *Under Western Eyes* gains further support from a few details in the story which, despite his declared effort to detach himself from "personal memories," contain suggestive echoes of Conrad's distant past. It is noteworthy, for example, that he gave the name Tekla to the "Samaritan" who rescues the stricken Razumov, for a girl by that name played a role of some importance in Conrad's adolescent years.

Following his return from his travels with his tutor, Mr. Pulman, in the autumn of 1873, Conrad lived in a boarding home in Lwow, under the care of a distant cousin, Antony Syroczynski. The latter had a daughter named Tekla with whom the young Conrad apparently fell in love.[p/62] Perhaps, as Baines suggests,[64] she was that "first love" to which Conrad later referred in a cancelled opening to *The Arrow of Gold*:

> From the nature of things first love can never be a wholly happy experience. But this man seems to have been exceptionally unlucky. His conviction is that, in colloquial phrase, he had struck something particularly wicked and even devilish. . . . I imagine that at first he amused her, then he bored her (perhaps was in the way of some more serious flirtation) and discovering that she could make him suffer she let herself go to her heart's content. She amused herself again by tormenting him privately and publicly with great zest and method and finally "executed" him in circumstances of peculiar atrocity—which don't matter here. . . . Perhaps he was unduly sensitive. At any rate he came out of it seamed, scarred, almost flayed and with a complete mistrust of himself, an abiding fear . . . he said to himself: if that's it then never, never again. In common parlance: once bit—twice shy. He had been bitten all over as it were, enough to make him shy of expressing himself forever.[65]

[p] Najder states that Conrad engaged in a flirtation with her for which he was severely reprimanded by her father.[63] It is interesting to note that Conrad applied her patronymic to another character in *Under Western Eyes*: Sophia Antonovna.

If indeed this is a description of the Tekla of Conrad's youth it must be admitted that, far from resembling her later namesake in *Under Western Eyes,* she appears more to have anticipated those biting cat-like creatures of Conrad's fiction who similarly succeed in inducing a state of "abiding fear": Aïssa, Amy Foster, Winnie Verloc, Clelia (*Suspense*), and the girl in "The Inn of Two Witches." Yet, despite the manifest differences between the two Teklas, the fictional one does possess certain characteristics which link her with Conrad's "cat women." A cat, as a matter of fact, is her constant companion. Referred to as the "woman with the cat,"[66] this maternal Tekla is often described as "pressing the cat to her breast,"[67] and in her "unselfish" devotion to Razumov she bears a resemblance to the "little cat," Winnie Verloc, shielding her beloved brother from their drunken father, and to Amy Foster, consumed by a single-minded dedication to her infant son.[q] "If you were to get ill . . . or meet some bitter trouble," she assures Razumov, "you would find that I am not a useless fool. You have only to let me know. I will come to you. . . . I would follow you with joy."[68]

It would be ironical if in fashioning this image of blind fidelity Conrad chose to name her after a childhood love who presumably treated him so cruelly, and who "finally 'executed' him in circumstances of peculiar atrocity." Yet on further consideration, perhaps it is not so strange after all, for is it not the essence of the daydreams of a spurned and disdained lover that one day his cruel tormentor will openly acknowledge her profound and abiding love?

Tekla Syroczynska, however, was apparently not the only girl on whom the youthful Conrad fixed his heart. As noted in an earlier chapter, in his First Note to *The Arrow of Gold,* and in the Introduction to *Nostromo,* Conrad referred to a girl, presumably Janina Taube, whom he had known in Cracow and whom he used as a model for Antonia Avellanos.[69] Unlike the devilish and flirtatious Tekla, Janina appears to have been a girl of lofty moral purpose: "an uncommon personality, the moral center of a group of young people on the threshold of life . . . she had the power of an exalted

[q] Or to her husband, Yanko Gooral, before the birth of their child.

character . . . how we used to look up to that girl . . . as a standard bearer of the faith to which we were all born but which she alone knew how to hold aloft with an unflinching hope."[70]

It is not necessary to point out that this is hardly the description of a frivolous and feminine girl, but rather of one of those Amazonian characters like Rita de Lastaola or the wife of Gaspar Ruiz, who are endowed more with gladiatorial than with maternal qualities. Such women do not conjure up fantasies of intimacy; they are worshiped from afar, secretly, as if they partake of awe-inspiring attributes. It is not difficult to find traces of the same model in the character of Nathalie Haldin whom Razumov addresses in his diary: "And your pure forehead! It is low like the forehead of statues—calm, unstained. It was as if your pure brow bore a light which fell on me, searched my heart and saved me from ignominy, from ultimate undoing . . . your light! Your truth! I felt that I must tell you that I had ended by loving you."[71] But this Razumov never does. He was like Conrad himself, who, speaking evidently of Janina Taube,[r] wrote: "He was in love with her. But he never betrayed that sentiment to her, to anybody. He rather affected resistance to her influence."[73]

Not unlike Janina, the "standard bearer," and those fictional women whom Conrad compared with sculpture, Nathalie possesses attributes which carry a distinct masculine stamp. Her voice, for example, is "slightly harsh, but fascinating with its masculine and bird-like quality,"[74] a somewhat paradoxical combination, it must be admitted, which reappears in another description: her "strong shapely hand had a seductive frankness, a sort of exquisite virility."[75] This attribution of a masculine quality to Nathalie's handshake is noteworthy, moreover, for in other respects as well it evokes comparisons with the handclasp of Razumov's *father*, suggesting that like a number of her fictional sisters Nathalie possesses a bisexual appeal.[s] No less striking is the similarity of the language

[r] If indeed Janina was the model for Antonia she must have been a rather formidable young lady, or at least appeared so to Conrad. " 'You know you were a very terrible person,' " Decoud tells Antonia. " 'A sort of Charlotte Corday in a schoolgirl's dress; a ferocious patriot.' "[72]

[s] Rita's handshake, which was "frank as a man's," would go through M. George "like a wave of heat."[76]

used to describe Razumov's reaction to his father's handshake—"his heart seemed to leap out of his throat"—and that employed by Conrad in recalling the farewell gesture of Janina Taube when he was about to leave Poland to become a French mariner: "That afternoon when I came in, a shrinking yet defiant sinner, to say the final goodbye, I received a hand squeeze that made my heart leap and saw a tear that took my breath away."[t/77]

Perhaps of all of Conrad's writings *Under Western Eyes* conveys most poignantly his own sense of isolation, his intense longing for human warmth and that unappeasable hunger for physical contact which confers such profound and unspoken significance upon the memory of a hand pressed by a father's hand and of a head cradled within the soft embrace of a mother's arms. What imparts to this work its special poignancy and renders it perhaps the most autobiographic of Conrad's stories would seem to be that here for the first—and last—time in his writing career he ventured boldly within the geographic, ethnic, and personal confines of his remote, unhappy past.[u] That he himself recognized the highly personal significance of this work seems certain from the Author's Note: "The obligation of absolute fairness was imposed on me *historically and hereditarily by the peculiar experience of race and family*."[79] (Italics mine)

For Conrad this evocation of memories of "race and family" must have been a heavy trial, and despite his efforts to keep his distance his own mournful shadow seems to move from time to time across the pages. Thus, when Razumov speaks to Nathalie in his diary, "And also I was afraid of your mother. I never knew mine.

[t] While Najder points out that there is no evidence to support the hypothesis that Conrad was in love with Janina Taube,[78] for present purposes the question of the precise identity of Conrad's adolescent loves is of minor importance. The essential point here is the correspondence between the two girls recollected from his youth and his fictional women. Of the latter many, if not most, would appear to be linear descendants of one or the other of these two girls: thus his stately heroines seem to be the counterparts of the awesome "Janina," while the aggressive and sensuous "cat women" appear to be related to the girl assumed to be Tekla Syroczynska.

[u] It may have been an inability to deal with this same material that was partially responsible for the failure of his earlier attempt to portray a lonely Slavic youth in *The Sisters*.

I've never known any kind of love. There is something in the mere word," etc.,[80] it is difficult to believe that the voice could be other than the voice of Conrad himself, revealing the source of his life-long sorrow in the untimely loss of his mother.[v]

Whether this open acknowledgment in a work of fiction of the cause of his suffering would alone have sufficed to induce a mental illness is unanswerable; as an accompaniment to the gathering storm occasioned by the separation from his friend Hueffer, his "life-long habit," it cannot be doubted that the writing of *Under Western Eyes* served to reinforce the pain of that new loss with its patent allusions to the earlier one. In the prophetic words of the narrator: "No human being could bear a steady view of moral solitude without going mad."[83] It is not surprising that in that madness Conrad spoke in his native tongue and held conversations with the Slavic personages of his story. Indeed it might be asserted that this aspect of his illness represented a continuation, as it were—albeit greatly altered in purpose, organization, and psychic control—of the same creative process that gave expression to the novel. At this moment there ceased to be a separation between "the mind that creates and the man that suffers," and like an enthralled spectator in the theater who after the final curtain is but vaguely and reluctantly cognizant of the real world about him, Conrad emerged from the creation of his Russian drama as if he had lost his bearings, unable to distinguish between fact and fiction. The flood of emotion that should have been contained within the confines of his art had overflowed its banks and threatened to engulf the author in his own creation, to the end that the boundaries between the crippled Razumov and the crippled Conrad were figuratively washed away. It is no wonder that he would later refer to his illness as a "horrible nightmare," nor can it be doubted that like all victims of the nightmare, Conrad dreaded the possibility of a repetition.

[v] In reply to a letter from Janina Taube (Baroness de Brunnow) in 1897 Conrad had written: "The sight of your signature has awakened all images of the past, of which the happiest moments were afforded by the kindness of your mother."[81] Some time later he begged to be remembered to Janina's mother, stating that he had retained "an almost filial regard for her."[82]

His fear of mental illness was of long duration. "I have long fits of depression that in a lunatic asylum would be called madness," he had written Garnett while on his honeymoon. "I do not know what it is. It springs from nothing. It is ghastly. It lasts an hour or a day and when it departs it leaves a fear."[84] A few months later he wrote, "I ask myself whether I am breaking up mentally. I am afraid of it."[85] There were others too who shared these anxieties. Some years later Sir William Rothenstein wrote that Conrad's "morbid fear of breaking down and leaving his wife and boy penniless is really tearing his nerves to shreds."[86] On another occasion Rothenstein wrote, "Last year I feared for his reason."[87]

That these fears were not unfounded must have been all too apparent to Conrad during the slow convalescence from his illness in 1910. Having skirted so precariously upon the rim of madness it is hardly surprising that he took measures to insure himself against a recurrence of that frightening experience. "I am keeping a tight hold on myself," he wrote in May, "for fear my nerves go to pieces."[88] In this he may be said to have achieved success, but it was a success for which he paid dearly, for it was secured by the adoption of psychological defenses, which, as will shortly become evident, exerted a profound and unfelicitous effect upon him as an artist, and, as some might believe, as a person too.

XII · The End of the Tether

IN CLOSING his perceptive study of Conrad, Moser observes: "It is indeed difficult to conquer the impulse to find greatness in all the works of a man we sense to be great."[1] Yet in the interest of discriminating criticism it is surely an impulse which should be resisted: not all of Beethoven is sublime and some of Shakespeare is quite dull.

A comparable unevenness in the quality of Conrad's art has been apparent to critics and readers almost from the beginning. Yet while the first half of his literary life—1894-1910—witnessed the occasional emergence of inferior writings, these were but islands of relative mediocrity set in a sea of literary grandeur. The second half of his writing life, however, from 1910 until his death in 1924, was marked by works, which, with the possible exception of *The Shadow-Line*, are regarded by many critics as uniformly inferior to the best of what had gone before. Guerard, for example, who considers *Victory* grossly overvalued and badly written, finds much of the later Conrad "indistinguishable from popular magazine romance."[2] Even if these opinions, which are shared in the main by Moser,[3] Hewitt,[4] and others, evoke an occasional dissent, there can be little disagreement that following his mental breakdown in 1910 a radical change took place in virtually all of Conrad's stories. The most striking manifestation of this change concerns a pronounced shift in the moral and psychological orientation of his stories which is characterized by an exteriorization of the source of suffering. As a consequence the poignant inner mental conflict of the early Conrad was replaced by conflict with the outer world, and doubting, troubled men, like Marlow of "Heart of Darkness," and hapless souls like Jim or Decoud, caught in a neurotic web of their own creation, gave way to simple innocent creatures who, as pawns of fate, struggle with indifferent success against external influence, external accident, and external malevolence. It is fitting that the first major work of this period was entitled *Chance*. Chance plays a role in the earlier Conrad, too, as Moser has emphasized, but there it remains a subordinate element, "a device for exploring moral failure."[5] In the later Conrad, this same critic observes, when trouble comes to the protagonist he is in no way responsible for it. "The fault lies elsewhere, in other people."[6] Guerard makes much the same point when he states: "Evil and failure in this new cleansed moral universe are presumed to come from outside rather than from within."[7]

The surrender of personal autonomy and the disavowal of personal authorship for the vicissitudes of life implicit in this new orientation is typical of the phenomenon of projection, that psychological device which consists in the attribution to influences or agencies beyond the self of those attitudes, feelings, impulses, and thoughts which reside within the subject's own mind. Carried to an extreme, projection may attain the proportions of paranoid thinking, characterized by delusions and other gross distortions of reality. Yet even in its less pronounced forms the recourse to projection as an attempted solution to intolerable inner contradictions must result in some warping of the sense of reality, particularly the reality that is implicit in a reasonable degree of self-knowledge. And if by such a process it is possible to attain a condition of relative conflict-free stability, it is at best a precarious stability, demanding constant vigilance and allowing neither searching introspection nor daring flights of imaginative fancy. In retreat from unsettling doubts and ambivalence, and in quest for comforting certainties, the subject tends to view the world in black and white simplicity, to the end that people are reduced to stereotypes, thoughts to platitudes, and the turmoil of life to a set of easy formulas.

Such was the course, it would seem, that Conrad took after his mental illness, turning his back upon his erstwhile skepticism, doubts, and introspection, and stepping forth resolutely as the cliché-ridden champion of solid virtue and duty with a capital "D." Thus the man who in 1897 had stated: "A sweeping assertion is always wrong, since men are infinitely varied,"[8] was able to declare in the later years: "Those who read me know my conviction that the world . . . rests on a few very simple ideas . . . it rests notably, among others, on the idea of Fidelity."[a/9]

[a] Although *A Personal Record* was written in 1909 the "Familiar Preface" from which this passage is taken was written in 1912.

In his fiction a freezing of his imagination manifested itself in a stereotypy that affected both his characters and his plots. His heroes became well-meaning but unmanly creatures, tentative and inert, and remarkably passive toward their women. The latter exhibit a comparable stereotypy, emerging as beings of monumental stature and incredible power—qualities which inevitably lend them a prominence in the narrative that was rarely evident in the earlier works. Prior to 1910, Conrad's fiction had been focused primarily on men (*The Nigger of the Narcissus*, "Youth," "Heart of Darkness," "The End of the Tether," and "The Secret Sharer"), or fairly equally on both sexes (*Almayer's Folly*, *An Outcast of the Islands*, *Lord Jim*, "Falk," "Amy Foster," *Nostromo*, *The Secret Agent*, and *Under Western Eyes*). Beginning with "A Smile of Fortune," written in the latter half of 1910, it is the women who dominate Conrad's fictional stage. Like ballerinas who traditionally comprise the main attraction of the dance, these fictional females perform breathtaking leaps and dazzling turns, while employing their submissive and often seemingly impotent partners as temporarily convenient accessories. With an inexorable consistency, moreover, the choreography turns out to be a dance of death in which the women usually emerge triumphant while their men are systematically unmanned and then destroyed. A review of some of Conrad's selected plot situations in his more important works after 1910 will illustrate this trend.[b]

"Freya of the Seven Isles"

Completed early in 1911, this story concerns the daughter of a retired sea captain who has insisted upon waiting until her twenty-first birthday before marrying her lover, Jasper Allen, ostensibly in order to dispel any doubts in the minds of others that she knows what she is doing. It might occur to the reader, however, that a more probable explanation for her postponing her wedding is to be found in her attachment to her father. She has many of the characteristic attributes of a standard post-1910 heroine, particularly a spectacular head of hair, so long that she could sit on it, "so

[b] "A Smile of Fortune" (1910) has been dealt with in an earlier chapter, and is omitted here.

glossy that it seemed to give out a golden light of its own."[10] Among her other accomplishments she plays the piano, but the description of her performance is more suggestive of an explosion than of an aesthetic experience. During rainstorms she "would play fierce Wagner music in the flicker of blinding flashes, with thunder bolts falling all around, enough to make your hair stand on end; and Jasper would remain stock still on the verandah, adoring the back view of her supple, swaying figure, the miraculous sheen of her fair head," etc.[11]

Although Jasper in turn is compared with a "flashing sword-blade perpetually leaping out of the scabbard,"[12] his actual behavior fails to mirror either this symbolic depiction of erotic readiness or the implied manly belligerence. For Jasper derives his total self-esteem and sense of masculinity from his brig, and when that ship is wrecked by the foul play of his rival, Lieutenant Heemskirk, Jasper's entire world crumbles. Belatedly recognizing his true inner weakness, he observes, "If I had been a man I would have carried her off, but she made a child, a happy child of me." (It is to be noted, in view of the passivity of these later heroes, that Jasper ascribes his becoming a child to Freya's influence, not because he wishes to become one.) "The day the only thing I had belonging to me in the world perished on this reef, I discovered that I had no power over her."[13] Freya herself acknowledges that there was something in her that refused to submit to her man. To her father she confesses that she has been "conceited, headstrong, capricious. I sought my own gratification. I was selfish or afraid . . . perhaps, when the day came [for her marriage] I would not have gone."[c/14]

Chance

Like Jasper Allen, Captain Anthony of this novel, finished in 1912,[d] does not loom as a conqueror of women. Although he

[c] Conrad did not think very highly of this story, if one may judge from a letter to Garnett, in which he wrote: "I daresay Freya is pretty rotten." He also appears to have had an intimation of what was wrong with it. Continuing in the same letter he said, "On the other hand, 'The Secret Sharer,' between you and me, is *it*. No damned tricks with girls there."[15]

[d] The major part of the writing of this work was begun in the summer of

rescues Flora de Barral from suicide and subsequently marries her, her relationship to her father, like Freya's, presents an almost insuperable barrier to a consummation of the marriage. Subjected to her jealous father's accusation that she is in love with her own husband, Flora finds herself unable to defend herself. "It might have made things worse; and she did not want to quarrel with her father, the only human being that really cared for her . . . she felt also helpless, as if the whole enterprise had been too much for her. . . . *She was becoming a fatalist.*"[19] (Italics mine) Faced by this patently adhesive union between father and daughter, Captain Anthony does nothing to assert his connubial claims: on the contrary, he shows a palpably supine willingness to give her up. "I own myself beaten," he tells Flora (although there is little evidence that he has fought for her). "You are free. I let you off since I must."[20] Unlike Freya, however, Flora refuses to accept her lover's inertia. Displaying a sudden and unwonted seductiveness, she falls into his arms, a gesture which succeeds in igniting a momentary spark of sexual initiative in Captain Anthony, who "burdened and exulting" leads her to his cabin. At this point, discovering that he has lost his daughter, De Barral commits suicide.

It must not be supposed, however, that Captain Anthony's action heralds his dramatic transformation into a man of aggressive virility. Like Jasper, he is merely a tool of a woman's whim and will, a pawn responding to the forces about him. Moreover, were it not for the *chance* discovery by the second mate, Mr. Powell, that Flora's father was preparing to poison his hated son-in-law,

---

1910 after the *New York Herald* offered to serialize a Conrad novel. Prior to this date Conrad had worked fitfully on the story—"tinkering" with it, as Baines put it[16]—for some six years. Conrad's stated opinion of this popular novel—"the biggest piece of work I've done since *Lord Jim*"[17]—is a good example of an artist's scotoma in judging the quality of his own work. For although *Chance* became a best seller and marked the turning point in Conrad's financial fortunes as a writer, it is likely that very few critics would think of comparing it with *Lord Jim* or gloss over *Nostromo* as Conrad obviously did in his evaluation of *Chance*. (Jean-Aubry sought to explain Conrad's statement as an error, presumably due to absent-mindedness, for in a footnote to the published letter in which the statement appears he added: "He means after *Nostromo*,"[18] but Jean-Aubry's correction seems to be based more on wish than on proven fact.)

Captain Anthony would never have survived long enough to be prodded into action by his wife. Even so, the idea that Captain Anthony should continue to enjoy his triumph was apparently unpalatable to Conrad, for he found it necessary to kill the captain off by having him go down with his ship at sea after a few years of married life, leaving the indestructible Flora to survive and marry Mr. Powell.

There is no mistaking the omnipotent role assigned to Flora. On board her husband's ship, the *Ferndale*, she evokes the general hostility of the crew because of her plainly demoralizing effect upon their captain. For, preoccupied with Flora, the once excellent Captain Anthony has become a prey to inefficiency and indecision. He is now absent-minded and forgets to issue orders, with the result that there is a near catastrophe—the *Ferndale* narrowly escapes collision with another ship at sea. Not surprisingly it is Flora herself who saves the *Ferndale*, for she succeeds in igniting a warning flare after the clumsy mate, Mr. Powell, proves unable to do so. Thus the all-powerful Flora is not only responsible for nearly wrecking the ship; she also is its savior. Some notion of her impressive power is conveyed by an aside of Marlow, the misogynous narrator of *Chance*. Speaking of Anthony's behavior toward her, he says, "He had dealt with her masterfully"—a sentiment to which the reader may have difficulty in subscribing. "But man has captured electricity too. It . . . lights him on his way, it warms his home, it will even cook his dinner for him—very much like a woman. But what sort of conquest would you call it? He knows nothing of it. He has got to be mighty careful what he is about with his captive. And the greater the demand he makes on it in the exultation of his pride the more likely it is to turn on him and turn him to a cinder."[21] In thus comparing Flora, and incidentally all women, with electricity, Conrad was repeating the image of the powerful Freya whose hair-raising piano-playing is accompanied by flashes of lightning and the roar of thunder.

"The Inn of Two Witches"

Written toward the end of 1912, this short story carries the image of women as destroyers of men to a point of willful and malicious brutality. It concerns "Cuba Tom," a British sailor assigned to a secret mission in French-held Spain in 1813. Stopping at an inn for the night he is murdered in bed by an infernal machine—a mechanically operated canopy which descends upon the unsuspecting sleeper and suffocates him. As might be expected, the inn is run by two old hags and the machine is operated by a voluptuous gypsy girl equipped with a typical Conradian coiffure and with characteristic feline attributes. Her face has "a wild beauty, voluptuous and untamed," and to gauge the power of her "steadfast gaze . . . you have only to observe a hungry cat watching a bird in a cage or a mouse inside a trap."[22] Although Tom has a reputation for manliness and courage—epitomized by a celebrated pigtail—he is no match for the gypsy girl, whose mode of annihilating him, by the way, is an almost literal enactment of the classic nightmare: the smothering incubus.

"The Planter of Malata"

This long short story, written in 1913, served as Conrad's next vehicle for the theme of the man-destroying woman. Like all of Conrad's fictional women of this period, Felicia Moorsom is a lethal force. She drives one man into drug addiction and another, Geoffrey Renouard, kills himself over her. Like her fictional sisters her power is epitomized by her hair, the description of which contains repeated allusions to armor, metal, and fire. Thus her head is "crowned with a great wealth of hair" which "appeared incandescent, chiselled and fluid, with the daring suggestion of a helmet of burnished copper and the flowing lines of molten metal."[23] Renouard does not deceive himself that he is any match for her. "Unnoticed, he looked at that woman so marvelous that centuries seemed to lie between them. He was oppressed and overcome at the thought of what she could give to some man who really would be a force. What a glorious struggle with this Amazon! What a noble burden for the victorious strength."[24] Renouard is no such force, and though he briefly entertains a wild fantasy of "seizing her in his arms, carrying her off in a tumult of shrieks . . . into some profound retreat as in the age of Cavern men," his actual behavior is quite different, for he is barely able to bring himself to look her in the face. Physically, no less than spiritually, Felicia is the stronger. Like Lena of *Victory*, who succeeds in overpowering the rapacious Ricardo with her "fingers like steel," Felicia is able to prevent Renouard from arising by exerting a "convulsive pressure on his wrist."[25] Even in a dream his weakness is revealed: he dreams he is traversing endless galleries, lofty halls, and innumerable doors. He becomes lost and the lamp which has been lighting his way goes out. He stumbles on the head of a statue, resembling Felicia, but as he holds it in his hands it "began to grow light in his fingers, to diminish and crumble to pieces, and at last turned into a handful of dust."[26]

An experience similar to this seeming symbolic depiction of detumescence takes place when briefly he holds her in his arms: "fire ran through his veins, turned his passion to ashes, burnt him out and left him empty, without force—almost without desire. He let her go before she could cry out."[27] What follows is characteristic of many of Conrad's later heroes: he kneels at her feet and kisses the hem of her skirt. Aware of her deadly power, he fears his love for her "instinctively as a sick man may fear death."[e/28]

Victory

Tentativeness, indecision, and passivity characterize Heyst, the hero of this novel of 1914. Like Captain Anthony and Geoffrey

[e] Leaving aside the question of the literary merit of this story, it is a work of particular interest in terms of its biographical and psychological significance in a study of Conrad. These matters are discussed elsewhere; see Chapter IV. Mention should be made here, however, that in the character of the Editor—a stoutish, fair-complexioned man, with a reputation for considerable professional vanity and a passion for discovering literary talent—Herndon has detected a probable portrait of Ford Madox Hueffer.[29] Support is lent to this conjecture by a letter which Conrad wrote to the editor of the *Sydney* (Australia) *Bulletin* in 1916, in which he broadly hinted that an episode described in the story was based upon a real event that had taken place in the editorial room of *The English Review*.[30] Since the Editor is presented in a generally sympathetic light, Herndon's thesis would provide additional evidence of Conrad's persistent attachment to his estranged friend. "The Planter" was written during the same year, incidentally, when Conrad wrote Hueffer a particularly cordial letter, containing allusions to their joint past, and addressing him as "Mon Très Cher." See Chapter VII, footnote *r*.

Renouard (and like Conrad himself after his marriage), Axel Heyst takes a girl away with him across the seas, but once he has installed Lena on his island retreat, his behavior, far from suggesting a man basking in a romantic idyl, reflects a state of extreme discomfort and remoteness. Like Captain Anthony and like Jasper Allen, moreover, Heyst is utterly passive in the face of external danger. When his island is invaded by the nefarious trio—Mr. Jones, Ricardo, and Pedro—Heyst not only does nothing to defend his girl or himself, but even the idea of doing so seems alien to him. Presented with an opportunity of overpowering the evil Jones, he seems paralyzed: "He did not even think of that. His very will seemed dead of weariness. He moved automatically, his head low, like a prisoner captured by the evil power of a masquerading skeleton out of the grave."[f/31] He is equally devoid of affectionate warmth and of sexual energy, and when the dying Lena cries out to him, "Why don't you take me in your arms?" he simply bends over her and remains sadly silent. Although in the end, Lena, like Freya, dies, it must not be supposed that this is a sign of weakness or defeat. On the contrary, the very title of the book symbolizes her triumph. She is possessed, moreover, of such prodigious, albeit improbable, strength that she overpowers the lust-ridden Ricardo when he tries to rape her.

The Shadow-Line

A break in this parade of romantic uniformity came with the writing of *The Shadow-Line* in 1915, a semifictionalized account of Conrad's only maritime command and the one work composed after his breakdown which has an exclusively male cast of characters. Guerard is undoubtedly right in claiming that it was the lack of land and love entanglements and the lack of the need for the author to invent a plot or setting which made *The Shadow-Line* a notable exception to the general inferiority of Conrad's post-1910 works.[33] As Conrad had said, accounting for the success of

[f] Compare a letter to Marguerite Poradowska which Conrad wrote from Africa in 1890. "For a long time I have been uninterested in the end to which my road leads. I have gone along it with head lowered, cursing the stones."[32]

"The Secret Sharer": "No damned tricks with girls there."[34] (See footnote *c*.)

The Shadow-Line was followed by two short stories, "The Warrior's Soul" and "The Tale," and then by *The Arrow of Gold*, a work which found Conrad committed more deeply than ever to the typical plot situations and the stock characters of this period of his writing: Rita, the all-powerful woman, M. George, her vulnerable lover, and Ortega, the grimacing lust-filled villain.

The Rescue

Although begun in 1898 this novel was not finished until 1919, by which time it came to resemble much of the writing of the later Conrad. "You have taken all the hardness out of me,"[35] exclaims Captain Lingard to Edith Travers, a remark which admits of little ambiguity, for his involvement with her has not only led to his utter ruin, but has also exposed his impotence. For despite Conrad's efforts to shore up his hero's virility by labeling him with such impressive titles as "red-eyed Tom," "King Tom," etc., Lingard's manliness, like that of Jasper Allen, is entirely contingent upon his brig, without which he is nothing. "Woman! That's just about the last touch," exclaims one of his men, shocked by Lingard's involvement with Mrs. Travers. "That you should leave your weapons twenty miles behind you, your men, your guns, your brig that is your strength, and come alone here . . . with a woman in tow!"[36] Like Captain Anthony on board the *Ferndale*, Tom Lingard's demoralization wrought by his association with a woman leaves "everyone dumb with astonishment at the change." From the moment when he embraces Mrs. Travers, he exhibits a progressive and steady deterioration in his once renowned mastery: his capacity to deal with "events, necessities, things—he had lost his grip on them all." This disorganizing effect produced by the embrace is hardly surprising, however, in view of Lingard's immediate reaction to it. For as he holds her in his arms he feels "as though she had suddenly stabbed him to the heart."[37]

The Rover

This novel, the last completed by Conrad, was written in 1922 and presents the same character types and the same peculiar relations between the sexes that have been noted in the preceding stories. When Lieutenant Réal embraces the beautiful Arlette, the sensations which he experiences are indistinguishable from those felt by Geoffrey Renouard or Captain Lingard under similar circumstances. "I am lost," he murmurs to himself, wondering whether he is about to die.[38] Like Lingard, Réal's reaction to the girl is that of one being passively penetrated by her: her words made him feel "like a man stabbed to the heart."[39] Nor is he the only victim of Arlette's power. For her sake the old sea captain, Peyrol, sacrifices his life, while Scevola, the "blood drinker," who lusts after her is as unsuccessful in fulfilling his sexual appetite as are his fictional villainous predecessors, Ricardo, Ortega, etc.

Suspense

Standard themes and standard character types recur in this last and unfinished novel. Obviously intended to be the villain of the story, Count Helion, equipped with an "inky black moustache," is a carbon copy of Ortega, Heemskirk, Ricardo, or Scevola. His wife Adèle, a counterpart of other "pure" Conrad heroines of this period, has "but a single sin: perfect frankness." His niece Clelia is a stock feline creature who bares her teeth and presents the appearance "of a cat ready to fly at one." Clearly a double for the gypsy girl in "The Inn of Two Witches," she regards Cosmo, the hero, as if he were good to eat. Completing the similarity to that story are Clelia's two black-robed aunts, who are depicted stirring something in a pot. In keeping with Conrad's view of human motivation in this period of his career, Cosmo and his half-sister Adèle are presumably a pair of good people menaced on all sides by evil persecutors.

From these examples taken from all of Conrad's major fiction written after his mental breakdown, it is evident that his fictional world became an apiary ruled by a succession of queen bees, who, luring their drones into the vertiginous and rarefied hazards of the nuptial flight, disembowel them in mid-air and return triumphant to the hive, clutching their entrails as souvenirs. Thus in *Victory* the dying Lena "looked drowsily about, serene, as if fatigued only by the exertion of her tremendous victory, capturing the very sting of death in the service of love. But her eyes became very wide-awake when they caught sight of Ricardo's dagger, the spoil of vanquished death . . . . 'Give it to me,' she said, 'It is mine!' "[40] Stripped of its disguise, Ricardo's fate, like the fate of all of Conrad's males of this period, is emasculation at the hands of a "castrating" woman. It is no accident that his knife is hidden in the folds of her skirt,[g] for the image of a woman concealing a symbolic phallus upon her person is a recurrent characteristic of Conrad's later heroines. Whether represented by a knife, by a gold hair ornament shaped like an arrow, by piercing glances or scorching hair, the phallic endowment of these women confers upon them the capacity for active penetration of their men: it is the latter, who, despite their seamanship, their weapons, and their reputation as "he-men," get "raped."

It should not be inferred, however, that the image of the phallic woman or the castrated man appeared in Conrad's fiction for the first time after 1910. Mrs. Hervey of "The Return" (1897) has much in common with the "Amazon," Felicia Moorsom, of "The Planter of Malata" (1913). Anticipating Lena's "victory" in fondling the knife of the villainous Ricardo is the picture of the wife of Gaspar Ruiz (1906) wearing a sword which she "loved to feel beating upon her thigh."[42] Her daughter's handgrip, moreover, is every bit as pulverizing as that of Rita. "I advise no one to ask for her hand," warns her guardian, "for if she took yours into hers it would be only to crush your bones."[43] Woman as the destroyer of man appeared in the earlier Conrad, too. Just as Felicia Moorsom drove her fiancé into drug addiction, so did Nina Almayer confer a similar fate upon her hapless father in Conrad's first published work in 1894. Willems is as surely wrecked by his love for Aïssa as is Captain Lingard through his entanglement with Edith Travers. Weak, vacillating, and passive men, moreover, are not lacking in the earlier Conrad fiction. Alvan Hervey is as hesitant and impotent as Axel Heyst, while Martin Decoud in *Nostromo* is every bit as tentative and submissive before Antonia as Captain Anthony is toward Flora de Barral.

[g] "There is death in the folds of her skirt and blood about her feet," says Catherine of the girl Arlette in *The Rover*. "She is for no man."[41]

Yet, despite these distinct traces of Conrad's post-1910 character types in his earlier work, there is a basic distinction between the gallery of portraits from these two periods of his creative work: a stamp of individuality and variety is discernible among the earlier characters which is conspicuously lacking among the later figures. Aïssa, of *An Outcast*, for instance, is not a Malayan version of Winnie Verloc, Willems bears no significant resemblance to the Capataz of *Nostromo*, and Jim is not easily confused with Martin Decoud or Razumov.

Except for Alice Jacobus and one or two others, however, Conrad's fictional characters after 1910 tend to be faceless stereotypes who attain their tenuous identity not from the brush strokes with which they are painted but rather from the topical plot situations in which they play their parts. There is little basic difference between the personalities of Captain Anthony, Axel Heyst, or Geoffrey Renouard; nor can one form a distinct individual mental image of Freya, Flora, or Felicia: they are as interchangeable as the initial letter of their names. Clelia in *Suspense* is the twin sister of the gypsy girl in "The Inn of Two Witches," and Edith Travers is a seafaring Rita de Lastaola. Indeed, these are scarcely individuals at all, but rather two-dimensional caricatures resembling personages in fairy tales or characters in a morality play. It is only necessary to compare a pre-1910 "villain" with a later one to appreciate the extent of change which took place in Conrad's characters after his mental breakdown. Mr. Kurtz, for example, entered the African wilderness equipped with the idealism of a dedicated social worker. It is only under the influence of the elemental brutality of the jungle that he sinks into a state of depravity as primitive as that which he had hoped originally to eradicate. Even so, echoes of his earlier moral sense are heard in his dying moments as he mutters a pitiful expression of remorse. Mr. Jones and his partner Ricardo of *Victory*, however, suggest no such shocking evolution into baseness. They are bad through and through and the reader is easily persuaded that they have never been anything else. "You are no more to me one way or another than that fly there," Ricardo tells Schomberg, the innkeeper. "I'd squash you or leave you alone. I don't care what I'd do[44] . . . you have been used to deal with tame people, haven't you? But we aren't tame."[45] Presented in terms of such simple villainy, it is inconceivable that Mr. Ricardo, at his moment of dying, would experience a sudden pang of conscience and cry out, like the dying Kurtz, "The horror! The horror!"

Moreover, despite their adventurous and dramatic experiences and despite their big talk, these later Conrad characters lack the vitality and guts of their predecessors. Willems, for instance, may be a weak man, but he is also a passionate man, endowed with an unmistakable capacity for loving and suffering. Falk, too, though he may be squeamish about his past, gives no hint of impotence or lack of purpose. Once he has won his girl it does not appear probable that like Captain Anthony he will hem and haw waiting to be seduced. And when Winnie Verloc, knife in hand, advances upon her recumbent husband, she does not stop to engage in a long harangue as Lena does in *Victory* when she has wrested Ricardo's knife from him. Caught between her feelings for her husband and for her baby, Amy Foster does not shilly-shally like Flora de Barral, who, torn between the claims of her father and husband, declares "I can't go on like this . . . between you two." Nor does Razumov passively permit the intrusion of the assassin Haldin to wreck his well-laid plans as Heyst does when his island retreat is invaded by Mr. Jones and his evil crew.

In short, Conrad's post-1910 fictional characters tend to be lacking not only in individuality but in spirit. The men are more than impotent: they seem devoid of desire, of motivation, and of purpose. Indeed, as Moser has emphasized, they are often depicted in attitudes of fatigue, even when, like M. George, they are in the very prime of life.[46] Afflicted with a kind of *tedium vitae* their aim would seem to be to seek "a love that will blot out all awareness of the world and bring the semblance of death."[47] As for their women, despite the iterated insistence upon their power, their destructiveness, or their awesome majesty, they are no more credibly alive than are their papier-mâché men.

It is hardly surprising that the verbal utterances of these characters are no more vital or subtle than are their portraits. What they say to or about each other often consists of a stream of banalities more reminiscent of slogans or propaganda than of conversation. Thus speaking of Rita de Lastaola, Dominic Cervoni suggests that "she ought to be set up on a high pillar for people that walk on the ground to raise their eyes up to."[48] And in *The Rescue,* D'Alcacer utters a comparable platitude about Edith Travers: "It is for such women that people toil on the ground and underground and artists of all sorts invoke their inspiration."[49] Along with these and kindred expressions idealizing women, however, Conrad has put into the mouths of his later characters an unrestrained spate of ill-tempered misogyny. Curiously these unflattering sentiments often appear in close juxtaposition to their seeming opposites. Directly after the speech just cited, for example, D'Alcacer goes on to generalize about women: "They lead a sort of ritual dance that most of us have agreed to take seriously. It is a very binding agreement with which sincerity and good faith and honour have nothing to do."[50]

Perhaps the most compelling example of the deterioration of Conrad as an observer and recorder of the human condition is supplied by the narrator, Marlow. The early Marlow is a thoughtful, troubled man endowed with a remarkable capacity for sympathy and understanding. Commenting upon Jim's pathetic efforts to justify his reprehensible conduct in the *Patna* affair, he tells his audience: "He was not speaking to me, he was only speaking before me, in a dispute with an invisible personality, an antagonistic and inseparable partner of his existence . . . another possessor of his soul."[51] Nor was he any less perceptive in recognizing the force of primitive impulse residing within every man.

By 1912, however, this Marlow had been transformed into a stuffy, cantankerous, and opinionated man, given to sweeping generalizations and particularly to intemperate misogyny. The Marlow of *Chance* says:

> As to honor, it's a very fine medieval inheritance which women never got hold of. It wasn't theirs. Since it may be laid as a general principle that women always get what they want, we must suppose they didn't want it. In addition they are devoid of decency. I mean masculine decency. Cautiousness too is foreign

> to them—the heavy, reasonable cautiousness which is our glory. And if they had it they would make of it a thing of passion, so that its own mother—I mean the mother of cautiousness—wouldn't recognize it. Prudence with them is a matter of thrill like the rest of sublunary contrivances. "Sensation at any cost" is their secret device. All the virtues are not enough for them; they want also all the crimes for their own. And why? Because in such completeness there is power—the kind of thrill they love most.[52]

Nor does Marlow conceal his hostility toward that power: "Mainly I resent that pretence of winding us round their dear little fingers as of right. . . . It is the assumption that each of us is a combination of a kid and an imbecile which I find provoking—in a small way. . . . And tenacious! When they once get hold you may uproot the tree but you won't shake them off the branch. In fact, the more you shake. . . ."[53]

In a word, the ordinary rules of conduct which men abide by simply do not apply to women according to this later Marlow: once seized by an impulse nothing can stop them. Speaking of the governess of Flora de Barral, he observes: "Hers was not a rare temperament except in its fierce resentment of repression; a feeling which like genius or lunacy is apt to drive people into sudden irrelevancy. A male genius, a male ruffian, or even a male lunatic would not have behaved exactly as she did behave. There is a softness in masculine nature, even the most brutal, which acts as a check."[54]

Conrad's generalizations about women were not limited to the narrator of *Chance*. Although somewhat less vituperative, similar misogynous expressions soon appeared again in "The Planter of Malata." Speaking of his daughter Felicia, Professor Moorsom speculates upon what might be driving her to seek out the man she had once wronged. "And I ask myself if she is obeying the uneasiness of an instinct seeking its satisfaction, or is it a revulsion of feeling, or is she merely deceiving her own heart by this dangerous trifling with romantic images? And everything is possible—except sincerity, such as only stark, struggling humanity can know.

No woman can stand that mode of life in which women rule, and remain a perfectly genuine, simple human being."[55]

In *Victory*, written in the following year, a renewed outburst of misogyny is voiced by the rabid woman-hater, Mr. Jones. When he discovers that his companion Ricardo has developed an interest in Lena his rage is unbounded. Denouncing him as a "woman lover," he avows his intention of killing him, that "prevaricating, sly, low class amorous cuss."[56] Apparently this was not the first time Ricardo had been "unfaithful"—"I had to shut my eyes many times to his little flings; but this is serious. He has found his soul mate."[57] At this point he launches into a diatribe against the fair sex which makes Marlow's asides pale in comparison. For far from concerning himself with spiritual qualities like honor and sincerity, Mr. Jones denounces women as basically dirty: "Mud souls, obscene and cunning! Mud bodies, too—the mud of the gutter."[58] This scatological outburst is especially arresting because it is inspired by the sight of Lena portrayed as a seated religious figure: "as if enthroned, with her hands on the arms of the chair. She was in black; her face was white, her head dreamily inclined on her breast.[h] . . . 'Can you understand their power?' whispered the hot breath of Mr. Jones. . . . 'Can there be a more disgusting spectacle? It's enough to make the earth detestable.' "[60]

Similar if more restrained unflattering generalizations about women appeared in two short stories written in 1917. In "The Warrior's Soul," the narrator asks: "But who is going to fathom their [women's] needs or their fancies? Most of the time they themselves don't know much about their innermost moods and blunder out of one into another, sometimes with catastrophic results."[61] The second story, "The Tale," has a special interest because the misogyny is intimately woven into a reference to the sexual act, itself a most unusual element in Conrad's fiction. The story begins directly after a couple has been making love; the woman asks

[h] Edith Travers in *The Rescue* is described in virtually identical terms: "She was leaning back again, her hands had fallen in her lap and her head with a plait of hair on each side of her face, her head incredibly changed in character and suggesting something medieval, ascetic, drooped dreamily on her breast . . . like a figure in a faded painting. . . . D'Alcacer's wonder approached a feeling of awe."[59]

her lover to tell her a story. "These words came with a slight petulance, the hint of a loved woman's capricious will, which is capricious only because it feels itself to be law, embarrassing sometimes and always difficult to elude. . . . But now he was a little angry with her for that feminine mobility that slips out of an emotion as easily as out of a splendid gown."[62]

From these and other examples it is apparent that after 1910 Conrad lost few opportunities to voice a series of sweeping and extreme generalizations about women. At their best they are described as objects of worship, pure and saintly, while in the words of their detractors they are vile and dirty creatures, bereft of true human feeling, conscience, or scruple. Bent upon the attainment of supreme power, they are disdainful and contemptuous of any obstacle—moral or sentimental—which may block their path. Viewed in either light—saint or devil—Conrad's image of woman during this era places her in a category which lies outside the pale of ordinary humans. They command that admixture of awe and fear evoked by the insane, or by victims of epilepsy, the "sacred disease" of the ancients. Indeed, prone to acts of "sudden irrelevancy" they are likened by Marlow to lunatics who are unchecked by moral codes or self-restraint. This same lack of inhibition, moreover, may manifest itself in their inexorable pursuit of thrills; as hoodlums in skirts, women are characterized by Marlow as beings whose motto is "sensation at any cost."

In her position as an alien, these women invoke the same attitudes of suspicion, hostility, and distrust with which a people or a community tends to regard the outsider, the foreigner, or the man whose skin is of a different color. Mr. Jones' denigration of women as dirty resembles the familiar use of that adjective in association with Jew, Frenchman, "nigger," etc. His vilification of Ricardo as a "woman-lover," moreover, recalls the invective hurled by racial bigots. Marlow's insistence upon women's lack of honor, sense of fair play, etc., corresponds to that brand of chauvinism which maintains that one's own nation (or the home team) fights clean, while the enemy is sly, devious, and dirty.[i]

[i] It should not be supposed that prior to 1910 Conrad's writing was free from all traces of hostility toward women. Mrs. Hervey of "The Return"

Such irrational attitudes are often consequences of a state of anxiety or a sense of danger. In times of war they are characteristic of the epithets flung at the foe, who is regarded as the epitome of all evil and of godlessness. Under other circumstances they may arise in response to an inner threat which is expelled from the self and projected upon alien objects. The Anglo-Saxon notion, for example, that Frenchmen are dirty, licentious, and parsimonious reflects in part, at least, a wish to dissociate nice English-speaking people with excrement, sex, and stinginess; for a number of nations syphilis is the "French disease." By the same token, the notion that all Negroes are rapists lusting after white virgins permits the fathers and brothers of these innocent girls to disown their own unacceptable sexual temptations.

From whatever quarter such a danger arises its very existence exerts a profound effect upon both the spirit and the mind. Thus, when a nation finds itself suddenly upon a war footing, all the energies of the state hitherto dispersed among various cultural, social, or industrial pursuits become cohesively mobilized for the common purpose of combat and defense. For the sake of creating an impregnable fortress and of arousing the nation into a spirit of homogeneous unity, paintings give way to posters, poetry is replaced by slogans, and love songs are supplanted by military

---

(1897) is characterized as possessing "not a thought of her own in her head."[63] Concerning honesty, her husband tells her that she doesn't "know the meaning of that word."[64] The wife of Captain MacWhirr of "Typhoon" is described as "a pretentious person with a scraggy neck and a disdainful manner,"[65] a seemingly gratuitous indulgence in misogyny insofar as she plays no significant role in the story and could just as well have been presented as a less unattractive person.

Despite these and other examples, Conrad's earlier work fails to present the unrelieved woman-worship and woman-hatred that broke out so conspicuously after his illness in 1910, and if traces of these attitudes are discernible prior to that time, they did not attain such prominence as to suggest an obsessional preoccupation. On the contrary, with few exceptions the earlier Conrad kept his misogyny within the bounds of artistic taste, exercising sufficient control over his dormant prejudices to prevent their dominating his material. Following his breakdown he appears to have lost that control, and what had been a random or minor nuance became a virtual rallying banner.

marches. So may the artistry of an individual be transformed in the face of danger, be it from the threat of an official censor or from storms brewing within the confines of his own mind. For such a one, as for a people at bay, all the resources of the spirit hitherto expended in the evocation of personal art may become channelized for the single and urgent task of defense, and the artist may yield to the propagandist within himself.

Such would appear to have been the fate of Conrad as an artist after his illness: he turned from a faithful depiction of sentient human beings to the creation of a gallery of puppets representing the good man, the bad man, the monumental goddess, and the cat-like woman.

Parallel with the deterioration of Conrad as a psychologist, a change took place in the mood and sensibility of his writing. As his fictional characters were transformed from complex personalities into cardboard figures of two-dimensional simplicity, so did the subtle shades of dreamy impressionism give way to pictorial images conceived in the full light of consciousness. The dream quality of the earlier Conrad is inescapable: "I did not see the man in the name any more than you do," says the narrator of "Heart of Darkness." "Do you see him? Do you see the story? Do you see anything? It seems to me I am trying to tell you a dream—making a vain attempt, because no relation of a dream can convey the dream sensation, that commingling of absurdity, surprise, and bewilderment in a tremor of struggling revolt, that notion of being captured by the incredible which is of the very essence of dreams."[66] The philosopher Stein in *Lord Jim* says, "A man that is born falls into a dream like a man who falls into the sea."[67] "All this must be life," writes Decoud to his sister in *Nostromo*, "since it is so much like a dream."[68]

Such allusions to dreams or dreaming are rare in the later Conrad novels, which read as if they were spawned in some layer of the mind remote from those deep recesses where dreams are born.

Like a writer of adventure yarns in which action and crisis hold the reader in his grasp, the erstwhile spinner of dreams forsook the penumbra of demisleep and in the unshadowed glare of daylight created a species of poster art. Surely it was no dreamer who entitled the two parts of *Chance*: "The Damsel" and "The Knight," and who bestowed such trite headings on its chapters as: "Young Powell Sees and Hears," and "Devoted Servants—And the Light of a Flare."[j]

Conrad's alienation from his own imaginative fancy after 1910 is discernible not only in his tales: it is also manifest in his retrospective comments on the earlier stories. Seemingly impelled to clothe these writings in a raiment of "normality" he found it expedient both in his correspondence and in his Author's Notes, written during the last seven years of his life for the first collected edition of his works, to deny, to minimize, and sometimes even to apologize for the subtle meanings and the very guts of some of his best writing. Thus while he told Garnett that in *Under Western Eyes* he had been concerned with "nothing but ideas,"[69] in the Author's Note to *Lord Jim* he summed up its theme as "acute consciousness of lost honor."[70] It is indeed fortunate for the world of letters that the Conrad who composed this feeble epitome was not the same man, psychologically speaking, who in 1900 had written that novel, for a post-1910 Jim would surely have emerged as a vacuous cliché. A retelling of the celebrated *Patna* episode might ultimately have found Jim in the lifeboat with his unsavory companions through no fault of his own but through the agency of an irresistible fate. He would have been represented, perhaps, standing resolutely on the *Patna*'s deck, proudly defying the beguiling and evil exhortations of the men in the lifeboat below, and fully prepared to remain aboard the doomed pilgrim ship in accord with the best traditions of maritime honor; then suddenly, fate, in the shape of a half-crazed snarling Arab would have descended upon him from behind to pitch him over the rail into the sea. At the Court of Inquiry Jim would have truthfully insisted: "Someone pushed me . . . it seems," and the Marlow of 1912, parenthetically confiding to his listeners that the mad Arab was undoubtedly a female, would have concurred.[k]

[j] A graphic confirmation of this analogy between Conrad's later writing and poster art is provided by the poster-like illustration which Conrad himself drew for *The Arrow of Gold*. See Illustration VIII.

[k] Ironically, this was allegedly the virtual fate of Chief Officer Williams of the SS *Jeddah*, who served as one model of the fictional Jim.[71]

The spectacle of artistic decline can hardly fail to arouse perplexity as well as regret, and it is only natural for both critic and biographer to try to account for it. Understandably, speculations concerning the causes of Conrad's decline have not been wanting. Guerard, for example, who acknowledges that "the ultimate psychological and perhaps biological *why* of Conrad's anticlimax may well be undiscoverable,"[72] has nevertheless suggested that physical and mental fatigue, compounded by financial worries, may have been responsible.[73] The plausibility of this explanation seems questionable, however, when it is recalled that ill health and neurotic suffering had dogged Conrad almost from the inception of his writing career, and that his financial state was at its worst during the years of his greatest artistic achievements. Indeed his growing popularity, which began with the publication of *Chance*, brought with it an increasing commercial success. In discussing the effect of Conrad's poor health upon his writing Moser points out that gout necessitated his dictating his last novels.[74] There is good evidence, however, that many years earlier portions of *The Mirror of the Sea* and *A Personal Record* had been taken down in dictation by Hueffer[75] without resulting in inferior writing. Furthermore the deterioration in Conrad's art preceded by several years his exclusive practice of dictation. It has also been suggested that Conrad's late novels suffered because of his relative physical isolation in Kent.[76] Virginia Woolf, who reluctantly labeled *The Rescue* as "stiff melodrama," not only subscribed to this view but enlarged upon it, pointing out that Conrad never saw anyone "who knows good writing from bad," that he was "a foreigner, talking broken English, married to a lump of a wife."[77] It should be pointed out that the influence of "relative isolation" on the creative imagination is quite unpredictable and varied; some artists, including Conrad, seem to have prospered under it. As for Conrad's being a foreigner and having a supposed "lump of a wife," neither of these factors originated in 1910, and neither had apparently interfered with his earlier artistic achievements.

In earlier pages in this work it has been suggested that the fluctuations in the quality of Conrad's writing were often closely correlated with his varying capacity to hold his art free from the contamination of immediate concurrent mental suffering. It would appear that the same principle would apply to the question of the cause of his ultimate deterioration as an artist, which was brought about, it would seem, not by physical ill health, mental fatigue, or financial worries, not by the necessity to dictate his novels, not by his "relative isolation" or by other environmental factors, but rather by the inevitable consequences of the specific psychological defenses adopted by him after his mental illness. Psychologically it would appear that he could no longer afford those introspective journeys into the self that constitute the greatness of the impressionistic art he created during the years of his close association with Hueffer. Deprived of that mirroring companionship which had sustained him in his earlier bold descent, and terrified by the mad devils leering at him during his illness, Conrad seems to have elected thereafter to confine his art to the surface of life, to become, as it were, a literary Captain MacWhirr, who had "just enough imagination to carry him through each successive day, and no more."[l/78] Hemmed in by such self-imposed restrictions it is hardly surprising that his creative artistry declined. Cut off from the dream source of poetic invention and unable to draw on the rich lode of his own well-guarded fancy, he was in time even reduced to picking over the slag of other literary prospectors: in the writing of *Suspense* there seems to be no question that he engaged in frank plagiarism.[80]

As might be expected, parallel with the deterioration of Conrad the artist, somewhat analogous changes were taking place in Conrad the man. These aspects of his personal history will be presented in the following chapter.

[l] Throughout Conrad's writings there is an implied envy of men like MacWhirr, Singleton, Captain Mitchell, and others, who seem to be endowed with a magic cap of invulnerability by virtue of their lack of what Conrad called imagination, which probably includes introspection, obsessional doubts and fears, and neurotic anxiety. Captain Mitchell, for example, "with all his small weaknesses and absurdities, was constitutionally incapable of entertaining for any length of time a fear of his personal safety. It was not so much firmness of soul as the lack of a certain kind of imagination—the kind whose undue development caused intense suffering to Señor Hirsch; that sort of imagination which adds the blind terror of bodily suffering and of death, envisaged as an accident to the body alone, strictly—to all the other apprehensions on which the sense of one's existence is based."[79] Characteristically when Captain Mitchell is being threatened by Colonel Sotillo, his entire concern is focused upon the fact that the Colonel's men have stolen his watch.

XIII · The Rover

The outstanding characteristics of Conrad's emotional make-up and behavior in the years following his mental illness in 1910, like the characteristics of his literary art during that period, were not new or unprecedented manifestations. They were rather an intensification of some of his least felicitous earlier traits so that they became the prevailing pattern of his style of life. The bouts of invalidism, for example, which had appeared intermittently throughout his adult life prior to his breakdown, were succeeded in the years that followed by a progressive trend toward chronic inaction. To some extent this trend was caused by the disease of his joints, but even in the gout-free intervals the one-time man of action showed an increasing disinclination for virtually any form of physical activity save for a nervous restlessness. Indeed, the extent to which gout contributed to his immobility is quite uncertain, for he became exceedingly childlike in his behavior and dramatized his suffering, making it difficult to gauge the degree of his actual discomfort or disability. "Often have I laboriously dragged him in his chair across the room," wrote his wife, "only to see him run back to the bed when he heard the doctor's car coming down the hill."[1] Typically his gout flared up in times of emotional crisis: upon the completion of a novel, during moments of stress or vexation, and, most strikingly, when he was confronted by the illness or disability of others, particularly his children, which characteristically caused him to respond in a "me-too" fashion. Upon her return from the sick bed of one of the children Mrs. Conrad would be asked for a report of the child's condition, "but almost before I could answer," she wrote, "my attention was claimed by my senior patient and it was pointed out that he required his share of my ministrations. There would be a pile of letters to answer, dressings for the painful foot or ankle, or some dainty dish to be cooked."[a/2]

Yet if Conrad reacted to environmental illness by an intensi-

[a] Conrad was not altogether unaware of the role he played with Jessie. "I really ought to have a nurse," he wrote to Meldrum during Borys' infancy, "since my wife must look after the other child."[3]

fication of his own helplessness, both his spirits and his health could suddenly prosper through a process, as it were, of contagion in an atmosphere charged with vigor and action. During the latter part of 1916 he was sent by the Admiralty to visit Dover and other ports and to observe naval activities. Then he joined a "Q" boat, *HMS Ready*, a sailing vessel engaged in hunting down German U-boats. Conrad's letters written on this tour of duty were full of bounce and high spirits. To his agent, Pinker, he wrote on November 8: "All well. Been practice firing in sight of coast. Weather improved. Health good. Hopes of bagging Fritz high. Have dropped a line to Jessie. Don't expect to hear from me for ten days."[4] His state of well-being at this time is further emphasized by an account given some years later by Captain Sutherland of the *Ready*, who, in deference to his distinguished guest, renamed her *Freya*. He depicted Conrad enjoying himself to the full, dashing up and down the stairs and pounding large-sized nails "with all the strength and power of a village blacksmith." On deck he located a quick-firing Gardner gun which he screwed down on the after skylight hatch and kept in a high state of perfection. "Bad weather or discomfort made not the slightest difference to Conrad. He was used to it—'brought up on it'—as it were."[b/5]

But in the space of less than four weeks, when he was once again home, both the gout and his low spirits had returned. "My psychology has been affected by way of inability to concentrate," he wrote to J. M. Dent on December 4th. "I am sorry, but helpless . . . I am more emotional, it appears, than I imagined myself to be."[6] And on the 3rd of January of the new year he told Cunninghame Graham that because of a swollen foot he could "just crawl across a room and no more."[7]

His need to create the illusion that he was the sole sufferer surrounded by a bulwark of strength and well-being was undoubtedly responsible for his behaving in a manner that appears callous or inconsiderate. During the Conrads' ill-fated Polish trip in 1914, when they were caught in the outbreak of World War I, many of their belongings were lost. The weather was cold and Conrad dressed

[b] A similar remission in his suffering was to occur again during his American tour in 1923.

himself in all the warm clothing available including some of his wife's apparel. Jessie cited this as an instance of his "complete absent-mindedness. Like a child he was quite irresponsible and I know well that he would have been terribly distressed to think that he was wearing literally all the warm outdoor clothing we had."[8] Inevitably while he wore more than his share of the clothing his wife bore more than her share of their burdens in periods of crisis and trial. When during the same trip, her endurance finally appeared to give way he reacted as if her fatigue were a personal attack launched upon him. "What had come to me?" he demanded to know. "Why had I given in like this? Such behavior was enough to rob him of all confidence; it made him anxious. It was not the thing to spring on a fellow."[9]

Needless to say he was sorely tried by his wife's chronic invalidism and by the several surgical procedures to which she was obliged to submit. Although in his letters to friends he gave evidence of his sympathy for her suffering, in his private behavior he often displayed a childlike refusal to admit that there was anything wrong with her. In words conjuring up images of some of his fictional women he is supposed to have told her: "Of course [the doctor] doesn't know you, my dear. You're not one of those frail, hysterical women who go to pieces at the mere idea of a little exertion. Bless you!"[10] Not surprisingly when she found it necessary to use crutches he assured her that she could get about just as well with a couple of canes,[11] and when she was obliged to be hospitalized he was evidently beside himself.

On one such occasion, while she was lying in a hospital bed, he found her engaged in making doll clothes for the granddaughter of her surgeon, who was at the bedside admiring her work. The scene evidently aroused Conrad's anger, for he blurted out, "Damn, isn't it time you began to grow up?," and like a neglected child he swept all the doll clothes onto the floor.[c/12] As was the case when his children were ailing it is not difficult to detect here Conrad's jealousy of the attention his bed-ridden wife was receiving from her doctor. At the same time it must be acknowledged that memo-

[c] There is an obvious similarity between this episode and his throwing the baby's clothes out of the train window. See Chapter X.

ries of a dying mother, and later of a father, must have conditioned him to react with terrible anxiety to any suggestion of disability or illness of his wife-mother, Jessie. Once when he was about to visit her in the hospital he met the matron and told her that Borys was suffering from influenza, which was true, but he added gratuitously the untruth that he himself was similarly afflicted. Upon hearing this the matron naturally refused to allow him to enter the hospital, at which he became incensed, declaring that if he were not to be permitted to see her, "no one else shall."[13] Inasmuch as his wife reported that Conrad was always extremely restless and ill at ease while visiting her in the hospital, it would seem plausible to conclude that his telling the matron about his nonexistent illness was motivated by a secret wish to be refused admission. A similar disinclination to pay sick calls was undoubtedly responsible for his bizarre behavior when, because of Jessie's disability, it was his lot to visit their ailing maid in the hospital. On entering the building he refused to give either his name or that of the patient he had come to see, with the result that he left angrily without visiting the maid at all.[14]

Naturally in the face of dying or death his childlike withdrawal was extreme. When summoned to the bedside of his dying friend Arthur Marwood he refused to go until Jessie, who had been invalided in her room for over a month, agreed to accompany him. "It always cost him an awful effort," she wrote, "to bring himself face to face with suffering in any form."[15] When the ailing maid finally died in January 1919, Conrad retired to an upstairs bedroom where he remained for a number of weeks. During this interval a little celebration was being planned for Borys' twenty-first birthday, but instead of participating in the festivities, Conrad wrote the following letter to his wife:

Dear Heart.

My soul is weary for the sight of you. I hope you will have a possible night. What a comfort it is to have the two kids with us in these trying times—and especially the big kid [Borys], who twines himself round my heart even more than when he was a small child.

I worry about you all, and I fret at being laid up on his 21st birthday. What must be will be—and after all, I have all possible confidence in the future. Good night, dearest, and give me a friendly thought before you go to sleep.

Your boy.

As Mrs. Conrad pointed out this letter "would give anyone the impression that he was ill miles away, whereas he was only lying in a room upstairs in the same house. I knew him so well," she added, "that I let him stay there until he elected to join again the family circle." On the next day, in fact, he confessed that there had been nothing wrong with him; yet he had stayed up there for nearly three weeks.[16]

What is remarkable about this little drama is not only Conrad's urge to seclude himself and play sick when confronted by the shadow of death, but also his equally childish refusal to join in the celebration of his son's coming of age. Typical of his need to be the only, or the most favored, child, he apparently sulked in self-imposed isolation rather than look on while Borys was being feted for arriving at his maturity. It is hardly remarkable that he signed his letter: "Your boy." (This was by no means an uncommon closing in Conrad's letters to his wife, who on one occasion responded appropriately by signing a letter to him: "Your loving wife and Mother.")[17] This birthday undoubtedly brought particular distress to Conrad, for it signified that his "kid" could from now on enjoy an independent existence, thereby threatening his father's role as lord of the manor. To some men the attainment of manhood by their sons is a source of pride, but if Conrad experienced such feelings they were swamped by another sentiment: the pain of losing a little boy whom he had been able to tolerate in the past, it would seem, only as long as he could hold him in complete subjugation as an unshared possession.[d] To Conrad it would appear that such a loss was as unsupportable as was a loss occasioned by death, and in his characteristic fashion he tried to deny both losses by withdrawing from the world to the room upstairs.

[d] Cf. Yanko Gooral's rivalry with his wife Amy Foster over their infant son.

In view of these observations it is clear why in his letter to Jessie, Conrad made such pointed and obviously wistful references to Borys as if he were still a small boy—who "twines himself round my heart." The phrase is striking for another reason: many years before, when Borys was not yet five years old, Conrad had used that identical expression in describing the relationship of old Captain Whalley to his daughter in "The End of the Tether." The Captain had named her Ivy[e]—apparently the mother had no role in naming her daughter—"because of the sound of the word and obviously fascinated by a vague association of ideas. *She had twined herself round his heart* and he intended her to cling close to her father as to a tower of strength."[19] (Italics mine) Now, clearly enough Captain Whalley (or Conrad) was deceiving himself as to who was actually to be the "tower of strength"—the father or the daughter. Surely, the father, like Conrad himself, hoped to maintain an exclusive and lasting possession of his child, forgetting "while she was little, that in the nature of things she would probably elect to cling to someone else" when she grew to womanhood. In light of this anticipation in fiction of the author's subsequent reluctance to accept the coming of age of his own son, it is noteworthy that Captain Whalley liked to refer jokingly to his daughter as "a good *boy* spoiled." (Italics mine)[f/21]

Throughout his adult life, and presumably earlier, Conrad was

[e] Ivy was the name of the five and one-half-year-old daughter of James Craig, captain of the SS *Vidar* when Conrad was chief mate of that ship. According to Allen, Captain Craig introduced her to Conrad in Singapore.[18] Inasmuch as the itinerary of the *Vidar* was closely followed by the SS *Sofala* in "The End of the Tether," it would seem likely that the fictional captain's daughter was named after the real one.

[f] This allusion to "The End of the Tether" in the context of Conrad's "de-thronement" has interesting ramifications. Moynihan has pointed out that the name of Captain Whalley's ship, *Sofala*, refers to a region in Africa known for its king-killing customs. Like Captain Whalley in the eyes of his daughter, the Sofala kings were regarded as gods by their people; however, upon the discovery of a bodily blemish, however slight, like the loss of a tooth (or Captain Whalley's blindness), they were expected to kill themselves.[20] Whether Conrad was acquainted with the Sofala region and took from it the name of Captain Whalley's ship is unknown to this writer.

Apropos of the subject of de-thronement, as will be mentioned later, Mrs. Conrad claimed that her husband's death was hastened by Borys' marriage.

obsessed by the idea of loss, which included not only the loss of persons but of material objects as well, of things often of insignificant importance. He was forever misplacing or losing objects, often insisting that they were irretrievably lost simply because he could not recall where he had put them. Once he had reconciled himself to the idea that they were gone he would become resentful if they were recovered. On one occasion when he was unable to find his wallet—which he frequently mislaid—he insisted that he had been robbed. When his wife suggested that it might be under his pillow, he retorted, "I tell you it isn't there. And if it is I will fling it out of the window."[22]

Toward his children he exhibited virtually identical attitudes. When they were small he was strongly opposed to their receiving praise or gifts from others,[23] presumably because he feared that through such enticements they might be lured away from him. Many years later, during the World War, he insisted that Borys had been killed in action.[g] When his wife remonstrated with him, declaring that there was no basis for his conviction, he retorted that it was true—"*he just knew it to be so*—he had a presentiment."[h/25] Happily his presentiment was without foundation; he did not lose Borys on the battlefields of France. Toward the close of the War, however, the relationship between the two began to cool—as is evident from the episode on Borys' twenty-first birthday —and "a barrier of restraint took the place of [their] intimate companionship,"[26] which persisted until the very eve of Conrad's death. Although many years later Borys blamed himself for this estrangement, chiding himself for being "foolish and irresponsible,"[27] this was clearly an oversimplified view of the problem, for, as previously noted, Conrad was somewhat lacking in warmth toward his grown son. In 1921 when a trip to Corsica was being planned, Mrs. Conrad earnestly requested that Borys be taken along, for she was

[g] Over her objections Conrad refused to alter the dedication for *The Shadow-Line* written in 1915: "To Borys and all the others who like himself have crossed in early youth the shadow-line of their generation." Jessie argued that it sounded as if Borys were indeed dead.[24]

[h] This conviction that Borys was dead is reminiscent of his assertion some years before that the cause for the absence of the hired hand was that he had committed suicide. See Chapter X.

eager for his company and for the physical assistance that he could lend her in her disabled state. She also felt it would be good for Borys who had undergone an emotional disturbance in the course of his war experience. "It would have made an enormous difference to me, and would have certainly had the most beneficial effect upon the young man's nerves and outlook on life," she wrote. Despite her entreaties, however, Conrad obstinately refused, and after accompanying his parents as far as Rouen, Borys turned back and returned to England alone.[i/28]

Conrad's rejection of Borys during these years stands in sharp contrast to his unconcealed warmth toward Richard Curle, a man 25 years his junior with whom he had begun a friendship in 1912 which persisted unimpaired until his death. There is no doubt that Conrad looked upon Curle as his son. "When I reflect that if I had made an early marriage," he wrote to Curle, "I could have been (easily) father of a man of your age."[j/30] On another occasion he told him "I am an old man and you might be my son," and Curle admitted, "He had a kind of paternal affection for me." Unlike Borys and John, moreover, whose disdain for literature was a source of grievous disappointment to their father, Curle was a "son" who looked upon his "father's" art with seemingly boundless admiration.[k] It was an enthusiastic review of *Nostromo* by Curle, in fact, which was initially responsible for bringing the two men together, and it is evident that Conrad derived deep satisfaction from the unwavering devotion which Curle continued to supply. "Outside my household," Conrad told him in 1917, "you are the person about whom I am most concerned, both in thought and feelings."[33]

Although he does not appear to have brought any of the stimulating effect on Conrad's writing which Hueffer had supplied,

[i] There was nothing new in this demand to have Jessie all to himself. When Borys was three years old his father forbade him to be present while his mother was getting dressed.[29]

[j] He closed a letter to Hugh Walpole: "Yours ever Paternally."[31]

[k] "I am not sure whether he understood his sons very well," wrote Curle, "or whether his sons understood him very well; but I am sure that the affection was mutual, and that though there was a certain fear mixed up with it on their part, there was never any kind of distrust."[32]

Curle's entrance into Conrad's life in 1912 undoubtedly filled some of the void left by Hueffer's defection a few years before. Just as he had once sought for similarities between Hueffer and himself Conrad now perceived an identity between himself and Richard Curle: "On the surface you and I are very different," he told Curle, "but *au fond* we are alike."[34] The parallels between the two relationships are further emphasized by the fact that on one occasion Conrad proposed that he and his new friend collaborate.[35]

From the foregoing observations it is evident that the progressive immobilization that characterized Conrad's life after his breakdown embraced mental as well as physical manifestations. Like his tired post-1910 heroes he seems to have lost the zest for action and adventure both of body and of spirit. What emerged was a nervous petulant man who sought to cling to those persons who would treat him and protect him as a favored only child, and who had little use for those who would not, or threatened to unseat him from that position. Such a pronounced regression in an adult, who has previously displayed a capacity for relatively mature functioning, can usually be interpreted as a defensive recoil in the face of danger, be it from without or from within. As an example of the former, a regressive trend may follow a traumatic experience, such as battle action, a civil disaster, mutilating surgery, or an unendurable personal loss. As a reaction toward a sense of inner danger, regression may appear as a defense against the threat of psychic upheaval or disorganization. In Conrad's case both of these elements apparently played a role: as previously noted his estrangement from Hueffer apparently re-kindled the trauma of childhood losses and reaffirmed his susceptibility to the loss of other key persons in his life, while his recent mental illness posed the danger of its possible recurrence. It would seem therefore that the regression in his psychological make-up was caused by the same factors which brought about the deterioration of his art.

Parallel with these changes it is not surprising that he seems to have lost that flexibility of the mind that had enabled him in the past to perceive the nuances, the subtleties, and the manifold intimate meanings of life as well as art. Apparently he attempted to suppress his feelings; in a letter to Galsworthy written in June 1910 he declared: "For myself I shall keep the lid down on my emotions. It's a question whether I even could lift it off. The hot spring boils somewhere deep within. There's no doubt of that; but if uncovered nothing would come out but a little vapour."[36] But in this he was mistaken, for, like the opinionated and crochety Marlow of 1912, Conrad became intemperate in his sentiments, somewhat pompous in his moral judgments, and faulty in his aesthetic taste. When in 1911 Edward Garnett made some mildly unfavorable comments about *Under Western Eyes*, Conrad turned on him and unleashed a barrage of epithets reminiscent of the xenophobia of a nation at war. "There's just about as much or as little hatred in this book as in *The Outcast of the Islands*," he wrote. "I don't expect you will believe me. You are so russianized my dear that you don't know the truth when you see it—unless it smells of cabbage soup, when it at once secures your profoundest respect. I suppose one must make allowances for your position of Russian Embassador to the Republic of Letters." Conrad followed this sarcasm with a protest against "being charged with the rather low trick of putting one's hate into a novel. If you seriously think that I have done that then my dear fellow let me tell you that you don't know what the accent of hate is." Advancing the curious claim that the novel was nothing more than an expression of pure thought, an intellectual exercise, he continued, "Is it possible that you haven't seen that in this book I am concerned with nothing but ideas, to the exclusion of everything else, with no *arrière pensée* of any kind? Or are you like the Italians (and most women) incapable of conceiving that anybody should speak with perfect detachment, without some subtle hidden purpose, for the sake of what is said, with no desire of gratifying some small personal spite—or vanity."[37]

Thus Conrad permitted himself to attack an old and faithful friend, the man who had recommended the publication of his first literary work, linking that very English Englishman with those alien creatures of evil and corruption—Russians, Italians, and, worst of all, women. (The only conspicuous omission on this occasion, but not on others, was Jew.) When it is realized with what unvarying respect Conrad had addressed Garnett in the past

—"I am now profoundly thankful to find I have enough sense to see the truth of what you say"[38]—the intemperance of his outburst becomes the more impressive and serves as true gauge of the profound change that had come over him. The element of xenophobia in his letter suggests, moreover, that his attack was based not only on Garnett's criticism of *Under Western Eyes,* but on a more subtle personal grievance as well. His sarcastic allusion to Garnett's "russianism" was probably prompted by the fact that the latter's wife, Constance, had been engaged in translating a number of Russian authors, notably Dostoevski, into English. To Conrad her activity must have been a red cloth waved before his (Western?) eyes, for by this time he had become consumed by an outspoken loathing for Dostoevski. Reviling the latter as a "grimacing, haunted creature,"[39] "too Russian for me,"[40] and as an author "whose works bore an unbearably bad odor,"[41] the man who had once declared that "the artist descends within himself . . . in that lonely region of stress and strife,"[42] dismissed *The Brothers Karamazov* as "fierce mouthings from some prehistoric ages."[43] Clearly something more fundamental than Polish chauvinism was responsible for these reckless judgments, nor can they be ascribed solely to professional jealousy, particularly in view of the generally accepted contention that in writing *Under Western Eyes* Conrad had been considerably influenced by *Crime and Punishment.*

Commenting on the subject of Dostoevski, Richard Curle observed that Conrad "did not despise him as one despises a nonentity; he hated him as one might hate Lucifer and the forces of darkness."[44] Seeking to account for this "dull fury which goes beyond the range of literary taste," Howe suggested that, for Conrad Dostoevski "meant a nagging memory, a sardonic challenge, an unsubdued pressure of rejected energies. Dostoievsky was his Smerdyakov."[45] Far from accepting Conrad's assertion that Dostoevski was "too Russian for me" Howe believes that Conrad understood him quite well although he did not really wish to. Hewitt too interpreted Conrad's professed hatred of Dostoevski as an expression of his need to dissociate himself from anything morbid.[46] Protesting to Galsworthy that he was "a plain man without tears or sensibility" Conrad appeared impelled to disavow any spiritual kinship with a writer whose example might dispel this patent illusion. In actuality, Hewitt observed, there are striking similarities between the two writers. "It seems certain," he wrote, "that Conrad attacked Dostoevsky so violently not because they were temperamentally dissimilar, but because Dostoevsky keeps always in the forefront of his work elements similar to those in Conrad's sensibility which he had thrust to the back and any suggestion of which he repudiated."[47]

In light of these observations it would appear that Conrad's rejection of Dostoevski was but another rivet in the armor by means of which he sought to ward off new psychological disasters. In doing so he was utilizing the familiar mechanism of projection previously cited as typical of the psychological orientation in his post-1910 writings.[l] No longer could he afford to admire, let alone imitate, introspective, intimate, or symbolic art. Not only did he need to proclaim his hatred for Dostoevski; he dismissed D. H. Lawrence as "filth; nothing but obscenities," and he flew into a rage on the subject of *Moby Dick*, asserting that Melville knew nothing of the sea and that the work was "fantastic and ridiculous."[49] In his flight from the "abnormal" within himself, it was necessary for him not only to shun "abnormal" writers, but to persuade himself that his own past writings were devoid of anything morbid or bizarre. Evidently this was not invariably an easy task, for while preparing *The Secret Agent* for theatrical presentation, he wrote to Pinker, "As I go on in my adaptation . . . I perceive more clearly how it is bound to appear to the collective mind of the audience a mere horrible and sordid tale, giving a most unfavorable impression of both the writer himself and of his attitude to the moral aspect of the subject."[50] And as noted in a previous chapter he utilized his Author's Notes, written long after his breakdown, as a means of belittling and disavowing any hint of subtle inner meanings in the great novels written many years before. Significantly when he was pressed by Lenormand in 1921 to discuss the question of guilt in *Lord Jim*, he became impatient and declared: "Je ne

[l] Evidence of a paranoid quality in his thinking is suggested by his wife's comment: "He had the most fantastic notions about one's motives, and he would attribute the most far fetched reasons for anything unexpected."[48]

veux pas aller au fond. Je veux considérer la réalité comme une chose rude et rugueuse sur laquelle je promène mes doigts. Rien de plus." (I have no wish to probe the depths. I prefer to view reality as a rough and rugged thing over which I can run my fingers. Nothing else.)[51]

No doubt it was this same disinclination to probe the depths that prompted him not only to alter the nature of his art but to revise his own personal history in a manner that might safeguard his tenuous mental equilibrium by excluding from his past anything that smacked of the eccentric or the abnormal, and by enveloping it in a mantle of conventional respectability. In 1916, for example, according to his friend, Joseph Retinger, Conrad refused "with vehemence" to sign a petition requesting clemency for the then notorious Sir Roger Casement, stating that he had once shared a hut in the Congo with Casement which ended in his "utterly disliking the man."[52] Now, while his decision to withhold his signature was surely his privilege, the gratuitously added derogatory comment was both irrelevant and at odds with a number of statements he had previously made about the condemned man. Thus in 1890 he had written in his *Congo Diary*: "Made the acquaintance of Mr. Roger Casement, which I should consider as a great pleasure under any circumstances and now it becomes a positive piece of luck. Thinks, speaks well, most intelligent and very sympathetic." A few days later he added: "Parted with Casement in a very friendly manner."[53] Indeed if Conrad ended his Congo acquaintance with Casement by "utterly disliking the man," it is hard to reconcile this with a letter to Cunninghame Graham written 13 years later in which he praised Casement with undisguised admiration, referring to his "limpid personality" and comparing him to the humanitarian missionary, Bartolomé de Las Casas.[54] Two years later, in the latter part of 1905, Conrad entertained Casement at his own home.[55] With Casement's downfall, however, Conrad abruptly revised both his memory and his opinion of his one-time Congo companion. The man of whom he had written in 1890 "thinks, speaks well, most intelligent" was now recalled as a man, "properly speaking, of no mind at all. I don't mean stupid. I mean that he was all emotion." And the Casement who had possessed "some particle of Las Casas' soul . . . in his indefatigable body" now became a "tragic personality: all but the greatness of which he had not a trace. Only vanity."[56] Evidently by 1916 Conrad could no more acknowledge his earlier high esteem for the traitorous and rumored homosexual, Casement, than for the "haunted and grimacing" author of Stavrogin's confession.

Yet despite these defensive devices and despite the gratification afforded by Curle's steadfast filial devotion, the years following the War were marked by increasing evidence of Conrad's mental suffering. His letters contained repeated allusions to depression, which was apparently little relieved by the trip to Corsica in 1921. He wrote to Garnett from Corsica that his head was empty and that he felt dead.[57] Following his return to England a few weeks later he told Galsworthy, "I am depressed and exasperated at the same time, and I only wish I could say to myself that I don't care. But I do care. A horrid state."[58] At the same time his irritability increased, sometimes to a point where he gave vent to outbursts of rage. Curle remarked upon these "paroxysms of fury," which would "sometimes smoulder for hours. It was very curious," he wrote. "He seemed like a man coming slowly back to life out of some hideous nightmare, and I am sure that he underwent at such times a kind of mental suffocation."[59] He also described phases of Conrad's behavior, especially at the start of the day, which for Curle had a bizarre ring: "an almost boisterous humor" at the breakfast table, "a bubbling stream of nonsense, in which each extravagance led to another and in which the ludicrous aspect of things held complete sway. . . . And yet to me there was, now and then, something almost painful about these wild bouts of fun. It was as if they had been consciously fomented as a momentary anodyne of forgetfulness. He had a strong sense of the bizarre, and he purposely let it run away with his talk when his mind was relaxed. But it was just like driving foam upon his thoughts, and one always knew that at any instant it might be blown away."[m/60]

[m] Compare Curle's description of Conrad's breakfast hypomania with Marlow's comments about Jim, exulting over his lordly position in Patusan: "He impressed, almost frightened, me with his elated rattle. He was voluble like a youngster on the eve of a long holiday . . . and such an attitude of

In light of the emphasis which has been placed in these pages upon the prominence of biting, devouring, cannibalism, and other "oral" activities in Conrad's emotional make-up as well as in his fiction, it is hardly surprising that it was notably at meal times and in relation to eating that his mental tensions appeared particularly strained. Alfred Knopf reported that when Conrad was annoyed with his family he would sit through an entire meal with the back of his chair to the table,[62] and Jessie Conrad described her husband's "absent-minded habit" of making pellets of bread, which, in the course of a meal, he would fire in all directions, often striking the guests and invading their plates and wine glasses[63]—behavior which leaves little doubt of the undercurrent of aggression which accompanied Conrad's consumption of food. Like Adolf Verloc, Conrad would become "awfully hungry . . . when under any strain."[64] (Not surprisingly he was a chronic nail biter and a prodigious smoker.)

But if meal times tended to become periods of thinly veiled excitement and aggressiveness, there were other moments when he appeared to drift off into a quiet world of his own, even in the midst of a conversation. Curle described such moods as characteristic of the late evening when Conrad would slip into a state of "dreamy softness, as if, in the intensity of his vision he was talking to himself aloud . . . his reminiscences . . . appeared to have no clear beginning or end . . . evidently provoked by some wandering thought, and Conrad always related them as though his listener had been present with him and could appreciate, to the full, the unfamiliar reference." Then suddenly in the midst of this "far away mood . . . he would make a kind of gesture of dismissal . . . one could almost feel his thought click back into the present."[n/65]

---

mind in a grown man and in this connection had in it something phenomenal, a little mad, dangerous, unsafe." It is noteworthy that Marlow's observations are gathered while Jim is eating, "or rather swallowing food, as it were, unconsciously."[61]

[n] If the excitement and tension of meal times were linked with Conrad's unappeased and aggressive hunger for love, these late evening reveries suggest the picture of the dreamy condition of a contented sleepy child. Curle's description of these states is also reminiscent of the "free association" of the psychoanalytic subject whose random wanderings of memory and thought

A major diversion in his depressing daily routine came in the spring of 1923 when Conrad accepted an invitation by his American publisher, F. N. Doubleday, to visit the United States. Shortly before his departure, however, Mrs. Conrad was shocked to learn that Borys had been secretly married. Aware of the strained relationship between father and son, and knowing that the news would undoubtedly evoke a violent reaction in Conrad, serious enough, perhaps, to ruin his trip, she decided to keep her secret to herself until his return to England.[66] The decision was probably a wise one, for Conrad's American tour was a personal triumph. Not surprisingly he seemed to enjoy relatively good health despite a rather strenuous schedule. Like the letters written during his tour of Naval duty in 1916, his communications from America reflected a state of relative well-being. In his letters to Jessie, however, he did not fail to mention various physical complaints. On board the S.S. *Majestic* he wrote her that he had accidentally hit his little finger, but he quickly reassured her that by the time of writing the pain had lessened.[67] Two weeks later he wrote to her from Oyster Bay, where he was staying with the Doubledays, "Don't be disturbed by the shaky handwriting. My wrist is slightly powerless[!] but it is getting better and indeed it was never very bad; and for the rest I feel tolerable."[68] Thus despite his efforts to appear reassuring he could not resist indulging in his familiar hypochondriasis. It is noteworthy that on the very day, May 14, 1923, when he was calling her attention to his "shaky handwriting" he wrote a letter to Jean-Aubry which the latter reproduced in facsimile in his 1927 biography of Conrad.[69] This letter not only fails to disclose any hint of tremor or awkwardness, but it bears a close resemblance to other and much earlier specimens of Conrad's handwriting.

Soon he was writing to his wife that "upon the whole I have improved in health."[70] In the distracting atmosphere of lively excitement and novel experience, and amidst an impressive demonstration of public acclaim, Conrad was enjoying what were probably his final moments of well-being and emotional satisfaction.

---

take place in the presence of a shadowy listener to whom the attribute of omniscience is also often imputed.

Upon his return home early in June, however, a bombshell awaited him, for Jessie Conrad had not overestimated the intensity of the reaction which would take place when her husband learned of their son's secret marriage. They had retired to bed when she found the courage to tell him. "Gripping my arm with cruel force," wrote Jessie, he cried out, " 'Why do you tell me that, why don't you keep such news to yourself!' "[71] Once the initial shock had passed he attempted to deal with the matter more realistically. That the intensity of his feelings of hurt and anger was undiminished, however, is revealed in a letter written on June 11: "Marrying is not a crime and one cannot cast out one's son for that . . . I . . . am not anxious to see his wife but I want to recognize his married status in some way or else it would be a complete break."[72] He then announced to Jessie the "terms" of his future relationship with Borys: " 'He shall know my conditions at once. Two hundred pounds a year, paid quarterly, not a penny more or less. They will come here to lunch on Sunday week—I don't care how, but mind they are not late.' "[73] It would seem that by laying down such stipulations he could persuade himself that he still exercised some semblance of control over his "disloyal" son.

Conrad's allusion to a "complete break" invites comparisons between this crisis and the earlier one with Hueffer when the latter began his liaison with Violet Hunt. Like Hueffer, whom Conrad had once liked to "recall" as a little boy, Borys had elected "in the nature of things . . . to cling to someone else."

In view of the apparent similarities of these two attachments it may be not without significance that not long after learning of Borys' "defection," Conrad, departing from his then habitual coolness toward Hueffer, wrote him a warm and conciliatory letter containing sentimental nostalgic recollections of their past association.[74] In February of the following year the two men met in order to discuss publication of *A Nature of a Crime*, which they had written together many years earlier. "We met as if we had seen each other every day for the last ten years," Conrad wrote to Eric Pinker.[o] "As we talked pleasantly of old times I was asking myself, in my cynical way, when would the kink come."[75]

[o] The son of Conrad's literary agent, James B. Pinker.

Conrad had recovered from his loss of Hueffer with considerable difficulty and at great cost; to some extent his friendship with Curle served as a partial replacement. Whether he ever really recovered from the "loss" of his son Borys is doubtful. "I am morally certain," wrote Mrs. Conrad "that the deception on the boy's part hastened his father's death."[p/76] True or not, from the moment he learned of Borys' marriage the decline in Conrad's health and spirit underwent an unmistakable acceleration. A crippling attack of gout promptly occurred which prevented him from writing, and he was obliged to dictate his letters. On July 7 he dictated a letter to Jean-Aubry to whom less than two months before he had written in faultless script. In November a medical examination is said to have revealed a "flabby heart" and a tendency toward occasional missed heart beats, although a month later Conrad wrote to Curle that his heart action had returned to normal.[78] His wife noted a progressive deepening of his depression: he showed little interest in anything and even eating seemed to hold no appeal. To her he proposed that as soon as their younger son John was established in a career they should leave both boys in England and return to Poland where he would live out his remaining days. "He had to be the supreme being in his own home," Jessie ventured to explain, "and there [in Poland] he would continue to do so."[q/79]

Aside from Jessie's explanation, there is reason to suspect that Conrad was motivated by deeper considerations in his wish to return to his native soil. In his last completed fictional work, *The Rover*, finished in 1922, he had, in fact, anticipated this very desire.

The Rover is named for its central character, Jean Peyrol, a seafaring man, who, after a life of "nearly fifty years" of "lawful and lawless" adventure, returns to his native land in southern France to live out his declining years. It was there that as a boy he had witnessed the death of his mother, after which he had

[p] Borys' "deception" was probably compounded by his becoming a father some six months before Conrad's death.[77]

[q] Although Curle dismissed the idea that Conrad thought of returning to Poland as "utter nonsense,"[80] there is no reason to doubt Jessie's word which was apparently accepted without reservation by Galsworthy[81] and by Morf.[82] Indeed Galsworthy characterized Conrad's wish to go "home" as "Birth calling to Death."

run away to sea. Modeled upon Conrad's idol of the Marseilles era, Dominic Cervoni, Peyrol is another version of the wanderer, the latter-day Ulysses, who held so strong an appeal for the author. But it is also clear that old Peyrol is a self-portrait of the wanderer, Konrad Korzeniowski, who after roving abroad for "nearly fifty years," was seized by a desire to return to the land where he was born, and where he had seen his mother die.[r]

But this dream of returning to his native soil never came to pass, for after his return from America Conrad stayed in England, dragging out the remainder of his time in a state of sterile melancholy. Complaining to André Gide that he had not written anything of value for four years, he asked: "Je me demande si c'est la fin? Peut-être."[83] He made a similar impression on Jacob Epstein, who, in the early part of 1924, was making a bust of him. "He was crippled with Rheumatism, crochety, nervous and ill," wrote Epstein. "He said to me 'I am finished.' There was pathos in his pulling out of a drawer his last manuscript [*Suspense*] to show me that he was still at work. There was no triumph in his manner, however, and he said that he did not know whether he would ever finish it. 'I am played out,' he said; 'played out.' "[84] Epstein saw him as a "lonely brooding man, with none too pleasant thoughts," who "gave . . . a feeling of defeat, but defeat met with courage."[85] He also noted Conrad's irritability, resulting at times in outbursts of rage, and at other moments in manifestations of extreme restlessness. "The house was roomy, and set among low hills. To Conrad it was a prison set in a swamp. He must move. He must find another house. He would set out in his car, one step from the door to the sealed vehicle to search for the new house. No outdoors for him. The sea captain hated out of doors and never put his nose into it."[86]

Early in the summer of 1924 Jessie Conrad was scheduled to re-enter the hospital for another operation, a prospect which was highly disturbing to her husband and only served to increase his irritability. Some days before the anticipated event he broke out in a storm of rage because of a new bed which she had procured for

[r] *The Rover* was finished in June 1922. Conrad died two years later, in August 1924, just two months short of the fiftieth anniversary of his departure from Cracow, in October 1874, for southern France.

him.[87] In his fury he screamed that the bed was a catafalque, and for the first time in their married life he went off to bed without kissing her goodnight.

During her convalescence in the hospital he was extremely impatient and displayed more than his usual exasperation. He seemed "disgusted that I was not making quicker progress," and he kept repeating, "I want you back home again, Jess, quickly." He insisted, moreover, that four, instead of the usual two, attendants be employed to fetch her home in the ambulance.[88]

Eleven days after her return he was suddenly stricken by a severe pain in the chest, which, erroneously ascribed to "indigestion," was evidently caused by coronary thrombosis. That night a reconciliation took place between Borys and his father, who on this occasion showed "his old affectionate warmth. 'You know,' he said, 'I'm really ill this time.' "[89] On the following morning, August 3, 1924, at about six o'clock, Conrad called out to his wife that he was feeling better. At half past eight another heart attack occurred and he was dead. The funeral took place at St. Thomas's Roman Catholic Church in Canterbury. Upon his tombstone were inscribed those lines from Spenser which he had selected as the epigraph to *The Rover*:

> Sleep after toyle, port after stormie seas,
> Ease after warre, death after life, does greatly please.

PART 3
Undercurrents

XIV · A Personal Record

"EVERY NOVEL contains an element of autobiography," wrote Conrad in the Preface to *A Personal Record*, "since the creator can only express himself in his creation."[1] In the preceding pages an attempt has been made to show how successive chapters in his life history were given fictional representation in various novels and short stories. Viewed individually these stories encompass a wide range of created personalities living amid a variety of geographic and temporal settings. Stripped of their peculiar costumes and scenery, however, the total array of Conrad's fictional output may be seen as a set of literary variations upon a rather simple theme. There is a basic and consistent formula underlying the biography of most of Conrad's invented characters—a formula which evidently possessed a highly personal significance for their creator.

The protagonist, to begin with, is usually an only child. In the few exceptions to this rule, the sibling is generally a shadowy unseen person, usually a sister, with whom the main character maintains a tenuous contact or none at all.[a] In the majority of cases the protagonist has been bereft of his mother at an early age. In two instances she has run away with another man;[b] when accounted for at all most of the other absent mothers are dead.[c]

[a] Captain Anthony and Mrs. Fyne of *Chance* are brother and sister, but his seafaring career prevents much interaction between them. The same is true of Nathalie and Victor Haldin of *Under Western Eyes*, who live a great distance apart. Decoud of *Nostromo*, like Cosmo of *Suspense*, has a sister far away to whom he writes letters. Neither of these sisters makes an appearance in the novels. Razumov in *Under Western Eyes* and Alice Jacobus in "A Smile of Fortune," both illegitimate, have legitimate sisters whom they never see, but whose lot is obviously a source of envy. Winnie Verloc is actually the sister of little Stevie, but her role toward him is decidedly that of a mother. Rita in *The Arrow of Gold* has a sister, Thérèse, who plays a minor role in the story (unlike what Conrad had apparently planned in the unfinished *The Sisters*).

[b] The mothers of Alice Jacobus and Lena.

[c] The mother of Victor and Nathalie Haldin is alive during the action of *Under Western Eyes*. Aside from her depiction as a grief-stricken woman, however, she has no convincing identity. The mother of Winnie Verloc is so weak and ineffectual a person that her little son Stevie has always regarded

The father nearly always outlives his wife and hence plays a far more influential role in the life and development of the child. Until the hero attains adolescence he may have lived with the father, but at that point either the latter dies or the son leaves him. The heroine's father, on the other hand, is often alive during the action of the story, maintaining a close attachment to the daughter.[d] This attachment is occasionally strengthened by some disability of the father.[e] Thus, characteristically, the hero becomes an orphan in his 'teens, literally or figuratively, while the heroine continues to maintain a relationship with her father or with a substitute for him.[f] In a few instances there is some doubt about the actual identity of the protagonist's parents, and especially of the father.[g]

Although her early death is responsible for the lack of a clear image of the fictional mother,[h] the father is often described in some detail. Typically he is portrayed as a man caught in the grip of an obsessional idea which engages such vast quantities of his attention as to bring misfortune upon himself and upon those around him, notably his child. In some instances he is obsessed with his daughter—almost never with his son[i]—to whom he clings with grasping tenacity, fiercely resisting the intrusion of any interloper who may threaten to take her away. In other instances the obsession is a cause, a principle, or an enterprise which he pursues with fanatic zeal, blind to the demands of reality and deaf to the needs and feelings of others. Such a man is the egocentric poet, Carleon Anthony of *Chance*, whom the narrator blames for the death of

---

his sister as his mother. Nina Almayer's mother is physically alive but she is depicted as a deteriorated nonentity who sits about chewing betel nuts.

[d] E.g., the fathers of Nina Almayer, Aïssa (*An Outcast*), Antonia (*Nostromo*), Flora (*Chance*), Alice Jacobus ("A Smile of Fortune"), Freya, Felicia Moorsom ("The Planter").

[e] The fathers of three of Conrad's fictional women are afflicted with blindness: Captain Whalley ("The End of the Tether") and the fathers of Aïssa and Bessie Carvil ("Tomorrow"). Lena's father is paralyzed.

[f] E.g., Jewel (*Lord Jim*), Hermann's niece ("Falk"), Rita (*The Arrow of Gold*), Arlette (*The Rover*).

[g] Alice Jacobus; Adèle (*Suspense*).

[h] Peyrol's single recollection of his mother was that she used a manure fork like a man.[2]

[i] Harry Hagberd ("Tomorrow") is an exception.

two wives and the misfortune of his two children, Captain Anthony and Mrs. Fyne. In the same novel the fierce passion for financial speculation of Mr. De Barral has equally baleful consequences: the death of his wife, his own ruin, and the misery of his daughter, Flora.[j] On more than one occasion it is hinted that these men are mentally deranged,[k] and to judge from Mrs. Gould's observation that "a man haunted by a fixed idea is insane,"[3] a similar impression might be justifiable concerning any of these fanatical men. Insane or not, they appear self-centered, remote, and friendless. Despite their many years of widowhood none of them remarry; those with daughters seem to find in the latter sufficient answer to their needs for female companionship. Adult sexual strivings are quite inconspicuous among these men who, despite a certain callousness and even cruelty, occasionally convey a faintly effeminate quality. Thus, although he "showed traces of the primitive cave dweller's temperament,"[4] the poetry of Carleon Anthony made one feel "as if you were being taken out for a delightful country drive by a charming lady in a pony carriage."[5] In two instances these fathers are abandoned by their wives, presumably for more exciting mates."[l]

The reader of Conrad's fiction cannot doubt that it was his intention to ascribe to these strange men the major responsibility both for the unhappy plight of their children and, in some instances, for the death of their wives.[m] Thus these fathers are doubly guilty: they have deprived a child of a mother and have subsequently subjected that child to the unhealthy and warping influence of their own bizarre personalities.

Occasionally it would appear that it is to escape from that baleful influence that the son leaves his native soil, usually in his late adolescence, never to return. Thereafter he becomes a wanderer who, though he may settle ultimately in a Patusan or a Samburan,

[j] Other examples of the fanatic are found in the fathers of Nina Almayer, Charles Gould, Axel Heyst, Alice Jacobus, and Harry Hagberd and Bessie Carvil ("Tomorrow"). Although he is a father only figuratively Verloc belongs in this catalogue.

[k] Carleon Anthony, Captain Hagberd.

[l] The fathers of Alice Jacobus and Lena.

[m] E.g., De Barral and Carleon Anthony of *Chance.*

never conveys the impression that he has truly found a new home. Moreover, despite his apparent desire to dissociate himself from his roots, he often seems to have acquired some of his father's least felicitous attributes, notably the latter's enslavement to a fixed idea. Charles Gould in *Nostromo*, for example, outdoes his father in his preoccupation with the silver mine of Costaguana, prompting his childless wife to realize that "he lives for the mine rather than for her," in the grip of a "cold and overmastering passion which she dreaded more than if it were an infatuation for another woman."[6] And although Captain Anthony of *Chance* had sought to escape his exacting and tyrannical father by running off to sea, "the inarticulate son had set up a standard for himself with that need for embodying in his conduct the dreams, the passion, the impulses the poet puts into arrangements of verses."[7] Yet far from enhancing his self-esteem the son's attempt to model himself upon his father appears to have had an opposite effect, "I do not think that there was in what he did a conscious and lofty confidence in himself," says Marlow of Captain Anthony. "Looked at abstractedly . . . his life had been a life of solitude and silence. . . ."[8] A similar life of "solitude and silence" is the legacy bestowed upon Axel Heyst, the hero of *Victory*, by his father. During the last three years of his father's life he and his father lived together—"three years of such companionship at that plastic and impressionable age were bound to leave in the boy a profound mistrust of life." Analytic and cynical, the father had taught the son to reflect—"a destructive process," for "it is not the clear sighted who lead the world. Great achievements are accomplished in a blessed warm mental fog, which the pitiless cold blasts of the father's analysis had blown away from the son."[9] On his deathbed the father cautions: "Look on—make no sound," and from that moment on the son decided to drift—"to drift without even catching on to anything. 'This shall be my defense against life,' he had said."[10]

In one form or another Heyst's determination to avoid emotional entanglements is typical of many of Conrad's fictional heroes: for example, Captain Anthony who is described as "a hermit withdrawn from a wicked world,"[11] or Lieutenant Réal of *The Rover* who seeks to achieve "a sense of remoteness from ordinary mankind." Like him, too, many of them succeed in believing that they have lost "all capacity for the softer emotions."[12] But in this they are mistaken, for in every instance this complacent policy of emotional detachment is doomed to failure. Drifting untroubled upon the calm waters of an isolated existence, the hero is suddenly confronted by an unforeseen accident of fate which bursts explosively upon the solitude and silence. From this moment on his detachment is at an end, his composure shattered forever. This intrusion takes on a variety of forms: it may be a submerged derelict that punches a hole in a ship during the quiet hours of the night; it may be a fugitive from the police seeking asylum; it may be the spoilage of the entire food supply on a foundering ship, exposing the crew to the peril of starvation. In the face of the crises presented by these unexpected and unwanted developments, the hero behaves in a manner which often reveals facets of his character that he had neither known nor suspected. Confronted by a test of his moral fiber the man who had once "laid for himself a rigidly straight line of conduct" discovers within himself depravity, cupidity, cowardice, corruptibility; with shock and disillusionment he learns that he is capable of dereliction of duty, betrayal, theft, murder, and even cannibalism.[13]

But the stroke of fate which rocks the hero's composure does not invariably assume the form of a crisis testing his moral quality. In a number of Conrad's stories the source of the disturbance of the hero's equanimity is a woman who arouses in him long-dormant emotions which he is now helpless to resist, and which in the course of time will lead to his undoing. Confronted by a woman's face he discerns his abject longing, his inner weakness, and his soft vulnerability.

But no matter from what quarter the invasion of his private world has arisen, the course of his life is irreversibly altered. No longer the confident master of his destiny, the hero, stripped of the armor of his "defence against life," becomes the pawn of forces residing within his own soul, an unstrung victim of gnawing remorse or of overpowering love. Nor are these two entities unrelated, for often it is to a woman that the hero seeks to make a confession of his crimes, hoping to evoke from her an expression of forgiveness and a sign of love.[n] Such guilt-ridden heroes are, moreover, inevitably tentative and restrained in seeking the fulfillment of their love, as if fearing that the commission of their dark deeds has rendered them unworthy of their suit. Yet even in those tales in which he is seemingly free of any taint of criminality (e.g., Heyst, Jasper Allen, Captain Anthony, Decoud), Conrad's fictional hero displays a striking awkwardness and flabbiness in his approach to the opposite sex. The very few who do marry[o] never achieve a condition of comfortable intimacy with their wives, nor do they manifest any desire to establish a family; with two exceptions[p] no babies are born in Conrad's fictional world, and nearly all of his married protagonists are childless. In truth, the behavior of Conrad's married heroes differs in no important sense from that of those who remain single—with women they are uniformly passive and helpless, and with one or two rare exceptions none of them evokes any convincing suggestion of passion or sexuality. Indeed, in situations of an erotic nature the hero—and the villain too, incidentally—usually appears paralyzed and devoid of either excitement or aggression. But the hero's path to romance is blocked not only by psychological forces within himself, but by the violent opposition of another man—the girl's father or his surrogate, or sometimes another—usually villainous—suitor. As a rule the hero survives the murderous designs of these rivals, but not because he prevails over them in manly combat.[q] On the contrary, faced by the threat of annihilation he is remarkably inert, often behaving as if he were passively courting his own destruction. If his life is saved in these crises, it is not by his own defensive action, but by

[n] E.g., Verloc, Falk, the Capataz (*Nostromo*), Razumov, Renouard. Kurtz's final cry of remorse places him too in this category.

[o] Anthony, Hervey, Yanko Gooral, Gould, Captain MacWhirr.

[p] "Gaspar Ruiz," "Amy Foster."

[q] In *Nostromo*, Georgio Viola murders his daughter's lover, the Capataz, under the mistaken impression that he is someone else. Since the old man had always regarded the Capataz as his adopted son, the pattern presents a close parallel to Verloc's destruction of *his* "adopted" son, in *The Secret Agent.*

the intervention of a third person, occasionally the girl herself.[r] Indeed, it is the heroine who is the only figure in Conrad's fiction who conveys a consistent and real impression of power, but hers is a power which can destroy as well as save, and although at one moment she may snatch her lover from the jaws of peril, she is ultimately the one who leads him to disaster.

This precariousness of the existence of Conrad's love-struck hero stands in sharp contrast with his seeming invulnerability during those earlier days when his life was unencumbered by any liaison with a woman. Like the men of the ill-starred ship *Judea* in "Youth," like the captain in "The Secret Sharer," like Captain MacWhirr in "Typhoon"[s] he had then possessed a combination of energy, courage, and resourcefulness which enabled him to survive unscathed the hazards and the storms of fate. But when there looms upon the hitherto untroubled horizon of his life the awesome and seductive outline of a female form, his course is doomed: lawless adventurer, solitary wayfarer, intrepid mariner—all are destined to be destroyed by the lethal force contained within virtually every woman in Conrad's fiction, heroine or villainess. From the encounter that ensues, the woman usually emerges unhurt, leaving in her wake a trail of broken hearts, drug addicts, suicides, and murdered men.[t] Indeed, the mortality rate among Conrad's principal male characters is appalling: in 31 stories (a list which includes all of his major fictional works and all but a few short stories)[u] the protagonist is emotionally involved with a

[r] Although in *Chance* it is Captain Powell who saves Anthony from being poisoned by his father-in-law, it is Flora who is responsible for rescuing her husband's ship from a collision at sea.

[s] In actuality Captain MacWhirr is a married man with two children. Conrad emphasizes, however, his almost total isolation from his family, who in turn are lacking both in interest and affection for the husband and father who is always away at sea.

[t] The appropriateness of the analogy between a woman and a destroying ship is supported by "The Brute," a short story about a ship that brings disaster upon everyone associated with her. In introducing her murderous propensities Conrad skillfully misleads the reader at the outset of the story into believing that the "she" he is describing is a woman.

[u] *Almayer's Folly*, "Amy Foster," *The Arrow of Gold*, *Chance*, "The End

woman in 25; in 17 of these he loses his life, in all but two instances directly or indirectly because of a woman.[v] In the remaining eight stories the hero escapes with his life, but with little else; a liaison with a woman is the direct cause of his ruin in three instances[w] and of the loss of his ship's command in another;[x] in a fifth case he is shot in a duel while defending a lady's honor,[y] while in two additional short stories an infatuation with a girl causes the hero to betray and kill his best friend in one and to slay her brother in the other.[z] In only one major story, "Falk," does the protagonist succeed both in winning the girl and in preserving body and soul.[a]

In contrast it is noteworthy that in Conrad's all-male stories[b]

---

of the Tether," "Falk," "Freya of the Seven Isles," "Gaspar Ruiz," "Heart of Darkness," "The Idiots," "Il Conde," "The Inn of Two Witches," "Karain," "The Lagoon," *Lord Jim, The Nigger of the Narcissus, Nostromo. An Outcast of the Islands,* "An Outpost of Progress," "The Planter of Malata," *The Rescue,* "The Return," *The Rover, The Secret Agent,* "The Secret Sharer," *The Shadow-Line,* "A Smile of Fortune," *Typhoon, Under Western Eyes, Victory,* and "Youth."

[v] Suicides (7): Kayerts ("An Outpost of Progress"), Jim, Decoud, Captain Whalley, Renouard, Heyst, Peyrol. (The "woman" in the case of Kayerts and Captain Whalley is a daughter.) The total incidence of suicide in Conrad's fiction is much higher—15—and includes Susan ("The Idiots"), Brierly (*Lord Jim*), Linda Viola (*Nostromo*), Winnie Verloc (*The Secret Agent*), Erminia ("Gaspar Ruiz"), Sevrin ("The Informer"), De Barral (*Chance*), Jorgenson (*The Rescue*).

Murdered by a woman (4): Willems, Jean ("The Idiots"), Verloc, and Cuba Tom ("The Inn of Two Witches").

Death caused by abandonment by a woman (2): Almayer, Yanko Gooral.

Death caused indirectly because of an involvement with a woman (2): Gaspar Ruiz, Razumov. (The Capataz of *Nostromo* belongs here; he has been omitted since Decoud, another protagonist of that story, has been listed under "suicide.")

Other deaths (2): Kurtz, Captain Anthony.

[w] Alvan Hervey ("The Return"), Lingard (*The Rescue*), and Jasper Allen ("Freya").

[x] "A Smile of Fortune."

[y] M. George (*The Arrow of Gold*).

[z] "Karain" and "The Lagoon."

[a] The same might be said of *Almayer's Folly,* but it is Almayer, not Dain Maroola, who is the true protagonist of this story.

[b] *The Nigger of the Narcissus,* "Youth," *Typhoon,* "The Secret Sharer," *The Shadow-Line,* and "Il Conde." The last named is the only woman-free story in which the protagonist is ruined.

there are no deaths save in *The Nigger of the Narcissus*, but James Wait, the dying man of that tale, is hardly a hero in the conventional sense.

Equally striking is the relative invulnerability of Conrad's heroines. In the aforementioned 25 stories all but five survive, and of these, three commit suicide after causing the deaths of their husbands.[c]

Despite the usual difference in their ultimate fate, however, there are a number of similarities among Conrad's heroes and heroines. As previously noted, the heroine resembles the hero in that she has lost her mother at an early age. Like him she has been subjected to the unsalutary influence of a father preoccupied by an obsessional idea. Like the hero, too, she is often a solitary and friendless creature, who at the time of her maturity is discovered living in a place far from her native land.[d] These women also exhibit traits of personality which recall their male counterparts; the emotional isolation of Alice Jacobus, for example, is reminiscent of a number of Conrad's heroes, particularly of Razumov.[e] As a "castaway" she evokes comparison with Yanko Gooral, and in her talk of suicide she recalls Martin Decoud, Renouard, and others. Another female character who contemplates suicide is the chronically depressed Flora de Barral. Remorse for past misdeeds and an insistent need to make amends occur among Conrad's heroines as well as among his heroes. Thus, somewhat reminiscent of Jim, Felicia Moorsom sets out upon a long voyage seeking to expiate a wrong she had committed in the past. Like Falk, Arlette (*The Rover*) is driven to confess her crimes before she can grant herself license to accept another's love. Nor are Conrad's heroines free of the fanaticism which characterizes such men as Charles Gould; the wife of Gaspar

[c] Susan ("The Idiots"), the wife of Gaspar Ruiz, and Winnie Verloc. Lena (*Victory*) is killed accidentally by a bullet aimed at a man, and Freya dies somewhat inexplicably after contributing to the ruin of her fiancé, Jasper Allen.

[d] E.g., Aïssa, Hermann's niece ("Falk"), Mrs. Gould and Antonia (*Nostromo*), Alice Jacobus, Nathalie Haldin, Felicia Moorsom, Lena, Edith Travers (*The Rescue*), and Rita.

[e] She resembles him also in being the illegitimate child of a man who has other children who are legitimate and privileged.

Ruiz, for example, was obsessed by "a burning sense of irreparable wrong" and "poured half of her vengeful soul into the strong clay of that man [Ruiz]."[14]

The nature of the relationship between the heroine and her father, which, as already noted, is more enduring than that between the hero and his father,[f] appears in varying patterns, ranging from captive and captor in the case of Mrs. Fyne and Carleon Anthony to a condition of virtual symbiotic union between Antonia Avellanos and her father. Mrs. Fyne is described, for example, as having remained "in bondage for several years, till she . . . seized a chance of escape,"[15] whereas "whenever possible Antonia attended her father . . . it was said that she often wrote State papers from her father's dictation, and was allowed to read all the books in his library."[16] When Martin Decoud proposes that she run off with him and get married, she brushes the idea aside and enters into a political discussion during which she says, "Leave poor papa alone."[17]

Between these extremes there are a number of girls whose feelings for their fathers are more ambivalent, making it difficult if not impossible for them to enter wholeheartedly into love or marriage, like Flora de Barral, who, although she is married to Captain Anthony, seems unable to shake off her jealous and possessive father. Similar conflicts between father and lover are implied in *An Outcast*, "A Smile of Fortune," "Freya," and "The Planter."

Just as in real life, the experience of maternal deprivation in early years and a persistent and sticky association with a father throughout childhood and adolescence seem to have produced severe distortions in the psychological aspects of the sexual development of these fictional women. In keeping with clinical experience the absence of a mother or of satisfactory maternal substitutes has deprived them of models through whom they might make healthy feminine identifications, with the result that they exhibit bizarre attitudes toward sexuality and a marked blunting

[f] Some of Conrad's heroes, e.g., Almayer, Willems, Nostromo, and M. George, enjoy a similar filial relationship with an older man. Almayer, for example, refers to Tom Lingard as "Father," just as Arlette in *The Rover* calls old Peyrol, "Papa."

of maternal feelings. These women seem to share with the heroes a pronounced disinclination to create children, and, except in rare instances, they manifest little convincing evidence of sexual arousal. For the most part they are frigid and several of them make no secret of their aversion toward sexuality altogether.[g] In those few passages in Conrad's fiction which depict erotic excitement, moreover, there is an unmistakable reversal of the polarity of sexual behavior; as noted earlier it is the woman who is seemingly endowed with some symbolic faculty for active penetration and the male who becomes the passive recipient of her aggression. An awareness on Conrad's part of this reversal was presumably responsible for certain contradictory and ambiguous passages in which it would appear that he tried, albeit unsuccessfully, to make his lovers conform to more conventional patterns. Thus, although Nina Almayer's erotic attitude toward her lover is termed "the look of woman's surrender,"[18] the actual description of that attitude is not that of a surrender at all, but of an attack: "She drew back her head and fastened her eyes on his in one of those long looks that are a woman's most terrible weapon; a look that is more stirring than the closest touch, and more dangerous than the thrust of a dagger."[19] A similar confusion over the active-passive aspects of sexuality is conveyed in an outburst by Ricardo addressed to Lena in *Victory*: "What you want is a man, a master that will let you put the heel of your shoe on his neck."[20] Even in his description of nonsexual attributes Conrad reveals the same lack of clear-cut differentiation between masculine and feminine characteristics. Thus, in *The Arrow of Gold*, M. George speaks of Rita's "adolescent, delicately masculine head, so mysteriously feminine in the power of instant seduction,"[21] while in *Under Western Eyes* the writer refers to the "masculine and birdlike quality" of Nathalie Haldin's voice,[22] and the "sort of exquisite virility" of her handshake.[23] This bisexual double-talk occurs again in *Nostromo* where it is stated, "It must not be supposed that Mrs. Gould's mind was masculine. A woman with a masculine mind is not a being of su-

[g] Susan in "The Idiots," Mrs. Hervey, Felicia Moorsom, and Rita de Lastaola.

perior efficiency; she is simply a phenomenon of imperfect differentiation—interestingly barren and without importance."[24]

Despite Conrad's efforts to endow his female characters with conventional femininity he is rarely convincing, for behind all the words contrived to convey an impression of yielding passivity, the majority of his fictional women emerge as hermaphroditic creatures armed with an assortment of military accoutrements and aggressive weapons. In some cases this reiterated emphasis upon their masculinity is underscored by frank transvestism. Thus, the wife of Gaspar Ruiz, who rode a horse astride and wore men's clothes as well as a sword, "for a long time was mistaken for a man,"[25] and Mrs. Fyne of *Chance* wore "blouses with a starched front like a man's shirt, a stand up collar and a long necktie."[26] Yet even when attired in women's clothes Conrad's heroines can evoke masculine images: "It's my belief, Edith," observes her husband in *The Rescue*, "that if you had been a man you would have led a most irregular life . . . a frank adventurer."[27] But insofar as the term "frank adventurer" is one of Conrad's favorite labels for Lingard (as well as for all the other heroes modeled upon the idol of his Marseilles days, Dominic Cervoni), one might suppose that he is hinting at an identification between Lingard and Mrs. Travers.

It would appear therefore that however laboriously Conrad strove to achieve a sharp differentiation between the sexes and an equally sharp delineation of individual personalities, his heroes and heroines tend to share an underlying single identity and a common gender much as they often share a common history. Indeed, even when he drew upon real personages in his past as models for his fictional characters, he introduced modifications in their actual histories in order to fit them into the formula typical of his hero or heroine. The real Almayer, for instance, had 11 children,[28] but the author's insistent concern with the problem of the only child apparently caused him to depict the fictional Almayer as the father of but one—his daughter Nina. Similar motivations were undoubtedly responsible for his depiction of Antonia Avellanos as a motherless and only child, although in the Author's Note to *Nostromo,* Conrad asserted that he had modeled her upon a school girl acquaintance who had two brothers and a living mother.[29]

Conrad's repetitive use of a set formula in depicting the histories and personalities of his characters was not restricted, however, to his heroes and heroines. For although he offers scant biographical data about his "bad" fictional people, what he does supply discloses some of the same familiar pattern which typifies his "good" characters. Thus, like so many of Conrad's heroes who leave home in their 'teens, the evil naval officer Heemskirk of "Freya of the Seven Isles" has been at sea since the age of fifteen; the "blood drinker" Scevola of *The Rover* left his parents during his youth; and the sinister Count Helion of *Suspense* quitted his native village to join an Irish regiment at seventeen. Described as a "military adventurer," his subsequent chequered career is a precise counterpart of the "lawless wandering" of the most approved Cervoni-like hero in Conrad's fiction. Count Helion is simply a Cervoni turned sour.

Conrad's villains and villainesses also share with his "good" characters their feelings of isolation from the rest of mankind. The portrait of Rita's perverse cousin Ortega, in *The Arrow of Gold,* could just as well apply to Alice Jacobus: "He had an unhappy mouth and unhappy eyes and he was always wretched about something."[30] Not surprisingly, he is an only child. Like Scevola of *The Rover*, who as a boy was "the butt of all the girls, mooning about amongst the people,"[31] Ortega is an object of both pity and derision in the eyes of his cousin. When as a grown man he seeks to invade her bedroom where she is closeted with M. George and succeeds in inflicting a severe wound upon himself with his sword, Ortega aligns himself with the typically awkward, love-struck Conrad hero. In general, Conrad's villains, for all their fire-breathing, suffer from the same lack of sexual competence as do his heroes. Despite his boast, "Ravish or kill—it was all one to him," the sinister Ricardo of *Victory* is overpowered by Lena's "fingers like steel" when he tries to rape her; and his partner, Jones, perhaps the greatest villain in all of Conrad's writing, hates all women and nourishes an undisguised homosexual interest in Ricardo. The wicked Count Helion, too, seems wanting in natural masculine strength, for "the only way he could make the power of his great fortune felt was by hurting the feelings of other people, of his servants, of his dependents, of his friends,"[32] a passage, incidentally, which bears a striking similarity to the characterization of the sexually inept Alvan Hervey ("The Return"), a man who is certainly no villain.[h]

From the foregoing it is evident that just as Conrad's fictional heroes and heroines share a number of common attributes, the boundary separating the identities of his good and evil characters is equally shadowy. The difference between hero and villain would appear to be not so much a matter of character as of their author's personal prejudice. In relating Alvan Hervey's rejection by his wife he is sympathetic, while Ortega's frustration at the hands of Rita invokes Conrad's derision. In some instances, moreover, the power of contrition and expiation permits a one-time "bad" person to achieve redemption and move into the ranks of Conrad's favorites, for example, Falk and Arlette (*The Rover*).

Thus, despite Conrad's efforts to create a variegated cast of characters who are endowed with a differentiation of gender and of moral sense and embossed by a stamp of individuality, and despite his use of living models upon which he strove to fashion his characters, a careful scrutiny of each indicates that they were virtually all cast from a single mold—a mold that was assuredly the writer himself. Nor would Conrad have disputed this conclusion. About his fictional characters he declared: "Writing about them he is only writing about himself."[34]

The autobiographical allusions in his fiction are self-evident. It was Conrad himself who had lost a mother at so early an age as to render her image nearly beyond recall. It was Conrad who spent much of his childhood in the solitary and doleful company of his father.[i] Again, it was young Conrad who some time after his

[h] Hervey has "that slight tinge of overbearing brutality which is given the possession of only partly difficult accomplishments; by excelling in games, or in the art of making money; by the easy mastery over animals and over needy men."[33] It is noteworthy that Conrad used the identical simile—a "grenadier"—in describing both Count Helion and *Mrs.* Hervey.

[i] The temporary separation from the father experienced by a number of Conrad's heroes, and some heroines, may correspond to periods in his childhood when Conrad stayed with his Uncle Thaddeus or with his grandmother. See Chapter XVII.

father's death left his native soil to wander to the far corners of the globe. Of particular interest is the image of his own father and the latter's influence upon him which Conrad apparently projected upon the many fathers created in his fiction. The picture of the fictional father as a self-centered man whose single-minded dedication to a fixed idea is responsible for widespread misery and even disaster must represent one facet, at least, of Conrad's judgment of Apollo Korzeniowski. In his portrait of the poet Carleon Anthony, for example, it is not difficult to discern Conrad's resentment toward the poet-patriot Apollo who, for all his high principles, left much to be desired as the head of his little family. Like De Barral and Carleon Anthony, Apollo pursued his own ends seemingly oblivious of any possible unhappy consequences this course might inflict on his wife and child. When his brother-in-law Thaddeus Bobrowski described him as "violent in emotions . . . unpractical in his needs, often helpless and unresourceful,"[35] he was anticipating almost literally what Conrad's narrator Marlow was later to say of Carleon Anthony: "Poets not being generally farsighted in practical affairs, no vision of consequences could restrain him."[36] Again speaking of Apollo, Bobrowski said, "I assert only that in general, poets, men of imagination and ideals, are not capable of clearly formulating the concrete postulates of existence."[37] As a result of his lack of practical responsibility, Conrad's father was continually dependent upon the help and handouts supplied by his wife's family. "That's your poet," comments Marlow again. "He demands too much from others."[38] But in his re-creation of his father in fiction, Conrad did more than merely charge him with neglecting his family; by inference he blamed Apollo for the death of his mother, just as Conrad's Marlow accuses De Barral of having caused his wife's death—"and there she died as some faithful and delicate animals die—from neglect, absolutely from neglect."[39] Moreover, such an accusation, implied through Conrad's fiction, is not altogether unjustified; there can be little doubt that Evelina's health was seriously and probably fatally undermined during the period when she accompanied her husband into exile.

Upon the subject of his father's fanatical Polish nationalism, however, Conrad was clearly very much on the defensive. No one can read *The Secret Agent* or *Nostromo* and his other political works without discerning his scornful regard for revolutionists, yet he vigorously protested the use of that term as a definition of his father: "No epithet could be more inapplicable to a man with such a strong sense of responsibility in the region of ideas and action and so indifferent to the promptings of personal ambition as my father," wrote Conrad in *A Personal Record*.[40] Yet a revolutionist is not necessarily driven by personal ambition, nor need he be devoid of a sense of responsibility. In point of fact, Morf asserts, Apollo was an undisguised "Red":

> an extremist among Polish patriots. He was all for violent methods; he organized obstruction (that foremost weapon of all revolutionary movements), he wrote pamphlets in which he urged for immediate action. When Conrad says that his father was not working for the subversion of any social or political scheme in existence, he is . . . simply playing with words. When a man belongs to a secret society with political ends, and prepares a civil war, his mentality becomes naturally that of a revolutionist.[41]

At some level of awareness Conrad himself may have realized that he was "playing with words," evidently in an effort to shield his father from his own intense resentment, for in *Nostromo* he put words into the mouth of Emilia Gould which admit no ambiguity concerning his estimation of the man "haunted by a fixed idea." Such a man is dangerous, she observes, "*even if that idea is an idea of justice*; for may he not bring the heaven down pitilessly upon a loved head?"[42] (Italics mine) The suspicion that the "loved head" was that of Conrad's own mother, and perhaps his own as well, gains further support from the probability that *Nostromo* represents in part, at least, a transplanted depiction of the politics and intrigue of Conrad's native Poland.[j] Morf has called attention

[j] Another possible reference to his father may be discovered in "The Informer": "The guiding spirit of that group was a fanatic of social revolution. . . . He began by being revolutionary in his art, and ended by becoming a revolutionist, after his wife and child had died in want and misery. He used to say that the bourgeois, the smug, overfed lot had killed them. That was his real belief."[43]

to several parallels between the turbulent history of Poland and the equally unstable political fortunes of Costaguana. He points out, for example, that the 3rd of May, the one date mentioned in *Nostromo*—the anniversary of an important battle—is the National Day of Poland.[44] Decoud's letters from Sulaco to his sister in Paris describe the typical Costaguanero in words that might have been uttered by Conrad's uncle about Polish nationalists: "There is a curse of futility upon our character. Don Quixote[k] and Sancho Panza, chivalry and materialism, high sounding sentiments and a supine morality, violent efforts for an idea and a sullen acquiescence in every form of corruption. We convulsed a continent for our independence only to become the passive prey of a democratic parody," etc.[47] Bobrowski wrote in a letter to his nephew: "Our nation unfortunately . . . is a 'peacock among nations,' which in simple prose means that we are a collection of proclaimed and generally unrecognized celebrities—whom no one knows, no one acknowledges, and no one ever will! So that if both Individuals and Nations were to make 'duty' their aim, instead of the ideal of greatness, the world would certainly be a better place than it is. . . ."[48]

Further indications that the author had Poland very much in mind in composing the drama of Sulaco is his admission that he had modeled the character of Antonia Avellanos on a girl he had been in love with during his school days in Cracow.[l] Viewed as a scornful commentary on Polish politics, then, *Nostromo* would appear to have served Conrad as a vehicle for leveling bitter accusations against the revolutionary activity of his father. Indeed, did he not have his mother in mind when he made the dying Señora Teresa Viola cry out: "Their revolutions, their revolutions. Look,

[k] The term Conrad's tutor is supposed to have applied to him at the Furca Pass. Another oblique verbal allusion to Conrad's Polish heritage may be discerned in Decoud's surprising willingness to assume the direction of the Sulaco newspaper: "Confronting with a sort of urbane effrontery Mrs. Gould's gaze . . . he breathed out the words, 'Pro Patria!' "[45] Conrad used the identical expression in explaining how his Great-Uncle Nicholas had reconciled himself to eating roast dog: "Pro Patria!"[46]

[l] Morf suggests that Sulaco, a city of by-gone importance, was modeled on Cracow.[49]

Gian' Battista, it has killed me at last . . . this one has killed me while you were away fighting for what did not concern you, foolish man."[50]

Yet if in these words and in the portrait of Charles Gould, Conrad was venting his resentment at his father's blind and destructive fanaticism, his depiction of the father of Antonia Avellanos may have represented Apollo in an altogether different light.[m] For in Don José Avellanos' relationship with his daughter, Conrad was able to recapture that tender attachment between father and motherless child which constituted, perhaps, the most vivid and the most cherished recollection of his own fragmented and melancholy family life. Indeed, in stating that Antonia was allowed to read all the books in her father's library, the author was probably alluding to a particularly poignant memory—his trepidation on being caught reading his father's translation of "Two Gentlemen of Verona," and his great relief on not being punished.[n/51] In thus depicting Antonia's affectionate intimacy with her father, Conrad was able to express another facet of his own filial feelings—his love and admiration for the man who had sought to educate him and who had introduced him to the wonderful world of literature.

There is at least a third likely portrait of Apollo in the rich pages of *Nostromo*—Giorgio Viola,[o] a one-time lieutenant and devoted follower of the great Garibaldi. In the character of Giorgio, Conrad was able to reveal the other side of the coin of his opinion of his father's political activity, for Conrad, like the offspring of many celebrities, was evidently torn between pride in being the son of a distinguished patriot and resentment at being the neglected child of a self-absorbed zealot.[p] Thus, in words reminiscent of Conrad's

[m] Don José establishes the newspaper, *El Porvenir*, just as Apollo had founded the fortnightly *Slovo*.

[n] "Perhaps I had earned, in my father's mind, the right to some latitude in my relations with his writing desk."

[o] Giorgio's role as father is emphasized by his relationship to the Capataz, Gian' Battista. The latter, an orphan, is regarded by the Violas as their adopted son. He is undoubtedly modeled upon Cervoni as well as being an alter ego for Conrad.

[p] Najder, too, emphasizes Conrad's conflict over his father. "On the one hand he could not escape the powerful appeal of Apollo's fascinating per-

remarks about his father in *A Personal Record* (cited above) Giorgio is represented as imbued with "the spirit of self-forgetfulness . . . simple devotion to a vast humanitarian idea which inspired the thought and stress of that revolutionary time," and endowed with "a puritanism of conduct, born of stern enthusiasm like the puritanism of religion."[54] (Here Conrad is skating on rather thin ice, as it were, since through Mrs. Gould he expresses the conviction that even nobly inspired zealots are dangerous people.)

By means of the device of creating a gallery of seemingly dissimilar fathers, Conrad was able to deal with his ambivalence toward his own father by separating his diverse and conflicting sentiments toward him much as a prism breaks up a complex light into a spectrum of discrete colors: in *Nostromo*, Charles Gould[q] receives his condemnation, José Avellanos his affection and gratitude, and Giorgio Viola his respect. But the versatility of Conrad's father-portraits transcends the three types identified in *Nostromo*. For just as Heyst declares: "There is something of my father in every man who lives long enough,"[55] Conrad might have said that there was something of his father in every story he had written: the self-centered poet Carleon Anthony who "wears out" two wives and causes his son to run off to sea; Adolf Verloc, the political agent who is the instrument of the death of his quasi-adopted son; the aristocratic father of the illegitimate Razumov, whom the latter has seen but twice in his life; the eccentric exiled writer, Heyst's father, who admonishes his son to stay clear of

---

sonality and of the heroic fidelity with which he had served to the tragic end the ideals of patriotism as he had conceived them. On the other hand he was by no means sure if these ideals had any reasonable basis. Conrad's father must have seemed to him at once awe-inspiring and absurd; his attitude towards him was a mixture of admiration and contemptuous pity. And he could never forgive his father the death of his mother."[52] Conrad's ambivalence toward his father may have been most succinctly expressed in *Chance* in the attitude of Mr. Fyne toward his father-in-law, the poet Carleon Anthony: "Proud of his celebrity without approving of his character."[53]

[q] Strictly speaking, Gould is not a father, much to his wife's regret. However, for the present purposes he can be regarded as such, particularly because he is presented as the embodiment of his own father, a man who too was obsessed by the silver-mine of Sulaco.

human relationships, and so on. But despite their seeming variety, virtually all of these men possess one quality in common: an unfortunate influence upon the development and welfare of their sons, who arrive at the threshold of manhood badly equipped for the establishment of adult relationships in general and for the achievement of intimacy with women, in particular.

Conrad's emphasis upon these unsalutary influences was in all likelihood rooted in his own experience. When, concerning Heyst's relationship to his father, he wrote: "Three years of such companionship at that plastic and impressionable age were bound to leave in the boy a profound mistrust of life,"[56] Conrad seems to be making an allusion to those painful years spent in the morbid company of his own ailing father, years of gloom and joint solitude in which the boy, afflicted by a variety and succession of bodily ailments, tried to drown his suffering in reading books. In such an atmosphere it is not surprising that like Heyst, whose dying father counseled him to "look on; make no sound," Conrad sought to acquire as his "defense against life" a capacity for emotional detachment.[r] If after his own father's death he waited longer than the two weeks that elapsed between the funeral of Heyst's father and Heyst's departure from home, Conrad's quitting his native soil was motivated by essentially the same considerations: to cut himself adrift from familiar connections, and to begin life anew as a silent spectator clad in the hard metal of insensitivity.

Like a number of his fictional characters, moreover, it would appear that he set out in quest of surroundings capable of providing him with the strength and certainty that were so conspicuously lacking in his childhood. In particular he seems to have

[r] When Conrad's narrator Marlow declares that there were some doubts about the sanity of Carleon Anthony toward the closing years of his life, it is quite possible that the author was voicing similar doubts about his own father. According to Conrad, the latter would sometimes spend an entire day fasting and gazing silently at the portrait of his dead wife, and while such behavior may be regarded as a manifestation of grief, it was at the time an indication of his capacity to withdraw into his own private world, detached from reality and deaf to the unspoken cries of distress of his lonely son. It is also possible that Apollo's behavior on such occasions was an expression of feelings of guilt toward both his wife and his son.

sought a powerful and splendid protector, like Dominic Cervoni, from whom he hoped to imbibe those qualities of physical might and mental stability so wanting in his father.

Like his fictional heroes, however, Conrad's quest was begun too late, as it were, for the new identification which he hoped to establish could not displace others which were already a built-in part of the structure of his character. Like Heyst, departing from his dead father, and like Captain Anthony, escaping from his living one, Conrad quitted his father's Poland carrying within his sailor's kit those very attributes which he hoped to shake off—a ready susceptibility to physical ailment, a disposition to recurring melancholy, a nervous distrust of human closeness, and a vague and fluctuating conception of who or what he really was. Burdened by this underlying frail and uncertain sense of self, Conrad's search for a new identity was doomed to failure. Instead, in the course of his wandering and in his restless changes of vocation, he acquired but a succession of façades, each accompanied by the language and the attitudes appropriate to the particular role he was enacting: adventurous French sailor, British Master Mariner, Belgian Congo river captain, English man of letters.

Nor was his quest for a new identity limited to the varied chapters of his actual life. In his fiction too he seems to have depicted himself in an almost endless array of personages. Thus he can be seen simultaneously as the virile Capataz and the neurotic Decoud in *Nostromo*, the faltering Anthony and the successful Powell in *Chance*, and the tired Peyrol and the dashing Réal of *The Rover*. But Conrad's fictional self-representations were not limited to his heroes, for just as he split up the complex images of his father upon a host of disparate fictional fathers, so could he depict himself in his writing in virtually any role: hero, heroine, villain, and observing narrator. Thus in "Heart of Darkness" he is Marlow, but he is also Kurtz; in "A Smile of Fortune" he is the captain-narrator, to be sure, but he is also the "castaway,"[s] Alice Jacobus; in *Chance* he is Marlow once more, but he is also Captain An-

[s] Conrad applied the same term to himself (as M. George) in *The Arrow of Gold*: "I was as much of a stranger as the most hopeless castaway."[57]

thony, Powell, and Flora de Barral; in *The Arrow of Gold* he is admittedly M. George, but he is also the perverse Ortega (whose first name is the Spanish form of *Joseph*) and the orphaned Rita. To paraphrase Pirandello, Conrad appears to have been an author in search of his own character.[t]

Inevitably this highly unstable and shifting conception of his true self affected his personal relationships, for a man given to such indiscriminate identifications with fictional characters—male, female, good and bad—and to such versatility of role playing in real life would hardly seem capable of a deep and unambiguous commitment to others. His hazy sense of his own identity, moreover, must have led to a comparable fuzziness and distance in the image he presented to others. How could they come to know intimately a man whose identity was an apparent enigma in his own eyes, and who strove to cover up the bitter memories of the past with a series of masks and a parade of adventures? Indeed, despite his exciting association with a Dominic Cervoni and his rather wide acquaintanceship with literary and other figures in England, Conrad's friendships rarely convey an impression of genuine intimacy. They tended, moreover, to take the form of protector and protégé, with Conrad occupying now one role and now the other, rather than to assume a pattern of a mutual exchange between two co-equal adults who are capable of enjoying each other's company with naturalness, candor, and good humor. Intent on maintaining his tenuous self-image, Conrad could rarely afford to permit such ingredients to enter into his human relationships. Humor, especially, seems to have occupied an inconspicuous position both in his real and in his imaginary world.[u] People were obviously fascinated by this extremely colorful and interesting man who could arrest them with the narration of his varied and dramatic experiences as well as with his literary genius, but in most of the personal

[t] Concerning Conrad's self-portraiture in fiction, Guerard writes, "The characterization [of Decoud] obviously belongs with those in which a writer attempts to separate out and demolish a facet of himself; attempts to condemn himself by proxy."[58]

[u] "One could always baffle Conrad by saying 'humour,'" wrote H. G. Wells. "It was one of our damned English tricks he had never learnt to tackle."[59]

accounts written about him a shadow of a wall appears which obscures the true image of the man. "For all his friendliness and sympathy," wrote his friend Curle, "there was something baffling about Conrad: the more one knew of him the more one perceived the limitation of one's knowledge."[60]

A similar impression was conveyed by his wife who, after living with him for nearly three decades, wrote: "One always felt that there was a depth within him that even after years of the closest friendship one had not reached."[61] This is not hard to believe, for if Conrad was guarded in his relationship with men, he had even more compelling reasons for being so with women.[v] Like his fictional heroes, he could not forever deny his hunger for a woman's love, but like them this yearning seemed to threaten his undoing. In Marseilles a presumed liaison with a woman ended with a bullet wound in his chest, apparently, like Decoud's, self-inflicted. Some years later an infatuation with a French girl on the island of Mauritius ultimately led to the loss of his one and only ship's command: like those proud skippers of his later fiction—Jasper Allen, Tom Lingard, and Captain Anthony—Captain Korzeniowski was undone by a woman's smiles. And if his ultimate marriage to Jessie George did not result in his actual ruin, his conduct toward her often suggested that he regarded her as bearing as great a potential for destruction as do his fictional women. Like a man on guard against an ever-present danger he seems to have avoided much show of sweetness toward her, not hesitating to criticize or belittle her in front of others and tending to side with them when they were in conflict with her. By exercising some kind of tyranny over her he evidently hoped to insure her harmlessness. Shorn of his defensive armor during states of delirium, however, his underlying general distrust of all women emerged and he then reviled her as if she were a witch. But even aside from such moments, his general bearing toward her often mirrored the same discomfort and restless irritability which his fictional heroes display when caught in the menacing and deadly web of a woman's embrace. Although his

[v] Cf. Decoud's assertion in *Nostromo* that friendship between a man and a woman is impossible save between brother and sister. See Chapter XI, footnote *c*, page 204.

span of life failed to conform to the fictional pattern of an early and a violent death, his married life was marred by chronic suffering and conspicuous hypochondriasis, unfolding the picture of a man who played with illness and toyed with doctors as if the attainment of sound health and a long life were alien to his secret desire. Psychologically it may well be that his chronic disability was an attenuated expression of an unconscious wish to die, for virtually until the very end of his life he seems to have played out the fictional drama of the hero who is ultimately destroyed by his woman. This seems to have been the unspoken meaning of the tirade he directed against his wife when he angrily accused her of having brought him a catafalque when he saw the new bed she had provided for him.

It goes without saying that such attitudes toward women are not especially compatible with either warm amiability or with felicitous sexual experience. As previously noted, neither Mrs. Conrad's account of their wedding night nor Conrad's complaints of loneliness addressed to his friends during the honeymoon conveys an impression of unencumbered erotic enjoyment.[w] But aside from these indications of his discomfort in the presence of sexual intimacy, his fictional portrayal of love and lovers suggests a subjective orientation toward sexuality which lies beyond the confines of the normal. Attaining particular prominence in this orientation is the conception of the androgynous or phallic woman and the phenomenon of fetishism.

These topics and their subtle relationship to the problem of the sense of personal identity will be discussed in the ensuing chapters.

[w] Like Conrad, who took his wife to an island off the coast of Brittany, a number of his fictional lovers seek to remove their women to a remote and isolated place: e.g., Captain Anthony, Heyst, Renouard, M. George.

XV · The Arrow of Gold

In the preceding pages it has been emphasized that despite Conrad's sporadic efforts to affix feminine qualities upon his fictional women, he rarely succeeded in dispelling a firm impression of their basic androgyny. Their symbolic endowment with tokens of masculine power is not limited to their aggressive use of knives, scissors, and knitting needles. Equally menacing to their lovers are their glances,[a] which are no less potent than Mrs. Verloc's kitchen knife. Like the look in Nina Almayer's eye—"more dangerous than the thrust of a dagger,"—Aïssa's sidelong glance is "hard, keen and narrow, like the gleam of sharp steel."[3] The glance of the wife of Gaspar Ruiz is "crushing," while Mrs. Hervey's glance makes her husband feel as if he has been struck down by a blow or penetrated. Indeed in "The Return" the notion of "penetration" attains the rank of an obsession: in page after page that word or some derivative of it recurs with such mounting frequency that in the last dozen pages it appears at least six times. When Hervey realizes, for example, that his wife has left him, he experiences "a shock—not a violent or rending blow, that can be seen, resisted, returned, forgotten, but a *thrust, insidious and penetrating*."[4] (Italics mine) After she changes her mind and returns to him she gives him a look which "penetrated . . . probed him; tampered with him."[5] Like many of Conrad's fictional males menaced by a woman's glance, he is patently impotent in his desire to return it: he feels "himself helpless before the hidden meaning of that look."[b/6] In vain he tries to "pierce her with his gaze." He muses upon the "impenetrable duplicity" of women, and their "feminine penetration—so clever and so tainted," etc.

No less characteristic of Mrs. Hervey's power is her identification

[a] In *Chance*, the narrator Marlow observes that "the general tradition of mankind teaches us that glances occupy a considerable place in the self-expression of women."[1] His predecessor in "Heart of Darkness" ascribes a yet more fundamental importance to the female glance. Speaking of Kurtz's Congo woman, he notes: "She looked at us all as if her life had depended upon the unswerving steadiness of her glance."[2]

[b] In *Suspense*, Cosmo tries to out-stare the evil Clelia, but soon regrets it, realizing that "she would not be the one to look away first."[7]

with flames and fire which on one occasion attains such a semblance of reality that her husband finds himself unable to touch her; instead he flings a glass of water in her face as if he were extinguishing a blaze. In this she resembles many of her fictional sisters who are charged with an incinerating potential of alarmingly high voltage.[c] Like many of these androgynous females, moreover, Mrs. Hervey conveys an image of male potency by virtue of her bearing and gait. She "strides like a grenadier," "is strong and upright like an obelisk," and is likened to a "gothic tower,"[8] recalling many similar comparisons between Conrad's heroines and erect monoliths.

The conception of the phallic woman, which reaches back into antiquity when it occasionally attained graphic expression in art, enjoys a wide appeal. Of its several determinants, the most compelling originates in the "castration complex" which, occurring in varying degrees of severity, is probably a universal phenomenon and often appears as a reaction to the child's discovery of the anatomical difference between the sexes. This discovery may lead to the belief that the girl once possessed a penis, but that it has somehow been lost or cut off. A logical consequence of this belief or "explanation" is that the same misfortune may befall the boy, particularly as a punishment for Oedipal fantasies of displacing his father in his mother's affections. Such "theories" are sometimes reinforced by overzealous parents or nurses in their attempts to impose discipline on small boys, especially in regard to masturbation.[d]

It is unlikely, however, that either such threats or the discovery of genital difference is a sufficient cause of the massive and enduring castration anxiety occurring in some individuals. In the latter instances it would appear more probable that a pre-existing condition of emotional vulnerability has set the stage for the powerful and lasting impact created by the visual "evidence" of castration. Thus, for a small boy who has a wavering conception of who or what he is, and an unsure knowledge of which sex he or his parents

[c] A combination of fire and glances is encountered in the blazing eyes of Mrs. Hervey and Felicia Moorsom, and in the firelight reflected in the ominous gaze of the gypsy girl in "The Inn of Two Witches."

[d] A literary monument to this type of pedagogy may be found in that awesome "children's" book—*Struwwelpeter*.

prefer him to be, as well as one who has already experienced psychic trauma as a result of environmental misfortune, the "evidence" of genital mutilation, corresponding too closely to already established fears and, no less important, to unconscious wishes, may lead to a severe and pervasive anxiety. Seen in this light the more severe expressions of castration anxiety and the psychologic mechanisms designed to allay it touch upon the fundamental problem of the strength or weakness of the sense of self. During their subsequent development such boys often create a variety of psychological defenses against the danger of castration, foremost among which is the mechanism of denial which, ignoring the evidence of reality, seeks to dispel that danger by insisting that all individuals—female and male alike—are equipped with a male genital.[e]

It goes without saying that insofar as the illusion of the female phallus is readily shattered, such males usually encounter serious disturbances in their adult sexual life. Matters may be made even worse, moreover, by the fact that the woman who is taken as a sexual object *because* she appears to have such attributes, may indeed have masculine aspirations of her own, originating in a childhood where envy of the apparent superior equipment of boys has fostered a highly competitive relationship with males whom she may seek, in one way or another, to "cut down." Thus the pursuit of the phallic woman may lead to the very danger of emasculation that she is supposed to ward off.

In some males, intent upon denying the insupportable facts of the female anatomy, however, the illusion of the female phallus is maintained, not by fostering a gross image of her androgyny (for example, via her athletic prowess or male attire), but by affixing symbolic phallic significance to some object pertaining to a woman —the fetish. In clinical experience this object, which becomes a necessary component in the sexual life of the fetishist, is characteristically a common article, like hair, footwear, furs, etc.

It is noteworthy that in Conrad's fiction these same objects attain an emphasis of such exaggerated proportion as to warrant giving them the designation of fetishes.

[e] A kindred psychological appeal is provided by the female impersonator, who creates the illusion of being a woman, although the viewer knows that "she" has a penis.

In his portraits of fictional women, for example, there is scarcely a single instance in which Conrad omitted a detailed and reiterated description of their hair. Indeed, it is not infrequently the woman's most striking feature, and the one most certain to be included in Conrad's description, however sketchy the remainder of the portrait. Hermann's niece in "Falk" is a case in point. After describing her in very general terms as an Amazon and an athlete—"she was constructed, she was erected, as it were, with a regal lavishness"—the author settles down, so to speak, to rhapsodize over her hair. "But what magnificent hair she had! Abundant, long, thick, of a tawny color. It had the sheen of precious metals. She wore it plaited tightly into one single tress hanging girlishly down her back and its end reached down to her waist. The massiveness of it surprised you. On my word it reminded one of a club."[f/9] In the next two short sentences we are told that she had a "good complexion" and "blue eyes." Another hair style to which Conrad devoted disproportionately detailed attention is the metallic helmet-like coiffure of such women as Kurtz's Congo woman, Felicia Moorsom, Mrs. Hervey, and Edith Travers.

The allusions to Rita's hair in *The Arrow of Gold* are virtually limitless and invariably coupled with the adjective "tawny"—a word undoubtedly intended to remind the reader of her leonine power. Indeed, the fetishistic element in the book is emphasized by its very title which is derived from the phallic-shaped gold ornament which Rita wears in her hair.

Some notion of the intensity of the emotion centered upon the fetish is conveyed in a passage describing M. George's reaction to Rita's departure, which he appears to regret less, it would seem, than her failure to leave something behind as a memento: "It was like the mania of those disordered minds who spend their days hunting for a treasure. I hoped for a forgotten hairpin, for some tiny piece of ribbon. Sometimes at night I reflected that such hopes were altogether insensate; but I remember once getting up at two in the morning to search for a little cardboard box in the bathroom, into

[f] The significance of the similarity between this "single tress" and the pigtail of Cuba Tom will be discussed later. See page 297.

which, I remembered, I had not looked before. Of course, it was empty."[g] Learning that prior to her departure Rita had used his hairbrushes he examines them "with the new hope of finding one of Rita's tawny hairs entangled amongst the bristles."[10]

A comparable fetishistic obsession pertains to Rita's furs, especially in the chapters when M. George is closeted with Rita in her bedroom. At the start of the scene George plays the role of a voyeur, gazing upon the reclining Rita who is clad in slippers and a fur coat which she wears over her nightgown. Despite the fact that the nature of the coat is established at the outset, Conrad seemed compelled to remind the reader at every turn that it is made of fur, much as he repeats the word "tawny" whenever he mentions her hair: "As she had no dressing gown with her she put on her long *fur* coat over her nightgown." In the next paragraph we are reminded again: "her other hand flew to the edges of the *fur* coat, gripping them together over her breast." Five sentences later he remarks: "her fingers still clutched the *fur* coat." Indeed, the sensuous pleasure associated with Rita's fur rivals the intense excitement displayed by George when he is engaged in hunting for traces of her hair in his brushes or for one of her hairpins. At one point, while kneeling at the side of her couch, her fur touches his cheek giving rise to feelings bordering on ecstasy: "I only breathed deeply the faint scent of violets, her own particular fragrance enveloping my body, *penetrating* my very heart with an inconceivable intimacy, bringing me closer to her than the closest embrace," etc.[11] (Italics mine)

As the scene progresses, the allusions to her furs multiply in frequency, reaching a climax when M. George puts the fur coat on Rita standing in the semi-darkness and clad only in her nightgown. "I buttoned all the buttons right down to the ground. It was a very long and splendid *fur.*[h] Before rising from my kneeling position I felt her feet."[12] In this final gesture the writer makes an allusion to other objects which commonly possess the significance of a fetish: the feet and its coverings. Thus, in one passage M. George observes Rita's feet "posed hieratically," and in another he says:

[g] The symbolism of the empty "box" in the bathroom is suggestive.

[h] Cf., The long braid of hair of Hermann's niece.

"I had the time to lay my infinite adoration at her feet whose white insteps gleamed below the dark edge of the fur coat out of quilted blue silk bedroom slippers, embroidered with small pearls. I had never seen them before; I mean the slippers. The gleam of her insteps too, for that matter." Indeed, George's reaction to her insteps is similar to that evoked by her fur: "I lost myself in a feeling of deep content."[13] Similar sensations are elicited by her slippers. "All that appertained to her haunted me with the same awful intimacy," he says, mentioning a number of features, including her "tawny" hair, and concluding with the "very shape, feel, and warmth of her high-heeled slipper, that would sometimes in the heat of the discussion drop on the floor with a crash, and which I would (always in the heat of the discussion) pick up and toss back on the couch."[14]

Although *The Arrow of Gold* is the most conspicuously fetish-laden work of Conrad, evidence of foot and shoe fetishism, in addition to hair fetishism, is discernible in other stories. Like Rita, for example, Alice Jacobus[i] wears high-heeled blue slippers which engage the unmistakable fascination of the captain. These slippers play an important role in the story, moreover, for when she is surprised by her father, Alice runs away from the captain's embrace and drops one of her slippers on the way. Somewhat later in a scene reminiscent of M. George's buttoning Rita's fur coat, the captain returns the slipper to Alice. "I bent low and groped for her foot under the flounces of the wrapper. She did not withdraw it and I put on the shoe, buttoning the instep-strap."[15]

That the dropped slipper contains an important, albeit unspoken, significance is indicated not only by the fact that it occurs in a number of erotic scenes, but by a statement of the author. When Mrs. Travers loses her sandal, for example, while she is held in Lingard's embrace, she is distinctly disturbed. "She would not have let him know of that dropped sandal for anything in the world. That lost sandal was as symbolic as a dropped veil," a simile which would impute to her sandal some barrier of defence against male sexuality,

[i] The similarities between these seemingly different women has been remarked upon before.

like a chastity belt. It is not surprising that when she finally retrieves it after some moments of anxiety, she almost immediately begins "to regain her sense of the situation and the memory of the immediate past."[j/16]

Fascination with a woman's foot and shoe is also depicted in "The Planter of Malata" where the infatuated Geoffrey Renouard gazes steadfastly at Felicia's shoe while talking to her; somewhat later he falls on his knees before her and kisses the hem of her skirt.

The most blatantly erotic example of foot fetishism, however, is supplied, surprisingly, perhaps, by the villainous Ricardo of *Victory*. Catching sight of Lena's foot peeping from under her skirt he throws "himself on it greedily." Later, clasping her ankle, he presses "his lips time after time to the instep, muttering gasping words that were like sobs, making little noises that resembled sounds of grief and distress."[17]

From these erotic scenes it is evident that the excitement and fascination induced by the look and feel of the several fetishes associated with Conrad's fictional women completely eclipse any hint of interest in normally attractive feminine sexual characteristics. Indeed, it would appear that it is precisely because of its lack of a specifically feminine signature that the fetish possesses its power of sexual arousal. For the fetishes in Conrad's fiction, like those encountered in clinical experience, are neuter objects which, pertaining equally to men and women, contribute to the illusion of their total anatomical similarity. Such an illusion is promoted, for example, by the similarity between the club-like single tress of the girl in "Falk" and the pigtail of Cuba Tom in "The Inn of Two Witches." The "finest for thickness and length of any man in the Navy," Tom's "appendage, much cared for and sheathed tightly in a porpoise skin, hung half-way down his broad back to the great admiration of all beholders and to the great envy of some."[18]

Insofar as the fetish represents, however, not only a highly prized illusory female phallus but also an emblem of its dangerous power, it is capable of arousing fear and recoil as well as awe and love. In the midst of Ricardo's seemingly orgastic experience with Lena's in-

[j] And her sense of identity? Cf. Marlow's comment on Kurtz's Congo woman in footnote *a*.

step, for example, he suddenly finds himself kicked "by the foot he had been cherishing—spurned with a push of such violence into the very hollow of his throat that it swung him back instantly into an upright position on his knees."[19] Thus, the fetishist, Ricardo, who but a short while before had told Lena that she needed "a master that will let you put the heel of your shoe on his neck," virtually achieves that position of distinction himself. A similar destructive potential is attributed to the feet of Rita in *The Arrow of Gold*: "You know how to trample on a poor fellow," Azzolati tells her. "But I don't mind being made to wriggle under your pretty shoes."[20]

The fetish may also give rise to attitudes of loathing and disgust on the condition that it fails to sustain the illusion of the female phallus and serves instead as an abhorrent reminder of the reality of the female genitalia. When Mrs. Hervey returns home with dirty boots, for example, her husband is "indignant, amazed and shocked."[21] Somewhat later, commenting upon her dishevelled appearance—especially the disarray of her hat and hair—the writer speaks of that "Ugliness of truth which can only be kept out of daily life by unremitting care for appearances."[22] As a rule in Conrad's writing such attitudes of revulsion toward hair (a fetishistic object) are directed not toward the neat, helmet-like coiffure, but toward the wild, disordered mass which is a typical attribute of Conrad's evil women. Of the gypsy girl in "The Inn of Two Witches," for example, he wrote, "the escaped single hairs from the mass, sombre and thick like a forest and held up by a comb, made a black mist about her low forehead."[23] This association of hair with ominous plant life can also be discovered in *An Outcast of the Islands* where Aïssa is identified with the deadly tentacles and creepers about her: "the slender spikes of pale green orchids streamed down from amongst the boughs and mingled with the black hair that framed her face."[24] Hair is compared to consuming fire in "The Planter of Malata" where Felicia Moorsom's coiffure is likened to "writhing flames," thus imparting to her the aspect of a Medusa. A comparable image is provided by Flora's governess in *Chance*, whose appearance affects the girl "exactly as if she had seen Medusa's head with serpentine locks."[25] It is characteristic of these Medusa-like women that they are without exception regarded as devourers:

both Clelia in *Suspense* and the gypsy girl in "The Inn of Two Witches" stare at the heroes of these tales as if they were planning to eat them, while the governess in *Chance* gives the appearance of wanting to bite Flora.[k] Thus, the same fetishistic object which in one form may be cherished as a reassurance against the danger of castration, can, in another form, serve as a renewal of the threat of that very danger. Just as the club-like braid or the helmet-like coiffure may represent the reassuring female phallus, so can the wild Medusa-like hair represent a symbol of the aphallic female genitalia, that mysterious and terrifying region filled with unknown and nameless perils: in *An Outcast of the Islands* these perils attain symbolic expression in the menacing vegetation and oppressive atmosphere of the environment surrounding the dangerous Aïssa. Peering above her head Willems looks into the "sombre brilliance of the night . . . into that *great dark place* odorous with the breath of life, with the mystery of existence, renewed, fecund, indestructible: and he felt afraid of his solitude, of the solitude of his body, of the loneliness of his soul . . ."[26] Holding her in his arms for the last time it seems to Willems "that he was peering into a sombre hollow, into a *deep black hole* full of decay and whitened bones; into an immense and inevitable grave full of corruption where sooner or later he must, unavoidably, fall."[27] (Italics mine) He foresees himself surrounded by "endless and minute throngs of insects, little shining monsters of repulsive shapes, with horns, with claws, with pincers, [which] would swarm in streams, in rushes, in eager struggle for his body."[28] Small wonder then, that faced by this terrifying image of devouring female sexuality he is seized by a desire to "clasp, to embrace solid things . . . for touching, pressing, seeing, handling, holding on, to all these things."[29] (Like Ricardo's passionate caress of Lena's fetish-like foot.) Dreaming of his escape he thinks of "ships, help, white men. Men like himself. Good men who would rescue him."[30] In "The Return" virtually identical thoughts occur to Alvan Hervey: "Women—nothing but women around him. . . . He experienced that heart-probing, fiery sense of dangerous loneliness,

[k] No less striking than the emphasis on the hair of his female characters is Conrad's preoccupation with their teeth, which undoubtedly should be included in the catalogue of fetishistic objects in his fiction.

which sometimes assails the courage of a solitary adventurer in an unexplored country. The sight of a man's face . . . of any man's face, would have been a profound relief. . . . He would engage a butler as soon as possible."[31]

In view of the intense castration anxiety implicit in these examples of Conrad's fiction, an anxiety which compares with that of the fetishist, other characteristics of the latter might logically be expected to appear in the writing. In his continual need to reassure himself of the universal existence of the phallus, for example, the fetishist engages typically in conspicuous practices of looking and self-display. Not surprisingly both voyeurism and exhibitionism are exceedingly common among Conrad's fictional people. Moser has called attention to the fact that peeping is virtually a standard attribute of Conrad's "bad" characters, citing De Barral, Ricardo, Ortega, Schomberg ("Falk," *Victory*), Heemskirk ("Freya"), Scevola (*Rover*), Clelia (*Suspense*), and others, as typical examples.[32] But a number of Conrad's "good" people are also voyeurs. Mr. and Mrs. Fyne in *Chance*, for example, station themselves at the window—"a most incredible occupation for people of their kind"—to watch the activities taking place in De Barral's house. Fyne appears to enjoy this activity as much as if he were a stock Conradian villain. "He confessed to me naïvely," says Marlow, "that he was excited as if watching some action on the stage."[33] D'Alcacer in *The Rescue* is another "good" voyeur. Whenever he sees Edith and Lingard together "he was much tempted to observe them. And he yielded to the temptation."[34] Spying or eavesdropping is also practiced by such "good" people as Powell (*Chance*),[l] Jacobus, the saintly Catherine (*The Rover*), M. George, and others. Perhaps the most undisguised voyeur of all is Marlow, the narrator of *Chance*, whose near encyclopedic knowledge of the private lives of the book's characters rivals that of a gossip monger. "For myself, without claim, without merit, simply by chance," he declares, "I had been allowed to look through the half-opened door and I had seen," etc.[35] Frank exhibitionism is far less common among Conrad's male characters than is their scopophilia. Ricardo, of *Victory*,

[l] Chapter 2, Part 2, of *Chance* is entitled "Young Powell Sees and Hears."

however, who is a voyeur and fetishist, is also a boastful exhibitionist. Following his unsuccessful sexual assault upon Lena, they hold a conversation in the course of which he lifts up his pajamas revealing the knife strapped to his leg. Even his manner of undressing in front of his woman-hating friend Jones has an exhibitionistic flavor.

It is Conrad's heroines, however, who show the most consistent tendency toward overt exhibitionism. Rita boasts of her health, Edith Travers of her strength, and Felicia Moorsom of her character. The most overt display of exhibitionism is furnished by Freya in a scene which also includes a strong voyeuristic content. Aware that she is being spied upon by the jealous Heemskirk who is hiding behind a door, Freya seizes her father's telescope in order to watch her lover Jasper on the deck of his brig. Jasper in turn directs his own long glass at Freya, who thereupon lays hers down and raises "her beautiful white arms" above her head. There she stands "glowing with the consciousness of Jasper's adoration going out to her figure held in the field of his glass away there, and warmed, too, by the feeling of evil passion, the burning, covetous eyes of the other, fastened on her back. In the fervour of her love, in the caprice of her mind, and with that mysterious knowledge of masculine nature women seem to be born to, she thought: 'You are looking on—you will—you must! Then you shall see something.' " Whereupon she flings "kisses by the hundred" toward her lover, before retiring behind the curtain. At this point Heemskirk emerges from his hiding place, "his hair rumpled, his eyes bloodshot." Departing, he has an unsteady gait, resembling "the last effort of waning strength." Freya is determined that he must be made to understand that she knows about his peeping. "She was excited, she tingled all over, she had tasted blood!" Her mode of humiliating him, however, is a little bizarre. Instead of screaming at him she dashes to the piano "and made the rosewood monster growl savagely in an irritated bass. She struck chords as if firing shots after that straddling, broad figure . . . and then she pursued him with . . . a . . . fierce piece of love music which had been tried more than once against the thunderstorms."[36]

It is evident that in this quasi-operatic scene Freya does not simply reject an unacceptable suitor; far from it. Against a contrapuntal background of peeping and self-display, she deliberately seeks to excite him before the final humiliation which she executes by firing bass notes at his broad retreating posterior. In this provocative and demeaning behavior Freya joins the ranks of the numerous Conradian females who, wittingly or not, succeed in emasculating, and sometimes physically wounding, their lovers. Her treatment of Heemskirk, likened to "tasting blood," is typical of the real or figurative cruelty that permeates so many of Conrad's erotic scenes. What is noteworthy about Heemskirk (and for that matter about all of Conrad's "bad" men) is that, for all his villainy, he is as vulnerable to symbolic castration and as sexually inhibited as is the noblest of Conrad's lovers. Paradoxically, in some instances there are hints of a sadistic component in the hero's thoughts about his girl. It is suggested, for example, that Falk's feelings toward Hermann's niece were not unlike his one-time cannibalistic hunger. Even more striking is a scene in *Suspense*: the hero, Cosmo, is shocked to discover that the lovely Adèle reminds him of a painting of a woman whose breast is pierced by a dagger. "He saw it there plainly as if the blow had been struck before his eyes. The released hilt seemed to vibrate yet . . . terror-struck, as if at the discovery of a crime, he jumped up, trembling in every limb."[37] One would suspect that Cosmo's perturbation arises from the terrifying thought of *his* stabbing the beloved Adèle.

No such recoil before the image of cruelty, however, is ascribed to her wicked husband, Count Helion, who, though he may be no great success as a lover, has a way of kissing her hand that causes her to fear he intends to bite it. The Count's sadism is also directed against his sensual niece, with whom he engages in some incestuous roughhousing capped by an impulse to grab her by the hair and pull her out of bed. Since Clelia's hair is no less impressive than that of any of her fictional sisters, the Count's gesture is aimed at one of Conrad's favorite fetishistic objects. A similar impulse is attributed to M. George in *The Arrow of Gold*, who on one occasion is seized by a desire to "pull out great handfuls" of the hair of Rita's sister, Thérèse.

This allusion to hair pulling is reminiscent of the behavior of boys whose tugging at girls' braids is sometimes related to castration anxiety. In older males similar motivations may lead to the perversion of braid-cutting or surreptitious hair-snipping, an activity which serves as a reassurance: "I am the one who cuts; not the one who is cut."[m] An additional reassurance against the threat of castration is supplied by the realization that unlike most body parts that are cut, hair will grow back.

Just as a variety of objects pertaining to the female may represent her penis to the fetishist, so may almost any part of himself play the role of the genital which is threatened by mutilation. This gives rise to what has been called "generalized castration hypochondria" which is characterized by recurring fears that various body parts will be cut off, injured, or fall off.[39] Such a diffuse "genitalization" of the body and even of clothing and of personal possessions can be repeatedly demonstrated in the portraits of Conrad's fictional males. When Jasper Allen's brig is wrecked by the jealous Heemskirk, for example, Jasper finds himself "disarmed . . . *unfit for love* to which he had no foothold to offer[40] . . . the day the only thing I had belonging to me in the world perished, I discovered that I had no power over her."[41] (Italics mine) Almost identical sentiments are attributed to Tom Lingard in *The Rescue*, who "cared for nothing on earth but his brig . . . he was aware that his little vessel could give him something not to be had from anybody or anything in the world; something especially his own. The dependence of that solid man of bone and muscle on that obedient thing . . . acquired from this feeling the mysterious dignity of love."[42] Significantly it is a woman who in both tales is ultimately responsible for the loss of these precious possessions.

Another example of symbolic castration is provided in "The Inn of Two Witches" when Cuba Tom—he of the long, envied pigtail—is murdered by two old crones and a gypsy girl for the sake of the brass buttons on his jacket. When Byrne sees that they have been cut off, he shudders "at the notion of the two miserable and repulsive witches busying themselves ghoulishly about the defenseless body of his friend. Cut off. Perhaps with the same knife which . . ."[n/43]

[m] Romm described a fetishist who forced his wife to submit to hair cutting during the sexual act.[38]

[n] The same theme of a woman cutting the buttons off a man's jacket is

Other forms of symbolic castration menacing the Conrad hero include injury to his eyes and to his mind. Attention has been drawn to the many "cat-women" in his fiction who are poised ready to scratch out the hero's eyes, while the fiery radiance of Felicia Moorsom threatens Renouard both with blindness and mental derangement. Thoughts of her traverse his mind "like a sharp arrow,"[45] much as in *The Arrow of Gold* M. George dreams that his beloved Rita is hurling her arrow-shaped hair ornament at him.[o]

In view of this pervasive preoccupation with the danger of castration, and in view of the tenuousness of the denial of female genital anatomy, Conrad's male characters, like the typical fetishist, exhibit sharply ambivalent attitudes toward women. They are regarded at one moment as objects of veneration—phallic goddesses—and at another, as objects of loathing. The aversion with which the typical fetishist uniformly regards the female genitals indicates that he considers them undistinguishable from excretory bodily orifices.[p] Such a view is implied by the misogynist Jones who finds Lena a "disgusting spectacle," and who denounces women in general as "mud souls . . . mud bodies . . . the mud of the gutter."[47] Renouard too is unable to separate his image of the beautiful Felicia from ideas of filth in the course of his wooing: "and if I saw you steeped to the lips in vice, in crime, in mud, I would go after you," etc.[48]

In his rejection of the aphallic woman whose "mutilated" genital rekindles his own fears of mutilation, the fetishist must find some token of phallic endowment in his sexual partner in order to achieve satisfaction in his erotic life. Like Willems he must be able to "clasp, to embrace solid things." This he may achieve by means of the fetish which fosters the illusion of the female phallus; failing in this he may renounce woman altogether as a sexual object, substituting

---

depicted in *Nostromo*, although here the atmosphere is one of love and gaiety. The Capataz invites a love-sick girl to cut off all the silver buttons from his coat, "so that everyone should know who is your lover today."[44]

[o] While suffering over the departure of Rita, M. George recalls once seeing a man in a lunatic asylum who had become mad "because he thought he had been abominably fooled by a woman."[46]

[p] Castration anxiety for such men is commonly heightened during the menses.

for her another man or himself. Both of these alternatives can be discovered in Conrad's fictional men.

There is no doubt, for example, that the misogynist Jones is sexually interested in his partner-in-crime Ricardo, and when he discovers that the latter has designs on Lena, Jones' boundless fury recalls the outrage of a jilted woman. Realizing that the faithless Ricardo has been grooming himself for Lena, Jones' indignation is supreme: "And he shaved—shaved under my very nose. I'll shoot him!"[49] It is also evident that the relationship between Jones and Ricardo partakes of the same voyeuristic and exhibitionistic ingredients which characterize Conrad's fictional heterosexual affairs. "For coolness Ricardo had thrown open his shirt . . . he moved stealthily across the room, barefooted, toward the candle, the shadow of his head and shoulders growing bigger behind him on the opposite wall, to which the face of plain Mr. Jones was turned. With a feline movement, Ricardo glanced over his shoulder at the thin back of the spectre reposing on the bed, and then blew out the candle."[50]

As for self-love, it is a sufficiently conspicuous element in Conrad's fiction to be commented upon by some of his more perceptive characters. Thus, when Alvan Hervey declares to his wife, " 'Pon my word, I loved you—I love you now," she replies, "You are deceiving yourself. You never loved me. You wanted a wife—some woman—any woman that would think, speak, and behave in a certain way—in a way you approved. You loved yourself."[51] Mrs. Travers entertains a rather similar view of her husband whom she married only to find him "enthusiastically devoted to the nursing of his own career," and leaving her "nothing to hope for."[52] In other instances the element of self-love is implied by the unmistakable similarity between the pair of characters experiencing mutual attraction. The narcissism of Conrad's characters attains a special emphasis, however, through the use of a mirror, itself a favorite word, a favorite image, and a favorite device in his writing. In *The Rescue,* Edith Travers holds a lengthy conversation with her husband while surveying her face in a looking glass, while in "The Return," it is upon looking into a mirror that Alvan Hervey first discovers the note announcing that his wife has left him. Moreover, it is by gazing upon his reflected image and by dwelling at length on his appearance that he seeks to regain his shaken composure. This curious method of physical introspection attains an even more explicit depiction in *The Arrow of Gold* when M. George seeks to understand his feelings for Rita while looking in a mirror: "Love for Rita . . . if it was love, I asked myself despairingly, while I brushed my hair before a glass. It did not seem to have any sort of beginning as far as I could remember. A thing the origin of which you cannot trace cannot be seriously considered. It is an illusion. Or perhaps mine was a physical state, some sort of disease akin to melancholia which is a form of insanity?"[53]

In a few instances it is hinted that this narcissistic love assumes a physical expression. Alluding to Razumov's secret diary, the narrator of *Under Western Eyes* remarks, "He was aware of that strange self-indulgence. He alludes to it himself, but he could not refrain. It calmed him—it reconciled him to his existence."[54] Even more explicit is the description of Heemskirk's appearance following his voyeuristic experience with Freya, notably the mention of his "last effort of waning strength," which suggests a caricature of the alleged untoward consequences of masturbation.

A final solution to the danger of castration lies in the attempt to eliminate sexuality altogether. An example of this may be found in the attribution of quasi-religious qualities to those fictional characters who threaten to arouse carnal desire. Thus, at the very moment when Mr. Jones finds Lena's image a "disgusting spectacle," she is seen through the eyes of Heyst as a nun or saint; and at one point in *The Rescue* Edith Travers is depicted in almost identical terms: "something medieval, ascetic . . . like a figure in a faded painting . . . D'Alcacer's wonder approached a feeling of awe."[55] A similar sentiment, equally interspersed with scopophilic asides, is conveyed by Marlow, the narrator of *Chance*, who says, "A young girl, you know, is something like a temple. You pass by and wonder what mysterious rites are going on in there, what prayers, what visions?"[56]

Similar allusions to a religious asceticism are not infrequently applied to the sexually inactive Conrad hero. Dominic Cervoni is recalled in *The Mirror of the Sea* as wearing a deep hood making him look "monkish." In *The Rover* Peyrol is mistaken for a priest.[q] Indeed, in the vocation of seafaring where women have no entry Conrad found a similarity to religious institutions. "I have observed," says the author in *Chance* "that profane men living in ships, like the holy men gathered together in monasteries develop traits of profound resemblance. This must be because the service of the sea and the service of the temple are both detached from the vanities and errors of a world which follows no severe rule."[r/58]

In light of these observations it is significant that in writing about his own initial venture into seafaring Conrad made an allusion to the priesthood. Speaking of the astonishment occasioned by his voicing his desire to go to sea, he wrote in *A Personal Record,* "it could not have been greater if I had announced the intention of entering a Carthusian Monastery."[59] Like his fictional seafaring characters Conrad himself undoubtedly saw in the exclusively masculine community of life at sea a bulwark protecting him not only against the threat of physical annihilation in general but against the dangers associated with romantic entanglements in particular. Such a view of the sea as a refuge is eloquently expressed by the captain in "The Secret Sharer": "I rejoiced in the great security of the sea as compared with the unrest of the land, in my choice of that untempted life presenting no disquieting problems."[60]

It will be recalled that Conrad's accounts of his adolescent experiences in love were characterized by unmistakable "disquieting problems" and sufficient pain to cause him to declare, "If that's it, then never, never again . . ."[61] Advancing upon the threshold of manhood one suspects that he was assailed by the apprehensions and perplexities characteristic of many adolescent children confronted by the burgeoning of sexual awareness, which not infrequently gives rise to a sudden flight into asceticism and even religiosity. Thus, in his entry into a "sea-going monastery" he sought perhaps a refuge not only from a repetition of his unhappy experi-

[q] A similar suspicion is directed at the villainous Jones of *Victory*. Ricardo says that girls would ask him if Jones was "a monk in disguise, or if he had taken a vow to the *santissima madre* not to speak to a woman, or whether——."[57] The deleted word is obviously "homosexual."

[r] Cf. Willems' longing to escape from Aïssa to a world of "ships, help, white men. Men like himself."

ences with girls, but also from those frightening images of sexuality, later expressed in his fictional romances, which were undoubtedly already woven into the fabric of his adolescent fantasies. There is some basis for suspecting, moreover, that like his childhood dreams of future deeds of adventure, these erotic reveries of his 'teens were influenced by his reading.

Writing to W. T. H. Howe in 1917 concerning some proposed illustrations for "The Planter of Malata," Conrad suggested that for the heroine, Felicia Moorsom, the model should be a "society belle . . . with a rare lot of Titian-red hair." He added, "But all this would hardly repay the trouble (though the search for the Titian-red hair would be amusing)."[62] There is something curious and enigmatic about these comments, for why need the model for Felicia be a "society belle" so long as she looked aristocratic, and why embark on a search for Titian-red hair when an illustrator could supply the color himself? The suspicion arises that these suggestions of Conrad were dictated not from considerations of artistic necessity but from some inner promptings rooted in his remote past. What might be "amusing" about the search for a girl with Titian-red hair would be that it struck a personal note of recollection concerning an "amusing" experience. Such an experience, it is suggested, may have been Conrad's discovery, presumably during his student days in Cracow, of Sacher-Masoch's book *Venus in Furs*. The heroine of the story, Wanda von Dunajew, is described as an aristocratic red-haired woman and is often likened to a painting by Titian. Indeed close attention to that book fosters the notion that Wanda became an important model for a number of Conrad's fictional women in addition to Felicia, and that he was more than a little indebted for the inspiration of scenes and dramatic situations to the Galician author whose name, as "masochism," has become immortalized in the lexicon of perversions.

Venus in Furs is a somewhat Victorian piece of pornography which, in addition to its serving as a primer of male masochism, is an essay on fur and foot fetishism, transvestism, and other assorted sexual deviations. The central male character, Severin, is a perverse sensualist who attains erotic excitement by seeing women, especially otherwise nude women, clad in furs. This arousing image is linked in his mind with a painting by Titian, known as "Venus with the Mirror," and represents to him the "symbol of the tyranny and cruelty that constitute woman's essence and her beauty."[63]

Severin lives on the ground floor of a house which stands in a park. On the floor above lives the wealthy aristocratic widow, Wanda, whose apartment has a balcony overgrown with green climbing plants. From time to time Severin peers up there and catches sight of her in a white gown gleaming "between the dense green network," a passage which recalls the familiar Conrad theme of equating creeping plant life with an ensnaring woman. The setting, moreover, is reminiscent of the situation in *The Sisters*, when Stephen and his presumed future beloved Rita are discovered living as close neighbors. In his studio—"a big stone cage"—the painter Stephen is likened to a bird that "cannot fly, whistle or sing."[64] "I, for my part," says the hero of *Venus in Furs*, "down below have a comfortable, intimate arbor of honeysuckle, in which I read and write and paint and sing like a bird among the twigs."[65]

At first Severin asserts that he is really not interested in the beautiful Wanda because he is in love with a piece of sculpture—a statue of Venus which is in the garden. "Often I visit that cold, cruel mistress of mine by night and lie upon my knees before her with my face pressed against the cold pedestal on which her feet rest, and my prayers go up to her."[66] Soon, however, the image of the statue and Wanda become united in Severin's mind, and he enters into a love affair with the woman he thinks of as "Venus in Furs." In "The Planter of Malata" a similar fusion of statue and woman takes place. In a dream Renouard stumbles against a cold and heavy object. "The sickly white light of dawn showed him the head of a statue. Its marble hair was done in the bold lines of a helmet, on its lips the chisel had left a faint smile, and it resembled Miss Moorsom."[67] Like Wanda, too, Felicia is identified with Venus: "Stealing a glance he [Renouard] would see her dazzling and perfect, her eyes vague, staring into mournful immobility, with a drooping head that made him think of a tragic Venus before him."[68]

Nor are these the only resemblances between Wanda and Felicia: both have abundant red hair—Wanda's is compared to "red flames," and Felicia's to "writhing flames"; both have an incinerating gaze—

Felicia's dazzling eyes threaten to destroy Renouard's wits, while Wanda's are likened to "green lightnings." (Her look, which enters Severin's heart "like a dagger," recalls an almost identical description of the glance of Nina Almayer—"more dangerous than the thrust of a dagger.")

Like many of Conrad's fictional heroes, Severin's love affair is marked by subservience to a woman at whose hands he endures terrible suffering. In the course of time he unhesitatingly signs an agreement with Wanda, moreover, freely acknowledging his willingness to be her slave. What follows is the abrupt and total transformation of the Galician nobleman and landowner, Severin von Kusiemski into the slave Gregor, who undergoes a process of inexorable degradation, torment, and emasculation: he is whipped, needled, harnessed to a plough, and forced to become an ear-witness to his mistress's love-making with another man. Interspersed with these episodes of torture, however, he is allotted sporadic moments of sexual rapture with his occasionally relenting tormentor, the fur-clad Wanda.

This image of the enslaved lover prostrating himself before the feet of a woman with flaming hair again recalls "The Planter of Malata"; "He [Renouard], *sensitive like a bond slave to the moods of a master*, was moved by the subtle relenting of her grace to an infinite tenderness. He fought down the impulse to seize her by the hand, lead her down into the garden . . . and throw himself at her feet uttering words of love."[69] (Italics mine)

The resemblance between *Venus in Furs* and Conrad's fiction gains its most striking expression, however, in the case of *The Arrow of Gold*.

The heroine of Sacher-Masoch's book, Wanda von Dunajew, for example, is compared to a consort of a royal personage, Madame de Pompadour, the mistress of Louis XV of France;[70] in *The Arrow of Gold*, Rita is likened to Louise de La Vallière, mistress of Louis XIV.[8/71] And although the color of Wanda's hair resembles Felicia's, the impression it conveys invokes the image of Rita's. Thus,

[8] In an early draft of the novel Conrad compared Rita to "a Mancini," instead of La Vallière.[72] Since Marie Mancini was also a favorite of Louis XIV the reason for the change is unclear.

the latter had "something of a lioness in the expression of her courageous face (especially when she let her hair down),"[73] while when Wanda's hair was loose it "fell like a lion's mane down her back." Rita's hair is graced by a jewelled arrow-shaped ornament; Wanda wears a diadem over her forehead. Their most striking similarity, however, is their penchant for appearing in furs, particularly in their bedrooms. There they are described in very similar language, reclining in almost identical poses. Thus Wanda is discovered "lying stretched out on cushions in her comfortable furs, covered up with the skins of animals. She is like an Oriental despot";[t/74] in Conrad's novel Rita is found lying on her side "enveloped in the skins of wild beasts like a charming and savage young chieftain [*sic*] before a camp fire."[u/75] The latter refers to the fireplace which is a prominently accentuated detail in the similar bedrooms of the two women. Rita's bed discloses a "magnificent combination of white and crimson . . . the room had an air of splendor with marble consoles, gilt carvings, long mirrors—and an eight branched candelabra standing on a little table . . ."[76] In Florence, where she has gone with Severin, Wanda is described "sitting in a negligee of white muslin and laces on a small red divan . . . the yellow lights of the candelabra which stand on projections, their reflections in the large mirrors, and the red flames from the open fireplace, play beautifully on the . . . smooth white skin and the red flaming hair of the beautiful woman."[77]

In comparison with the heroines their lovers at first glance appear to have less in common. Although M. George makes no secret of his suffering at the hands of Rita, there is no hint of the violent physical torment endured by his fictional brother Severin. Indeed the lovers in *The Arrow of Gold* seemingly engage in little love-making at all, confining most of their bedroom activity to rather vapid conversation. Rita is plainly frigid—"Just what I expected," says M. George, "you are a cold illusion"—,[78] and her young lover behaves like a tired old man—"I detected in myself

[t] As the model of Henry Allègre, Rita poses for a painting of the Byzantine Empress Theodosia.

[u] A drawing of Rita sketched by Conrad could serve equally well as a portrait of the reclining Wanda. See Drawing I.

an immense fatigue," he observes, while kneeling at the side of the couch where Rita is reclining.[79] Unlike his frankly voyeuristic counterpart, Gregor, moreover, M. George has some misgivings about looking at his lady in furs: "The edges of the fur coat had fallen open and I was moved to turn away."[80]

Yet on closer inspection the differences between Gregor and George are more apparent than real: both men are obviously intoxicated by their fur-clad women and both reveal that their erotic sensations are inseparably bound with the fur itself as well as with other fetishistic objects. Both men, too, dress their negligee-clad women in their furs: upon Wanda's command Gregor takes her furs and "holds them while she slowly and lazily slides into the sleeves."[81] Allegedly because she is cold in her thin negligee, George performs the same service for Rita: "I had actually to put her arms into the sleeves myself, one after another."[82] After buttoning her fur coat from her neck down to the ground, George kneels and feels her feet, which gesture is an exact duplicate of Gregor's action, for no sooner does he finish putting Wanda in her furs than, responding to her command to remove her shoes and put on her slippers, he obeys and kneels down. When he encounters some difficulty in the process she whips him, and then, like Lena with the kneeling Ricardo, gives him a lusty kick.

Indeed, the frequency of the allusions to feet and shoes in *Venus in Furs* rivals that already noted in Conrad's fiction. At one point early in their relationship Severin kneels before Wanda and, like Renouard with Felicia, kisses the hem of her gown and then her foot. To this she responds flirtatiously by running away, but in her flight "her adorable slipper remained in my hand. Is it an omen?" asks Severin, recalling the loss of Edith Travers' sandal while she is in Lingard's embrace: "as symbolic as a dropped veil."[v]

Rita too drops a slipper while M. George carries her in her furs upstairs to her bedroom: "I lifted her from the ground so abruptly that she could not help catching me round the neck."[83] In *Venus in Furs* Gregor carries Wanda, naked under her fur coat, down a flight of stairs to her bath: "I lifted her up, so that she rested in my arms,

[v] The scene with Wanda is also reminiscent of the episode of the dropped shoe in "A Smile of Fortune."

while she twined hers around my neck."[84] At this point she orders him to fetch a ribbon for her hair, recalling a scene in *The Arrow of Gold* where, seeking to console himself for Rita's temporary absence, M. George searches for some memento of her—"a forgotten hair pin . . . some tiny piece of ribbon."

If Rita does not treat M. George with the brutality that Wanda directs at her lover, there are other men in *The Arrow of Gold* who believe her fully capable of doing so. Azzolatti, with evident pleasure, tells her that she knows "how to trample on a poor fellow," and her cousin Ortega shouts at her through the locked door of her bedroom, "Oh, you know how to torment a man!"[85] Nor do Ortega's complaints seem entirely baseless, for in response to his pleadings and jealous ravings, Rita retorts contemptuously that he was "born to be laughed at," a sentiment of dubious charity which recalls Wanda's reaction to seeing Gregor whipped by her latest lover, the Greek Alexis—she is "convulsed with laughter." During the beating, Gregor catches a glimpse of a painting on the wall representing Samson lying at Delilah's feet and about to have his eyes put out by the Philistines. In Conrad's story, known at one time, incidentally, as "The Laugh,"[86] Ortega's humiliation culminates not in his being beaten by his successful rival, but by his accidentally stabbing himself with a knife—a Nubian (i.e., "slave") knife. No painting of Samson blinded by the Philistines stands as a witnessing mirror to this climax of his debasement, but in the pages which follow there are more than faint overtones of that ancient drama of abundant hair, a woman's cruelty, and a man undone; and in the ensuing scene, when M. George removes the clasp holding Rita's hair, allowing the "tawny" mass to fall about her shoulders, she looks at the arrow "sparkling in the gas light," and mutters, "Ah! that poor *Philistinish* ornament!"[87] (Italics mine) This is the same object which in M. George's dreams seems about to pierce his heart as it comes flying at him but, unlike Gregor, M. George is menaced by his "Venus in Furs" only in his dreams.

In *The Arrow of Gold* it is Ortega, not M. George, who is the actual target of the sadism which in Sacher-Masoch's book is directed at the hapless Gregor. Just as the latter is obliged to spend the night in an anteroom to the chamber in which Wanda is making love with her Greek "strong man," so is it Ortega's lot to be an ear-witness to the amorous activities of Rita and M. George. Both men respond to their humiliation in a similar fashion: Ortega nearly kills himself with a knife; Gregor contemplates suicide with poignard. Moreover, the two men hold still another trait in common—a past reputation for cruelty toward women. Thus, early in the "Venus" story Severin is discovered menacing his young housekeeper with a weapon because he is displeased with her manner of serving him eggs; and when Rita was a young girl we are told that her cousin Ortega used to pelt her with stones and threaten to whip her.

"Man has but one choice," observes Severin: "To be a tyrant *over* or the *slave* of woman."[88] *Venus in Furs* is therefore a tale which, like many of Conrad's love stories, discloses a wavering and uncertain image of love, of the sexual role, and of the distinguishing characteristics of masculinity and femininity. Even Wanda's Greek lover, whom she calls her "strong man" and a "lion," and who is famed for his cruelty and bravery as a warrior, does not quite measure up to this description: in actuality he is a transvestite who once appeared in Paris wearing woman's clothing and was assailed by love letters from numerous men.[w] Nor does he fare much better in the end than Rita's lover, M. George. Both men become involved in duels, and although M. George is merely wounded, Wanda's lover is killed.

Woman, says Wanda, "has the nature of a savage, who is faithful or faithless, magnanimous or cruel, according to the impulse that dominates at the moment. . . . Man even when he is selfish or evil always follows *principles*, woman never follows anything but impulses. Don't ever forget that, and never feel secure with the woman you love."[89]

"As to honor," says Marlow in *Chance* "it's a very fine medieval inheritance which women never got hold of. . . . In addition they are devoid of decency. I mean masculine decency. . . . 'Sensation at any cost' is their secret device."[90]

[w] As mentioned in footnote *e*, the attraction of transvestism for the fetishist is caused by the knowledge that the "woman" really possesses a penis.

The hypothesis implicit in the foregoing discussion, namely, that a number of elements in *The Arrow of Gold* as well as scenes and descriptions in other Conrad writings were "inspired" by *Venus in Furs*, may be challenged on two counts: first, that there is no evidence that he was familiar with Sacher-Masoch's book, and second, that the resemblances between the latter and Conrad's stories are purely coincidental. Concerning the first point, while it is true that there is no proof that Conrad ever read *Venus in Furs*[x]—and it is doubtful whether such proof will be forthcoming—it should be noted that when it first appeared in 1870 Conrad was in his thirteenth year and attending the gymnasium in Cracow. Although published originally in German,[y] by the following year the book was making its way all over Europe and in the course of time could hardly have escaped the notice of 'teen-aged boys and young men, who could be counted on to devour this racy story and pass it around among themselves. As for the second point, while it must be admitted that coincidence cannot be ruled out, the several and sometimes minute similarities between Conrad's writings and *Venus in Furs* appear too remarkable to be so lightly dismissed. In any event further evidence must be awaited in order to confirm or deny the validity of the hypothesis.

Yet even if the hypothesis should ultimately prove to be unfounded, the similarities between the two writers are instructive; they reveal Sacher-Masoch's book as a blatant expression of the same sexual fantasies which Conrad expressed in a veiled and restrained manner. A comparison of *Venus in Furs* and *The Arrow of Gold*, for example, offers evidence of the pains that Conrad took to attenuate and censor the perverse sexuality implicit in his novel. Thus, although the heroes of both novels dress their scantily-clad lady-loves in their luxurious furs, M. George performs this service for Rita not because it excites him but because she is shivering with cold. By the same token, through the use of metaphor and

[x] The fact that it was not listed among the contents of his library after his death is of course no proof that he was unfamiliar with it.[91]

[y] Although German was Sacher-Masoch's literary language, his mother was Polish and that was his native tongue. Like Conrad, too, he mastered French at an early age.[92]

other literary devices, Conrad succeeded in partially de-sexualizing the image of the phallic woman and in dulling the impact of the sado-masochism and other erotic deviations implicit in his fetish-ridden romances.

Yet despite these efforts to obscure his meaning, the underlying fantasies emerge with enough insistence to warrant the suspicion that they represent revelations of his own sexual psychology. Indications that this conjecture is not without foundation will be presented in the following chapter.

XVI · The Black Mate

IN VIEW OF the redundant emphasis on hair which pervades the descriptions of Conrad's fictional characters, it is noteworthy that what Conrad claimed to be his first literary effort, "The Black Mate"[1] is a story of a seaman who dyes his white hair black in order to appear young enough to procure a position on a ship as mate.[a] Here, presumably on the threshold of his career as a writer, Conrad dealt with the theme which was to recur repeatedly in his later fiction: the attribution of power, notably masculine power, to an impressive abundance of youthful-appearing hair. It should come as no surprise to discover that Conrad's own hair played a significant role in his emotional life.

In an earlier chapter mention has been made of Conrad's violent reaction to the news that his son Borys had secretly married. After his outburst at his wife—"Why do you tell me that? Why don't you keep such news to yourself?"—he leapt from the bed and went swiftly to the dressing table where he seized his hairbrushes in both hands. "*This was such a familiar habit* [brushing his hair when at all perturbed]" observed his wife, "that it seemed to lift some of the weight of oppression off my mind." (Italics mine) Somewhat later he exclaimed, "I don't want to know anything more about it. It is done and I have been treated like a blamed fool. Damn!"[4]

Almost 26 years before this episode Conrad had composed a scene of remarkable similarity in the short story, "The Return." Upon his return home one afternoon, Mr. Hervey looks into a mirror and discerns the reflection of a note pinned to the dressing table by his wife which announces that she has left him for another man. His composure shattered, Mr. Hervey peers at his image in the mirror as if expecting to discover some alteration in his appearance.

[a] There is some uncertainty about the exact date of the writing of this story. Although Conrad declared that he had written it in the late eighties, his wife denied this, claiming that she had supplied him with the material for the story at a much later date.[2] For the present purposes the truth of the matter is irrelevant, for, like the inexact memories of his past of the psychoanalytic subject, the *impression* of the truth may be more revealing than are the actual facts. "Only in man's imagination," wrote Conrad, "does every truth find an effective and undeniable existence."[3]

> On the whole he looked very much as usual. Only his hair was slightly ruffled, and that disorder, somehow, was so suggestive of trouble that he went quickly to the [dressing] table, and began to use the brushes, in an anxious desire to obliterate the compromising trace, that only vestige of his emotion. He brushed with care, watching the effect of his smoothing; and another face, slightly pale and more tense than was perhaps desirable, peered back at him from the toilet glass. He laid the brushes down and was not satisfied. He took them up again and brushed, brushed mechanically—forgot himself in that occupation.

Ultimately somewhat calmer, he slapped the brushes on the table and said in "a fierce whisper: 'I wish him joy . . . damn the woman!' "[5]

What is noteworthy about these two strikingly similar episodes is that in both instances the hair brushing is undertaken as an urgent and immediate reaction to an unexpected and shocking loss: in the story, the desertion of Alvan Hervey by his wife; in the author's personal life, his "desertion" by his marrying son.[b] How fixed a habit this brushing must have been[b1] is further emphasized by its reappearance in *The Arrow of Gold*, where, as in "The Return," it occurs in relation to a loss: peering into a mirror, M. George brushes his hair while thinking of the absent Rita. In both fictional descriptions of the hair brushing Conrad reveals the identification between the subject and the absent loved one. Looking upon his own image, M. George thinks of Rita's face; brushing his own hair, he thinks of her hair. Love for her seems indistinguishable from self-love; loss of her is a loss of a part of himself. It is no wonder that when a search among the bristles of his brushes reveals no trace of her hair, he is seized by a fit of melancholy. He lights a cigarette and slowly de-

[b] It should be recalled that Conrad composed "The Return" during his wife's first pregnancy—which event, it would seem, was also experienced by Conrad as a desertion—the desertion of his wife-mother for an unborn rival, Borys.

[b1] As an illustration of the fact that even his children sensed the irritation discharged in Conrad's hair brushing, Mrs. Conrad mentioned an occasion when the three-year-old John rushed into her room exclaiming: " 'Good morning, Mum! I can't stop a minute. Dada's brushed his hair three times already!' "[5a]

scends the stairs, his unhappiness "dulled, as the grief of those who mourn for the dead gets dulled in the overwhelming sensation that everything is over, that *a part of themselves is lost beyond recall* taking with it the savour of life."[6] (Italics mine) It should be pointed out that during this scene M. George is well aware of the fact that Rita's absence is temporary. In "The Return" Mrs. Hervey's absence too turns out to be temporary; exercising a woman's privilege of changing her mind, she decides to return to her husband, who, suddenly aware of her presence, feels as if "*some essential part of himself had in a flash returned to his body*."[7] (Italics mine)

It is clear from these passages that the compulsive hair brushing signifies not only a reaction to a loss, but a denial of it as well, and an affirmation that everything and everyone is in its place, that nothing, or no one, is really missing. Implicit in this formulation is a fluid and amorphous sense of personal identity, a vagueness of the boundaries of the self. Mrs. Hervey is perceived as an integral part of her husband's body, which is consequently depleted by her departure and replenished by her return. Yet in her absence the stroking of his hair provides Hervey with the illusion of her presence, much as if he were stroking some part of her, or as if she were patting his head.[c] In a like manner a thumb in a child's mouth may console him for an absent mother as if the thumb were a physical extension of her as well as a part of himself. Children may also seek to assuage their anxieties by clutching a furry toy animal or by clinging to a blanket whose satin border is fingered and caressed as if it too possessed a double significance, representing both the self and the soft clothing and smooth skin of the mother.[d] Inasmuch as such

[c] Not surprisingly several scenes of a parent stroking a child's head can be found in Conrad's writings: in his first novel, Almayer is discovered caressing the hair of his beloved Nina; in his last, *Suspense*, the same action takes place between Sir Charles Latham and the child Adèle.

[d] One is reminded here of the behavior of anxious little boys, who, in unfamiliar or frightening situations clutch and rub their genitals as if to reassure themselves of their total intactness. Indeed it is hardly possible to avoid a recognition of the masturbatory nature of Hervey's compulsive stroking of a body part. This impression is supported not only by the phrase: "brushed, brushed mechanically—forgot himself in that occupation," but by the sentences immediately following: "The tumult of his thoughts ended in

objects, animate or inanimate, may become the precursors of a fetish, it may be readily understood how the latter, occupying a wavering position on the boundary of self and nonself, is intimately related to the problem of individual and separate identity. Viewed in such terms the significance of the fetish may transcend the restricted meaning of the female phallus; it may serve as well as a symbolic corrective for any subjective sense of incompleteness or defect, including the defect wrought by the absence of a "key" person.[e]

The intimate relationship between fetishism and the sense of identity is further emphasized by another detail in Conrad's hair-brushing scenes. This activity, it will be recalled, takes place before a mirror into which the subject gazes while seeking to regain his composure, much as if he were saying to himself: "Look! You see you are still there, and in one piece!" Similar behavior has been observed in clinical practice in which compulsive and intense staring into a mirror appears to take place in moments of great inner stress, specifically when individuals seem to be threatened by a sense of inner dissolution or loss of self.[f] Under such circumstances, Elkisch noted, the subjects appear to be seeking "to retrieve, as it were, in their mirrored images what they felt they had lost, or might lose; their ego, their self, their boundaries."[g/11]

---

a sluggish flow of reflection, such as, after the outburst of a volcano, the almost imperceptible progress of a stream of lava, creeping languidly over a convulsed land," etc.; "his moral landmarks were going one by one, consumed in the fire of his experience, buried in hot mud, in ashes"; "A crowd of shapeless, unclean thoughts crossed his mind in a stealthy rush . . . he put his hands deep into his pockets."[8] Compulsive masturbation, it should be noted, is a characteristic symptom of fetishists.

[e] In *The Rescue* Edith Travers is at one point likened to an *arrow*, itself a fetishistic ornament worn in the hair of her fictional near-twin sister, Rita.[9]

[f] It is stated that in his dotage Dean Swift used to peer at himself in the glass and mutter, "I am what I am; I am what I am."[10]

[g] A mythological depiction of a somewhat related conception may be discovered in one version of the Narcissus legend, according to which, in order to console himself for the death of a favorite twin sister (his exact counterpart), he sat gazing into the spring to recall her features by looking at his own.[12] Frazer has pointed out that far from having a restorative effect, in many cultures peering at one's reflection is held to jeopardize one's life

That Conrad was intensely preoccupied by mirrors and reflections needs no emphasis. Undoubtedly his most explicit "mirror" story is "The Secret Sharer" which is, in essence, the story of a double or mirror image of the self. Gazing upon Leggatt it seemed to the Captain "as though I had been faced by my own reflection in the depths of a somber and immense mirror."[14] Like most of Conrad's "secret sharers," moreover, Leggatt represents an externalized facet of the Captain's personality, a dark reflection that reveals aspects of the man invisible in the cold light of day.[h] What is implied in "The Secret Sharer," and for that matter in all of Conrad's kindred tales, is the complementary role played by the "other," the double, or the mirror image in rounding out the incomplete self of the protagonist. It is such a quest for completeness or inner unity that prompts the forsaken Alvan Hervey to gaze upon his reflection in the glass, and that presumably caused his creator to do likewise when, "deserted" by his son Borys, he enacted a virtually exact duplication of Hervey's behavior.

From these observations it would appear certain that the tenuousness of the sense of self and the reparative reliance on fetishism pervading Conrad's fiction was a projection of identical elements in his own personality.[i] Foot and shoe fetishism, too seems to have

---

or soul. Similar ill effects have been ascribed to having one's likeness made, concerning which, there is reason to believe, as will be noted presently, Conrad entertained kindred prejudices.[13]

[h] "And since you know you cannot see yourself
So well as by reflection, I, your glass
Will modestly discover to yourself
That of yourself which you yet know not of."—*Julius Caesar*, I:2.

[i] Whether Conrad's decision to wear an impressive beard during the greater part of his adult life was a manifestation of hair fetishism is conjectural. In any event the question should not be easily dismissed with the observation that wearing beards was a common convention at the time, for while this is quite true, there were many clean-shaven men in those days—friends of Conrad too—who did not conform to that convention. Like the present-day fashion of wearing sunglasses indoors and out, rain or shine, night and day, an individual's mode of dress and grooming may be encouraged by a prevailing custom that happens to correspond to deep-seated emotional needs.

There is a small piece of evidence suggesting that, like some hair fetish-

played a role in Conrad's personal life. In an earlier chapter attention has been drawn to the almost magical effect on him of the sight of the "marble-like" calves and the laced boots of the Englishman at the Furca Pass when as a fifteen-year-old schoolboy he was engaged in what seemed a losing battle with his tutor over his wish to go to sea. A complement to this experience took place in 1914 when the Conrads were about to embark on a visit to his native Poland. During the trip from their home to London, his wife reported, Conrad broke into a "violent fury" because John was not wearing his leather gaiters, although she had deliberately dressed both boys as lightly as possible because of the intense July heat.[16] It would appear that in returning to his fragile and uncertain homeland Conrad required the same visual manifestations of sturdy English legs encased in tough English leather that had sustained him many years before in facilitating his departure from that country. Like Mrs. Travers after retrieving her lost sandal, Conrad appears to have endowed footwear with a capacity for maintaining his bearings, for providing him with "a sense of the situation and the memory of the immediate past."[j]

---

ists, Conrad may have harbored fantasies akin to braid-cutting. Writing to Galsworthy about the latter's novel, *Fraternity*, Conrad criticized the characterization of the protagonist Hilary, declaring, "You have refined and spiritualized the poor wretch into a remote resemblance to those lunatics—there are such—who try to cut off locks of women's hair in crowds."[15] This reference to hair snipping is surprising for there is nothing in Galsworthy's description of Hilary that might conceivably evoke such an impression. Conrad's allusion to this particular perversion, moreover, seems quite gratuitous—he could have selected any other from a wide variety of pathological types. The possibility presents itself, therefore, that Conrad was making a covert confession that he himself might be one of those "lunatics."

[j] The psychoanalyst might discern echoes of this aspect of Conrad's fetishism in random and seemingly fortuitous allusions to his own feet and boots. Replying to H. G. Wells's criticism of *An Outcast*, he wrote to his publisher: "My style may be atrocious—but it produces its effect—is as unalterable as—say—the size of my feet—and I will never disguise it in the boots of Wells's (or anybody else's) making . . . I shall make my own boots or perish."[17] On a much later occasion he replied with irritation to the suggestion that *Moby Dick* was "symbolical and mystical" by retorting: "Mystical. My eye. My old boots are mystical."[18] In view of the phallic significance of the fetish it is noteworthy that in both instances when Con-

Like the fetishist, Conrad too gave evidence of a tendency to deny or ignore the anatomical differences between the sexes. Mrs. Conrad related how on one occasion her husband had been sent out to find a new home for his family where a plentiful supply of milk would be available for the children. He found a place and rented it, but the animals on the premises turned out to be bullocks. "This really tried my fortitude," she wrote, "but at the same time I excused my husband: I did not expect him to know a cow from a bullock."[19] She conveyed a similar impression in her account of the trip to Poland in 1914, when, "absent-mindedly" appropriating all the available warm clothing, Conrad displayed no apparent concern about wearing his wife's sweater, "unmistakably a feminine garment," she wrote, "which fastened from right to left."[k/20] Not only was he unable to distinguish a bullock from a cow, but Conrad seemed confused about the gender of some of his fictional characters. Thus, in "The Planter of Malata" Geoffrey Renouard's appearance is likened to the "profile of Pallas," and in a letter containing recommendations for an illustration for that story, he wrote that for a model for Renouard "you'll want a young man with a Minerva profile."[22] (Minerva and Pallas are names for the same goddess.)[l]

Like many of his fictional characters and like the typical fetishist, Conrad suffered from a diffuse "castration hypochondria." He had fears of going blind, becoming paralyzed, being unable to write, and going mad—eventualities which he projected upon a number of

---

rad defiantly invoked his boots he was clearly on the defensive as if his reputation both as a writer and as a man was being questioned.

[k] It will be recalled that in a letter expressing regret that his new-born child was not a girl he had written, "I can't help thinking she would have resembled me more."[21]

[l] A further indication of a lack of a clear-cut differentiation of gender of this character, and of others too, is suggested by the ease with which Conrad formed masculine names out of feminine ones, and vice versa. Thus, as noted in an earlier chapter, it seems quite possible that "Renouard" was fashioned out of "Renouf," the surname of the French girl with whom Conrad fell in love in Mauritius. Both her initials as well as her first name reappear in the person of the French naval lieutenant, Eugène Réal, of *The Rover*. It may be that Conrad's sensitivity to the bisexual potentiality of names (e.g., Anthony-Antonia) was enhanced by his identification with his near-namesake, his cousin Josefina.

his fictional characters. His concern over the impairment or loss of his faculties, moreover, extended beyond his physical person and embraced personal possessions as well. Thus, he fretted repeatedly over the real or imaginary loss of objects which often were of trifling importance. Just as the family was about to depart for Capri, for instance, he suddenly insisted upon retrieving what he then claimed were his "favorite" spectacles, although Jessie Conrad stated they were an old, cracked, and rusty pair for which he had no need.[m/23] And when his wife was about to go into labor during her second pregnancy he insisted upon her going on a long and arduous trip to find a book which he had misplaced.[24] From these examples it can be seen that his anxieties over retrieving seemingly unimportant objects were heightened upon the eve of major changes in the pattern of his daily life.[n] Similar considerations were undoubtedly responsible for his behavior when the family moved to a new home: he would refuse to allow the moving van people to remove a single picture or a rug until he himself had left the old premises and could thus not be a witness to its dismantling.[25]

Serving apparently as another defense against his fear of loss was his habit of appropriating objects which did not belong to him. Thus, a silver pin tray which his wife had received as a cherished birthday present was commandeered by him to serve as an ash tray,[26] and when someone in the household chanced to lay a book aside for a moment it was a common practice for Conrad to carry it off and start reading it himself.[27] As previously noted he also protected himself against possible misfortune or loss by imagining and believing in the very worst. Thus he could announce with conviction that the hired hand had committed suicide, that his misplaced wallet had been stolen, and that his son Borys had been killed in action. Like Señor Hirsch, Conrad seems to have been endowed with that "kind of imagination whose undue development caused intense suffering."[28]

In view of this evidence of Conrad's kinship with the fetishist, it is probable that he also possessed a wavering regard for women which was determined in no small measure by their capacity to in-

[m] The relevance of this to his fear of blindness seems self-evident.

[n] Cf., the episode of the leather gaiters, page 322.

fluence the fluctuations of his own castration anxiety. Thus, while at one moment he might revere his "Aunt" as a beloved figure mounted on a pedestal, at another he could echo the fetishist's disgust over women's "dirty apertures." On one occasion, for example, when a woman brushed past the table where Conrad and Garnett were eating, the latter, ostensibly to test Conrad's powers of observation, asked him what he had noticed in particular about her, eliciting the reply, "the dirt in her nostril."[29] It would seem that in the course of time such an excremental view of women included sexuality altogether: he denounced the writings of D. H. Lawrence (several years before the appearance of *Lady Chatterley's Lover*) as "Filth. Nothing but obscenities."[30] The comment recalls Mr. Jones's summing up of the fair sex: "Mud souls, obscene and cunning."[o]

In light of this evidence of the several points of similarity between Conrad and the typical fetishist it might be suspected that like the latter he too manifested a tendency toward voyeuristic and exhibitionistic behavior. Confirmation of such a suspicion is not difficult to find, although it is apparent that Conrad's voyeurism and exhibitionism were in themselves subjects of neurotic conflict. As a consequence these tendencies emerged either in a covert fashion or in the form of their exact opposite wherein the impulse toward looking was replaced by a neurotic fear of blindness and the desire for self-display was concealed behind a façade of exaggerated shyness. Although he was evidently an accomplished raconteur—often alter-

[o] Evidently Conrad was somewhat perplexed by Mr. Jones's misogyny. In a letter to Macdonald Hastings, who was engaged in dramatizing *Victory*, he wrote: "As to his [Jones's] dislike of women I am damned if I know what to say. They have spoiled so many of his little games before perhaps?" Then he suggested that Jones is somewhat insane: "Don't forget, however, that there is a strain of peculiar craziness about the gentleman. The novel only faintly suggests it. On stage, it may pay if Irving [Henry Irving] will try honestly. Something temperamental rather than mental. He's in fact an unusual sort of crank. Voyez-vous ça?"[31] In a subsequent letter he left no doubt about Jones's insanity as he gave a sketch for an alternative ending to the novel: Heyst and Lena survive and leave the island where Jones is now entirely alone. "Completely crazed now" Jones sets fire to the bungalow and runs around "shouting crazily, 'Ashes! Ashes! Ashes! I am a force!' " as he burns to death.[32] One cannot avoid the impression that in this portrayal of the psychotic Jones, Conrad was unconsciously revealing his worst fears about himself.

ing the "factual" details of his experiences to a degree which amazed his wife—he was ill at ease in the presence of a formal audience. During his American visit in 1923 he refused an invitation to lecture, allegedly because he feared his voice might fail and because of self-consciousness over his foreign accent. Neither of these explanations appears to have been the real reason for his refusal, however, for although his larynx may have been temporarily affected by gout some years before, there is no indication that there was anything wrong with his voice in his later years. On the contrary he wrote to Jessie describing a reading from *Victory* before some 200 people in New York, making no mention of any difficulty with his speech, aside from some initial nervousness which he overcame by the help of a watch his wife had given him and which he placed beside him on the table. Reminiscent again of the fetishist, he wrote, "That watch was the greatest comfort to me. Something of you."[33] He then proceeded to read for an hour and a quarter undeterred either by the feared "extinction" of his voice or by his accent. It would appear therefore that the real reason for his reluctance to lecture in public was stage fright, that pathognomonic sign of a conflict over exhibitionistic impulses. Nor was this the only evidence of such a conflict.[p] He insisted that he loathed actors and the theater, yet he dramatized several of his stories and saw them mounted on the stage, thereby indicating a persistence of an interest in the theater which he had displayed as early as the age of eleven when he wrote and directed plays for his friends.[q] Moreover, from his wife's account of his personal behavior, especially his behavior during his bouts of illness, it is clear that Conrad was given to self-dramatization in the extreme—"a consummate actor," Jessie called

[p] Echoes of this conflict are audible in the Author's Note to *Notes on Life and Letters,* which he called "a one-man show—or is it merely the show of one man?" Pursuing this theme he remarked that "the only thing that will not be found amongst those Figures and Things that have passed away, will be Conrad *en pantoufles*. . . . This volume (including the introductory remarks) is as near as I shall ever come to *deshabille* in public; and perhaps it will do something to help toward a better vision of the man, if it gives no more than a partial view of a piece of his back."[34]

[q] In the present context of voyeurism the title of one of these youthful efforts is arresting: "The Eyes of John Sobieski."[35]

This was Joseph Conrad's own — impression of Dona Rita in the 'Arrow of Gold' and was sketched in my presence.

Jessie Conrad.

DRAWING I

This little sketch was done by
Joseph Conrad in his rooms
in Wilton Road Victoria in
1896. To show me how the girls
for the ballet were engaged.

DRAWING II

This original drawing was
done by Joseph Conrad in 1891
Jessie Conrad

DRAWING III

DRAWING IV

DRAWING V

This sketch must have been done between the years of 1892-1894. They came into my possession at my marriage in 1896.

Jessie Conrad

DRAWING VI

This little girl was a maid
in a Country house and
always brought his hat and
stick to Joseph Conrad.
Jessie Conrad.

DRAWING VII

Authentic drawing by Joseph Conrad intended as a design for paper jacket for "The Arrow of Gold" Jessie Conrad

Authentic drawing by Joseph Conrad intended as a design for paper jacket for "The Arrow of Gold" Jessie Conrad

him. Yet in public he demanded that his wife and children remain as inconspicuous as possible.[r]

A striking manifestation of Conrad's recoil from self-display was revealed in his attitude toward portraiture and photography. For many years he resisted sitting for painters and sculptors and he was notoriously uncomfortable posing for pictures. Although one might be tempted to ascribe his attitude to self-consciousness or embarrassment, there is reason to believe that it was prompted by more complex causes. His objection to photography, it should be noted, was not limited to pictures of himself but included his family as well. Thus, when his son Borys was an infant and it was proposed that a picture be made of the baby and his mother, Conrad objected vigorously: "I am very unwilling to have their photographs taken," he wrote, adding, "I hate photographs anyhow."[36] This, one might say, was a rather excessive reaction to so seemingly innocent a proposal, so vehement, in fact, as to create the impression that what was being proposed was felt by him to be harmful and even dangerous.

Such an attitude bears a close resemblance to that of many primitive people who regard with distrust portraiture of any kind. Frazer mentions a number of instances of a taboo on creating likenesses based on the belief that since a picture contains the soul of the person portrayed, having a picture made will cause his death.[37] A modified version of this same superstition can be discovered even in contemporary America: in a 1964 issue of *Time* magazine mention is made of the "cover jinx"—the belief that any sports figure who "gets on the cover of *Time* . . . is doomed to defeat—in a phrase, has had it."[38]

A similar prejudice against being photographed has been reported by several writers. Frazer mentioned individuals in the West of Scotland who claimed they had not had a day's good health after having their pictures taken,[39] and Gill stated that the Indians of Ecuador believe that the camera takes away a part of the soul. He further remarked that photography could prove to be a most un-

[r] Similar considerations were undoubtedly partially responsible for his refusal to acknowledge any connection with his howling infant during the train trip to the Cranes, and for his later insistence, en route to Capri, that his crippled wife use canes instead of her conspicuous crutches.

popular procedure if for any reason the subject were to become ill after his picture was taken, and that in any event photography was only possible when conditions of friendship had been established.[40]

In view of these observations it is noteworthy that Conrad finally permitted himself to be photographed only when it was suggested that the picture be taken by someone whom he knew personally, "not by one of the regular professionals of his dislike." Not surprisingly during the initial efforts to take his picture he wore "an expression of such enduring sadness" that the project had to be abandoned.[41] Many years later, following his arrival in New York in 1923, he wrote to his wife: "I will not attempt to describe to you my landing . . . to be aimed at by forty cameras held by forty men is a nerve shattering experience.[8/42]

But if in response to his deep-seated primitive fears Conrad felt threatened by having his, or his family's, picture taken, he evidently had no aversion to making pictures of others. Especially during the years just prior to his marriage he made or copied a number of sketches of women, some of which are "sexy" pictures done in the style of the "naughty" French magazines. In characteristic fashion he attempted to destroy some of these pictures, and actually succeeded in doing so on one occasion when his wife was in a nursing home. Mrs. Conrad succeeded however in preserving a number of his sketches on several of which she wrote explanatory notes prior to offering them for sale following her husband's death. Whether there was a tongue-in-cheek element in some of these inscriptions or whether they reflect a genuine naïveté is a matter of conjecture. Be that as it may, it is difficult to accept the latter explanation for her writing at the bottom of a drawing of three dancing "can-can" girls with uplifted skirts that Conrad drew them "to show me how the girls for the ballet were engaged." (Drawing II) For whether this was an original drawing, or whether it was copied from a mag-

[8] The offensive implications of photography are underscored by its peculiar vocabulary: One *loads* a camera, *aims* at a subject, *shoots* a picture and *captures* a scene. In toy cameras these aggressive figures of speech combined with sexual overtones become a reality: water squirts at the unsuspecting victim, as from a water pistol, or a snake pops out at him. Of interest in this context is a line from "The Return": "The eternal preoccupation of sex came out like a toy demon out of a box."[43]

azine, it offers clear evidence of a fascination with women's legs, thighs, and nether garments, and of an interest in peeping and exhibitionism that could hardly have escaped the notice of his usually perceptive wife. Similar scopophilic allusions are apparent in Drawing III which shows a dancing girl whose diaphanous costume exposes a generous view of legs and thighs. Reminiscent of the artist's fetishism is the streaming mass of black hair ending in a serpentine fringe which all but obscures her head and neck. The feline attributes of some of Conrad's fictional women is suggested by the hands which resemble a pair of claws.

Although most of Conrad's drawings are concerned exclusively with women, there are two pictures portraying a man and a woman together. Engaged in seeming romantic intimacy these couples provide a remarkable pictorial re-affirmation of the bizarre and distorted relationships encountered in his love stories. In both pictures the woman is depicted as if in pursuit of the man who, like the artist himself, wears a monocle. In the seated picture (Drawing IV), the man, who has a "Milquetoastish" aspect, appears to be warding off the lady as she crowds him into a corner of the sofa. In the foreground on the floor is an enormous animal skin, presumably of a tiger, which, extending beyond the width of the sofa, is undoubtedly dead, although its head displays an attitude of aroused ferocity and seems very much alive. As if retreating from both beast and lady, the man sits retracting his pigeon-toed feet, his knees pressed firmly together like a well-behaved girl, with his left forearm guarding the vicinity of his genitals. In view of the patently Victorian atmosphere it is noteworthy that the lady is smoking while he is not, a detail repeated in the standing picture (Drawing V), in which the lady holds on to the man's sleeve, seemingly less out of affection than in order to prevent his running away. Her powerful right arm carries a brief case of impressive proportions, which, together with her forthright posture and a general appearance of uncompromising rectitude, suggests that she intends one day to become the British Prime Minister, although the man will undoubtedly not live long enough to see it.

Thus, in these seemingly innocent pictures Conrad succeeded in conveying the same image of the aggressive woman who menaces the vulnerable man that attained such prominence in his fiction. The inclusion of a not-so-dead "cat," moreover, serves as a forceful reminder of Conrad's penchant for equating his fictional women with such predatory beasts. Even an allusion to the incinerating quality of so many of his heroines gains expression in the depiction of the women smoking.

An even more dramatic example of one of Conrad's overpowering women is provided in another sketch done before his marriage; it bears no explanatory inscription by his wife and perhaps for good reason since it is difficult to imagine what Conrad could have told her about it. (Drawing VI) It is a drawing of a woman whose massively top-heavy hair, overwhelming her face, recalls the descriptions of many of Conrad's fictional women. In her hair she wears a sparkling ornament, a diadem reminiscent of Rita's jewelled "arrow of gold."[t] A more striking aspect of the picture, however, is a huge serpent which, encircling her right arm and torso, finally curves about as if emerging from her body in such a way that its head, supported by the lady's rather hefty left arm and hand, is poised directly opposite her mouth, toward which it extrudes its tongue.

Although the subject of Drawing VII is said to have been a servant girl who often brought Conrad his hat and walking stick, the depiction of a woman bearing masculine attire may also be interpreted as a veiled expression of transvestism. The head of the cane which she is carrying is noteworthy, moreover, because of its resemblance to an animal head—perhaps a bird, perhaps a snake.

Bird or snake, both are among the commonest and oldest objects symbolizing the phallus in the recorded history of human thought and fantasy. The erotic significance of the serpent is as old as the Book of Genesis, while the occurrence of winged phalli in the sculpture of antiquity bears witness to an ancient symbolic association between creatures that fly and a bodily organ which too is mysteriously endowed with the power of defying gravity.[u]

In light of the preoccupation with tokens of reassurance against

[t] And of Wanda von Dunajew's hair ornament.

[u] Additional comments on the phallic significance of birds have been made in Chapter IX, footnote *n*.

the danger of castration that Conrad evidently shared with the fetishist, it is not surprising that both his writings and his drawings are liberally sprinkled with references to birds and snakes. Usually, but not always, the snake has an evil or bestial connotation, while the bird generally represents an innocent creature whose freedom is imperiled by capture or destruction. Thus, Stephen of *The Sisters* is likened to a bird in a cage, Yanko Gooral and his infant son are described as the fluttering caged victims of Amy Foster, and Cuba Tom is compared to a bird stalked by the feline gypsy girl in "The Inn of Two Witches." The claustrophobia implicit in these and other examples gains a particularly overt expression in the latter story when Tom is smothered to death by the bed canopy that descends upon him during his sleep. In *Victory*, on the other hand, before his fateful liaison with Lena, Heyst is referred to as "a bird that had never had a nest,"[44] and when Ricardo proposes to her that she run off with him, he tells her: "You are no cage bird. We'll rove together, for we are of them that have no home. We are born rovers!"[45]

Ricardo himself, however, is compared to a snake, for when Lena finally succeeds in inducing him to surrender his knife, the writer observes: "The very sting of death was in her hands; the venom of the viper in her paradise, extracted, safe in her possession—and the viper's head all but lying underneath her heel."[46] In short, Ricardo has been "de-snaked." Another hated reptilian character is Dominic Cervoni's perfidious brother César, of "The *Tremolino*," who is likened to something "clammily cold to the touch, like a snake."[47]

In keeping with the fuzziness of Conrad's differentiation between the sexes it is understandable that he applied the same symbolic designation to female personages as well. Rita's cousin Ortega, barred from the room in which she is closeted with M. George, screams at her that her "body is cold and vicious like a snake,"[48] while in *An Outcast of the Islands* the untidiness of Willems' despised wife Joanna is emphasized by a torn flounce that followed "her like a snake as she moved languidly about."[49]

It is not surprising to discover that in his nonfictional writing too, Conrad often employed bird and snake similes, applying the former to himself and the latter to others. In the semi-autobiographic *The Shadow-Line*, for example, while commenting on his restless boredom on the steamship *Vidar*, which led to his resigning his position, he wrote, "And suddenly I left all this. I left it in that, to us, inconsequential manner in which a bird flies away from a comfortable branch."[50] An identical simile is voiced in "Heart of Darkness" by his mouthpiece Marlow, who describes how in his childhood the map of the Congo fascinated him "as a snake would a bird—a silly little bird."[v/51]

Winged creatures, however, did not always signify innocence to Conrad: in "Autocracy and War" he likened Napoleon to a vulture,[53] and in a drawing designed for *The Arrow of Gold* he depicted a powerful sphinx before which stands a statuesque woman, who presumably represents Rita. (Drawing VIII) Evidently modeled upon the ancient custom of portraying the face and head of a king upon the body of a winged beast, the sphinx was undoubtedly supposed to represent Don Carlos de Bourbon, although to this writer, at least, the face bears more than a passing resemblance to Joseph Conrad.[w] (Drawing IX)

Marlow's comment in "Heart of Darkness," however, makes it clear that at times Conrad's references to snakes reflected feelings of attraction, awe, and fascination. In a letter to Garnett, written not long after the birth of Borys, in which he announced an imminent visit to Stephen and Cora Crane,[x] Conrad wrote: "My wife shall want to show the blessed baby to your wife. I hate babies. Will you manage to see me while I am there? I want to hear you speak—

[v] In a letter urging him to become a British subject, Conrad's Uncle Thaddeus reminded him: "You can't live forever like a bird on a twig."[52]

[w] In keeping with Conrad's propensities for multiple identifications it is also possible to view the sphinx as alluding to Rita: "She listened to me—as if carved six thousand years ago in order to fix forever that something secret and obscure which is in all women. Not the gross immobility of a Sphinx proposing roadside riddles, but the finer immobility, almost sacred, of a fateful figure seated at the very source of the passions that have moved men from the dawn of ages."[54] Jewel, in *Lord Jim*, also evokes an allusion to the sphinx "propounding childish riddles to wayfarers."[55]

[x] In a letter to Cora Crane anticipating the difficulty of transporting the two-week old Borys, Conrad suggested that "perhaps a strong iron cage would be the most effective expedient."[56]

I do. I want to come in contact with your thought. . . . I won't do anything [about publishing] without giving you information in time for a last word of advice. For after all you are the serpent and I am a bedraggled silly dove."[57] And in 1923 when he overcame his bitterness toward Hueffer long enough to wish him well in his new venture—the *Transatlantic Review*—he wrote: "Unlike the serpent (which is wise), you will die in your original skin. So I have no doubt that the Review will be truly Fordian."[58]

In these seemingly contradictory attitudes toward birds and snakes, wherein the former are endowed with qualities ranging from preying aggression to innocent chirping, and the latter connote both loathsome sexuality and an alluring and hypnotizing symbol of power and support, it is possible to discern a reflection of the ambivalence traditionally accorded to the male genital, which can serve both as the epitome of a hostile epithet and as an object of awe-struck veneration. However it is represented, whether as the threatened member of his vulnerable fictional heroes, as the menacing instrument of female aggression, or as the impressive attribute of protective power, the symbolic phallus appears as an almost ubiquitous element both in Conrad's writings and in his drawings. Through their depiction of snakes, birds, cats, androgynous women, and fragile men, moreover, his drawings provide a graphic confirmation of his fetishism and other distortions of sexuality, as well as of his ill-defined conception of the self that is so widely implicit in his fiction.

Yet if like the typical fetishist Conrad employed these manifold defenses against the danger of genital mutilation and in a broader sense against total destruction, something of a paradox must be acknowledged in the realization that in his actual behavior he often gave the appearance of openly encouraging these same dreaded eventualities. It will be recalled, for instance, what an uncooperative patient he was, and how subtly and slyly he attempted to controvert the efforts of the doctors to make him well. He was notoriously neglectful of his teeth, moreover, those body parts which in his fiction he held in such high esteem. Nor was he more careful of his clothes and personal possessions than of his body and health. In view of his preoccupation with the incendiary female there is irony in the fact that he repeatedly burned holes in his garments and bedclothes with cigarettes;[y/59] money, too, seems to have burned holes in his pockets, for even after he had become successful financially, he seemed to find it difficult to save money. As previously noted a portion of "The End of the Tether" was destroyed by fire when a lamp exploded for some undisclosed reason, and on another occasion Mrs. Conrad hid the manuscript of *Under Western Eyes*, fearing that her husband's "passion for burning manuscripts" was about to be directed at that work.[z/61]

From these and other examples of his self-injuring behavior it would appear that Conrad often courted these very calamities which he ostensibly dreaded. In this he recalls those fictional re-creations of himself, men like Willems, Jim, Heyst, Tom Lingard, and others, who, faced by the seeming threat of annihilation from without, display a posture of passivity and a stance of inertia which strongly suggest some secret complicity with their supposed enemies. In common with these fictional self-representations, the real danger which Conrad sought to ward off appears to have resided less in a hazardous environment than in dark purposes within himself bent on his own ruin. In this he seems to have shown once again his kinship with the fetishist, who, despite the magnitude of his defenses against the danger of castration, quite commonly displays a paradoxical penchant for self-injury and emasculation, particularly in his erotic life. For, like the hero Severin of *Venus in Furs*, the typical fetishist often appears to express a concealed wish to relinquish both the

[y] On one occasion when Conrad put an unextinguished cigarette lighter into his pocket, his secretary exclaimed, "Oh, Mr. Conrad, there's a nasty smell of cooking in here!" In relating this incident Mrs. Conrad made the interesting comment that in some way it caused her to recall her feelings of disgust with the story of Captain Falk's cannibalism![60]

[z] Conrad left the unfinished manuscript of *Almayer's Folly* in a railroad station restaurant in Berlin while en route to the Congo in 1890. It was only because of the vigilance of a station employee that he succeeded in retrieving those chapters that were ultimately destined to launch him on his literary career.[62]

That Conrad was aware of some kinship between burning manuscripts and self-destruction is apparent in a letter to Madame Poradowska in which he informed her that despite his opinion of *An Outcast*, he had "burnt nothing. One talks like that and then courage fails. People talk this way of suicide."[63]

adult and the masculine role, and to become the helpless plaything of a strong woman with whom he seeks to re-discover the boundless "one-ness" of mother and child. In his pursuit of this goal he may exploit events or situations in the environment much in the same way as Conrad's fictional hero utilizes the play of chance or the machinations of his adversary to implement his secret wish for self-annihilation.

As a consequence of this complicity those Conrad tales which depict an undisguised rivalry between an older and a younger man for a woman's love rarely convey the impression that this "Oedipal" conflict is the nuclear, psychological center of the story. It is true that in *An Outcast* a father tries to murder his daughter's lover, that in *Nostromo* he actually succeeds in doing so, and that in *Chance* De Barral attempts to poison his son-in-law. Yet throughout these and similar clashes, one seldom gains an impression of a grim fight to the finish of two determined adversaries. The hero, despite his youth, often behaves like a tired man, weighted down with excess psychological baggage which tends both to obscure his purpose and to dampen his vigor. Conrad's heroes make a point, almost a virtue, in fact, of going through life unarmed. Thus, neither Willems nor Heyst possesses a weapon more formidable than a penknife; M. George boasts to Rita that he will go through life "without as much as a switch in my hand,"[64] and Tom Lingard, the "red-eyed" bold adventurer, refrains from carrying firearms for the reason that he was "much too quick tempered . . . on the chance of a row"[65]—an explanation hardly consistent with his inert behavior in *The Rescue*. Nor is the hero's adversary a particularly formidable threat: blind, awkward, or incompetent he lunges at his unarmed opponent, and what purports to be an "Oedipal" fight often emerges as a mock battle between a faint-hearted hero and a foolish older man. Nor do these fights engage the serious and breathless concern of the reader, whose fears for Willems, for example, are not that he will be impaled by the blind thrusts of Omar's kriss, but that he will be destroyed by the "gleam of sharp steel" in the eye of his daughter. For what menaces Willems is the same force that threatens most of Conrad's fictional heroes—an unconscious longing to be pierced by the shafts of the golden arrows of their beloved phallic women. This wish indeed would seem to be the ground bass of Conrad's sad songs of love, for these are songs of male masochism in which an intense suffering both of body and of spirit constitutes the essential condition for erotic arousal and satisfaction. Such an image of love, however, can be tolerated only as long as the elements of cruelty and tyranny can be safely contained within the boundaries of reasonable control. Without such limits the game of surrender soon ceases to be a sport at all—the hapless lover discovers that the rules have been abandoned and the stakes are now his ruin and his death. Cognizant of his plight he is seized with a claustrophobia that drives away all thoughts of love and transforms the image of his pretty girl into that of a devouring witch. Thus while longing to escape from the beautiful Aïssa, Willems thinks of her eyes as "a pair of jailers."[a]

It is not surprising therefore that in those unguarded moments occasioned by a transient psychosis, Conrad's dormant enmity toward women broke out in a furious denunciation of his wife, nor is it any less astonishing to learn that when the creator of *Venus in Furs* became psychotic he killed a furry cat of which he had been exceedingly fond, and some time later attempted to strangle his wife. During the night of the cat-killing he is said to have awakened in a state of violent excitement, shrieking, "I am being eaten alive! I am being eaten alive! It's the cats—the cats—they are after me."[b/67]

These words might have been uttered by any of Conrad's heroes

[a] The association of claustrophobia with sleep (and death) is clearly depicted in *An Outcast of the Islands*. Lying in Aïssa's arms Willems dreams of a man who appears to be going away. Suddenly he realizes that the man is himself. On awakening he "felt indignant. It was like an evasion, like a prisoner breaking his parole—that thing slinking off stealthily while he slept."[66] Another allusion to claustrophobia may be discerned in Jimmy's "entombment" in his cabin in *The Nigger*.

[b] "A woman in furs," exclaims the heroine of *Venus in Furs*, "is nothing else than a large cat."[68] The several elements of these stories—cats, women, claustrophobia, and death—are combined in Edgar Allan Poe's "The Black Cat." Of interest in the context of the present discussion is Marie Bonaparte's suggestion that Poe's great literary concern with horror, death, and love of the dead was a manifestation of a necrophilic type of love for his mother who died when he was three years old.[69]

menaced by his devouring "cat-women." By implication they were uttered by Conrad himself, when toward the close of his life, he angrily accused his wife[c] of bringing him a "catafalque-bed," thereby linking her with the feline gypsy girl who murders Cuba Tom in "The Inn of Two Witches."[d]

Like *The Arrow of Gold* and a number of other tales by Conrad, *Venus in Furs* is a quasi-autobiographical story revealing an immense ambivalence toward women. That in both writers these inconstant sentiments sprang from a similar origin is strongly suggested by the following pair of episodes taken from their writings.

While staying in Florence with Wanda, her "slave" Severin contemplates the idea of escaping from her. Sitting alone on the banks of the Arno he recollects his mother, "whom I loved so deeply and whom I had to watch waste away beneath a horrible disease."[74] Thinking of her and of others now dead and reviewing his life of misery, he suddenly falls into the water but saves himself by grasping a branch of a willow tree. "As in a vision, I see the woman who has caused all my misery. She hovers above the level of the water, luminous in the sunlight as though she were transparent, with red flames about her head and neck. She turns her face toward me and smiles."[75]

Thoughts of his mother occupy Renouard's mind, too, as he contemplates his beloved Felicia. Like his fellow-sufferer, Severin, he too slips into the water, but not by an accident from which he saves himself. Like Martin Decoud weighted down with silver ingots, Renouard enters the water to commit suicide.

There can be no misunderstanding the meaning of these thoughts and actions. The fact that in the unhappiness endured for the sake

[c] It is noteworthy that some of Conrad's letters to her bore the salutation "Kit"[70] or "Kitty,"[71] and that in one letter he referred to her as "a pretty kitty-faced girl."[72]

[d] There is good reason to suspect that Conrad's lifelong restlessness represented in part, at least, a defense against claustrophobia. Some confirmation of that suspicion may be detected in a passage in "Geography and Some Explorers": "Of all the sciences," he wrote, "geography finds its origin in action, and what is more, in adventurous action of the kind that appeals to sedentary people who like to dream of arduous adventure in the manner of prisoners dreaming behind bars of all hardships and hazards of liberty dear to the heart of man."[73]

of a woman each of these men recalls his own mother emphasizes her role in shaping his later fortunes in love. Presumably it is of his mother that Severin is dreaming when in his reverie he sees "the woman who has caused all [his] misery"; it may have been no less of Conrad's own mother, "wasted away beneath a horrible disease," that the author was thinking when he directed Renouard and those other hapless fictional selves to seek a final peace in death. Swimming out to sea Renouard is overcome by a "mournful fatigue. . . . It was as if his love had sapped the invisible supports of his strength. There came a moment when it seemed to him that he must have swum beyond the confines of life. He had a sensation of eternity close at hand, demanding no effort—offering its peace."[76]

"I resemble Geoffrey Renouard," wrote Conrad, "in so far that once engaged in an adventure I cannot bear the idea of turning back."[e/77] Yet it is plainly evident that however consciously Conrad strove to fight off the impulse to "turn back" it was for him and for the numerous fictional re-creations of himself an impulse that was well-nigh irresistible. His own life, peppered by bursts of spectacular and varied actions, was punctuated by increasingly impressive phases of physical and psychological "turning back," manifested notably in bouts of invalidism, in personal behavior which his wife likened to that of the "smallest infant,"[79] and by a desire, toward the close of his life, to live out his remaining years in his native land.

In this too he resembled Renouard, whose suicide, viewed symbolically, must be regarded as the ultimate expression of a "turning back." Indeed the resemblances between them would seem to cover other traits as well, particularly those concerning intimate personal relationships. In the following pages an attempt will be made to discover the genesis of these elements in Conrad's history, and to find there as well the origins of those several adventures in his life from which, like Renouard, he could not bear the thought of turning back.

[e] This sentiment, incidentally, he assigned to another fictional character, Charles Gould: "What should be perfectly clear to us," the latter tells his wife about his decision to re-open the silver mine, "is the fact that there is no going back."[78]

XVII · Poland Revisited

PSYCHOANALYTIC INVESTIGATION of the problem of fetishism points to disturbances in the earliest years of life in the genesis of this condition.[1,2] These disturbances occur characteristically in two main periods of childhood development: the first eighteen months, or so, and again around the third and fourth years. In the earlier period of development the principal factor involved is usually a disharmony between mother and infant, often arising as a consequence of the mother's failure or disinclination to provide her baby with loving warmth and physical handling. As a result the infant may exhibit a tendency to excessive clinging to the mother and an inability to tolerate normal intervals of separation from her. Such "separation anxiety" is understandably an obstacle to the development of autonomy in the growing child, for it fosters a shadowy conception of the self and a tendency toward a persistently "sticky" identification with the mother instead of a progressive sense of independent identity.

It is this tenuousness of the sense of self which appears to increase the vulnerability of some children to the psychic traumas of the second period, notably castration threats. The severity of the castration complex in some pre-fetishists, moreover, appears to be enhanced by the occurrence of other traumas during these critical years, for example, tonsilectomies and other surgical operations, the witnessing of accidents, mutilations, childbirth, abortions, etc. Individuals sensitized by such experiences are poorly equipped for the later vicissitudes of life, and they arrive at the threshold of sexual maturity with a reinforcement of long-standing anxieties concerning physical intactness in general and the danger of castration in particular. Seen in this light the fetish may be viewed both as a talisman or safeguard against the recognition of the reality of the "castrated" female, and as the legacy of the inexorable clinging to the mother that characterizes the earliest years.

In seeking to discover such influences in Conrad's life the present study labors under something of a disadvantage. The voices of his distant past are muffled, and what little can be heard sounds faint indeed to the ears of the clinician who is accustomed to the insistent and reiterated songs of childhood of his patients. Least clear of all is an image of Conrad's mother, the most important figure in those critical moments of his childhood. Owing partly to her early death and partly to other reasons, one suspects, Conrad wrote almost nothing about her, and what her brother Thaddeus had to say about her has a somewhat fuzzy quality that prevents her coming into focus as a person of flesh and blood. In his memoir Bobrowski drew a contrasting picture of Evelina Korzeniowska and her younger sister who died, presumably of consumption, at the age of seventeen. The latter, though lacking Evelina's intelligence, was praised by Thaddeus for her good sense, "the admirable sweetness of her nature, her exceptional facility and ease . . . that endeared her to everybody." Had she lived, he continued, "she would have brought the greatest blessings to the house it would have been her lot to enter, as wife, mother and mistress of a household. She would have created round herself an atmosphere of peace and contentment which only those who can love unselfishly are able to evoke."[3] Evelina, on the other hand, drew no such encomiums from her brother, who, far from describing her as endowed with a capacity for unselfish love, spoke of her "less easy-going nature, making far greater demands, and at that period [i.e., prior to her marriage] requiring more attention from others than she was ready or able to give them." Behind the façade of fraternal tact one suspects that Thaddeus saw Evelina as a disturbed, self-centered, and possibly depressed girl, who, "struggling between love for her future husband and the expressed will of her father, whose memory and judgment she respected, was unable to maintain her moral balance."[4] Even when her emotional turmoil apparently subsided after her marriage, the sentiments which she evoked in her brother were less clearly warmth and affection than respect and admiration. Thus while he spoke of the "modest, lovable qualities" of the younger sister, he described Evelina in the rather awesome and majestic terms of one who fulfilled "the role imposed by the duties of a wife, mother and citizen, sharing her husband's exile and worthily representing the ideal of Polish womanhood," thereby gaining "the respect and veneration of her own people and of others."[5]

Conrad's few comments about her evoke a similar image of quiet dignity rather than of maternal playfulness and warmth. Thus he spoke of her "silent, protecting presence," and referred to "a sort of commanding sweetness of her eyes,"[6] a curious combination of attributes, one might say, which he repeated almost verbatim in describing the frigid heroine of *The Rescue*, Edith Travers.[a]

Although it is admittedly impossible to tell whether Conrad's sketchy description of his mother was based on actual memory or upon a reconstructed image of her conforming to his fictional ideal, an impression of cool austerity nevertheless clings to this woman, who for one reason or another did not marry until the age of twenty-three—a ripe age for a bride in those days. It may well be that like Flora de Barral and other fictional heroines created by Conrad, Evelina's somewhat protracted spinsterhood was the outcome of her being caught in a struggle not simply between respect for her father's wishes and her love for Apollo Korzeniowski, but between her wish to remain a father's daughter and to become a man's wife.

If this conjecture is valid, Evelina may have possessed still another characteristic common to most of Conrad's fictional women, namely, a recoil from sensuality and physical intimacy. It is well known that when such women attain the state of motherhood they often tend to display discomfort in the fondling and caressing of their children, particularly their boys. Whether this was true of Conrad's mother cannot be affirmed, but there are hints that it may have been so. Conrad's recollection of his nearly devouring affection for a childhood doll, from whose cheeks he had licked off all the paint and whose nose he had bitten off "dans un accés de folle tendresse,"[8] hardly conjures up the picture of a child basking in the lavish warmth of a mother's embrace; it suggests, rather, the behavior of one starved for physical affection and closeness.

Admittedly this is pretty tenuous evidence on which to base an impression of Evelina's personality, and until something more definitive comes to light what has been said about her must remain within the realm of conjecture.

No such reliance on hunch or hypothesis is necessary, however, in assessing the impact upon Conrad's emotional development of

[a] When Lingard asks Mrs. Travers to summon his man Carter she does so, "and Lingard thought her voice very commanding and very sweet."[7]

a series of misfortunes which began when he was not yet three and a half years old: the protracted absence of his father; the raiding of his home by the Russian police; his father's arrest and imprisonment (possibly his mother's too); and finally the long journey into exile under the custody of Russian guards to an icy and unfamiliar land, where strangers spoke a foreign tongue and where the Korzeniowskis and other exiles—mostly Polish priests—bore numbers as their mark of identification.[9] Amidst these frightening and bewildering upheavals in his life, the child was seriously stricken with pneumonia. Hardly had he recovered from this near-fatal illness, moreover, when his mother, who had nursed him during these anxious days, collapsed and became so weak, it is said, that she had to be carried in and out of the carriage in which they were traveling.[b] An interruption of the journey was evidently beneficial to her, for after a few days' rest, the little party proceeded toward its remote destination. It was not long after their arrival, however, when Evelina began to show signs of the tuberculosis that soon would end her life.

Such a parade of misfortunes, it cannot be denied, would be a heavy burden for any child. Occurring as they did during an era in Conrad's life that has already been cited as a time of exceptional vulnerability, they undoubtedly made an indelible imprint on his sensitive mind and played an important role in fashioning his future emotional make-up. That such a series of traumas might lead to an elaborate system of psychological defense is hardly surprising, nor is it remarkable that occupying a conspicuous position in that system, designed to deny the danger of bodily mutilation or destruction,

[b] Although a few months later it was realized that Conrad's mother was afflicted with tuberculosis, the nature of her illness during the journey to Vologda is unclear. The seemingly abrupt onset of profound weakness and her apparent prompt recovery after a few days' rest suggests some acute process. A later statement by her husband that she was suffering from "an internal tumor, the result of bad circulation, which calls for an operation,"[10] suggests the occurrence of periodic bleeding, caused, perhaps, by some gynecologic condition. It is also remotely possible that her collapse during the journey was the result of a spontaneous abortion of a brief pregnancy.

was the concept of the phallic woman and the phenomenon of fetishism.

These, however, were not the only devices by which Conrad sought to counteract the impact of early traumas or to ward off the threat of future ones. In a seeming effort to blot out the memory of what he would later call his "hazardous childhood"[11] it would appear that he enveloped those events in a veil of amnesia—at least if one can judge from his writings. It may be significant, for example, that when writing *A Personal Record* Conrad placed his earliest "distinct" memories of his mother in the summer of 1863, a time when he was approaching his sixth birthday.[c] Because of her failing health, Evelina was permitted to leave her exile temporarily during the summer of 1863, and she spent some months with her son at her brother's estate in Novofastov. Here Conrad met his cousin and namesake, Josefina Bobrowska, with whom he experienced what were probably the first carefree happy days of his short but troubled life. The implied amnesia for the frightful events preceding this summer is especially noteworthy since Conrad claimed to have retained a memory, dating from before the age of four, of the room in the house in Warsaw where the Secret National Committee held meetings; he recalled that the persons involved in these activities were "beyond the usual stature of mankind" and that his mother was dressed in the illegal black of national mourning.[13] Since these meetings preceded his father's arrest, it is evident that the "blackout" imposed by Conrad in his written reminiscences embraces all the disturbing and frightening events taking place between October 1861 and the summer of 1863: the removal of his father, the loss of his home, the long journey into exile, his own near-fatal illness, the collapse of his mother, and the miserable months in Vologda. Whether all of these unhappy events were actually forgotten, or simply omitted from his written recollections, Conrad was displaying a formula for dealing with insupportable realities which he had undoubtedly begun to employ at a very early age and would

[c] It is noteworthy that Conrad gave the wrong date to this holiday, naming the year 1864, a mistake which would serve to remove it even further in his mind from the shocking events occurring during the journey into exile.[12]

continue to use throughout his life: the denial of intolerable "truths" and their replacement by "memories," perceptions, and actions designed to create an illusion of invulnerability. As a further safeguard it would appear that Conrad strove not only to cultivate an attitude of aloofness from human attachments in order to spare himself the pain of future losses, but also to adopt a stance of heightened vigilance in order to anticipate any unforeseen distressing happenings.

That these defenses exacted an exorbitant price has already been indicated. Emotionally cramped and inflexible, remote in human relationships, nervous, irritable, and generally humorless, Conrad appears to have been encased in a psychological straitjacket which permitted only a limited scope for the pursuit of pleasure and for the enjoyment of that personal closeness for which secretly he so plainly thirsted. Indeed, not only did this psychological armor dull his capacity for a full-throated engagement with life, but in some respects it would seem as if it warded off the realization of his deepest strivings. Vying equally with his pursuit of manly inviolability, it is suspected, was his susceptibility to the beckoning enticements unfolded before his hungry eyes during the idyllic summer holiday in Novofastov. Here, in the person of his cousin Josefina, he caught a glimpse of a child whose lot in life could hardly have failed to excite his wonder and his envy. Although motherless since birth,[d] she was evidently an object of lavish affection and attention. "A small princess attended by the women of her own household," her secure position must have presented a striking contrast to the uncertain, fragile, and nomadic existence of her cousin and namesake. For some three months little Conrad shared in her "aristocratic" environment, presided over by her sober, reliable, and level-headed father and peopled by kindly female retainers.[e] Of the latter, one

[d] Probably an additional determinant in the almost unvarying motherlessness of Conrad's fictional characters.

[e] Conrad's recollection of the "small princess" living in a seeming state of grace with a loving father may have contributed to his undisguised fascination with the relationship between fathers and daughters, expressed overtly many years later and revealed repeatedly in his fiction. Unhappily the privileged Josefina died in her 'teens in 1871, which misfortune Conrad may have alluded to in his poignant autobiographic tale of human isolation,

in particular, the French governess Mlle Durand, was singled out by Conrad for her loving devotion. When the unhappy day arrived when he and his mother were forced to return to their place of exile, it was Mlle Durand whose "good natured eyes . . . were dropping tears." "N'oublie pas ton français, mon chéri," she called out in a sobbing voice, he wrote, adding that "simply by playing with us she had taught me not only to speak French but to read it as well. She was an excellent playmate,"[16] commented this man whose dreary and chaotic childhood so far had not been conspicuously graced or enlivened by any playmates, large or small.

With this departure it must have seemed to him as if a door had slammed shut upon an all too fleeting joyous dream, a sweet and peaceful dream nestled softly between two nightmares. Just as misery and disaster had preceded this interlude, so now upon the return to exile they were to reappear with renewed force; by the summer of 1863 it was apparent that his mother was seriously ill.

The varied and distorting influences of all these experiences on the sexual development of young Conrad can hardly be exaggerated. As already noted, neither his fiction nor his personal life appears to project a hard core of aggressive "Oedipal" rivalry, which is hardly surprising in light of the magnitude of his castration anxiety. A slowly dying mother is hardly a fit object for the nascent sexual fantasies of a small boy, and an absent and imprisoned father is not a very credible rival for her love. Indeed it may be asked whether powerful and aggressive heterosexual strivings could have played an important role in the life of this man whose childhood was characterized by such profound maternal deprivation. What emerges as the dominant aggressive drive both in his fiction and in the accounts of his personal life is not so much the wish for genital union as for the gratification of an apparently insatiable oral appetite. In the short story "Falk" (and elsewhere) this impulse is expressed by frank cannibalism; in *Nostromo* by the rapacious assault upon the

---

"Amy Foster." Among the bodies washed upon the shore following the shipwreck in which Yanko Gooral is the sole survivor, only one—"a little fair-haired child in a red frock"—is singled out for description.[14] Since in *A Personal Record* Conrad recalled his cousin wearing "a short skirt of a tartan pattern with a deal of red in it,"[15] it may well be that she was the original model for this little girl.

silver of the mine; in "Heart of Darkness" by a devouring greed for ivory. But, whatever its object, it is clear that this hunger is incompatible with adult sexuality. Like Charles Gould, whose preoccupation with the silver leads to "that conjugal infidelity through which his wife was no longer the sole mistress of his thoughts,"[17] Kurtz forsakes and forgets his "intended" as a consequence of his unappeasable passion for ivory. Despite their obvious differences, both of these men are driven by the same hunger for the treasures that nature conceals within the hills and valleys of her person.[f] Small wonder, then, that in dying Mr. Kurtz presented a vision of a man "opening his mouth voraciously, as if to devour all the earth with all its mankind."[21]

Cheated out of the sweetmeats of childhood affection, so lavishly bestowed, it might have seemed, on his cousin Josefina, Conrad appears to have suffered for the rest of his life from the torments of a gnawing hunger that neither time nor change of circumstance could assuage. Yet here as elsewhere Conrad seems to have sought to re-

[f] The writer is indebted to Dr. Joseph D. Lichtenberg for the interesting suggestion that among its other meanings the silver of *Nostromo* symbolizes the dead and buried mother. Seen in this light it is she who bars the way to love for all who are involved with the treasure: Charles Gould, whose childless wife dreads his preoccupation with the mine "*more than if it were an infatuation for another woman*";[18] Decoud, who, despite his love for Antonia, drowns himself in the sea, weighted down by silver ingots; and the Capataz, whose passion for Giselle is thwarted by his enslavement by the metal. After his death the embittered Mrs. Gould tells Giselle: "Console yourself, child. Very soon he would have forgotten you for his treasure."[19] Support for Dr. Lichtenberg's conjecture may be found in a passage where the silver is virtually personified. Just after the Capataz has declared his love for Giselle and gains a momentary sense of freedom, she reminds him of the silver. He becomes suddenly agitated, realizing that "he had not regained his freedom. The spectre of the unlawful treasure arose, standing by her side *like a figure of silver, pitiless and secret with a finger upon its pale lips*."[20] (Italics mine) Viewing the silver in such terms, Decoud's suicide assumes the significance of joining a mother in death. It is noteworthy, as was pointed out in an earlier chapter, that two other characters in Conrad's fiction drown, weighted down by metal: César Cervoni in "The *Tremolino*," and Captain Whalley in "The End of the Tether." A variation on this theme may be found in *The Rover* when old Peyrol drops his gold-lined jacket down a well just before setting out to sacrifice his life at sea. Insofar as this is the story of the return of the wanderer to the land of his origin, the "burial" of the jacket may contain a symbolic significance similar to that of Decoud's suicide.

lieve his pain through the artistry of his creative imagination. In his fiction it was in all likelihood himself—the deprived and envious onlooker—that he depicted through such characters as Razumov and Alice Jacobus, whose isolated and lonely lives stand in such sharp contrast to the richly endowed lives of their wellborn half-sisters.

Indeed in this picture of contrasts it is possible to discern the seeds of that yearning for another origin, or for a rebirth from other parents, which is known as the fantasy of the Family Romance.[22] Although this rather common childhood fantasy assumes a variety of forms, it always reflects a single goal: the wish for reunion with the "real" parents or creators, who characteristically are imagined as persons of famous or illustrious stature. Among these variations, therefore, are fantasies of being the rightful child of parents of noble lineage, e.g., *The Prince and the Pauper*; of being rescued from a humble or lowly condition by a powerful or wealthy patron, e.g., Cinderella, Eliza Doolittle; and of being the raw uncut material out of which a great artist creates a living soul, e.g., Pygmalion.

As noted previously in these pages, all these variations can be found repeatedly in Conrad's fiction: characters suspected of being of noble birth include Razumov, the alleged son of a Prince, and Cosmo, of *Suspense*, who is said to be descended from the Medici; Almayer, Willems, Jim, Lena, Alice Jacobus, and others are examples of persons slated for rescue from disgrace or lonely isolation; while Rita de Lastaola, who belongs to this second category is also an epitome of the Pygmalion version of the Family Romance.[g]

In the transformation of the poor shepherd girl into the protégée of an artist and ultimately into the consort of a "king," the Family Romance theme in *The Arrow of Gold* offers a remarkable resemblance to the stereotyped, apocryphal accounts of the childhood history of a number of great artists, especially of the Renais-

[g] It is noteworthy that when she is discovered in his garden by the wealthy artist Allègre, Rita is seated upon a stone, identified as "a fragment of some old balustrade,"[23] thus conferring upon the combined seated girl and chiselled stone an image of statue and pedestal. Equally pertinent to this theme of re-creation is the attribution of godlike qualities to her discoverer, who looks "down thoughtfully over that ambrosian beard of his, like Jove at a mortal."[24]

sance. According to this formula, the future artist is characteristically depicted as a poor child, often a shepherd, who is accidentally discovered by an established and renowned artist, who subsequently becomes his patron and genius father. Ernst Kris, who called attention to the persistent appearance of this legend in the history of art even into the present century, cited as its prototype the story of the discovery of the shepherd boy Giotto by Cimabue.[25]

Now, while the one-time shepherdess Rita does not become an artist, she does become the favorite model and mistress of the god-like painter Allègre, and hence represents both the source of his inspiration and his creation. In light of Conrad's apparent identification of himself with Rita—as well as with virtually the entire roster of his "adopted" fictional heroes and heroines—one may assume that his reiterated depiction of the Family Romance was a projection of his own wish to achieve a fulfillment of that fantasy himself. Indeed, virtually every chapter of his multifaceted life can be viewed in such terms: as the disciple of Dominic Cervoni, whose powerful paternal image appears throughout Conrad's fiction; as the protégé of his beloved "Aunt," Madame Poradowska; and as the adopted child of English literary circles. It was in his relationship with Hueffer, however, where Conrad's personal Family Romance gained its clearest expression, and where, it is suspected, it evoked a reciprocal response. In one way or another each of these men "rescued" the other, and indeed much of the heat of the Hueffer-Conrad controversy was generated by a failure to recognize the subtle interaction between these two men—now one and now the other played the role of protector and discoverer. Conrad's playful invention of their common past, their pre-history, so to speak, bears a striking resemblance to the "discovery" theme in the myth of the artist's biography: his fancy, for example, that upon his initial arrival in England as a common sailor in June 1878 he discovered little "Fordie," then four years old, playing with his shovel on the beach at Lowestoft, an activity, by the way, which may be viewed as an early expression of a child's essays in sculpture.[26] A reversal in the polarity of this theme can be found in Conrad's claim that it was a glimpse of one of Hueffer's novels in the railroad station in

Geneva, many years later, that first instilled in him the idea of becoming an English writer.[h/27]

Yet if becoming the protégé of a Corsican adventurer, the reincarnation of a Captain Marryat, a second Henry Morton Stanley,[i] the adopted child of English letters, and a subject of the British Crown are to be viewed as varied expressions of Conrad's personal Family Romance, how is one to explain the nervous and unsatisfied restlessness of these pursuits? How can one explain the fact that after he had attained an unquestioned triumph in his coveted goal, he spoke toward the close of his life of returning to the land of his origins? To understand this as well as other seeming inconsistencies in his life it is necessary to examine the psychological genesis of the Family Romance itself.

Viewed through the insights of psychoanalytic experience it is evident that ulterior to the search for new and all-powerful parents lies a wish to return to that early period of life when the true parents, seen through the eyes of a little child, did indeed appear as the embodiment of omnipotence, goodness, and perfection. "Indeed," wrote Freud, "the whole effort at replacing the real father by a superior one is only an expression of the child's longing for the happy vanished days when his father seemed to him the noblest and strongest of men, and his mother the dearest and loveliest of women."[31]

[h] Another manifestation of a wish to "share" in his friend's earlier history may be discerned in Conrad's use of vignettes from Hueffer's past in his fiction. In the short story, "The Informer," a brother and a sister are engaged in printing (in the cellar of their London house) an anarchist leaflet, known as *The Firebrand*. In the basement of William Rossetti's house, the Hueffer children and their Rossetti cousins printed an anarchist newspaper, called *The Torch*.[28] As was noted in an earlier chapter newspapers bearing that same title are discovered in the window of Mr. Verloc's shop in *The Secret Agent*. The Editor in "The Planter of Malata," who was apparently modeled on Hueffer (Chapter XII, footnote *e*, page 228) signs his weekly articles: *The Slave of the Lamp*.[29]

[i] Stanley's life was itself an enactment of a Family Romance fantasy. Born in Wales as John Rowlands, an illegitimate child whose father died shortly after his birth, he ultimately became the protégé of an American merchant, named Henry Morton Stanley, whose name young Rowlands adopted as his own.[30]

It is for this reason that the actual attainment of "rebirth" through the acquisition of a new parent may sometimes seem a hollow victory and as devoid of lasting satisfaction as were the successive achievements of Conrad's several careers. In the far-off soundproof places of his real and fictional life he was plainly out of earshot of the voices of his native soil; yet he was never entirely deaf to the unanswered longings of a muted past. Of this duality in his nature he was not unaware. "My point of view, whether on land or sea," he wrote to a compatriot, "is English, but you must not conclude from that that I have become an Englishman. By no means. The *homo duplex* has, in my case, more than one meaning."[32]

Manifestations of this "homo duplex" and its accompanying ambivalences are not hard to discover. As a good British subject he denounced Bonaparte as "a sort of vulture preying upon the body of Europe,"[33] but no one familiar with his fiction can ignore the evidence it contains of the fascination and awe aroused in him by the famous Corsican, whose life and times constituted the background for a number of his stories. His Uncle Thaddeus was well aware of this admiration. Writing to his friend Buszczynski after Conrad's Marseilles debacle, he said, "We Poles . . . have an inborn liking for the French and the Republic, but he [Conrad] . . . is for the Emperor. De gustibus non est disputandum."[34] Mrs. Conrad conveyed a similar impression: "He always declared that he was no admirer of Napoleon, but the fact remains that this tragic personality exercised a spell over the author."[35] And although his trip to Corsica in 1921 was undertaken ostensibly to gather material for the Napoleonic novel *Suspense* ("in search of 'climate' "),[36] one suspects that it was also in the nature of a pilgrimage. His wife claimed that a visit to Napoleon's birthplace had been "a cherished dream," an "obsession" of her husband since his early childhood.[37] On another occasion Conrad denied that he had gone to Corsica "for the sake of any novel."[38] His professed antipathy toward Bonaparte is similarly inconsistent with the report that he was fond of discovering resemblances between himself and the Emperor, which, in light of the pattern already noted, suggests that like a number of other famous persons Napoleon played a role in Conrad's personal Family Romance.[j] Support for this conjecture may be found in *Suspense* in the quasi-filial relationship of Adèle (the unhappily married heroine) to the French Emperor, who, acting as a vicarious progenitor, at one point counsels her to have a child out of wedlock.[39] Like the divine impregnation of the Virgin, the begetting of a child through the agency or sponsorship of a godlike or demigodlike paternal figure constitutes a distinctive expression of the Family Romance fantasy, of which the ultimate origin lies again in the reveries of childhood, namely, in the nearly ubiquitous wishes of little girls to be given a child by their fathers. In light of his admitted fascination with father-daughter intimacies it cannot be doubted that this version of the fantasy would have a particular appeal for Conrad. The easy mobility of his self-representations, moreover, would make it seem certain that through the character of Adèle he could attain vicariously a similar position of the privileged confidante and beneficiary of a great person, and the adopted child of a near deity. It will soon become apparent that *Suspense* was not the only vehicle through which he voiced such aspirations.

The subject of Bonaparte was not the only one on which Conrad's expressed opinions were sharply opposed to the sentiments implicit in his fiction. In his personal behavior as well as in his correspondence he professed to have repudiated at the age of fourteen the Catholic faith into which he had been born. "I am not blind to its services," he wrote to Garnett about Christianity, "but the absurd oriental fable from which it starts irritates me. Great, improving, softening, compassionate, it may be, but it has lent itself with amazing facility to cruel distortion and is the only religion which, with its impossible standards, has brought an infinity of anguish to innumerable souls on this earth."[k/40] Yet this sober and sophisticated statement was but one side of a coin, for in his fictional writings it requires little discernment to discover powerful and poignant overtones of a deep and abiding devotion to that early Catholic faith.

[j] Pictorial evidence of this penchant for identifying himself with the illustrious has already been noted in the suggestive self-portraiture manifest in his drawings of Don Carlos: Drawings VIII and IX.

[k] According to Jessie Conrad he asserted that he was "a hater of priests . . . and a determined atheist." She noted that during their stay in Catholic Brittany Conrad never removed his hat when passing a church.[41]

Indeed, true to the theme of the Family Romance, there is some reason to suspect an identification of himself with Jesus.

In *Victory*, the rescue of the girl Magdalen (later renamed Lena) bears an unmistakable allusion to the fate of her namesake in the New Testament. Like Magdalen, Conrad's heroine, who describes herself as "not what they call a good girl,"[42] attains an ultimate state of grace through the redeeming action of Heyst (which rhymes with Christ), another ostensible self-portrait of the author. It is in "Amy Foster" (the story of the Catholic central European, Yanko Gooral, who is washed up on the shores of England as the sole survivor of a shipwreck) that allusions to the Christ legend attain a particular force.[l] Aside from the Christlike portrait of Yanko, whose long hair flows over his shoulders and who is reviled and pelted with stones by the natives, the story abounds in references to the Church and to Yanko's sense of religious estrangement in a land where tokens of his native Catholic faith were so scarce that when he discovered someone wearing a crucifix he "used to cast stealthy glances at it and feel comforted."[43] His final hour resounds with echoes of the Crucifixion. Parched with thirst and burning with fever, the abandoned Yanko begs his wife for water, but his cries go unheeded, and like Christ on the Cross crying "My God, my God, why hast Thou forsaken me?," Yanko calls out " 'Why?' . . . in the penetrating and indignant voice of a man calling to a responsible Maker."[44]

Not surprisingly Conrad exhibited evidence of anti-Semitism. Concerning *The Outlook*, he wrote: "It's price: threepence sterling: it's attitude: literary: it's policy—Imperialism, tempered by expediency: it's mission—to make money for a Jew."[45] On one occasion he referred to his publisher Heinemann as "that Israelite,"[46] and on another as "The Patron Jew."[47] Similar innuendoes can be found in his fiction; Moser has called attention to the depiction of some of the villains as caricatures of the stereotyped Jew. Thus the evil Heemskirk does not look like a Dutchman; he is dark and swarthy and has a "hooked nose." The conventional defamation of

[l] It will be recalled that Yanko escapes from drowning by clinging to a hen coop containing 11 ducks, which number plus the surviving man may have reference to the number of the Apostles.

the Jew as a usurious financial speculator is also suggested in *Chance* where it is hinted that the criminal De Barral may have changed his original name.[48] The most explicit example of Conrad's anti-Semitism is to be found in his characterization of the Jewish merchant Hirsch in *Nostromo*, whose "whining voice," "hooked beak," and mercenary soul epitomize the typical caricature of the central European Jew. Yet, as Gillon has pointed out, the complete portrait of Hirsch indicates that Conrad's anti-Semitism possessed a complexity and an ambivalence that give it a dimension beyond traditional Polish attitudes towards Jews.[49] For in his ultimate fate Hirsch assumes an identity typical of the isolated "outsider" that pervades Conrad's fictional world: the Negro, James Wait; the European castaway, Yanko Gooral; the Swede, Heyst. Although his unforeseen and unwanted presence on the lighter imperils the safety of Nostromo and Decoud when they are engaged in hiding the silver ingots, like so many of Conrad's thirsting "castaways"—indeed, like Conrad himself, if one is to believe his Congo experience with the succouring native woman—the despised Hirsch is given water to drink by the compassionate Don Martin. Indeed, even the latter may be viewed as sharing something of Hirsch's identity, for the half-French, half-Costaguanero Decoud is "neither the son of his own country nor of any other"[50]—a patent allusion, one suspects, to Conrad's view of himself. Like Hirsch, Decoud is figuratively stateless. With his horrible death Hirsch takes on a new and more subtle identity. "No longer does Conrad refer to his thick lips, his hooked nose, his side whiskers or his practical mercantile soul," observes Gillon. "In death Hirsch has attained a new dignity, and one wonders whether the 'signal in the night' is not meant to be an expression of that other Conrad, capable of infinite compassion and understanding, who has at length come to realize that in death, at least, Hirsch resembled the mystery of Christ."[51] This "compassion" and "understanding," one suspects, was based upon an identification of Conrad with Hirsch, and with Christ too. Seen in this light the reviled Jew may be viewed as another self-portrait of Conrad, whose anti-Semitism, like much racial prejudice, was in large measure a manifestation of projection, the displaced hatred of one's own kind, and of one's own self. Speaking of Charles

Gould, the engineer-in-chief remarks to Doctor Monygham, "He must be extremely sure of himself," to which the Doctor replies, "If that's all he's sure of, then he is sure of nothing. . . . It is the last thing a man ought to be sure of."[m/52]

Like other inconsistencies in Conrad's pronouncements, his conflicting attitudes toward Christianity mirror the conflict between Joseph Conrad, the English man of letters, and Konrad Korzeniowski, the child of Catholic Poland. It is hardly remarkable that he suffered keenly over his attempts to straddle his twin allegiances. Perhaps it was to diminish his Anglophilia in Polish eyes that prompted him to decline an offer of knighthood in 1924.[n/54] Surely it was an effort to curry favor with his compatriots that caused him to announce, falsely, it would seem, the christening of Borys in the Chapel of the Cloister of the Carmelites in Southwark (London).[o/56] It was undoubtedly also for home consumption that he belittled his literary gifts, declaring, "I write novels to amuse the English."[58] Nor is it surprising that he begged his cousin Karola Zagorska to forgive him for the fact that his sons could not speak Polish,[59] and that he rejoiced at being called an "author-compatriot" by the Polish writer, Zeromski.[60]

Like Yanko Gooral, a Catholic living in an alien land who felt comforted by the sight of a crucifix, so, it may be suspected, did Conrad, a wanderer and a self-imposed exile, nourish secret longings for signs and emblems of his native land. Like his declared scorn for England's enemy, Bonaparte, his professed rejection of Catholicism could be construed as an expression of his very British persona, from which vantage point he sought to view the religious and political institutions of Eastern Europe with Anglo-Saxon detachment, or, as he put it, "under western eyes." Yet beneath this

[m] Conrad's anti-Semitism did not prevent his having a Jewish publisher, being on apparently amiable terms with Sir Jacob Epstein, and befriending a young Polish writer of Jewish extraction, Bruno Winawer.[53]

[n] Najder attributes the refusal to the fact that the Korzeniowskis had been noblemen for generations.[55]

[o] Najder asserts that there has never been such a Cloister in Southwark, and that there are no documents concerning Borys Conrad in the baptismal records of St. George's Cathedral.[57]

façade of contrived aloofness and of professed estrangement from Slavic sentiment and tradition, there was a heart warmed by the passions that quickened the pulse of the most Polish of Poles, a heart that might leap at the name of Bonaparte, the promised deliverer of Conrad's native land, a heart that might even echo the doctrine of Polish National Messianism, the credo espoused by Mickiewicz and other Polish literary figures, including the poet-patriot Apollo Korzeniowski.[p] Viewed in such terms the deepest meaning of Conrad's personal Family Romance fantasy has the same significance that psychoanalysis accords it in general: the quest for reunion with the idealized parents of early childhood.

In the Christ story, the model *par excellence* of the Family Romance, the child Jesus shares in the attributes of his omnipotent Father, particularly the power of creation. There are legends which depict the Savior as a supreme artist, endowed with the capacity for fashioning birds out of clay with such skill that they come to life and fly away.[q/65] As an artist who caused the written page to bring forth vivid images of storms and living portraits of men, Conrad too shared in the attributes of a creator-father, and in-

[p] Najder has called attention to the influence of Mickiewicz on Conrad's writings. In the character of Jacek Soplica of *Pan Tadeusz*, who is shown trying to atone by many years of heroic service to Poland for a moment of weakness in his youth when he neglected his national obligations, Najder discerns a "perfect forerunner of Conrad's Jim."[61] This same critic asserts that the plot of "Karain" is based on Mickiewicz's ballad *Czaty*, and notes "verbal echoes" of *Konrad Wallenrod* in *Almayer's Folly* and in *An Outcast of the Islands*, as well as borrowings from "Forefather's Eve" in *Under Western Eyes*.[62] "Polonism I have taken into my works from Mickiewicz and Slowacki," wrote Conrad in 1914.[63]

It will be recalled that Conrad was named after the hero of one of Mickiewicz's epic poems. It is noteworthy that the latter was so ardent an admirer of Napoleon that he added the Emperor's name to his own when he registered at the University.[64]

[q] Even on the Cross the conception of Christ as the creator-artist is maintained: a robin, hitherto a totally gray bird, pecks a thorn from the brow of the Savior, whose blood, flowing upon the bird's chest, stains it red and causes all robins thenceforth to be red-breasted.[66] In view of these and other allusions to birds in the Christ legend, it is not surprising to find abundant references to these creatures in "Amy Foster" (Conrad's "Christ-story"), as well as in his other writings. Conrad's numerous references to birds have been pointed out in an earlier chapter.

deed, for all his restless roaming about the world in search of those lordly parents in whose shadow he hoped to catch the mantle of greatness, it was his own father who apparently remained the fixed star in the firmament of Conrad's aspirations.

An interest in emulating his father's literary leanings began at an early age. In *A Personal Record* Conrad recounted a childhood incident which bears a striking resemblance to a characteristic element in the myth of the history of the artist as described by Kris. The latter called attention to a typical experience in which the future artist is discovered engaged in some "childish activity" for which he receives his "father's" encouragement and support instead of an anticipated punishment.[67] One day, wrote Conrad, his father suddenly came upon him while he was looking at some manuscript pages of a translation of *Two Gentlemen of Verona*. "I was greatly confused," wrote Conrad, "expecting to get into trouble. . . . [My father] stood in the doorway looking at me with some surprise, but the only thing he said after a moment of silence was 'Read the page aloud.' When I got to the end [of the page] he nodded and I flew out of doors thinking myself lucky to have escaped reproof for that piece of impulsive audacity."[68] Having survived unscathed this poaching on his father's literary preserve, young Conrad showed further signs as time went on of wishing to follow his footsteps, and by the age of eleven he was boasting openly of his great talent and proclaiming prophetically that one day he would become a famous writer.[r] What is surprising, perhaps, in view of the "Oedipal" significance of his aspirations to be a writer, is that he postponed a serious engagement with that *métier* until the rounding out of his thirty-third year, in the late summer of 1889; no less striking is his confining his literary art to the English language.

As noted earlier in these pages, the year 1889 was a momentous one in Conrad's life. Aside from the fact that it witnessed the beginning of *Almayer's Folly*, it was also the year in which he set in motion his bizarre impulse to venture into the Congo, which, in

[r] The title of one of Conrad's stories—"Because of the Dollars"—is somewhat reminiscent of the name of one of his father's plays: "For the Love of Money."

turn, led to the strange "love affair" with Madame Poradowska, the "Aunt" who was eleven years his senior.

Like the writing of his first novel, Conrad's journey to the Congo was also a fulfillment of a childhood boast: "When I grow up I shall go there!" If the latter symbolized an entry into that mysterious region where little boys aspire to go on attaining manhood, his venturing upon a literary career signified an even more explicit invasion by this small-boy-grown-up of his father's private domain. Viewing these gestures as delayed expressions of "Oedipal" impulses, his quasi-incestuous relationship with the recently widowed Mme Poradowska falls into place as an appropriate piece in the total picture. That he waited until this moment for the symbolic expression of these strivings might be ascribed to chance, but mindful of Conrad's tendency to engage in rather precise imitation of his real as well as his "Family Romance" fathers, it should be recalled that Conrad was then approaching the age at which his father had married. Indeed at the time of his own marriage in 1896 Conrad was two years older than Apollo had been when he married, while their brides were precisely the same age—twenty-three. Another echo of his father's example, who died after 12 years of marriage, could be heard in Conrad's statement at the time of his marriage proposal that he had not long to live.

Although this gloomy prediction fortunately failed to materialize, the several manifestations of Conrad's figurative and realistic emulations of his father in the year 1889 were somewhat less than immediately or completely successful. The writing of *Almayer's Folly* limped along for more than five years, and the book was not completed—significantly, it may be judged—until shortly after the death of Conrad's surrogate father, his uncle Thaddeus Bobrowski. The "love affair" with Mme Poradowska came to naught, and really never got off the paper on which it was written. As for the fulfillment of his childhood boast to enter the heart of Africa, this ended in disaster and near self-destruction. Viewed against the background of the established pattern of his life, this outcome is hardly surprising, for despite his quest for manly adventure, dressed in the borrowed trappings of those men whose powerful example would lend him the armor of invulnerability, he labored in vain. At nearly every crucial turn his body betrayed his inner softness: an infection, the heritage of a succession of childhood illnesses, interrupted his apprenticeship as a French sailor, and an apparently self-inflicted bullet wound ended his career in Marseilles; a back injury, followed by bizarre, probably hysterical, symptoms immobilized him not long after his certification as British Master Mariner; and tropical illness put an end to his venture in the Congo. What might have been his ultimate fate had he persisted in a life of action is conjectural, but in view of these indications of a proneness to injury and illness as the concomitance to his virile achievements, it is not unlikely that, like many of his fictional heroes, he would have met an early death through sickness, accident, or suicide.

Happily for him and for the world of art he forsook the perils of active adventure for the writing desk, and from this protected station he unfolded the full spectrum of his varied and contradictory impulses. There, in the safety of his art, he could fancy himself not only as the descendant of a Medici, the confidant of Bonaparte, a latter-day Galatea, and perhaps even the Son of God, but also as the hapless victim of an androgynous woman who leads her lover inexorably to his doom. By means of this vicarious and unchecked expression of his self-destructive aim he was able to survive, although even in that survival he could not quite conceal his morbid longing to share his heroes' fate. Like them, it would appear he sought out suffering and courted his own ruin as an inevitable component of a wish for complete surrender to a beloved and ideal woman. The depiction of this wish in fiction may again be viewed as an expression of the fantasy of the Family Romance; here, as in its male counterpart, there can be little doubt of its meaning, for in this fusion of love with death, Conrad was surely voicing his deepest and most poignant yearnings—the wish to be reunited with his mother. Often ailing and melancholy from the time of her death until his own, it seems as if he sought to make himself one with her, sharing her ill health, her physical deterioration, and her untimely end.

Seen in this light the nearly rhythmic oscillation of Conrad's life between the twin poles of action and collapse would appear to correspond synchronously with an alternation between masculine and feminine identifications. However vigorous he seemed in the pursuit of a goal—upon the high seas, in the Congo jungle, or even at his writing desk—once he had attained it, Conrad behaved as if his ultimate purpose was not to crown his action with exultant triumph but to offer himself as a willing though broken victim to that very prize.

That in the telling of his tales Conrad confined himself to an alien tongue is not surprising in view of his recurring quest for a new identity. At just what point he began to link that new identity with England is uncertain, but it cannot be doubted that he was greatly influenced by his childhood reading of the exploits of Captain Marryat, Mungo Park, and others. Surely the invigorating effect upon him created by the sight of the "unforgettable Englishman" at the Furca Pass could have been facilitated by some pre-formed ideal. Having gazed upon this ideal in the flesh it may have been as urgent for Conrad to acquire that man's language as to possess for himself the sturdiness of his marble-like calves.

But aside from the fact that it constituted an essential element in his personal Family Romance, the English language served an important and probably indispensable function in Conrad's writing, for it aided him in placing a psychological distance between the dramas of his fictional world and their origins within the memories and experiences of his unhappy past. The English language was admirably suited to help him achieve such a distance, for his extraordinary mastery of that tongue occurred when he was already a grown man, long years after the form and content of his personality had been fixed, and hence too far removed in time and place for it to have served as the literal verbal text for the mournful and poignant tunes of childhood.[8] To have written in the language of his

[8] Psychoanalytic experience with patients who have adopted a second language in adult life has revealed striking differences in the significance and importance of verbal utterances depending upon which language is being employed. Characteristically, speaking in the new language serves to detach the speaker from the psychic traumas of childhood, while verbalizing experiences in the language spoken at the time of their occurrence makes them become real.[69] A patient whose native tongue was German told her psychoanalyst: "I don't want to talk German. I have the feeling that in talking German I shall have to remember something I wanted to forget." In speaking

early youth—his *mother tongue*—would have imparted an element of immediacy and a quality of autobiographic proximity to his tales which, causing his tongue to stammer and his pen to tremble, might well have wrecked his art upon the shoals of personal involvement. Conrad himself was not unaware of his dependence upon the language of his adult life for the tool of his literary art; he acknowledged that despite his intimate knowledge of both Polish and French, the languages of his childhood, had he not written in English he would not have written at all.[t/71]

Furthermore, it was not in his fiction alone that Conrad employed his adopted English tongue as a screen to veil the vividness and the depth of his feelings. It will be recalled that during his uneasy flirtation with Mlle Renouf, the shy and guarded Captain Korzeniowski replied in English to her French questionnaire. A fictional counterpart of this phenomenon, although reversed, occurs in "The Planter of Malata" when, in a scene highly charged with emotion, the English Felicia Moorsom suddenly and unaccountably uses French in replying to Renouard's passionate declaration of love: "Assez! J'ai horreur de tout cela."[73] Ignoring the question of the plausibility of Felicia's linguistic switch at such a moment, the author's explanation for it—to "soften the harshness of expression"—is in keeping with the contention offered here that the use of a language foreign to the scenes of childhood may serve as a means of blunting the intensity as well as blurring the early origins of the emotions of later life. There is indeed something affected and prim about Felicia's use of French in this outburst as if it were part and parcel of her psychological armor, for stripped naked of her de-

German she thought of herself as a "scared, dirty child"; when she spoke English she pictured herself as a "nervous, refined woman."[70]

[t] It seems unlikely that Conrad fully understood his reasons for writing exclusively in English. Surely one cannot accept his explanation to a compatriot: "I hold our beautiful Polish literature in too high esteem to introduce to it my poor writing. But for the English my abilities are sufficient and secure my daily bread."[72] Retinger reported that in 1914 he and Conrad began to write a play based on *Nostromo*. "A fancy took Conrad to use French for this purpose. He always wished to write something in French." Apparently this joint venture did not progress very far.[72a]

fenses she would surely have cried out in her native tongue.[u] This, to be sure, is exactly what happened to Conrad on his honeymoon: in the course of a febrile delirium he raved and shouted imprecations at his bewildered wife in his native Polish.

Although Conrad avoided writing in Polish and never wrote about Poland explicitly in any major work, there may be significance in the fact that toward the close of his life his fiction became increasingly focused on France—the country of his "second" mother tongue. Conrad turned to France and Frenchmen in all but one of his last four novels as if in obedience to Mlle Durand's sweet command—"N'oublie pas ton français, mon cheri!"—issued so long ago by that "excellent playmate" of his happy days at Novofastov. The single exception to this trend was *The Rescue* which was actually the completion of a work begun in 1896. Perhaps this literary return to the shades of Bonaparte (the hero of his Great-Uncle Nicholas), to the land of Hugo (whose works his father had translated into Polish), and to the language of the kindly Mlle Durand was as near as Conrad dared to go in exposing in his fiction the poignant longings hidden in the draperies of the Family Romance.[v] A similar significance might be ascribed to his toying during that time with the idea of making an extended stay in France.[74] Seen within the context of the Family Romance there is something fitting in the fact that the unfinished Napoleonic story *Suspense* became his swan song. In keeping with the ultimate meaning of that theme, there is irony in the realization that in composing that work he was obliged to moisten the dried lips of his inspiration at the fount of a woman's writings, a woman long since dead and a noble woman at that—the Countess de Boigne.[w] In this sym-

[u] One is reminded here of the French obstetrician who fails to concern himself seriously about the cries of his Jewish patient as long as she keeps moaning, "Ah Mon Dieu! Comme je souffre!" etc. It is only when he hears the shrill "Gewalt!" of her native Yiddish that he acknowledges that the hour of her delivery is at hand.

[v] Not only is *The Rover* concerned with France, but with Frenchmen at war with England. Indeed, the political theme of the book deals with the successful "outsmarting" of England's naval hero, Lord Nelson.

[w] Conrad's plagiarism in this work stands in sharp contrast to his earlier use of source materials. His use of Alfred Wallace's *The Malay Archipelago*

bolic gesture he gave oblique expression to a wish voiced in the final phase of his life, when he spoke of going home to Poland to live out what days or months remained, and no doubt to die, too, for he began to speak of death "with great serenity, as of a secret desire."[78] Returned to his native soil he might at last recapture that elusive sense of self for which he had searched in vain over the four corners of the earth. There, no longer a castaway who lived as a homeless exile in distant lands and on stormy seas, he could reclaim his rightful name, and, firm in the conviction of his "true-est" self, could look with tranquility upon the day when he might at last close his tired eyes and rest his head upon the bosom of her who all too briefly had once turned on him the "commanding sweetness" of her eyes.

In a short essay entitled "The Life Beyond," Conrad quoted some lines from Joséphin Peladan, a French mystic, which seem particularly appropriate to the conclusion of the present study:

"O Nature, indulgent Mother, forgive! Open your arms to the son, prodigal and weary. . . . I have attempted to tear asunder the veil you have hung to conceal from us the pain of life, and I have been wounded by the mystery. . . . Oedipus, half way to finding the word of the enigma, young Faust, regretting already the simple life, the life of the heart, I come back to you repentant, reconciled, O gentle deceiver!"[79]

(his "favorite bedside book")[75] and of material concerning the Rajah James Brooke of Sarawak[76] for the writing of *Lord Jim*, for example, can hardly be considered piracy. His use of these sources may be viewed in the same terms that prompted the publisher Novello to reply to the charge that George Frederick Handel had engaged in plagiarism: "He picked up a pebble and changed it into a diamond." It is noteworthy, too, that in his earlier writing life Conrad was troubled about the use of literary sources for his works. Speaking of *Nostromo*, he wrote in 1904, "In regard to that book I feel a great fraud."[77]

Bibliographical Notes

ALL REFERENCES TO Conrad's writings are to the 26-volume Canterbury Edition of his Complete Works, published by Doubleday, Page and Company in New York in 1924, except for *The Sisters*, *The Nature of a Crime*, and the dramatized version of *The Secret Agent*. The corresponding English edition was published by J. M. Dent & Sons, Ltd., and the pagination is identical with the American edition.

A short list of the books cited most often in the Bibliographical Notes follows.

Allen, Jerry. *The Thunder and the Sunshine: A Biography of Joseph Conrad* (New York, G. P. Putnam's Sons, 1958).

———. *The Sea Years of Joseph Conrad* (Garden City, Doubleday, 1965).

Baines, Jocelyn. *Joseph Conrad, A Critical Biography* (London, Weidenfeld and Nicolson, 1960).

Conrad, Jessie. *Joseph Conrad As I Knew Him* (Garden City, Doubleday Page, 1926).

———. *Joseph Conrad and His Circle* (New York, Dutton, 1935).

Garnett, Edward. *Letters from Conrad—1895-1924* (Indianapolis, Bobbs Merrill, 1928).

Goldring, Douglas. *Trained for Genius* (New York, E. P. Dutton, 1949). (American title of *The Last Pre-Raphaelite*).

Guerard, Albert, *Conrad the Novelist* (Cambridge, Harvard University Press, 1958).

Hay, Eloise. *The Political Novels of Joseph Conrad* (Chicago, University of Chicago Press, 1963).

Hueffer (Ford), Ford Madox. *Joseph Conrad, A Personal Remembrance* (London, Duckworth, 1924).

Jean-Aubry, G. *Joseph Conrad. Life and Letters* (Garden City, Doubleday Page, 1927).

———. *The Sea Dreamer* (New York, Doubleday, 1957). (Originally *Vie de Conrad*).

Morf, Gustav. *The Polish Heritage of Joseph Conrad* (London, Sampson Low, 1930).

Moser, Thomas. *Joseph Conrad: Achievement and Decline* (Cambridge, Harvard University Press, 1957).

Najder, Zdzislaw. *Conrad's Polish Background* (London, Oxford University Press, 1964).

BIBLIOGRAPHICAL NOTES

NOTES TO THE INTRODUCTION

1. *A Personal Record*, p. xv.

2. L. Edel, *Literary Biography* (Toronto, University of Toronto Press, 1957), p. 45.

3. S. Freud, "Creative Writers and Day-Dreaming" (1908), *Standard Edition* (London, Hogarth, 1957), IX, 141-53. Hereafter referred to as *S.E.*

4. *The Nigger of the Narcissus*, Preface, p. xiv.

5. G. Morf, *The Polish Heritage of Joseph Conrad* (London, Sampson Low, 1930).

6. A. J. Guerard, *Conrad the Novelist* (Cambridge, Harvard University Press, 1958), p. xi.

7. J. Baines, *Joseph Conrad* (London, Weidenfeld and Nicolson, 1960), p. 54.

8. *Ibid.*, p. 288.

9. D. Beres, "The Contribution of Psycho-Analysis to the Biography of the Artist," *International Journal of Psycho-Analysis*, XL (1959), 26-35.

10. L. Edel, *op.cit.*, p. 57.

11. S. Freud, "Leonardo Da Vinci and a Memory of His Childhood" (1910), *S.E.*, XI, p. 63.

12. E. Garnett, ed., *Letters from Conrad, 1895-1924* (Indianapolis, Bobbs Merrill, 1928), p. 14.

13. Jessie Conrad, "Conrad's Skill As an Artist," *Saturday Review of Literature*, II (April 10, 1926), 700-01.

14. G. Jean-Aubry, *Joseph Conrad, Life and Letters* (Garden City, Doubleday Page, 1927), II, p. 336. Letter to Charles Chassé, Jan. 31, 1924.

15. E. Kris, "The Image of the Artist," *Psychoanalytic Explorations in Art* (New York, International Universities Press, 1952), pp. 64-84.

16. E. and R. Sterba, *Beethoven and His Nephew: A Psychoanalytic Study of Their Relationship* (New York, Pantheon, 1954), p. 15.

17. Jean-Aubry, *Life and Letters*, II, p. 86. Letter to Galsworthy, Sunday 1908.

18. H. R. Lenormand, "Note Sur Un Séjour En Corse," *La Nouvelle Revue Française* (Dec. 1, 1924), 666.

19. J. Rickman, "On the Nature of Ugliness and the Creative Impulse," *International Journal of Psycho-Analysis*, XXI (1940), 294.

20. J. Allen, *The Sea Years of Joseph Conrad* (Garden City, Doubleday and Company, 1965), pp. 120-50.

21. *Ibid.*, pp. 20-46.

22. *Ibid.*, pp. 306-07.

23. Edel, *op.cit.*, p. 55, cites C. A. Sainte-Beuve, *Nouveaux Lundis* (Paris, 1865), III.

24. T. S. Eliot, *The Sacred Wood* (New York, Barnes and Noble, 1928), p. 54.

25. Jean-Aubry, *Life and Letters*, I, pp. 221-22. Letter to R. B. Cunninghame Graham, Jan. 14, 1898.

26. D. Hewitt, *Conrad: A Reassessment* (Cambridge, England, Bowes and Bowes, 1952), p. 2.

27. S. Freud, Preface to Marie Bonaparte's *The Life and Works of Edgar Allan Poe: A Psychoanalytic Interpretation* (London, Imago, 1949). First printed in French as *Edgar Poe, Etude Psychanalytique* (Paris, Denöel et Steele, 1933).

28. G. B. Shaw, *London Music* (New York, Dodd Mead, 1937), p. 337. Entry of March 7, 1890.

29. *Ibid.*, p. 314. Entry of Jan. 31, 1890.

30. Hewitt, *op.cit.*, p. 2.

31. Freud, "Leonardo Da Vinci and a Memory of His Childhood" (1910) *S.E.*, XI.

32. *A Personal Record*, A Familiar Preface, p. xxiii.

NOTES TO CHAPTER I

1. Baines, *op.cit.*, p. 5, cites T. Bobrowski, *Pamietniki* (Lwow, 1900), I, p. 362.

2. Baines, *op.cit.*, p. 2, cites Bobrowski, *op.cit.*, I, p. 363.

3. Baines, *op.cit.*, p. 1, cites Bobrowski, *op.cit.*, I, p. 363.

4. Baines, *op.cit.*, p. 2, cites Bobrowski, *op.cit.*, I, p. 364.

5. Baines, *op.cit.*, p. 4, cites Bobrowski, *op.cit.*, I, pp. 361-62.

6. Z. Najder, *Conrad's Polish Background* (London, Oxford University Press, 1964), p. 7.

7. *Ibid.*, p. 18.

8. *A Personal Record*, pp. 34-35.

9. Baines, *op.cit.*, p. 6, cites Bobrowski, *op.cit.*, II, p. 14.

10. Baines, *op.cit.*, p. 5.

11. Lenormand, *op.cit.*, 666.

12. Baines, *op.cit.*, p. 11.

13. G. Jean-Aubry, *The Sea Dreamer* (Garden City, Doubleday and Company, 1957), p. 25.

14. Najder, *op.cit.*, p. 6.

15. *Ibid.* Letter from Apollo Korzeniowski to Karol and Aniela Zagorski.

16. Baines, *op.cit.*, pp. 13-14. Letter to the Zagorskis.

17. *Ibid.*, p. 16. Letter to Casimir Kaszewski, Feb. 26, 1865.

18. *Ibid.*

19. Jean-Aubrey, *Life and Letters*, I, p. 16. Letter to John and Gabriela Zagorski, Jan. 18, 1866.

20. Najder, *op.cit.*, p. 9. Letter to Kaszewski, summer 1868.

21. *Ibid.*, pp. 9-10.

22. Baines, *op.cit.*, pp. 21-22. Letter to Kaszewski.

23. Najder, *op.cit.*, p. 10.

24. *Ibid.*, p. 10.

25. Baines, *op.cit.*, p. 23.

26. *Notes on Life and Letters*, pp. 167-68.

27. Najder, *op.cit.*, p. 11.

28. *A Personal Record*, p. 42.

29. Najder, *op.cit.*, p. 41. Letter from Bobrowski to Conrad, Oct. 26, 1876.

30. *A Personal Record*, p. 44.

31. *Ibid.*

32. "The *Tremolino*" in *The Mirror of the Sea*, p. 163.

33. *The Arrow of Gold*, p. 12.

34. *Nostromo*, p. 554.

35. *Ibid.*, p. 498.

36. E. H. Visiak, *The Mirror of Conrad* (London, Werner Laurie, 1955), p. 69.

37. F. M. Hueffer (Ford Madox Ford), *Joseph Conrad: A Personal Remembrance* (London, Duckworth, 1924), p. 152.

38. Baines, *op.cit.*, p. 31.

39. "Poland Revisited" in *Notes on Life and Letters*, p. 167.

40. *Ibid.*, p. 145.

41. Morf, *op.cit.*, p. 164.

42. *A Personal Record*, p. 36.

43. "The Nursery of the Craft" in *The Mirror of the Sea*, p. 154.

NOTES TO CHAPTER II

1. Najder, *op.cit.*, pp. 175-78. Letter from Bobrowski to Stefan Buszczynski, March 24, 1879.

2. *Ibid.*

3. *Ibid.*

4. *Ibid.*

5. J. Allen, *The Thunder and the Sunshine* (New York, G. P. Putnam's Sons, 1958), p. 166.

6. *The Sisters* (New York, Crosby Gaige, 1928), pp. 1-16. With an Introduction by Ford Madox Ford (Hueffer).

7. Najder, *op.cit.*, pp. 53-56. Letter from Bobrowski to Conrad, July 8, 1878.

8. J. Allen, "Conrad's River," *Columbia University Forum*, V, No. 1 (Winter 1962), 29-35.

9. Najder, *op.cit.*, pp. 53-56.

10. *Ibid.*, p. 196. The "Bobrowski Document."

11. *Ibid.*, pp. 175-78. Letter from Bobrowski to Buszczynski.

12. *Ibid.*

13. *Ibid.*

14. *Ibid.*, p. 198. The "Bobrowski Document."

15. Baines, *op.cit.*, p. 52.

15a. *The Arrow of Gold*, First Note, p. 4.

16. Baines, *op.cit.*, p. 47n.

17. *Ibid.*, p. 69.

18. Allen, *Sea Years*, p. 152.

19. Allen, *Thunder and Sunshine*, p. 133.

20. *Ibid.*

21. Baines, *op.cit.*, p. 55.

22. *Ibid.*, p. 57.

23. Allen, *Thunder and Sunshine*, p. 163.

24. *Ibid.*, p. 227.

25. *Ibid.*, p. 218.

26. *Ibid.*, p. 118.

27. *Ibid.*, p. 178, cites the Count de Melgar, *Veinte Años con Don Carlos*, Memorias de su Secretario el Conde de Melgar (Madrid, Espasa-Calpe, 1940).

28. *Ibid.*

29. Baines, *op.cit.*, p. 290n.

30. *Ibid.*, p. 57.

31. Allen, *Thunder and Sunshine*, p. 123.

32. *Ibid.*, p. 125.

33. *Ibid.*, p. 178.

34. *The Arrow of Gold*, pp. 57-58.

35. Allen, *Thunder and Sunshine*, p. 124.

36. Jean-Aubry, *Life and Letters*, II, p. 229. Letter to Sir Sidney Colvin.

37. Allen, *Thunder and Sunshine*, p. 123.

38. *The Arrow of Gold*, p. 348.

39. *Ibid.*, pp. 224-25.

40. *Ibid.*, p. 333.

41. *Ibid.*, pp. 255-56.

42. *Ibid.*, First Note, p. 3.

43. MS "The Laugh," pp. 1-3, Yale University Library. Courtesy Estate of Joseph Conrad.

44. *The Arrow of Gold*, First Note, p. 3.

45. *Ibid.*, p. 4.

46. *Ibid.*

47. *Nostromo*, Author's Note, pp. xiii-xiv.

48. *The Sisters, op.cit.*, pp. 1-16.

49. *Ibid.*, p. 28.

50. T. Z. Skarszewski ("T. S."), "Conradiana," V. *Poland* (New York, American-Polish Chamber of Commerce, 1927), p. 22.

51. *The Sisters, op.cit.*, p. 8.

52. Allen, *Thunder and Sunshine*, p. 211.

53. "The *Tremolino*" in *The Mirror of the Sea*, p. 161.

54. *Nostromo*, p. 46.

55. Jean-Aubry, *Life and Letters*, II, p. 229. Letter to Sir Sidney Colvin.

56. *The Arrow of Gold*, p. 64.

57. Najder, *op.cit.*, p. 78.

58. *Ibid.*, pp. 134, 139.

59. J. Retinger, *Joseph Conrad and His Contemporaries* (London, Minerva Publishing Company, 1941), p. 98.

60. *A Personal Record*, p. xvii.

61. Najder, *op.cit.*, pp. 175-78. Letter from Bobrowski to Buszczynski.

NOTES TO CHAPTER III

1. Najder, *op.cit.*, p. 198. The "Bobrowski Document."

2. *Ibid.*, pp. 62-63. Letter from Bobrowski to Conrad, May 30, 1880.

3. Jean-Aubry, *Life and Letters*, I, pp. 79-80. Letter to Spiridion Kliszewski, Nov. 25, 1885.

4. "The Weight of the Burden" in *The Mirror of the Sea*, p. 55.

5. Najder, *op.cit.*, p. 117. Letter from Bobrowski to Conrad, Aug. 20, 1887.

6. Najder, *op.cit.*, p. 56. Letter from Bobrowski to Conrad, Sept. 14, 1878.

7. Baines, *op.cit.*, p. 97. Extracts of a letter from Paul Langlois to Savinien Mérédac (pen name of Auguste Esnouf), Feb. 2, 1931.

8. "The Weight of the Burden" in *The Mirror of the Sea*, p. 56.

9. Paul Wohlfarth, "Der Kranke Joseph Conrad," *Sudhoff's Archiv*, XLI (1957), 68. Letter from Jean-Aubry to Wohlfarth.

10. *Typhoon*, p. 39.

11. *Ibid.*, p. 40.

12. *The Shadow-Line*, pp. 3-4.

13. *Ibid.*, p. 4.

14. *Ibid.*, p. 5.

15. *Ibid.*, p. 7.

16. J. Galsworthy, "Reminiscences of Conrad" in *Castles in Spain and Other Screeds* (New York, Scribners, 1927), p. 117.

17. *Lord Jim*, p. 341.

18. *Ibid.*, p. 11.

19. *Ibid.*, p. 266.

20. H. Deutsch, "Lord Jim and Depression," *Neuroses and Character Types* (New York, International Universities Press, 1965), p. 356.

21. *Lord Jim*, p. 218.

22. *Ibid.*, p. 232.

23. *Ibid.*, p. 236.

24. Allen, *Sea Years*, pp. 120-150.

25. Morf, *op.cit.*, pp. 163-64.

26. *A Personal Record*, p. 121.

27. *Ibid.*, p. 35.

28. W. Weintraub, *The Poetry of Adam Mickiewicz* (The Hague, Mouton & Company, 1954), pp. 194-207.

29. L. Krzyzanowski, "Joseph Conrad. Some Polish Documents," in *Joseph Conrad Centennial Essays* (New York, Polish Institute of Arts and Sciences in America, 1960), p. 114. Quotation from Eliza Orzeszkowa.

30. Jean-Aubry, *Sea Dreamer*, p. 21.

31. Personal communication from Alexander Janta.

32. Krzyzanowski, *op.cit.*, p. 137.

33. C. Milosz, "Joseph Conrad in Polish Eyes," *Atlantic Monthly*, CC (Nov. 1957), 219.

34. *A Personal Record*, p. 110.

35. "Poland Revisited" in *Notes on Life and Letters*, p. 149.

36. *The Sisters*, *op.cit.*, p. 37.

37. *Lord Jim*, p. 79.

38. *Ibid.*, p. 223.

39. *The Rescue*, p. 10.

40. *Lord Jim*, p. 214.

41. *The Sisters*, *op.cit.*, p. 42.

NOTES TO CHAPTER IV

1. Baines, *op.cit.*, p. 97. Extracts of a letter from Paul Langlois to Savinien Mérédac (pen name of Auguste Esnouf), Feb. 2, 1931.

2. "A Smile of Fortune" in *'Twixt Land and Sea*, p. 34.

3. Jean-Aubry, *Sea Dreamer*, p. 142.

4. "A Smile of Fortune" in *'Twixt Land and Sea*, p. 46.

5. Jean-Aubry, *Sea Dreamer*, pp. 143-44.

6. *Ibid.*, p. 145.

7. *Ibid.*, pp. 147-49.

8. Jessie Conrad, *Joseph Conrad As I Knew Him* (Garden City, Doubleday Page and Company, 1926), p. 45.

9. Jean-Aubry, *Life and Letters*, I, p. 113.

10. *'Twixt Land and Sea*, p. ix.

11. "A Smile of Fortune" in *'Twixt Land and Sea*, pp. 42-43.

12. *Ibid.*, pp. 43-44.

13. *Ibid.*, p. 46.

14. *Ibid.*, p. 65.

15. *Ibid.*, pp. 53-54.

16. *Ibid.*, pp. 56-59.

17. *Ibid.*, p. 78-79.

18. *Ibid.*, p. 79.

19. *Ibid.*, p. 87.

20. MS "The Planter of Malata," the Albert and Henry Berg Collection, New York Public Library. Courtesy Estate of Joseph Conrad.

21. "The Planter of Malata" in *Within the Tides*, p. 78.

22. *Ibid.*

23. MS "The Planter of Malata," the

Berg Collection, New York Public Library. Courtesy Estate of Joseph Conrad.

24. R. J. Herndon, "The Collaboration of Joseph Conrad and Ford Madox Ford" (Ph.D. thesis, Stanford University, 1957), microfilm, Yale University Library.

25. Jean-Aubry, *Sea Dreamer*.

26. Jean-Aubry, *Life and Letters*, I, p. 113.

27. Jessie Conrad, *C. As I Knew Him*, p. 139.

28. "A Smile of Fortune" in *'Twixt Land and Sea*, p. 48.

29. *Ibid.*, p. 53.

30. *Ibid.*, p. 11.

31. *Ibid.*, p. 19.

32. S. Freud, "A Special Type of Choice of Object Made by Men" (1910), *S.E.*, XI, p. 165.

33. "The Planter of Malata" in *Within the Tides*, p. 78.

34. "Geography and Some Explorers" in *Last Essays*, p. 15.

35. Garnett, *op.cit.*, p. 14.

36. "A Smile of Fortune" in *'Twixt Land and Sea*, p. 88.

NOTES TO CHAPTER V

1. *A Personal Record*, pp. 73-74.

2. *Ibid.*, pp. 69-70.

3. J. A. Gee and P. J. Sturm, *Letters of Joseph Conrad to Marguerite Poradowska, 1890-1920* (New Haven, Yale University Press, 1940), pp. 8-9. Letter of March 23-25, 1890.

4. Baines, *op.cit.*, p. 22, cites Stanislaus Czosnowski's "Conradiana," *Epoka*, No. 136 (1929).

5. *A Personal Record*, p. 68.

6. Jean-Aubry, *Life and Letters*, I, p. 98.

7. Jessie Conrad, *Joseph Conrad and His Circle* (New York, Dutton, 1935), p. 9.

8. *A Personal Record*, p. 13.

9. "Heart of Darkness" in *Youth and Two Other Stories*, pp. 52-53.

10. *Ibid.*, p. 148.

11. "Geography and Some Explorers" in *Last Essays*, p. 16.

12. "Heart of Darkness" in *Youth and Two Other Stories*, p. 53.

13. *Ibid.*, p. 131.

14. "Well Done" in *Notes on Life and Letters*, p. 183.

15. Hueffer (Ford), *A Personal Remembrance*, pp. 90-91.

16. R. Curle, *The Last Twelve Years of Joseph Conrad* (Garden City, Doubleday Page and Company, 1928), p. 123.

17. *A Personal Record*, p. 13.

18. "Geography and Some Explorers" in *Last Essays*, p. 17.

19. Gee and Sturm, *op.cit.*, pp. 11-13. Letter of June 10-12, 1890.

20. *Ibid.*, pp. 15-18. Letter of Sept. 26, 1890.

21. *Ibid.*, pp. 72-73. Letter of July (?) 25, 1894.

22. *Ibid.*, pp. 37-39. Letter of Oct. 16, 1891.

23. Najder, *op.cit.*, p. 148. Letter from Bobrowski to Conrad, July 30, 1891.

24. *An Outcast of the Islands*, p. 29.

25. Garnett, *op.cit.*, pp. 35-36. Letter of May 1, 1895.

26. *A Personal Record*, pp. 15-18.

27. Gee and Sturm, *op.cit.*, p. 63. Letter of Feb. 18, 1894.

28. *Ibid.*, p. 64. Letter of March 29 or April 5, 1894.

29. *Ibid.*, pp. 65-66. Letter of April 24, 1894.

30. Guerard, *op.cit.*, p. 11.

31. *The Shadow-Line*, p. 100.

32. *Nostromo*, pp. 65-66.

33. *Ibid.*, p. 497.

34. *Ibid.*, p. 496.

35. Gee and Sturm, *op.cit.*, pp. 73-74. Letter of July 30 (?), 1894.

36. Najder, *op.cit.*, p. 148. Letter from Bobrowski to Conrad, July 30, 1891.

37. Jessie Conrad, *C. and His Circle*, p. 70.
38. Baines, *op.cit.*, p. 171.
39. *Ibid.*
40. *Ibid.*
41. Gee and Sturm, *op.cit.*, pp. 52-53. Letter of Sept. 14, 1893.
42. *Ibid.*, pp. 55-56. Letter of Dec. 18, 1893.
43. *Ibid.*, pp. 63-64. Letter of March 2, 1894.
44. *Ibid.*, p. 95. Letter of May 6, 1895.
45. *Ibid.*, pp. 39-40. Letter of Oct. 22, 1891.
46. Garnett, *op.cit.*, p. 3.
47. Jean-Aubry, *Life and Letters*, I, p. 185.

NOTES TO CHAPTER VI

1. Najder, *op.cit.*, p. 215. Letter from Conrad to Karol Zagorski, March 10, 1896.
2. Jessie Conrad, *C. and His Circle*, p. 24.
3. Jean-Aubry, *Life and Letters*, II, p. 183. Letter to Christopher Sandeman, March 14, 1917.
4. T. C. Moser, *Joseph Conrad: Achievement and Decline* (Cambridge, Harvard University Press, 1957), p. 62.
5. *Romance: A Novel* (with F. M. Hueffer [Ford]), p. 487.
6. *An Outcast of the Islands*, p. 145.
7. *Chance*, p. 424.
8. *An Outcast of the Islands*, p. 17.
9. *Ibid.*
10. Najder, *op.cit.*, p. 175. Letter from Bobrowski to Stefan Buszczynski, March 24, 1879.
11. *An Outcast of the Islands*, p. 25.
12. *Ibid.*, p. 327.
13. Gee and Sturm, *op.cit.*, pp. 83-85. Letter of Oct. 29 or Nov. 5, 1894.
14. *An Outcast of the Islands*, p. 270.
15. *Ibid.*, p. 277.
16. *Ibid.*, p. 332.
17. Jessie Conrad, *C. As I Knew Him*, p. 105.
18. Jessie Conrad, *C. and His Circle*, p. 19.
19. *Ibid.*, p. 20.
20. *Ibid.*, p. 22.
21. Garnett, *op.cit.*, pp. 48-49. Letter of April 9, 1896.
22. *Ibid.*, pp. 52-54. Letter of May 24, 1896.
23. Jessie Conrad, *C. and His Circle*, p. 27.
24. *An Outcast of the Islands*, p. 77.
25. *The Rescue*, p. 287.
26. *An Outcast of the Islands*, p. 278.
27. *Ibid.*, p. 271.
28. Baines, *op.cit.*, p. 177n.
29. *Ibid.*, p. 184.
30. "Stephen Crane" in *Last Essays*, p. 94.
31. Jean-Aubry, *Life and Letters*, II, p. 342. Letter to Henry Canby, April 7, 1924.
32. Garnett, *op.cit.*, p. 83. Letter of Jan. 10, 1897.
33. *The Nigger of the Narcissus*, p. 24.
34. *Ibid.*, pp. 72-73.
35. F. Karl, *A Reader's Guide to Joseph Conrad* (New York, Noonday, 1960), p. 112.
36. *The Nigger of the Narcissus*, p. 43.
37. Garnett, *op.cit.*, p. 44. Letter of Feb. 22, 1896.
38. *Ibid.*, pp. 54-56. Letter of June 2, 1896.
39. *Ibid.*, pp. 66-68. Letter of Aug. 14, 1896.
40. *Ibid.*
41. *Tales of Unrest*, p. ix.
42. Jean-Aubry, *Life and Letters*, II, p. 342. Letter to Henry Canby, April 7, 1924.
43. *The Nigger of the Narcissus*, p. xiii.
44. *Typhoon*, p. 19.
45. *The Rover*, p. 4.
46. *Victory*, p. 90.
47. Baines, *op.cit.*, p. 61.

48. "Tomorrow" in *Typhoon and Other Stories*, p. 265.

49. "The Return" in *Tales of Unrest*, p. 123.

50. *Ibid.*, p. 120.

51. *Ibid.*, p. 140.

52. Moser, *op.cit.*, p. 75.

53. "The Return" in *Tales of Unrest*, p. 178.

54. "The Planter of Malata" in *Within the Tides*, p. 78.

55. Garnett, *op.cit.*, p. 100. Letter of July 18, 1897.

56. *Ibid.*, p. 109. Letter of Oct. 8, 1897.

57. Jean-Aubry, *Life and Letters*, I, pp. 206-07. Letter to Edward Sanderson, July 19, 1897.

58. Jessie Conrad, *C. and His Circle*, p. 51.

59. *Ibid.*, p. 53.

60. *Ibid.*

60a. Jean-Aubry, *Life and Letters*, I, pp. 216-18. Letter to Angèle Zagorska, Dec. 20, 1897.

61. Jessie Conrad, *C. and His Circle*, p. 85.

62. *Ibid.*, p. 80.

63. *Ibid.*

64. Jean-Aubry, *Life and Letters*, II, p. 69. Letter to Major E. Dawson, June 25, 1908.

65. Jessie Conrad, *C. and His Circle*, p. 67.

66. Jean-Aubry, *Life and Letters*, I, pp. 206-07. Letter to Edward Sanderson, July 19, 1897.

67. Garnett, *op.cit.*, p. 106. Letter of Sept. 27, 1897.

68. *Ibid.*, p. 109. Letter of Oct. 8, 1897.

69. *Ibid.*, p. 107. Letter of Sept. 29, 1897.

70. Jean-Aubry, *Life and Letters*, I, pp. 222-23. Letter to R. B. Cunninghame Graham, Jan. 14, 1898.

71. Jessie Conrad, *C. and His Circle*, p. 56.

72. Jessie Conrad, *C. As I Knew Him*, p. 43.

73. Jean-Aubry, *Life and Letters*, I, p. 227. Letter to R. B. Cunninghame Graham, Jan. 31, 1898.

74. *Stephen Crane's Letters*, R. W. Stallman and Lillian Gilkes, eds. (New York, New York University Press, 1960), p. 170. Letter from Conrad to Cora Crane, Jan. 25, 1898.

75. Jessie Conrad, *C. and His Circle*, pp. 57-58.

76. Letter from Joseph Conrad to R. B. Cunninghame Graham, Feb. 16, 1898, Dartmouth College Library. Courtesy Estate of Joseph Conrad.

77. Jessie Conrad, *C. and His Circle*, p. 63.

78. Garnett, *op.cit.*, p. 135. Letter of March 29, 1898.

79. Jean-Aubry, *Life and Letters*, I, p. 241. Letter to R. B. Cunninghame Graham, July 19, 1898.

80. Garnett, *op.cit.*, p. 144. Letter of Sept. 29, 1898.

81. Jean-Aubry, *Life and Letters*, I, p. 253. Letter to R. B. Cunninghame Graham, Nov. 9, 1898.

82. Baines, *op.cit.*, p. 215.

83. D. Goldring, *Trained for Genius* (New York, E. P. Dutton, 1949), p. 64.

NOTES TO CHAPTER VII

1. Goldring, *Trained for Genius*, p. 24.

2. *Ibid.*, p. 23.

3. *Ibid.*

4. J. Soskice, *Chapters from Childhood* (New York, Harcourt Brace, 1922), p. ix.

5. Goldring, *Trained for Genius*, pp. 33-37.

6. Personal communication from Marvin Lowenthal.

7. D. Goldring, *South Lodge: Reminiscences of Violet Hunt, Ford Madox Ford, and the English Review Circle* (London, Constable & Company, 1943), p. 9.

8. Goldring, *Trained for Genius*, p. 52.

9. F. M. Hueffer (Ford), *Return to Yesterday* (New York, Horace Liverright, 1932), p. 119.

10. N. Douglas, *Late Harvest* (London, Drummond, 1946), p. 45.

11. Goldring, *Trained for Genius*, p. 28.

12. *Ibid.*, pp. 51-52.

13. *Ibid.*, p. 161.

14. H. G. Wells, *Experiment in Autobiography* (London, Gollancz, 1934), II, p. 617.

15. Goldring, *South Lodge*, p. 88.

16. *Ibid.*, p. 83.

17. *Ibid.*, p. 122.

18. Goldring, *Trained for Genius*, p. 250.

19. *Ibid.*

20. Goldring, *South Lodge*, p. 54.

21. Baines, *op.cit.*, pp. 217-19. Letter from Conrad to W. E. Henley, Oct. 18, 1898.

22. *Ibid.*, p. 220.

23. Hueffer (Ford), *A Personal Remembrance*, p. 92.

24. *Ibid.*, pp. 92-93.

25. *Ibid.*, p. 258.

26. *Ibid.*, p. 36.

27. Jessie Conrad, *C. and His Circle*, p. 70.

28. *Ibid.*, p. 72.

29. *Ibid.*

30. *Ibid.*, p. 114.

31. Goldring, *Trained for Genius*, p. 77.

32. *Ibid.*, p. 93. Letter from Conrad to Hueffer, July 1902.

33. T. Gautier, *Histoire de l'Art Dramatique* (Leipsig, Durr, 1858), I, pp. 82-83.

34. E. Noble, *Five Letters by Joseph Conrad to Edward Noble in 1895* (London, privately printed, 1925), Introduction.

35. *The Inheritors* (with F. M. Hueffer [Ford]), p. 205.

36. *Ibid.*, p. 210.

37. F. M. Hueffer (Ford), *Women and Men* (Paris, Three Mountains Press, 1923), p. 25.

38. *Romance* (with F. M. Hueffer [Ford]), p. 487.

39. Moser, *op.cit.*, p. 218.

40. Goldring, *Trained for Genius*, p. 115.

41. Jessie Conrad, *C. As I Knew Him*, p. 51.

42. Goldring, *Trained for Genius*, p. 130.

43. Baines, *op.cit.*, p. 351. Letter from Conrad to Pinker, probably July 1909.

44. *Ibid.*, pp. 349-50.

45. *Ibid.*, p. 350. Letter from Conrad to Galsworthy, Sept. 7, 1909.

46. Hueffer (Ford), *Return to Yesterday*, p. 131.

47. F. M. Hueffer (Ford), *Portraits from Life; Memories and Criticisms* (Boston, Houghton Mifflin Company, 1937), p. 34.

48. Jean-Aubry, *Life and Letters*, II, p. 25. Letter to H. G. Wells, Oct. 20, 1905.

49. Herndon, *op.cit.*, p. 265.

50. Baines, *op.cit.*, p. 351n.

51. *The Nature of a Crime* (with F. M. Hueffer [Ford]), (London, Duckworth, 1924), pp. 79-80.

52. *Ibid.*, p. 23.

53. *Ibid.*

54. Goldring, *Trained for Genius*, p. 161.

55. Goldring, *South Lodge*, p. 89.

56. *Ibid.*, p. 41.

57. Herndon, *op.cit.*, pp. 265-67.

58. F. M. Hueffer (Ford), *It Was the Nightingale* (Philadelphia and London, Lippincott, 1923), pp. 271-77.

59. Goldring, *Trained for Genius*, p. 42.

60. *Ibid.*, p. 23.

61. *Ibid.*, p. 135.

62. *Ibid.*, p. 64.

63. R. A. Cassell, *Ford Madox Ford: A Study of His Novels* (Baltimore, Johns Hopkins Press, 1961), pp. 277-79.

64. Letter to Perceval Gibbon (dated "Sunday"), the Berg Collection, New

York Public Library. Courtesy Estate of Joseph Conrad.

65. Letter to the Galsworthys, Aug. 14, 1906, the University of Birmingham (England). Courtesy Estate of Joseph Conrad.

66. Jean-Aubry, *Life and Letters*, II, pp. 36-37. Letter to the Galsworthys, Aug. 14, 1906.

67. Goldring, *Trained for Genius*, p. 76.

68. V. Hunt, *The Flurried Years* (London, Hurst and Blackett, 1926), p. 204.

69. Jean-Aubry, *Life and Letters*, II, p. 138. Letter to Galsworthy, end of March, 1912.

70. J. Morey, "Joseph Conrad and Ford Madox Ford: A Study in Collaboration" (Ph.D. thesis, Cornell University, 1960), microfilm Yale University Library, p. 48 cites a letter from Conrad to Hueffer (Ford), March 3, 1913 in the Ashley Library of the British Museum. Courtesy Estate of Joseph Conrad.

71. Letter from Conrad to Violet Hunt, Jan. 7, 1914 (?), Yale University Library. Courtesy Estate of Joseph Conrad.

72. Hunt, *op.cit.*, p. 262.

73. R. Ludwig, ed., *Letters of Ford Madox Ford* (Princeton, Princeton University Press, 1965), pp. 75-76. Letter to Conrad, Sept. 7, 1916.

74. Morey, *op.cit.*, p. 31. Letter from Conrad to Hueffer, Dec. 6, 1921. Courtesy Estate of Joseph Conrad.

75. Baines, *op.cit.*, p. 433. May 1, 1924.

76. Galsworthy, "Reminiscences," pp. 109-10.

77. Guerard, *op.cit.*, p. 254.

78. Hewitt, *op.cit.*, pp. 4-5.

79. Moser, *op.cit.*, p. 2.

80. Baines, *op.cit.*, p. 272. Letter from Conrad to Hueffer, undated.

81. Jessie Conrad, *C. and His Circle*, p. 87.

82. Goldring, *South Lodge*, p. 29.

83. Jean-Aubry, *Sea Dreamer*, p. 232.

84. Simon Pure, "The Londoner," *The Bookman* LXI (March 1925), 49.

85. J. Collins, "The Doctor Looks at Biography," *The Bookman* LXI (April 1925), 173.

86. Morey, *op.cit.*, p. 94.

87. Hueffer (Ford), *Return to Yesterday*, p. 114.

88. *The Secret Agent: A Drama in 4 Acts* (Garden City, Doubleday Page and Company, 1926), Act I, p. 16. (Published with *The Nature of a Crime* [with Hueffer] and two other plays.)

89. Baines, *op.cit.*, p. 432. Letter from Conrad to Hueffer (Ford), Oct. 13, 1923.

90. Hueffer (Ford), *A Personal Remembrance*, p. 42.

91. Hueffer (Ford), *Return to Yesterday*, p. 287.

92. H. L. Mencken, "The Conrad Wake," *The American Mercury*, IV, No. 16 (April 1925), 505.

93. Jessie Conrad, *C. and His Circle*, p. 199.

NOTES TO CHAPTER VIII

1. Jean-Aubry, *Life and Letters*, I, p. 249. Letter to H. G. Wells, Sept. 11, 1898.

2. "Heart of Darkness" in *Youth and Two Other Stories*, Author's Note, p. xi.

3. Baines, *op.cit.*, p. 227. Letter from Conrad to Elsie Hueffer, Dec. 3, 1902.

4. Hewitt, *op.cit.*, p. 14.

5. "Heart of Darkness" in *Youth and Two Other Stories*, p. 51.

6. Hewitt, *op.cit.*, p. 26.

7. "Heart of Darkness" in *Youth and Two Other Stories*, p. 85.

8. *Ibid.*, p. 92.

9. *Ibid.*, p. 118.

10. *Sémaphore de Marseille*, Jan. 16, 1878.

11. Allen, *Sea Years*, pp. 277-81.

12. "Heart of Darkness" in *Youth and Two Other Stories*, p. 131.

13. *Ibid.*, p. 144.

14. *Ibid.*, p. 96.

15. Jean-Aubry, *Life and Letters*, I, p. 269. Letter to R. B. Cunninghame Graham, Feb. 8, 1899.

16. "Heart of Darkness" in *Youth and Two Other Stories*, p. 97.

17. *Ibid.*, p. 114.

18. *Ibid.*, p. 105.

19. *Ibid.*, p. 82.

20. Baines, *op.cit.*, p. 212.

21. *Lord Jim*, p. 111.

22. *Ibid.*, p. 80.

23. S. Freud, "Some Character Types Met With in Psychoanalytic Work: III. Criminals from a Sense of Guilt" (1916), *S.E.*, XIV, p. 332.

24. *Lord Jim*, p. 386.

25. *Ibid.*, p. 387.

26. *Ibid.*, p. 130.

27. *Typhoon*, p. 14.

28. *Ibid.*, p. 19.

29. W. S. Maugham, *Tellers of Tales* (New York, Doubleday Doran, 1940), p. xxx.

30. Baines, *op.cit.*, p. 356. Letter to Pinker, undated (Dec. 1909?).

31. "The Secret Sharer" in *'Twixt Land and Sea*, p. 101.

32. *Ibid.*, p. 125.

33. *Ibid.*, p. 142.

34. *Ibid.*, p. 96.

35. *Ibid.*, p. 93.

36. *Ibid.*, p. 94.

37. *Ibid.*, p. 130.

38. *Lord Jim*, p. 93.

39. *The Nigger of the Narcissus*, Preface, pp. xi-xii.

NOTES TO CHAPTER IX

1. *A Personal Record*, p. 34.

2. *Ibid.*

3. "Falk" in *Typhoon and Other Stories*, pp. 145-46.

4. *Ibid.*, p. 224.

5. *Ibid.*

6. *Ibid.*, p. 162.

7. *Suspense*, p. 134.

8. *Victory*, p. 75.

9. *Chance*, p. 120.

10. "The Inn of the Two Witches" in *Within the Tides*, p. 150.

11. *Suspense*, p. 92.

12. *The Secret Agent: A Drama in 4 Acts*, *op.cit.*, Act I, p. 4.

13. *An Outcast of the Islands*, p. 47.

14. "The Return" in *Tales of Unrest*, p. 178.

15. Morf, *op.cit.*, p. 70n.

16. "Amy Foster" in *Typhoon and Other Stories*, p. 109.

17. *Ibid.*

18. *Ibid.*, pp. 139-40.

19. *Ibid.*, p. 141.

20. *Ibid.*, p. 142.

21. *An Outcast of the Islands*, p. 77.

22. *Ibid.*, p. 332.

23. "The Return" in *Tales of Unrest*, p. 174.

24. *Ibid.*, p. 166.

25. "The Planter of Malata" in *Within the Tides*, p. 35.

26. "The Return" in *Tales of Unrest*, p. 124.

27. "Tomorrow" in *Typhoon and Other Stories*, p. 268.

28. Morf, *op.cit.*, p. 55.

29. "Amy Foster" in *Typhoon and Other Stories*, p. 123.

30. *Ibid.*, p. 205.

31. Jean-Aubry, *Life and Letters*, II, p. 65. Letter to Galsworthy, Jan. 6, 1908.

32. "Amy Foster" in *Typhoon and Other Stories*, p. 136.

33. Najder, *op.cit.*, p. 27.

34. "Falk" in *Typhoon and Other Stories*, p. 152.

35. Baines, *op.cit.*, p. 265.

36. Jessie Conrad, *C. As I Knew Him*, p. 118.

37. W. Blackburn, *Joseph Conrad: Letters to William Blackwood and David S. Meldrum* (Durham, N.C., Duke

University Press, 1958), p. 137. Letter to Meldrum, Jan. 7, 1902.

38. *Ibid.*, p. 158. Letter to Blackwood, about June 24, 1902.

39. Goldring, *Trained for Genius*, p. 115.

40. Jessie Conrad, *C. As I Knew Him*, p. 51.

41. Jessie Conrad, *C. and His Circle*, p. 92.

NOTES TO CHAPTER X

1. Jessie Conrad, *C. and His Circle*, p. 109.
2. *Ibid.*
3. *Ibid.*, p. 113.
4. *Ibid.*, p. 114.
5. *Ibid.*
6. *Ibid.*
7. *Ibid.*, p. 69.
8. *Ibid.*, pp. 118-19.
9. *Ibid.*, p. 122.
10. Jessie Conrad, *C. As I Knew Him*, p. 53.
11. V. Woolf, *A Writer's Diary* (London, Hogarth, 1953), p. 27.
12. Jean-Aubry, *Life and Letters*, I, p. 336. Letter to William Rothenstein, Sept. 3, 1904.
13. Letter to Ada Galsworthy, Oct. 31, 1905, the University of Birmingham (England). Courtesy Estate of Joseph Conrad.
14. Baines, *op.cit.*, p. 329.
15. *Ibid.*, p. 330.
16. *The Secret Agent: A Drama in 4 Acts*, *op.cit.*, Act I, p. 4.
17. *The Secret Agent*, p. 253.
18. *Ibid.*, p. 263.
19. *Ibid.*, p. xii.
20. *The Secret Agent: A Drama in 4 Acts*, *op.cit.*, Act I, p. 34.
21. *Ibid.*, p. 39.
22. *Nostromo*, p. 372.
23. *The Secret Agent*, p. 60.
24. *Ibid.*, pp. 262-63.
25. *The Sisters*, *op.cit.*, pp. 1-16.
26. *Victory*, p. 186.
27. Baines, *op.cit.*, p. 154.
28. *Ibid.*, p. 5.
29. *Under Western Eyes*, p. 23.
30. Jean-Aubry, *Life and Letters*, I, p. 271. Letter to Mrs. E. L. Sanderson.
31. *Ibid.*
32. Letter to Galsworthy, Jan. 10, 1908, the University of Birmingham (England). Courtesy Estate of Joseph Conrad.
33. *The Secret Agent*, p. 42.
34. *Ibid.*, p. 69.
35. *Ibid.*, p. 92.
36. *The Secret Agent: A Drama in 4 Acts*, *op.cit.*, Act IV, Scene 3, p. 99.
37. Morf, *op.cit.*, p. 91.
38. Baines, *op.cit.*, p. 340.
39. "Il Conde" in *A Set of Six*, p. 280.
40. Najder, *op.cit.*, p. 245.
41. Jean-Aubry, *Life and Letters*, II, p. 66. Letter to Sir Algernon Methuen, Jan. 26, 1908.
42. *Lord Jim*, p. ix.
43. "The Duel" in *A Set of Six*, p. 207.
44. *Ibid.*, p. 266.
45. *Ibid.*, p. 191.

NOTES TO CHAPTER XI

1. Baines, *op.cit.*, p. 347.
2. E. Hay, *The Political Novels of Joseph Conrad* (Chicago, University of Chicago Press, 1963), pp. 267-68n.
3. *Under Western Eyes*, p. 39.
4. *Ibid.*, p. 12.
5. *Ibid.*, p. 341.
6. *Nostromo*, p. 223.
7. *Under Western Eyes*, p. 359.
8. Jean-Aubry, *Life and Letters*, II, pp. 64-65. Letter to Galsworthy, Jan. 6, 1908.
9. *Under Western Eyes*, p. 355.
10. *Ibid.*, p. 296.
11. *Ibid.*
12. Baines, *op.cit.*, p. 370.

13. *Under Western Eyes*, p. 371.

14. *Ibid.*

15. *Ibid.*, p. 379.

16. Jessie Conrad, *C. and His Circle*, p. 140.

17. Jessie Conrad, *C. As I Knew Him*, p. 136.

18. *Ibid.*, p. 137.

19. Blackburn, *op.cit.*, p. 192. Letter from Jessie Conrad to Meldrum, Feb. 6, 1910.

20. Jessie Conrad, *C. and His Circle*, p. 146.

21. Jean-Aubry, *Life and Letters*, II, p. 107. Letter to Galsworthy, May 17, 1910.

22. *Ibid.*, p. 109. Letter to Sir Hugh Clifford, May 19, 1910.

23. *Ibid.*, p. 113. Letter to Norman Douglas, June 28, 1910.

24. *Ibid.*, pp. 115-16. Letter to E. L. Sanderson, Sept. 2, 1910.

25. Jessie Conrad, *C. and His Circle*, p. 26.

26. *Henderson and Gillespie's Textbook of Psychiatry*, 9th edn., revised by Sir David Henderson and Ivor Batchelor (London, Oxford University Press, 1962), p. 370.

27. Hunt, *op.cit.*, p. 18.

28. Goldring, *South Lodge*, p. 87.

29. Hunt, *op.cit.*, p. 21.

30. Goldring, *South Lodge*, pp. 87-88.

31. Herndon, *op.cit.*, p. 267.

32. Hunt, *op.cit.*, p. 25.

33. Morey, *op.cit.*, cites a letter from Conrad to Hueffer, Dec. 17, 1908, in the Ashley Library of the British Museum. Courtesy Estate of Joseph Conrad.

34. Jean-Aubry, *Life and Letters*, II, pp. 101-12. Letter to Hueffer (Ford) July 31, 1909.

35. Goldring, *Trained for Genius*, p. 140.

36. Morey, *op.cit.*, p. 73.

37. Hunt, *op.cit.*, pp. 86-89.

38. Blackburn, *op.cit.*, p. 191. Letter to Meldrum, Dec. 31, 1909.

39. Goldring, *Trained for Genius*, p. 90.

40. *Ibid.*

41. *Nostromo*, p. 66.

42. Jean-Aubry, *Life and Letters*, I, p. 321. Letter to H. G. Wells, Nov. 30, 1903.

43. *Under Western Eyes*, p. 339.

44. *Ibid.*, p. 293.

45. I. Howe, *Order and Anarchy in Politics and the Novel* (New York, Horizon Press, 1957), p. 89.

46. *Under Western Eyes*, p. viii.

47. Baines, *op.cit.*, pp. 369-70.

48. Hay, *op.cit.*, pp. 279-82.

49. Jessie Conrad, *C. As I Knew Him*, p. 56.

50. Baines, *op.cit.*, p. 372.

51. Hay, *op.cit.*, pp. 283-84.

52. *Ibid.*, p. 283.

53. Garnett, *op.cit.*, p. 240. Letter of May 27, 1912.

54. Jean-Aubry, *Life and Letters*, II, p. 198. Letter to Sir Sidney Colvin, Nov. 12, 1917.

55. *Ibid.*, p. 64. Letter to Galsworthy, Jan. 6, 1908.

56. Guerard, *op.cit.*, p. 244.

57. Hay, *op.cit.*, p. 298.

58. "A Note on the Polish Problem" in *Notes on Life and Letters*, pp. 135-36.

59. Jean-Aubry, *Life and Letters*, II, p. 289. Letter to George T. Keating, Dec. 14, 1922.

60. Najder, *op.cit.*, p. 13.

61. *Ibid.*, p. 223n.

62. Baines, *op.cit.*, p. 28.

63. Najder, *op.cit.*, p. 13.

64. Baines, *op.cit.*, p. 30.

65. Canceled opening to *The Arrow of Gold* in MS "The Laugh," pp. 1-3, Yale University Library. Courtesy Estate of Joseph Conrad.

66. *Under Western Eyes*, p. 140.

67. *Ibid.*, p. 158.

68. *Ibid.*, p. 233.

69. *Nostromo*, p. xiv.

70. *Ibid.*

71. *Under Western Eyes*, p. 361.

72. *Nostromo*, p. 180.

73. Canceled opening to *The Arrow*

of Gold in MS "The Laugh," pp. 1-3, Yale University Library. Courtesy Estate of Joseph Conrad.

74. *Under Western Eyes*, p. 141.

75. *Ibid.*, p. 118.

76. *The Arrow of Gold*, p. 242.

77. *Nostromo*, p. xiv.

78. Najder, *op.cit.*, p. 218n.

79. *Under Western Eyes*, p. viii.

80. *Ibid.*, p. 360.

81. G. Jean-Aubry, *Joseph Conrad, Lettres Françaises* (Paris, Gallimard 1930), p. 31. Letter to Baroness de Brunnow (Janina Taube), Aug. 9, 1897.

82. Najder, *op.cit.*, p. 249. Letter to Baroness de Brunnow (Janina Taube), Feb. 19, 1908.

83. *Under Western Eyes*, p. 39.

84. Garnett, *op.cit.*, p. 56. Letter of June 2, 1896.

85. *Ibid.*, p. 64. Letter of Aug. 5, 1896.

86. William Rothenstein, two letters to Edmund Gosse, June 31 [*sic*], 1904. Keating Collection, Yale University Library. Courtesy Estate of William Rothenstein.

87. *Ibid.* Letter of May 20, 1905.

88. W. Rothenstein, *Men and Memoirs, 1900-1922* (New York, Coward McCann, 1932), pp. 159-60. Letter of May 20, 1910.

NOTES TO CHAPTER XII

1. Moser, *op.cit.*, p. 212.
2. Guerard, *op.cit.*, p. 255.
3. Moser, *op.cit.*, p. 2.
4. Hewitt, *op.cit.*, pp. 4-5.
5. Moser, *op.cit.*, p. 135.
6. *Ibid.*, p. 140.
7. Guerard, *op.cit.*, p. 257.
8. Blackburn, *op.cit.*, p. 14.
9. *A Personal Record*, A Familiar Preface, p. xxi.
10. "Freya of the Seven Isles" in *'Twixt Land and Sea*, pp. 149-50.
11. *Ibid.*, p. 152.
12. *Ibid.*, p. 158.
13. *Ibid.*, p. 236.
14. *Ibid.*, p. 238.
15. Garnett, *op.cit.*, p. 243. Letter of Nov. 5, 1912.
16. Baines, *op.cit.*, p. 379.
17. Jean-Aubry, *Life and Letters*, II, p. 146. Letter to J. Pinker, June 2, 1913.
18. *Ibid.*, p. 146n.
19. *Chance*, p. 380.
20. *Ibid.*, p. 429.
21. *Ibid.*, p. 327.
22. "The Inn of the Two Witches" in *Within the Tides*, p. 150.
23. "The Planter of Malata" in *Within the Tides*, pp. 9-10.
24. *Ibid.*, p. 42.
25. *Ibid.*, p. 50.
26. *Ibid.*, p. 31.
27. *Ibid.*, p. 77.
28. *Ibid.*, p. 34.
29. Herndon, *op.cit.*
30. Jean-Aubry, *Life and Letters*, II, p. 171. Letter to the editor of the Sydney *Bulletin*, March 1916.
31. *Victory*, p. 390.
32. Gee and Sturm, *op.cit.*, pp. 11-13. Letter of June 10-12, 1890.
33. Guerard, *op.cit.*, p. 254.
34. Garnett, *op.cit.*, pp. 242-43. Letter of Nov. 5, 1912.
35. *The Rescue*, p. 339.
36. *Ibid.*, pp. 255-56.
37. *Ibid.*, p. 395.
38. *The Rover*, p. 222.
39. *Ibid.*, p. 223.
40. *Victory*, p. 405.
41. *The Rover*, p. 225.
42. "Gaspar Ruiz" in *A Set of Six*, p. 48.
43. *Ibid.*, p. 70.
44. *Victory*, p. 129.
45. *Ibid.*, p. 113.
46. Moser, *op.cit.*, p. 195.
47. *Ibid.*, p. 143.
48. *The Arrow of Gold*, p. 140.
49. *The Rescue*, p. 411.
50. *Ibid.*, p. 412.
51. *Lord Jim*, p. 93.
52. *Chance*, p. 63.
53. *Ibid.*, pp. 150-52.

54. *Ibid.*, p. 100.

55. "The Planter of Malata" in *Within the Tides*, p. 41.

56. *Victory*, p. 387.

57. *Ibid.*, p. 392.

58. *Ibid.*

59. *The Rescue*, pp. 315-16.

60. *Victory*, p. 391.

61. "The Warrior's Soul" in *Tales of Hearsay*, p. 10.

62. "The Tale" in *Tales of Hearsay*, p. 60.

63. "The Return" in *Tales of Unrest*, p. 120.

64. *Ibid.*, p. 145.

65. *Typhoon*, p. 14.

66. "Heart of Darkness" in *Youth and Two Other Stories*, p. 82.

67. *Lord Jim*, p. 214.

68. *Nostromo*, p. 249.

69. Garnett, *op.cit.*, pp. 232-33. Letter of Oct. 20, 1911.

70. *Lord Jim*, Author's Note, p. ix.

71. Allen, *Sea Years*, p. 132.

72. Guerard, *op.cit.*, p. 255.

73. *Ibid.*, p. 256.

74. Moser, *op.cit.*, p. 208.

75. Morey, *op.cit.*

76. Moser, *op.cit.*, p. 209.

77. Woolf, *op.cit.*, p. 27.

78. *Typhoon*, p. 4.

79. *Nostromo*, p. 338.

80. M. Atkinson, "Conrad's *Suspense*," *Times Literary Supplement* (London), Feb. 25, 1926, p. 142; M. H. Wood, "Source of Conrad's *Suspense*," *Modern Language Notes*, 50 (1935), 390-99.

NOTES TO CHAPTER XIII

1. Jessie Conrad, *C. As I Knew Him*, p. 138.

2. Jessie Conrad, *C. and His Circle*, p. 106.

3. Blackburn, *op.cit.*, p. 82. Letter to Meldrum, Jan. 9, 1900.

4. Jean-Aubry, *Life and Letters*, II, p. 179. Letter to J. Pinker, Nov. 8, 1916.

5. J. G. Sutherland, *At Sea with Joseph Conrad* (Boston, Houghton Mifflin, 1922), 78.

6. Jean-Aubry, *Life and Letters*, II, p. 180. Letter to J. M. Dent, Dec. 4, 1916.

7. *Ibid.*, p. 181. Letter to Galsworthy, Jan. 3, 1917.

8. Jessie Conrad, *C. and His Circle*, p. 176.

9. Jessie Conrad, *C. As I Knew Him*, p. 65.

10. Jessie Conrad, *C. and His Circle*, p. 119.

11. *Ibid.*, p. 222.

12. *Ibid.*, p. 210.

13. *Ibid.*, p. 211.

14. *Ibid.*, p. 213.

15. Jessie Conrad, *C. As I Knew Him*, p. 135.

16. Jessie Conrad, *C. and His Circle*, p. 213.

17. *Joseph Conrad's Letters to His Wife* (London, privately printed, 1927), p. 108. With a Preface by Jessie Conrad Korzeniowska.

18. Allen, *Sea Years*, p. 47.

19. "The End of the Tether" in *Youth and Two Other Stories*, p. 174.

20. W. T. Moynihan, "Conrad's 'The End of the Tether': A New Reading," *Modern Fiction Studies* (Lafayette, Ind., Modern Fiction Club of Purdue University, 1958), IV, No. 2, p. 173.

21. "The End of the Tether" in *Youth and Two Other Stories*, p. 174.

22. Jessie Conrad, *C. and His Circle*, p. 125.

23. Jessie Conrad, *C. As I Knew Him*, p. 4.

24. *Ibid.*, p. 15.

25. *Ibid.*

26. Borys Conrad, "Reminiscences," *New York Times Magazine*, Dec. 1, 1947.

27. *Ibid.*

28. Jessie Conrad, *C. and His Circle*, p. 223.

29. Jessie Conrad, *C. As I Knew Him*, p. 139.

30. Curle, *Last Twelve Years*, p. 9.

31. Letter to Hugh Walpole, undated, University of Texas Library. Courtesy Estate of Joseph Conrad.

32. Curle, *Last Twelve Years*, p. 134.

33. *Ibid.*, p. 9.

34. *Ibid.*, p. 6.

35. *Ibid.*, p. 101.

36. Letter to Galsworthy, June 26, 1910. University of Birmingham (England). Courtesy Estate of Joseph Conrad.

37. Garnett, *op.cit.*, pp. 232-33. Letter of Oct. 20, 1911.

38. *Ibid.*, pp. 66-68. Letter of Aug. 14, 1896.

39. *Ibid.*, pp. 248-51. Letter of May 2, 1917.

40. *Ibid.*, pp. 240-41. Letter of May 27, 1912.

41. Lenormand, *op.cit.*, p. 666.

42. *The Nigger of the Narcissus.* Preface, pp. xi-xii.

43. Garnett, *op.cit.*, pp. 240-41. Letter of May 27, 1912.

44. Curle, *Last Twelve Years*, pp. 28-29.

45. Howe, *op.cit.*, p. 77.

46. Hewitt, *op.cit.*, p. 126.

47. *Ibid.*, p. 127.

48. Jessie Conrad, *C. As I Knew Him*, p. 155.

49. J. Epstein, *Let There Be Sculpture* (New York: G. P. Putnam's Sons, 1940), pp. 62-67.

50. Jean-Aubry, *Life and Letters*, II, p. 233. Letter to J. Pinker, Nov. 11, 1919.

51. Lenormand, *op.cit.*, p. 666.

52. J. Retinger, *op.cit.*, p. 49.

53. "The Congo Diary" in *Last Essays*, p. 161.

54. Jean-Aubry, *Life and Letters*, I, p. 325. Letter to R. B. Cunninghame Graham, Dec. 26, 1903.

55. Jessie Conrad, *C. and His Circle*, p. 103.

56. Letter to John Quinn, May 24, 1916, Margaret McKim Maloney Collection, New York Public Library. Courtesy Estate of Joseph Conrad.

57. Garnett, *op.cit.*, pp. 277-78. Letter of March 18, 1921.

58. Jean-Aubry, *Life and Letters*, II, p. 257. Letter to Galsworthy, May 10, 1921.

59. Curle, *Last Twelve Years*, p. 29.

60. *Ibid.*, p. 47.

61. *Lord Jim*, p. 234.

62. *Life* (July 23, 1965), p. 40.

63. Jessie Conrad, *C. As I Knew Him*, p. 19.

64. Letter from Jessie Conrad to Hugh Walpole, Feb. 10, 1922, University of Texas Library. Courtesy Estate of Joseph Conrad.

65. Curle, *Last Twelve Years*, p. 46.

66. Jessie Conrad, *C. and His Circle*, p. 250.

67. Jean-Aubry, *Life and Letters*, II, p. 306. Letter to Jessie Conrad, April 29, 1923.

68. *Ibid.*, p. 312. Letter to Jessie Conrad, May 14, 1923.

69. *Ibid.*, opposite pp. 310-11.

70. *Ibid.*, p. 313. Letter to Jessie Conrad, May 24, 1923.

71. Jessie Conrad, *C. and His Circle*, p. 256.

72. Baines, *op.cit.*, p. 431. Letter to E. Pinker, June 11, 1923.

73. Jessie Conrad, *C. and His Circle*, p. 260.

74. Jean-Aubry, *Life and Letters*, II, p. 323. Letter to Hueffer (Ford), Oct. 23, 1923.

75. Baines, *op.cit.*, p. 423. Letter to E. Pinker, Feb. 4, 1924.

76. Letter from Jessie Conrad to W. T. H. Howe, Nov. 15, 1926, the Berg Collection, New York Public Library. Courtesy Estate of Joseph Conrad.

77. Jessie Conrad, *C. and His Circle*, p. 264.

78. R. Curle, *Conrad to a Friend: 150 Selected Letters from Joseph Conrad to Richard Curle* (London, Sampson Low, Marston & Company, 1928), p. 222.

79. Jessie Conrad, *C. and His Circle*, pp. 263, 271.

80. Curle, *Last Twelve Years*, p. 165.

81. J. Galsworthy, *Two Essays on Conrad* (Privately printed, 1930), p. 60.

82. Morf, *op.cit.*, p. 201.

83. Jean-Aubry, *Lettres Françaises*, p. 200. Letter to André Gide, May 30, 1924.

84. Epstein, *op.cit.*, p. 63.

85. *Ibid.*, p. 64.

86. *Ibid.*, p. 65.

87. Jessie Conrad, *C. and His Circle*, p. 272.

88. *Ibid.*, p. 273.

89. Borys Conrad, *op.cit.*

NOTES TO CHAPTER XIV

1. *A Personal Record*, pp. xvii-xviii.
2. *The Rover*, p. 7.
3. *Nostromo*, p. 379.
4. *Chance*, p. 38.
5. *Ibid.*
6. *Nostromo*, p. 245.
7. *Chance*, p. 328.
8. *Ibid.*
9. *Victory*, pp. 91-92.
10. *Ibid.*, p. 92.
11. *Chance*, p. 221.
12. *The Rover*, p. 209.
13. *Ibid.*
14. "Gaspar Ruiz" in *A Set of Six*, p. 52.
15. *Chance*, p. 39.
16. *Nostromo*, p. 150.
17. *Ibid.*, p. 182.
18. *Almayer's Folly*, pp. 171-72.
19. *Ibid.*
20. *Victory*, p. 397.
21. *The Arrow of Gold*, p. 317.
22. *Under Western Eyes*, p. 141.
23. *Ibid.*, p. 118.
24. *Nostromo*, pp. 66-67.
25. "Gaspar Ruiz" in *A Set of Six*, p. 47.
26. *Chance*, p. 39.
27. *The Rescue*, p. 268.
28. J. D. Gordan, *Joseph Conrad; the Making of a Novelist* (Cambridge, Harvard University Press, 1940), p. 36.
29. *Nostromo*, pp. xii-xiv.
30. *The Arrow of Gold*, p. 111.
31. *The Rover*, p. 92.
32. *Suspense*, p. 137.
33. "The Return" in *Tales of Unrest*, p. 119.
34. *A Personal Record*, p. xv.
35. Baines, *op.cit.*, p. 4. Quotation from the "Bobrowski Document."
36. *Chance*, p. 62.
37. C. Milosz, "Apollo N. Korzeniowski," *Kultura* (Paris), Feb. 1956, 70.
38. *Chance*, p. 328.
39. *Ibid.*, pp. 71-72.
40. *A Personal Record*, p. ix.
41. Morf, *op.cit.*, pp. 38-39.
42. *Nostromo*, p. 379.
43. "The Informer" in *A Set of Six*, p. 83.
44. Morf, *op.cit.*, p. 147.
45. *Ibid.*, p. 158.
46. *A Personal Record*, p. 35.
47. *Nostromo*, p. 171.
48. Najder, *op.cit.*, p. 154. Letter from Bobrowski to Conrad, Nov. 9, 1891.
49. Morf, *op.cit.*, p. 146.
50. *Nostromo*, p. 253.
51. *A Personal Record*, pp. 71-72.
52. Najder, *op.cit.*, p. 11.
53. *Chance*, p. 184.
54. *Nostromo*, p. 31.
55. *Victory*, p. 196.
56. *Ibid.*, p. 91.
57. *The Arrow of Gold*, p. 69.
58. Guerard, *op.cit.*, p. 199.
59. Wells, *op.cit.*, II, pp. 615-622.
60. Curle, *Last Twelve Years*, p. 11.
61. Jessie Conrad, *C. and His Circle*, p. 278.

NOTES TO CHAPTER XV

1. *Chance*, p. 170.
2. "Heart of Darkness" in *Youth and Two Other Stories*, p. 136.
3. *An Outcast of the Islands*, p. 71.
4. "The Return" in *Tales of Unrest*, p. 133.
5. *Ibid.*, p. 141.
6. *Ibid.*, p. 142.
7. *Suspense*, p. 116.
8. "The Return" in *Tales of Unrest*, pp. 120-22.
9. "Falk" in *Typhoon and Other Stories*, p. 151.
10. *The Arrow of Gold*, p. 233.
11. *Ibid.*, pp. 294-95.
12. *Ibid.*, p. 329.
13. *Ibid.*, p. 288.
14. *Ibid.*, pp. 163-64.
15. "A Smile of Fortune" in *'Twixt Land and Sea*, p. 77.
16. *The Rescue*, p. 396.
17. *Victory*, p. 401.
18. "The Inn of Two Witches" in *Within the Tides*, p. 134.
19. *Victory*, p. 401.
20. *The Arrow of Gold*, p. 100.
21. "The Return" in *Tales of Unrest*, p. 140.
22. *Ibid.*, p. 167.
23. "The Inn of Two Witches" in *Within the Tides*, p. 147.
24. *An Outcast of the Islands*, p. 76.
25. *Chance*, p. 118.
26. *An Outcast of the Islands*, pp. 336-37.
27. *Ibid.*, p. 339.
28. *Ibid.*, p. 332.
29. *Ibid.*, p. 331.
30. *Ibid.*, p. 329.
31. "The Return" in *Tales of Unrest*, p. 173.
32. Moser, *op.cit.*, p. 115.
33. *Chance*, p. 114.
34. *The Rescue*, p. 310.
35. *Chance*, p. 311.
36. "Freya of the Seven Isles" in *'Twixt Land and Sea*, pp. 205-6.
37. *Suspense*, pp. 195-96.
38. M. Romm, "Some Dynamics of Fetishism," *Psychoanalytic Quarterly*, XVIII (1949), 137-53.
39. P. Greenacre, "Certain Relationships between Fetishism and Faulty Development of the Body Image," *Psychoanalytic Study of the Child* VIII (New York, International Universities Press, 1953), pp. 79-98.
40. "Freya of the Seven Isles" in *'Twixt Land and Sea*, p. 229.
41. *Ibid.*, p. 236.
42. *The Rescue*, pp. 10-11.
43. "The Inn of the Two Witches" in *Within the Tides*, p. 157.
44. *Nostromo*, p. 129.
45. "The Planter of Malata" in *Within the Tides*, p. 33.
46. *The Arrow of Gold*, p. 238.
47. *Victory*, p. 392.
48. "The Planter of Malata" in *Within the Tides*, p. 78.
49. *Victory*, p. 387.
50. *Ibid.*, p. 277.
51. "The Return" in *Tales of Unrest*, p. 177.
52. *The Rescue*, p. 152.
53. *The Arrow of Gold*, p. 163.
54. *Under Western Eyes*, p. 339.
55. *The Rescue*, pp. 315-16.
56. *Chance*, p. 311.
57. *Victory*, p. 160.
58. *Chance*, pp. 32-33.
59. *A Personal Record*, pp. 41-42.
60. "The Secret Sharer" in *'Twixt Land and Sea*, p. 119.
61. Canceled opening to *The Arrow of Gold* in MS "The Laugh," pp. 1-3, Yale University Library. Courtesy Estate of Joseph Conrad.
62. Letter from Conrad to W. T. H. Howe, April 20, 1917, the Berg Collection, New York Public Library. Courtesy Estate of Joseph Conrad.
63. Leopold von Sacher-Masoch, *Venus in Furs* (New York, privately printed by the Sylvan Press, 1947), p. 21.
64. *The Sisters*, *op.cit.*, p. 48.
65. *Venus in Furs*, *op.cit.*, p. 24.

66. *Ibid.*, p. 25.

67. "The Planter of Malata" in *Within the Tides*, p. 31.

68. *Ibid.*, p. 36.

69. *Ibid.*, p. 47.

70. *Venus in Furs, op.cit.*, p. 53.

71. *The Arrow of Gold*, p. 24.

72. MS "The Laugh," pp. 59-60, Yale University Library. Courtesy Estate of Joseph Conrad.

73. "The *Tremolino*" in *The Mirror of the Sea*, p. 160.

74. *Venus in Furs, op.cit.*, p. 79.

75. *The Arrow of Gold*, p. 288.

76. *Ibid.*, p. 286.

77. *Venus in Furs, op.cit.*, p. 82.

78. *The Arrow of Gold*, p. 297.

79. *Ibid.*, p. 295.

80. *Ibid.*

81. *Venus in Furs, op.cit.*, p. 97.

82. *The Arrow of Gold*, p. 329.

83. *Ibid.*, p. 331.

84. *Venus in Furs, op.cit.*, p. 108.

85. *The Arrow of Gold*, p. 318.

86. MS "The Laugh," Yale University Library. Courtesy Estate of Joseph Conrad.

87. *The Arrow of Gold*, p. 332.

88. *Venus in Furs, op.cit.*, p. 22.

89. *Ibid.*, pp. 62-63.

90. *Chance*, p. 63.

91. *A Catalogue of Books, Manuscripts and Corrected Typescripts from the Library of the Late Joseph Conrad* (London, Hodgson, March 13, 1925).

92. J. Cleugh, *The Marquis and the Chevalier* (New York, Duell, Sloan and Pearce, 1951).

NOTES TO CHAPTER XVI

1. Jean-Aubry, *Life and Letters*, II, p. 264. Letter to J. Pinker, Jan. 19, 1922.

2. R. L. Megroz, *Joseph Conrad's Mind and Method* (London, Faber and Faber, 1931), p. 88.

3. *A Personal Record*, p. 15.

4. Jessie Conrad, *C. and His Circle*, pp. 255-56.

5. "The Return" in *Tales of Unrest*, pp. 136-37.

5a. Jessie Conrad, *C. As I Knew Him*, p. 140.

6. *The Arrow of Gold*, pp. 233-34.

7. "The Return" in *Tales of Unrest*, p. 140.

8. *Ibid.*, pp. 136-37.

9. *The Rescue*, p. 338.

10. P. Greenacre, *Swift and Carroll: A Psychoanalytic Study of Two Lives* (New York, International Universities Press, 1955), p. 58.

11. P. Elkisch, "The Psychological Significance of the Mirror," *Journal of the American Psychoanalytic Association*, V (April 1957), 235-44.

12. *Encyclopaedia Britannica*, XVI (1954), p. 117.

13. J. G. Frazer, *The New Golden Bough*, T. H. Gaster, ed. (Garden City, Doubleday, 1961), p. 93.

14. "The Secret Sharer" in *'Twixt Land and Sea*, p. 101.

15. Jean-Aubry, *Life and Letters*, II, p. 78. Letter to Galsworthy, Wednesday 1908 (?).

16. Jessie Conrad, *C. As I Knew Him*, p. 63.

17. Baines, *op.cit.*, p. 167. Letter to Unwin, May 28, 1896.

18. Epstein, *op.cit.*, p. 66.

19. Jessie Conrad, *C. As I Knew Him*, p. 134.

20. Jessie Conrad, *C. and His Circle*, p. 176.

21. Jean-Aubry, *Life and Letters*, I, p. 272. Letter to Mrs. E. L. Sanderson, Feb. 26, 1899.

22. Letter from Conrad to W. T. H. Howe, April 20, 1917, the Berg Collection, New York Public Library. Courtesy Estate of Joseph Conrad.

23. Jessie Conrad, *C. and His Circle*, p. 91.

24. *Ibid.*, p. 118.

25. *Ibid.*, p. 134.

26. *Ibid.*, p. 154.

27. Jessie Conrad, *C. As I Knew Him*, p. 22.

28. *Nostromo,* p. 338.

29. Garnett, *op.cit.*, p. 13.

30. Epstein, *op.cit.*, pp. 62-67.

31. Letter from Conrad to Macdonald Hastings, 1916,-17,-18 (?). Colgate University Library. Courtesy Estate of Joseph Conrad.

32. *Ibid.*

33. Jean-Aubry, *Life and Letters,* II, p. 310. Letter to Jessie Conrad, May 11, 1923.

34. *Notes on Life and Letters,* p. vi.

35. Baines, *op.cit.*, p. 22.

36. Letter from Conrad to Mrs. Brooke, no date, University of Texas Library. Courtesy Estate of Joseph Conrad.

37. Frazer, *op.cit.*, p. 93.

38. *Time,* Nov. 20, 1964. Letter from the publisher.

39. Frazer, *op.cit.*, p. 93.

40. R. C. Gill, *White Water and Black Magic* (New York, Henry Holt, 1940), p. 59.

41. W. Cadby, "Conrad's Dislike of the Camera and How It Was Conquered," *The* (London) *Graphic,* Nov. 1, 1924, p. 728.

42. Jean-Aubry, *Life and Letters,* II, p. 307. Letter to Jessie Conrad, May 4, 1923.

43. "The Return" in *Tales of Unrest,* p. 178.

44. *Victory,* p. 32.

45. *Ibid.*, p. 397.

46. *Ibid.*, p. 399.

47. "The *Tremolino*" in *The Mirror of the Sea,* p. 166.

48. *The Arrow of Gold,* p. 318.

49. *An Outcast of the Islands,* p. 25.

50. *The Shadow-Line,* pp. 3-6.

51. "Heart of Darkness" in *Youth and Two Other Stories,* p. 52.

52. Jean-Aubry, *Sea Dreamer,* p. 84.

53. "Autocracy and War" in *Notes on Life and Letters,* p. 86.

54. *The Arrow of Gold,* p. 161.

55. *Lord Jim,* p. 307.

56. *Stephen Crane's Letters, op.cit.*, p. 170.

57. Garnett, *op.cit.*, pp. 130-32. Letter of Feb. 2, 1898.

58. Baines, *op.cit.*, p. 432. Letter to Hueffer (Ford), Oct. 13, 1923.

59. Jessie Conrad, *C. As I Knew Him,* pp. 144-45, 154-55.

60. *Ibid.*, p. 118.

61. Jessie Conrad, *C. and His Circle,* pp. 140-41.

62. *A Personal Record,* p. 19.

63. Gee and Sturm, *op.cit.*, pp. 87-88. Letter of Dec. 6 (or 13?), 1894.

64. *The Arrow of Gold,* p. 302.

65. *The Rescue,* p. 70.

66. *An Outcast of the Islands,* p. 145.

67. Cleugh, *op.cit.*, p. 279.

68. *Venus in Furs, op.cit.*, p. 49.

69. M. Bonaparte, *The Life and Works of Edgar Allan Poe: A Psychoanalytic Interpretation* (London, Imago, 1949).

70. *Conrad's Letters to His Wife, op.cit.*, p. 35.

71. *Ibid.*, p. 51.

72. *Ibid.*, p. 37.

73. "Geography and Some Explorers" in *Last Essays,* p. 2.

74. *Venus in Furs, op.cit.*, p. 126.

75. *Ibid.*

76. "The Planter of Malata" in *Within the Tides,* p. 62.

77. *Within the Tides,* p. x.

78. *Nostromo,* p. 85.

79. Jessie Conrad, *C. and His Circle,* p. 278.

NOTES TO CHAPTER XVII

1. R. Bak, "Fetishism," *Journal of the American Psychoanalytic Association,* I (April 1953), 285-98.

2. Greenacre, *op.cit.*, "Fetishism and Body Image," pp. 79-98.

3. *A Personal Record,* p. 28.

4. Baines, *op.cit.*, p. 6, cites Bobrowski, *Pamietniki*, *op.cit.*, II, p. 14.

5. *Ibid.*

6. *A Personal Record*, p. 24.

7. *The Rescue*, p. 229.

8. Gee and Sturm, *op.cit.*, pp. 37-39. Letter of Oct. 16, 1891.

9. Skarzewski, "Conradiana," *op.cit.*, V, p. 22.

10. Baines, *op.cit.*, p. 16. Letter to Casimir Kaszewski, Feb. 28, 1865.

11. *A Personal Record*, p. ix.

12. *Ibid.*, p. 23.

13. *Ibid.*, p. xii.

14. "Amy Foster" in *Typhoon and Other Stories*, p. 184.

15. *A Personal Record*, p. 64.

16. *Ibid.*, pp. 64-65.

17. *Nostromo*, p. 365.

18. *Ibid.*, p. 245.

19. *Ibid.*, p. 561.

20. *Ibid.*, p. 542.

21. "Heart of Darkness" in *Youth and Two Other Stories*, p. 155.

22. S. Freud, "Family Romances" (1909), *S.E.*, IX, pp. 237-41.

23. *The Arrow of Gold*, p. 34.

24. *Ibid.*

25. Kris, "Image of the Artist," *op.cit.*, p. 64.

26. Hueffer (Ford), *A Personal Remembrance*, p. 92.

27. *Ibid.*, pp. 92-94.

28. Soskice, *op.cit.*, p. 4.

29. "The Planter of Malata" in *Within the Tides*, p. 49.

30. P. Greenacre, "The Family Romance of the Artist," *Psychoanalytic Study of the Child*, XIII (New York, International Universities Press, 1958), pp. 9-36.

31. Freud, "Family Romances," *op.-cit.*, pp. 240-41.

32. Jean-Aubry, *Sea Dreamer*, p. 240. Letter from Conrad to Casimir Waliszewski, Dec. 1903.

33. "Autocracy and War" in *Notes on Life and Letters*, p. 86.

34. Baines, *op.cit.*, p. 59. Letter from Bobrowski to Buszczynski, March 24, 1879.

35. Jessie Conrad, *C. and His Circle*, p. 219.

36. Jean-Aubry, *Life and Letters*, II, p. 253. Letter to C. Sandeman, Jan. 17, 1921.

37. Jessie Conrad, *C. and His Circle*, p. 219.

38. Jean-Aubry, *Sea Dreamer*, p. 278.

39. *Suspense*, p. 146.

40. Garnett, *op.cit.*, pp. 244-45. Letter of Feb. 23, 1914.

41. Jessie Conrad, *C. As I Knew Him*, p. 29.

42. *Victory*, p. 198.

43. "Amy Foster" in *Typhoon and Other Stories*, p. 129.

44. *Ibid.*, p. 141.

45. Jean-Aubry, *Life and Letters*, I, p. 227. Letter to E. L. Sanderson, Feb. 3, 1898.

46. Garnett, *op.cit.*, pp. 110-14. Letter of Oct. 11, 1897.

47. *Ibid.*, p. 116. Letter of May 5, 1897.

48. Moser, *op.cit.*, p. 122.

49. A. Gillon, "The Merchant of Esmeralda—Conrad's Archetypal Jew," *Polish Review*, IX (1964), 3.

50. *Nostromo*, p. 198.

51. Gillon, *op.cit.*, p. 19.

52. *Nostromo*, p. 310.

53. Gillon, *op.cit.*, p. 12.

54. Baines, *op.cit.*, p. 435.

55. Najder, *op.cit.*, p. 28.

56. *Ibid.*, p. 223.

57. *Ibid.*

58. *Ibid.*, p. 225. Letter to Aniela Zagorska, Dec. 4, 1898.

59. *Ibid.*, p. 27.

60. *Ibid.*

61. *Ibid.*, p. 15.

62. *Ibid.*, p. 30.

63. *Ibid.*, p. 15.

64. Weintraub, *op.cit.*, p. 12.

65. S. Lagerlöf, *Christ Legends* (New York, Henry Holt, 1908), pp. 87-93.

66. *Ibid.*, pp. 193-202.

67. Kris, *op.cit.*

68. *A Personal Record*, pp. 71-72.

69. E. Buxbaum, "The Role of a Second Language in the Formation of

Ego and Superego," *Psychoanalytic Quarterly*, XVIII (1949), 279-89.

70. R. Greenson, "The Mother Tongue and the Mother," *International Journal of Psycho-Analysis*, XXXI (1950), 18-23.

71. *A Personal Record*, p. viii.

72. Krzyzanowski, *op.cit.*, p. 113.

72a. Retinger, *op.cit.*, p. 144.

73. "The Planter of Malata" in *Within the Tides*, p. 78.

74. Jean-Aubry, *Sea Dreamer*, pp. 285-86.

75. F. Clemens, "Conrad's Favorite Bedside Book," *South Atlantic Quarterly*, XXXVIII (1939), 305-15.

76. Gordan, *op.cit.*, pp. 57-73.

77. Jean-Aubry, *Life and Letters*, I, p. 337. Letter to R. B. Cunninghame Graham, Oct. 31, 1904.

78. Jean-Aubry, *Sea Dreamer*, p. 282.

79. "The Life Beyond" in *Notes on Life and Letters*, p. 70.

Index